Days of Sorrow and Pain

Days of
LEO BAECK

Sorrow and Pain

AND THE BERLIN JEWS

by LEONARD BAKER

OXFORD UNIVERSITY PRESS
New York   Toronto

First published by Macmillan Publishing Co., Inc.,
New York, 1978

First issued as an Oxford University Press paper-
back, New York, 1980, by arrangement with Macmillan Publishing Co., Inc.

Library of Congress Cataloging in Publication Data

Baker, Leonard.
      Days of sorrow and pain.

      Bibliography: p.
      Includes index.
      1. Baeck, Leo, 1873–1956. 2. Rabbis—Germany—
Biography. 3. Jews in Germany—History—1933–
1945. 4. Germany—History—1933–1945. I. Title.
BM755.B32B34 1978   296.6′1′0924 [B]   77–28872
ISBN 0–19–502800–7 pbk.

Printed in the United States of America

To the memory of my grandfather
Rabbi Abraham Baker

CONTENTS

ACKNOWLEDGMENTS

IN RESEARCHING THIS book I traveled in ten countries and visited the homes of approximately a hundred people who had known Leo Baeck. The admiration and warmth these people felt for the man who had been their *seelsorger* in their time of agony are perhaps the best source of inspiration for a biographer of Rabbi Baeck.

Rabbi Bernard H. Mehlman of Temple Micah in Washington, D.C., was, from the beginning, counselor, guide, and friend.

Leo Baeck's granddaughter, Marianne Dreyfus, and her husband, Rabbi A. Stanley Dreyfus, made available to me the vast amount of material about Leo Baeck in their possession.

The following persons read this book either in part or in its entirety, in one or more of its several early forms, and offered suggestions, comments, and criticisms: David Baker, Liva Baker, Rabbi Bernard J. Bamberger, Rabbi Gustav Buchdahl, Rabbi Ernst Ludwig Ehrlich, Kenneth C. Judd, Rabbi Bernard H. Mehlman, Margaret Koeber Merzbach, and Uta C. Merzbach.

In translating the original material from German, French, and Hebrew, I was helped by Verna E. Groo, Kenneth C. Judd, Dahlia Luttwack, and Renate Vendel.

Special contributions were made by Larry Bernstein, Arnost Lustig, Sybil Milton, and Douglas Thurman.

Wendy H. Waddell assisted me with the editorial preparation of this book.

GANDHI'S ADVICE ... was consistent with his philosophy of *Satyagraha*—a form of passive resistance. All the German Jews at a given moment should commit suicide. The collective action, Gandhi insisted, would shock the conscience of the world. After the war Gandhi defended that advice, saying there had been no hope for the German Jews anyway—most had lost their lives without the positive value that the human, collective sacrifice would have had.

Leo Baeck received Gandhi's advice but did not pass it on to his fellow Jews; he could not say to them there was no hope. *"Wir Juden wissen,"* he said, *"es ist ein Gebot von Gott, zu leben"*—"We Jews know that the commandment of God is to live."

Days of Sorrow and Pain

1 RETURN

Patrick Dolan spat out the words: "Who the hell," he demanded, "is Leo Baeck!"

The answer came quickly. "Leo Baeck is the pope of the German Jews."

Dolan glared at the shortwave radio. After risking his life to cross Nazi lines, he had arrived safely in Prague, where his job, he thought, was working with the Czechoslovakian underground until the city had been cleared of Nazis. Now new orders were given him by an unknown voice at the other end of his radio linkup: Slip out of Prague, travel forty kilometers to Theresienstadt, a city turned into a Jewish ghetto by the Nazis, and find somebody named Leo Baeck. Damn army![1]

This was early May 1945, and the days of the German occupiers of Czechoslovakia were dwindling. As the Russians approached, the underground forces Dolan had contacted were coming into the open to join in fighting the Nazis. On May 4 there had been a premature hoisting of Czechoslovakian flags at several spots in Prague, and the SS troops had retaliated by driving through the streets in their armored cars and shooting at civilians. This brought out the partisans, and skirmishes grew into battles. By May 8 the roads leading from the city had become jammed with Nazi soldiers trying desperately to find American units to which they could surrender before the onrushing Soviet troops, demanding revenge, captured them.

Between May 4 and May 8, while Prague was a battleground, an estimated 3,600 civilians were killed there by Germans. It was a time of murder, rape, and thievery. Even those who claimed to see a grandeur in war could not find it here, where men murdered for a crust of bread.[2]

1

Against this background and through these people Major Patrick
Dolan of the United States Army was to travel to Theresienstadt and
find Leo Baeck. His mission had begun weeks earlier, when Jewish
leaders in England and the United States realized that Theresienstadt
soon might be caught in the crossfire of opposing armies and, fearing for
Baeck's life, appealed to the Allied command for his rescue. They were
heard, and the responsibility was turned over to the Office of Strategic
Services. Patrick Dolan, the OSS man in Prague, then was ordered to
rescue the man described as "the pope of the German Jews."[3]

Never before had Leo Baeck been called pope—cardinal, yes. "There
was something about the man that recalled a prince of the church,"
said many who had known him in the 1930s when he had led the
Berlin Jewish community in its encounter with Nazism. Although it was
an encounter the Jews could not win, because of Leo Baeck there was a
feeling that some remnant of Israel still would emerge from that holocaust, from that destruction of civilization. There was the feeling that
this rabbi, this *seelsorger*—one who cares for the soul—would bring
them through, some of them at least.

Leo Baeck had become the symbol, both of the Jews he had led in
Berlin and of the Jews imprisoned at Theresienstadt. For many it was
difficult to articulate whether Baeck symbolized the durability of Judaism, the courage of its leaders, or the triumph of the civilized man. But
they understood the excitement of his symbolism. A few months after
Baeck had disappeared from Berlin in 1943, when no one was certain
whether he was alive or dead, there was a gathering of Jewish leaders
in New York City. Suddenly the room became charged with excitement
as Stephen S. Wise, president of the American Jewish Congress, moved
from table to table with the news: "Leo Baeck is alive. He is in Theresienstadt."

A man who had known Baeck well in Berlin in the 1930s, Robert
Weltsch, was living in Jerusalem in 1943 when he also heard that Baeck
was in Theresienstadt. He approached the Apostolic Delegate in Jerusalem, Cardinal Hughes, and asked about the possibilities of the Vatican
arranging a trade—a prominent German interned in an allied country
for Leo Baeck. Cardinal Hughes listened, "deeply moved and with reas-
suring kindness in his eyes," as Weltsch and his associates told him
of Leo Baeck. Cardinal Hughes understood Leo Baeck perhaps better than they did. "My friends," he told them, "your mission is
in vain; if the man is such as you have described him, he will never
desert his flock."[4]

Cardinal Hughes was right. Leo Baeck had many opportunities to escape from Berlin in the 1930s and early 1940s. In those years, as he neared his seventieth birthday, no one could have criticized him if he had chosen to spend the remainder of his time with his only family— his daughter, son-in-law, and granddaughter in England. But he had stayed. For almost five decades he had been a rabbi to the Jews in Germany; he would not leave in the last hours.

The Nazis sent him to Theresienstadt. "*Das war, als ich ein Pferd war*"—"That was when I was a horse"—Baeck said later of those years and of being forced to do manual labor. There was something else he recalled. "I was in Theresienstadt the number 187894," he said. "I had only this one thought: never to resign before rudeness, never to become a mere number, and always to keep my self-respect." At Theresienstadt, as in Berlin, he represented not only the survival of Israel but also that the Jew would survive unbent, without capitulating before the degradation or the rudeness, not as a mere number, but always as a person with self-respect. That was the man with whose safety Patrick Dolan now was charged.[5]

When Patrick Dolan arrived at Theresienstadt in early May, it was an ugly, desolate city. "What struck the eye immediately in Theresienstadt," said one visitor at the time, "were the trunks of the trees, without branches, always overrun with thousands of starving sparrows." Theresienstadt consists of two parts. One is a small fortress that the Nazis had turned into a political prison, and the other is an actual city, surrounded by a high wall, from which the Nazis had expelled the Czechoslovakian residents. This city, which once had housed 8,000 people, was turned into a "model" ghetto for prominent Jews. Almost 200,000 people were sent there. At one time 68,000 people were crushed into an area built to house 8,000. Figures cannot be exact, but reasonable estimates list 120,000 men, women, and children deported from Theresienstadt and between 33,000 and 40,000 dying there. Despite that figure, Theresienstadt never had been a death camp, never a rival to Auschwitz as a site for mass murder.[6]

Almost it had come to that. In January 1945, when many Nazis realized they were going to lose the war, they had begun eliminating evidence of the cruelties at Theresienstadt by eliminating the witnesses. Deep tunnels were dug beneath the town fortifications; for store rooms, the Nazis said. "That did not appear likely," said Baeck later, reflecting the fear of most inmates. "Their real purpose could only have been gas chambers. We spread the word that if the SS ordered any groups to go to these tunnels, they should lie down—simply lie down—wherever they were. There were perhaps 300 SS men attached to Theresienstadt, and it would have taken two of them to carry one of us to a gas chamber." Whether Baeck believed such resistance could have effectively blocked any SS efforts or whether Baeck, by giving the advice, was only attempting to spur his fellow Jews to continue hoping, he never explained. "Fortunately nothing happened," Baeck continued, "no doubt owing to the approach of the American and British armies."[7]

But Theresienstadt, if spared the gas chambers, still was not spared a final Nazi thrust. As the Germans in charge of the death camps realized not only that they were losing the war but that their crimes were about to be discovered—crimes that would add the word *genocide* to the vocabularies of the civilized world—they worked frantically to clear the death camps. Records were destroyed, alibis fashioned, and the survivors of the concentration camps were crammed into cattle cars and shipped away, anywhere.

Some of the survivors—lice-infested, sick, almost dead from starvation—arrived at Theresienstadt. Fifteen hundred of them came on April 20, and 13,000 the next week. According to an American army report at the time of Patrick Dolan's rescue assignment,

> ... there were about 35,000 Jews in Theresienstadt. In April and May the Nazis dealt this community a final blow. They proceeded to dump the most miserable, diseased, and humiliated prisoners of other concentration camps, mostly from Auschwitz, Belsen and Buchenwald in Theresienstadt. . . . To cover their tracks the Nazis did not send any documents or personal papers along. Thus it was impossible to list or parcel out these unhappy men and women. All of them were veterans of many years of Nazi torture; many of them had lost all human dignity. The Czech doctor, now in charge of medical aid, mentions cannibalism as one of the things happening among them. They were quartered in a special enclosure on the ground or in small huts. They were sick. The worst diseases were three types of typhus: spotted typhus, black typhus and vomiting typhus. The epidemic immediately spread over the rest of the town. The hospital with its thousand beds is jammed and there is no room for hundreds of cases. At this moment there are said to be 12,000 people sick of the three kinds of typhus. About 140 doctors, all inmates, are trying to cope with the situation . . .

The sick were taken to the buildings that had been barracks for the imprisoned Jews; soon one-third of the town was quarantined. "We will never know the exact number of infections and the number of people who actually died of the disease," said a doctor who was there.

Even after Theresienstadt was liberated in early May, the transports from the death camps still came. On the afternoon of May 6, 2,000 adults and children arrived in open railroad cars. They had been traveling for thirty days and had had no food for twelve days. Eighty-seven people in those cars had died; most of the survivors had typhus.[8]

Leo Baeck once said that the worst experience at Theresienstadt was the typhus epidemic at the end and the problems of isolating the afflicted. "We were in two prisons in reality," he said. "One made by the Germans and one because of the typhus." As the epidemic spread, the Jews' passion to burst from their barracks and head for homes existing now only in their memories became increasingly powerful. But if the Jews succumbed to that passion and broke through those gates, they would be carrying a typhus epidemic with them throughout all of Europe.[9]

It was when Baeck was wrestling with this threat that Patrick Dolan arrived in Theresienstadt. He had no difficulty finding Baeck. After the Germans had left, the International Red Cross took command and then turned the leadership over to a council drawn from the Jewish inmates. Leo Baeck represented the German Jews on this council.

The man Patrick Dolan found was almost six feet tall, but his hunched walk made him look shorter. His hair was white—actually he now was partially bald with tufts of hair at the side of his head—and he had a small beard. Both hair and beard were neatly trimmed, as they always had been when he had stood before throngs in the cathedral-like synagogues of Berlin. The dark suit, shirt, tie, and traditional vest of the burgher hung loosely on the painfully thin body. In his two years and four months at Theresienstadt Leo Baeck had lost more than fifty pounds. But it was not his thin body that was most noticeable, but his eyes, which continued to reflect the intelligence and comprehension of the scholar's mind as well as the tenderness of the rabbi's soul. Each man is a product of his experience, and now Leo Baeck's eyes glowed with the pain of having witnessed the death of friends and relatives, seen cruelty beyond understanding, watched a society disintegrate. In a photograph of Leo Baeck taken a few months before Theresienstadt was liberated his eyes show astonishment and anger, but mostly pain. This man had expected more of his fellow men.[10]

Baeck refused to leave with Patrick Dolan. The man who had not abandoned his fellow Jews in Berlin would not leave them in Theresienstadt. Baeck saw the epidemic as his responsibility; the typhus must be contained. He returned to the barracks and passed through those doors. What he saw was hardly human. Once healthy bodies now were bones with skin pulled tightly over them. Eyes stared vacantly and with unawareness at a neighbor. People who once had faith in the decency of their fellow man now trusted no one. For them there had been too many years of imprisonment. No one had cared for them in those years; now they saw no reason to worry about strangers outside the barracks. They had been imprisoned too long. They wanted out.

Drawing on a reputation that spanned a half-century, Leo Baeck offered to trade his liberty for theirs, his health for others'. If they remained in the quarantined area until the threat of an epidemic ended, he would remain with them. "Stay here and don't infect the rest of the camp," he pleaded. "Infecting the rest of the camp is what the Nazis want." He assured them there would be medical care and, once they were well, there would be transportation away from Theresienstadt. They knew him. They remembered hearing his sermons and reading his books before the war. They recalled him striding through the streets of Berlin in the 1930s, oblivious to the threats of the Nazis. To them he was a symbol of the people they once had been, a symbol of what they could become again. Because they trusted him, they listened to him and they stayed. Once calmed, they assured him that he could leave the area of the sick. They understood and they trusted.

Leo Baeck left the quarantined area, but not Theresienstadt. Until the end of June, until all the German Jews either had left or had received assurances of being cared for, Baeck stayed. There was considerable assistance in those weeks from the Russian army, which opened five hospitals in the city, helped isolate the sick, and set up delousing stations. Of the more than 30,000 inmates at Theresienstadt at the time of liberation, only about 4,000 remained when June ended. Some had gone into the displaced-person camps that would pock the face of Europe for years after the war. A few returned to their home towns, wondering if they could resume lives that once had been so rich and so full. Others began the long journey to Palestine; with old ways of life destroyed, they would begin anew.[11]

Theresienstadt had been a ghetto primarily for elderly Jews, and many now had no relatives, no papers, no proof of identity. Leo Baeck's last task at Theresienstadt, as his family urged him to join them in London and as Patrick Dolan waited for him in Prague, was to give these people some record, some endorsement. Those who had worked with Baeck, those with whom he had shared the agonies of Theresienstadt, these people received letters from him attesting to their praiseworthy work and high character. Armed with a paper carrying a signature that would be recognized and honored by Jews around the world, these people had the beginnings of a formal identity. It was a first step for many of them back to a normal existence.[12]

As he worked in that May and June of 1945 to help those near him, Leo Baeck could not forget his daughter Ruth, her husband Hermann, and his granddaughter Marianne. *"Geliebte Kinder!"* was how he wrote them on June 4—the same way he had addressed them in his letters from Berlin before his imprisonment. He had gone to Prague for a day on June 4 to arrange the details of moving some German Jews from Theresienstadt, and he wrote them: "I have been for the first time in a very long time on a way that goes between fields and meadows." To prevent his children from worrying, he quickly told them, "Above all I have remained healthy, and I hope that I can depart this month," not mentioning his weight loss. There was sad news also. "The sacrifices in Theresienstadt were terribly hard," he said. "My sisters Frieda, Lisa, Anna and Rose have died there from illness." There were old friends, names his children would recognize, who *"sind nach dem Osten verschleppt"*— were transported to the east, the euphemism for being sent to a death camp.[13]

Finally, the work was done and Theresienstadt was almost empty. The military, the International Red Cross, and the various Jewish groups involved in helping the people there assured Baeck that he no longer was needed. On July 1, 1945, Hermann Berlak, Leo Baeck's son-in-law, received a telegram from Prague: "Baeck started to Paris by airplane . . ." Patrick Dolan had fulfilled his orders. In an army jeep he had picked up Baeck in Theresienstadt and driven him to the airport near Prague, where the two men had boarded a lumbering Flying Fortress, the American plane that, with loaded bombbracks, had preceded much of the Allied armies' advance across Europe. Leo Baeck later recalled his reintroduction to western civilization as he left Prague: An enlisted American soldier helped him to climb into the airplane and then offered him some chewing gum for the trip back.[14]

On that day in July 1945 there were perhaps a hundred Jews alive in Prague. Before the war, in 1939, the city had had a community of 60,000 Jews which traced its roots there back almost a thousand years. Despite expulsions, physical attacks, and denials of civil rights during that thousand-year history, the Jews in Prague not only had survived, but they had made the city a focal point for eastern European Jewry. Prague was the first city north of the Alps in which Hebrew books were printed. It became a center of Jewish learning and continued so until the Nazis destroyed its Jewish population.

Poland also had been a Jewish center. In the city of Lodz, for example, eleven Jews had begun a community in 1793 that in less than 150 years numbered 200,000 people, one-third of the city's population. These Jews had worked hard, built their homes and synagogues, and prospered. Then came the Nazi invasion. In the late 1930s Leo Baeck sent an emissary to the Lodz Jews to warn them and to help them. It had not worked. The Nazis shot some of the Lodz Jews in the streets, sent others to death camps, left many to die of starvation. Years later a Polish Jew walked through the Jewish cemetery in Lodz, pointing out the filled-in moat that went around its perimeter. Speaking in German, he explained that the moat had been used as a mass grave by the Nazis, pointing: *"Ein tausend, zwei tausend, drei tausend."*

Even more than Lodz, Warsaw, further west, had been an important Jewish center. A half-million Jews had lived there before the war. They had their own newspapers, theaters, neighborhoods. When the war began, they too had been transported to death camps, starved, and shot. On April 19, 1943, the Jews in Warsaw had begun a revolt against the Nazis— one of the first organized efforts by a captured people to resist the Nazis with arms—an effort as doomed as it was brave. As Leo Baeck's airplane flew toward Paris, the report was that about 200 Jews survived in Warsaw.

And so it was throughout most of the European countries the Nazis had conquered. In all of Czechoslovakia there had been 250,000 Jews when the war had begun; 25,000 when it ended. Austria had 185,000 Jews when the Nazis had entered in 1938; perhaps one-tenth survived. In the Netherlands there had been 140,000 Jews; 75 percent perished. France was one of the saddest of the many sad stories. Of the 350,000 Jews in France, almost one percent of the country's population, 90,000 died. Most of those deaths took place with the complicity of the French authorities. The French government had bowed to the Nazi occupiers and enacted laws restricting Jewish civil rights. French police had arrested the Jewish citizens for deportation.

There were exceptions to these tragedies. Finland refused Nazi demands to deport its Jewish citizens. Half of the Jews in Norway escaped with the help of the Norwegian government and that country's underground. Denmark helped its Jewish citizens to escape, all except 400 who were sent to Theresienstadt, and those the Danish government watched over constantly, demanding reports on their health; not one Danish Jew was executed by the Nazis.

And then there was the tragedy of the German Jews. So much of the lives of the German and the Jew had been intertwined. "To be German and Jewish was to be written in the stars," exalted one who had been both. Jews and Germans had created together a product that represented both societies. The traditions of scholarship and precision associated with the Germans had combined with the traditions of industriousness and compassion associated with the Jews to produce a Marx, a Freud, an Einstein. And a Leo Baeck. Beyond even the killing of individuals, beyond the premeditated planning of Adolf Hitler and the Nazis to make Europe *Judenrein*—free of Jews—there was the added tragedy that institutions and society stood impassive before the attempted murder of a whole people and the denial of an entire civilization. When help was needed, friends had not answered doors. When neighbors glimpsed tortures and abominations, they looked away. When churches were asked to help, they refused.

People always had killed before in wars. That was not the new element in this war. Previously, however, killing had not been the goal, the killers had said, but the means toward a goal—booty, territory, trade routes, the glory of God. Always before there had been hope that if some other means could be found, war would not be necessary. But in this war of the Germans against the Jews, killing had been the goal, not the means. When the figures were totaled, the sum was six million Jews —noncombatants, children, women, and elderly among them—dead. They had been killed only because they were Jews. Such an event, 3,000 years after Moses and 2,000 years after Jesus, could not be comprehended.[15]

As the plane carrying Leo Baeck crossed the Rhine River—moving in a straight line from Prague toward Paris—Patrick Dolan turned and studied the elderly man with the thin, hunched body beside him. Dolan was a former newspaperman—in Chicago during the 1930s, its rough and tumble days—and then an officer with the Office of Strategic Services, fighting his way across Europe. He was intrigued by the elder man, not having met many like him. He thought he could understand the hate and revulsion, the bitterness Leo Baeck must feel at this moment. Gently he reached over and placed his hand on the older man's arm. "That's the Rhine down there," he said. "You'll never have to see that again."

In the course of his life Leo Baeck had built around himself certain barriers, specific ways of thinking that came to him from Judaism. These he had learned, practiced, and taught. It was of these which he thought when he described himself as a Jew who believed in salvation—a salvation that is not man's due but his obligation, not something that comes to him but something he must earn, not something that he finds at the end of his life but something he achieves throughout his life.

The barriers were three. They were to love mercy, to do justly, and a third that grew out of what has come to be known as *lex talonis*, an eye for an eye. This biblical law commanded that an injured person be compensated fairly by the one who injured him. It held that a just punishment could not be more severe than the crime committed. It was an Hebraic plea for justice arising in a time of barbarism, a plea that permeated Jewish tradition. Leo Baeck interpreted the first line of the Ninety-fourth Psalm—"O Lord God, to whom vengeance belongs . . ."—to mean that man had no right to vengeance. Vengeance was denied him by God.

There was then only one way Leo Baeck could answer the soldier that day as they flew over the remains of the dead Jews and of a destroyed civilization, as they passed above a ravaged continent and the millions of people whose lives had been shattered. "Patrick," he said, "do not have revenge in your heart. Only love and justice."[16]

2 BEGINNINGS

"JEWS SETTLED in Europe comparatively early," Leo Baeck wrote, "probably in the time of Alexander the Great and his followers." The arrival of the Jews in Europe and their development there followed the general pattern of European civilization. The first Jews probably were mercenaries who came with the armies from the south and were given land or positions in Europe as a reward. Others were prisoners of war who made the land of their captors their own homeland.

Those trailblazers were followed in the first century after Jesus by Jews who, after the destruction of their Temple in Jerusalem, wandered from their homeland seeking a place to live, prosper, and to practice their religion. By the third century of the Christian era Jewish colonies ringed the Mediterranean Sea. Later, Jews followed the roads inland to the north, crossing the Rhine, the Danube, Elbe, and Oder rivers, building their own communities within the Christian ones. They moved often because of persecutions, denial of civil liberties, and restrictions on their religious practices. Many of them ultimately settled in central and eastern Europe. "Here they had," said Leo Baeck, "despite the violent incidents of the first Crusade, a steady development."[1]

One of these settlers was Leo Baeck's ancestor. The name Baeck is an abbreviation of the Hebrew "Ben Kodesh," son of a pious man or a martyr. According to family tradition, a Baeck ancestor had been persecuted, probably killed, in southern Germany during one of the many pogroms of the Middle Ages. Moving eastward then, along with many other Jewish refugees, cherishing a hope to live in peace, the Baeck family settled in Moravia, part of modern Czechoslovakia. Their written records begin to emerge in the eighteenth century, and they are the rec-

ords of a rabbinical family. There is Abraham Bäck, rabbi in Lundenburg
and Holitsch, a famous Talmudic scholar. One of his sons, Nathan, was
a rabbi in Maehrish-Kromau. Nathan's son was Samuel Bäck, the
father of Leo Baeck and an interesting man in his own right.

A cousin of Leo Baeck's once recalled, "When I was a child, I knew
I was the granddaughter of Samuel Bäck, and that was something." Another of Leo's cousins remembered that when one of her professors
learned she was the granddaughter of Samuel Bäck, he immediately
stood, bowed toward her, and announced she was the daughter of a
Fürst—a prince. Samuel Bäck had an unusual rabbinical education for
his time. Not only had he studied for the rabbinate in the traditional eastern European way with famous Jewish scholars, but he also had pursued a formal German secular education, something almost unheard of
then for prospective rabbis. He attended gymnasiums in Pressburg and
Nikolsburg, where he took his rabbinical training in the yeshiva, the
Jewish academy. He continued these studies with Lazar Hurwitz, a famous rabbi of the time, in Vienna; while there, he also was a student at
the University of Vienna, receiving a doctorate in philosophy, an unusual achievement for a rabbi in the mid-nineteenth century. Following a family tradition, one that his son Leo also would continue, Samuel
married the daughter of a rabbinical family, Eva Placzek.

Samuel Bäck's first rabbinical post was in Bohemia; in 1864, when
he was thirty years old, he moved to Lissa in eastern Germany, where
he stayed until his death in 1912. In Lissa he re-established his family's
German roots and built a career that earned him the respect of both Jew
and non-Jew. When he died, the bells of the town hall and of all the
Christian churches of Lissa rang out in sorrow.[2]

His first reception, however, was not warm. The elders of the Lissa
Jewish community were suspicious of a rabbi with a university education and a doctorate and proud of their community's reputation as a
center of Talmudic teaching. They called Samuel Bäck before them and
questioned him sharply about the Talmud. The Hebrew word *talmud*
means learning or study, and the Talmud, next to the Hebrew Bible, is
the greatest literary achievement of the Jewish people. It is the written
record of the study of Jewish laws, ritual, and life style. Intertwined
within it are two elements—*Halakah*, the legal, and *Aggadah*, dealing
with the religious and ethical. Its purpose is to adapt the teachings of
the Bible to contemporary life. Talmudic scholars examine each word,
to fathom why one word instead of another was chosen; to analyze each
anecdote, to understand why it was used. The Talmud is a maze of dis-

courses, stories, explanations, debates, analyses, unravelings of some mysteries, posings of more mysteries. Its volumes support and contradict, seem clear and then, suddenly, are murky. Studying the Talmud is a constant search through the practical and the mystic, seeking guidelines and advice for living in a moral way. The challenge to the Talmudic scholar is to work through all the stories, conflicting interpretations, and citations, then to emerge not only knowledgeable but also incisive. The scholar must be able not only to cite the Talmud but to apply it. When questioned by the elders of the Jewish community of Lissa, Samuel Bäck demonstrated his ability to meet that challenge. He was retained as their rabbi, and the reputation of that city as a center for Talmudic learning increased in the half-century he was there.

The rabbi's role in the nineteenth century was principally that of teacher, and Samuel Bäck became famous throughout Germany as the teacher of the Lissa Jews. Many of his students spoke in later years of the stern taskmaster waving his finger at them and shouting, "You receive a five!"—the lowest mark in the school. Many also recall, however, that in their final reports he adjusted the lower marks somewhat higher.

The secular schools in Germany offered religious instruction only for Christians. Samuel Bäck insisted that the Prussian schools, of which the Lissa schools were part, allow religious instruction for Jewish students by Jewish teachers in the same way that the Protestant and Catholic students received religious instruction by clergymen of their faith. He carried his point, but it was not a complete victory; Prussian law required the local communities to offer religious instruction for the Christians but only suggested that they offer instruction for the Jews. Still, it was a step forward, and Lissa was one of the towns where Jews learned about their religion in the state schools. Samuel Bäck himself taught in these classes, and wrote the textbook for them; no other existed. In the course of his rabbinate he wrote several books on Jewish history and cultural life, in addition to contributing to the *Jewish Encyclopedia*. One of his community activities involved Jews drafted into the Prussian army. Lissa was the military center for that area, and the draftees reported there to take the oath of allegiance administered by a clergyman of their faith; Samuel Bäck was the rabbi who administered the oath for the Jewish draftees.[3]

In at least one respect the Jewish clergy were similar to the clergy of other faiths. They did not have much money. Samuel Bäck rented his house from the Calvinist minister in Lissa. Years later Samuel Bäck's children spoke of the long-standing dispute between the rabbi and the minister. The rabbi wanted to pay a reasonable rent, but the minister did not wish to accept any rent, being fully aware of the financial difficulties faced by his Jewish brother. The minister actually tried to give the house to the rabbi, who never would accept it. The two men played out their scenario of kindness and pride for years, never resolving the matter. Much later, when Leo Baeck spoke to his friends of the minister's kindness, he added that he had a preference for Calvinism among the Protestant sects. He said that with its emphasis on the moral act it was similar to Judaism. His friends did not dispute his interpretation of Calvinism but suspected the preference had its roots in the kindness of that minister toward Rabbi Samuel Bäck.[4]

An account of Samuel Bäck's rabbinate in Lissa describes it as "graceful." Written in 1912, after his death, this account credited him with transforming "a community of the Middle Ages into a modern one." It continued:

> Gracefully he expressed his deep religiousness and spoke to the heart. He did not push away the conservatives. He did not push away the liberals. He collected the entire community around him because everybody knew that he was not an opportunist, but that he was a man of belief, of loyalty, of duty and of loving mildness.

Leo said the prayer at his father's grave, where he spoke of him as belonging to no party but to Judaism.[5] As the father had been, so the son could be. Throughout all of Leo Baeck's life as a rabbi he attempted to represent Judaism rather than any faction. He was a person with whom Liberal and Orthodox Jews could meet, a man trusted by Zionists and anti-Zionists, one respected for his Judaism and admired for his Germanism. It was this quality of relating to all Jews that was Leo Baeck's strength in 1933 when the Jews of Germany needed a single leader.

Leo Baeck was born on May 24, 1873, in Lissa. One of eleven children, he was part of a typical German-Jewish middle-class family in which the father dominated the household and the sons were dominant among the children. Leo was the only child to carry on the family tradition of becoming a rabbi. His brothers became doctors and dentists, and his sisters married rabbis and successful merchants. The family was typical of the families of the time—without much money but with an educational and cultural background, each generation climbing farther up the ladder of economic success and educational achievement.

Lissa was one of the most influential factors in shaping Leo Baeck's later life. Part of the province of Posen, the town historically had belonged to Poland. Leo Baeck described the eighteenth-century Lissa ghetto this way: "The Jews insulated themselves in the essentials. They held unconditionally to their religion and often withdrew themselves into it. They knew and felt their uniqueness; they had in it their own life forms and also their own mystique, which they cherished."

In 1793, however, the Posen province became part of Prussia, and suddenly these isolated eastern Jews were linked to Berlin, the Prussian capital, at a time when the Berlin Jews were merging into German cultural, social, intellectual, and professional life. As Berlin increasingly attracted the Lissa Jews away from their ghetto, the Jewish elders in Lissa countered by forbidding the reading of non-Jewish materials and prescribing penalties for Jews who read the new German translation of the Hebrew Bible.

Out of this conflict between the ghetto and the world beyond the ghetto a different Jew emerged, one who combined

on one hand, the love for the rich treasury of the old Jewish literature which for centuries had been the only means of Jewish education; and on the other hand, the burning desire to assimilate the great works of western thinkers and poets and, in particular, German classics.[6]

Leo Baeck was one of these new Jews of the Posen province, embracing both the traditions of the eastern Jews and the intellectuality of western scholarship. Never could he escape the eastern tradition, the feeling of being enveloped in Jewish life. A contemporary wrote, "Through every [Lissa] street, by day and night, the cadence of talmudic study echoed, and it often happened that a simple citizen without any special merit rose in later years to fame because of his talmudic knowledge." Jewish businessmen in the community, as a matter of course, spent part of each day in Jewish studies. There was a saying that "It is easy in any Jewish home in Lissa to convene a *bet din*" —a court of three Talmudic scholars capable and authorized to make religious decisions. There were Jewish educational facilities for the youth, Jewish bookstores, and—in keeping with a German society in which public welfare was controlled by religious organizations—there was a variety of Jewish hospitals, orphanages, and homes for the aged. The Jews "represented a world of their own," said the account by Leo Baeck's contemporary, "in which all the concerns of life, from the cradle to the grave, were regulated and determined by the Jewish religion."

While not rejecting this traditionalist background, Leo Baeck also was attracted to Berlin and the western world it represented, as were other Lissa Jews. For him it was the lure of universities and an intellectual milieu. For others it was the lure of commercial and professional success. The Jews wanted to think of themselves as Germans, to enjoy themselves, and to thrive. Years later one whose grandparents had come from the province recalled, "The Jews supported Germany rather than Poland because the Germans were more sophisticated and cultured than were the Poles." An associate of Leo Baeck's suggested this snobbism was one reason for Samuel Bäck's acceptance in Lissa during the last half of the nineteenth century. "The Jews there withstood Polish influence," he said, "and wanted a rabbi who had the stamp of Germany about him. Samuel Bäck's sermons were pearls of German construction and wisdom."[7]

Civil rights had been granted to Prussian Jews during the nineteenth century, and various laws appeared to strengthen those rights. However, the enactment of laws could not overcome the anti-Semitic feelings of many Germans and Poles. Their attitude showed particularly in the rural areas surrounding the cities, and the Posen province was no exception. "The time came for every one of us Jewish children," recalled one who had grown up in the area during the latter part of the nineteenth century, "when we were first hit by the word *Jew* as a term of abuse from German or Polish lips. The dreamy security of our childhood was shattered." Others spoke of children who wanted to play being pulled away: "Don't stop here, that's a Jew"; of being taunted in school with "Jew, hep, hep"; of being charged with "nailing our Savior to the Cross"; of being accused of belonging to a people who murdered non-Jewish children in order to use their blood in the manufacture of Passover matzo.

This anti-Semitism rarely intruded into the city of Lissa. One of Leo Baeck's cousins who grew up there recalled many years later, "I didn't hear of anti-Semitism there. I didn't know of it." Perhaps this was because of the influence of Calvinism, still strong in the city; perhaps because of the solid roots the Jews had in Lissa; or perhaps because of the middle-class quality of the city's non-Jewish residents; for whatever reason, when Leo Baeck lived there, Lissa was both a peaceful and a pleasant city for a Jew growing up, one of the few in Europe. Because it was a center for Jewish learning, it produced many of Germany's Jewish leaders of the twentieth century; because of their inexperience with anti-Semitism, many of them would be unable to understand the virulence that anti-Semitism could take on. To understand anti-Semitism better than did his fellow Jews would be one of the challenges for Leo Baeck in his later years.[8]

The Jews in Lissa developed as Germans. The broad-brimmed black hat and the long, dark coat that had been the Jew's costume in eastern Europe was replaced by the Berliner's business suit. The Lissa Jews attempted to speak a pure German, leaving Yiddish to the Polish and Russian Jews. Polish was available to their children for study in the local schools, but only as an elective. They began to enter the German civil service and sided with their German neighbors against the Poles in political disputes. If they lost some favor with the Poles, they assumed they would earn some with their fellow Germans. It was a city where, said one commentator, "The Poles regarded the Jew as one who had enjoyed the protection of the old Poland and had curried favor with the Germans," and "The blood Germans saw him as an unreliable 'betwixt and between.' "[9]

A child in the closing decades of the nineteenth century was growing up in the last years before technology would destroy all geographic barriers between peoples. When Leo was five years old, for example, his father took him to see the opening of the railway line in the area. Not wishing to miss the first railroad train, they awoke early and walked for miles, running at the end, to watch the train race through without stopping. To a little boy this shape of the modern world was a juggernaut, frightening everything out of its way and crushing anything that did not move fast enough. It was a power beyond comprehension.[10]

The end of the nineteenth century was a time when scholarship was prized, the hope being that education liberated and elevated the mind. In Germany, if one forgot a person's name, one could call him *Herr Doktor* and be correct, or so a joke at the time went. And there was the German gymnasium—an elitist high school for students with demonstrated academic qualifications or with parents who could buy academic places for them. The gymnasium system was undemocratic. Those not accepted were denied access to the professional world and relegated to the life of the mechanic and workman. For the individual who was accepted, however, the opportunity for a formal education could scarcely be paralleled. Many years later, as an old man, Leo Baeck told a group of rabbinical students that one of the most important influences on his life was the gymnasium.

The gymnasium in Lissa had been founded by Amos Comenius in

the seventeenth century. Only in the twentieth century are Comenius's theories of education becoming accepted. He himself was educated in schools he described as "a terror for boys and slaughterhouses of the mind." He resolved to develop an educational system that had as its object "to seek and to find a method of instruction by which teachers may teach less, but learners may learn more; by which schools may be the scene of less noise, aversion, and useless labour, but of more leisure, enjoyment, and solid progress." At its simplest the Comenius system was one of better trained teachers and better teaching facilities plus an organized approach to learning. At a more sophisticated level it was a method of teaching subjects so that the learner could see the relationship between them and their relationship to a unity. This, hopefully, could open for the student the way to wisdom.

Comenius also was a bishop of the Moravian and Bohemian Brethren of the Unity, a Protestant sect that renounced war and class distinctions. Such beliefs not being popular among Christians at the time, the Brethren ultimately disappeared, but not before Comenius had implanted at the Lissa gymnasium a humanistic tradition that became a part of the students' lives.

Leo Baeck was a brilliant student in the gymnasium, but the story recalled by one of his classmates was neither of his brilliance nor of his religious tradition. Rather, it was almost a typical incident for the son of a poor family in a school catering primarily to the children of upper-middle-income families. As the outstanding student in the gymnasium, Leo Baeck had to make the usual speech at the graduation ceremony, extending the thanks of the class to the staff of the school. The event required his wearing a cutaway coat; traditional German formality allowed no less. Unfortunately, Samuel Bäck could not afford to buy his son a coat for the occasion, and Leo had to wear his father's. The father's coat was too big, and the family stuffed the shoulders with stockings to fill them out. During the talk one of the stockings unrolled, slipped down the voluminous sleeves, and dropped into the speaker's hand. Undaunted, Leo Baeck continued the speech—the first demonstration of his ability to remain calm before an audience when the unexpected happens.[11]

His religious education began early and was primarily under his father's supervision. It is not known when it was decided that he would be the son to carry on the family's rabbinical tradition, except that it never seemed in doubt. When Leo was six years old, according to family tradition, he already was a scholar of an elementary kind, and could discuss with some authority parts of the Talmud with his father. The only question about his career as he grew up was which rabbinical seminary he would attend.[12]

As Leo's father had learned in the middle of the nineteenth century, there was a suspicion among Jews of rabbis educated in a university-type setting rather than in a yeshiva. However, the yeshiva system of students clustering around an individual renowned for his knowledge was no longer acceptable at the end of the century because of several developments. The first of these was the organization of Jewish knowledge in a scientific manner. Scholars had pulled the history of the people together, studied it, and produced systematic works about it. Chief among these scholars was Heinrich Graetz, whose eleven-volume work on the history of the Jewish people became a basic research tool. The result was a requirement that teaching be organized; communities no longer relied on the ability of their rabbis to absorb this information by chance.

The second development was the emergence of the Jews from their ghettos, their increasing contact with non-Jews, and the pressures on them to surrender their traditional ways. In 1845, for example, a group of rabbis from all over Germany, meeting in Frankfurt, announced that the use of Hebrew, although advisable, was not necessary for the conduct of religious services. There was more to that announcement than the words indicate. To the Jewish people Hebrew was not just an ancient language. For 5,000 years it had been one of the cords that tied Jews together, a means by which the religion passed through the generations. A Jew from any land could walk into a synagogue and participate in a religious service even though completely ignorant of the language of the country in which the synagogue was located. The Jew could do this because the service—at least its most significant parts—was in Hebrew. The 1845 proposal to push Hebrew out of the service would have diluted that unifying tendency and destroyed that tradition of welcoming the Jew from the strange land. A counterforce was needed to pursue the tradition in an organized way.

One rabbi supporting the retention of Hebrew was Zacharias Frankel, who argued that an understanding of religious customs and ceremonies was necessary for them to be preserved. A few years later Frankel became head of a new rabbinical seminary in Breslau, the Jewish Theological Seminary, the first in Germany to include the word *theological* in its name. Apparently this represented a Christian influence of the time; Christians studied theology in their seminaries, while Jews studied the Talmud in theirs.

Frankel developed a seven-year program for students in conjunction with studies at the University of Breslau. The students studied the Hebrew and Aramaic languages, Bible, geography of Palestine, historical and methodological introduction to rabbinic literature, the Talmudic writings, homiletics (the art of preaching), Jewish law, and philosophy. One of the first to join the faculty was Heinrich Graetz, the historian whose research had done so much to challenge the traditional method of rabbinic instruction by placing Jewish scholarship on a scientific basis.

Four decades later this school seemed the logical choice for Leo Baeck's rabbinic education. The Breslau seminary had become the center of traditional Judaism. Such teachers as Graetz and other academic luminaries—Rosin, Lewy, Brann, for example—were known throughout the Jewish world for their scholarship. It encouraged freedom of investigation but maintained the traditional practices of Judaism. Zacharias Frankel had indicated that, despite fears of some Jewish scholars, the seminary never would stray too far from the path of the accepted. "It is inconceivable," he had written, "that a community in its totality, or even in its majority, should follow tendencies which are subversive, which shake its foundations and threaten its existence . . . [A rabbi's] desire for improvement must not be based on imitation or concessions to the spirit of the times, but rather must have its origin in truly religious needs." (Despite all of Frankel's protestations the traditional wing of Judaism never trusted his inclinations and established its own seminary in Berlin.)[13]

Neither as a student nor as an adult could Leo Baeck surrender his religious tradition. He did, however, believe that the responsibilities of a modern rabbi in Germany would place demands upon him for which he felt he could not be prepared at Breslau. Most of his fellow students were from eastern Europe, the ghettos of Poland and Russia. Leo Baeck had grown up in Lissa, where the Jews lived in their own community but where there were no ghetto walls, either actual or figurative, between them and their Christian neighbors. His direction was toward Berlin, where Jews did not live in isolation but as Prussian citizens.

After three preparatory years in Breslau, Leo Baeck left for Berlin. On April 16, 1894, the seminary certified that he had been a properly registered student from May 3, 1891, to the end of the winter semester of

1892–1893. Shortly after that, the University of Breslau, where he also was enrolled, gave him a certificate attesting to his attendance for seven semesters (with a major in philosophy) and to his eligibility for the examination that would allow him to begin work on his doctoral dissertation. He took the examination and on July 31, 1894, was given the mark of *sehr gut*, the highest of three categories.

His goal in Berlin was the Lehranstalt für die Wissenschaft des Judentums—the Teaching Institution for the Science of Judaism. Over this change in schools has hung the shadow of parental disapproval and of rebellion against the harsh strictures of the Breslau school. According to one story a student was expelled from the Breslau seminary because he had not obeyed all the Sabbath requirements; he had, in fact, broken the rule against Sabbath labor by shaving that morning rather than merely powdering his face. Leo and a third student were incensed at the treatment of their friend and, supposedly, resigned from the school in protest. One of those three students was Hermann Vogelstein, who later, ironically, became chief rabbi of the Jewish community of Breslau. Many years later his son, Max Vogelstein, confirmed that his father had indeed left the seminary under such circumstances. Max recalled his father saying that Leo Baeck also had objected to such intrusion into the personal lives of the students. There is no confirmation, however, that Baeck left as a result of those objections.

Several family accounts indicate that Leo's father objected to the move; according to these accounts there was a rift between father and son over the son's leaving Breslau. Again, there is no confirmation, but this story seems more unlikely than the first. Father and son remained close over the years, and Samuel Bäck, with his open-mindedness, certainly would have understood his son's seeking better educational opportunities. If the Lehranstalt had been in existence when Samuel Bäck was a student, he probably would have gone there himself. The better opportunities for education plus the ease with which students could shift from one school to the other are the probable reasons for the son's change.[14]

When Leo Baeck arrived at the Lehranstalt to complete his rabbinic education, he began an association with it that would last through most of the next half-century. The Lehranstalt had been founded in 1872 because of the dissatisfaction with the Frankel school in Breslau. Not only was it a school for the training of rabbis as was the Breslau seminary, it also was a site for the study of Jewish culture and tradition at the university level. Teachers there were required to have the same scholarly qualifications as those in German universities. Entering students had to have the same qualifications as did entering students at any German university. Nonrabbinical students were admitted, including non-Jews and—what may have been the ultimate reform in a Jewish educational institution—women.

The school was autonomous, free from control by any of the differing Jewish groups in Germany and of any public authority. The result was reliance by the school on private contributions, and this led to a name change early in its career. Originally its founders had called it Hochschule, a name that connotes university status in Germany. A few years later, however, the school had to be incorporated to receive some foundation bequests. The Prussian government, swayed by anti-Semitism, insisted as a condition of incorporation that the school change its name from Hochschule to Lehranstalt, a lesser designation. The change took place formally in 1883. To the students and faculty members, however, the school continued as Hochschule.

Without any particular faction backing it, the Hochschule was always short of funds and at odds with every group in the Jewish community; avoiding control by any one of them meant angering all of them. Students were counted by the handfuls and faculty members on the fingers of one hand. The school was located on Unter den Linden—a distinguished address but not a distinguished facility, housed in three dark rooms on the third floor of a building far back from the street. A student who preceded Leo Baeck there by several years described the Hochschule's rooms as "a disgrace to an unpretentious elementary school" and said that "When I visited the building for the first time in order to enroll, I was simply shocked. This, then, was the respect with which wealthy German Jewry treated the Jewish Torah!"[15]

The Hochschule, with its shabby quarters, began during the flowering of German Judaism and lasted until well into the Nazi years, when Leo Baeck was one of the last teachers remaining. It contributed perhaps more than any other institution to the development of what later was called the German-Jewish culture. The two could not be separated. The German Jews who emerged from this school embodied the middle-class respectability of the German burgher, the devotion to knowledge and education that became a pride of the German citizen, and the respect and love for the Jewish faith. It was not only that the students spent much of their time at the University of Berlin, actually receiving their doctorates there. It was more the mingling of the values of the two groups, the development of an understanding that, for many, the German and the

Jew were not only compatible, they were inseparable. This mixture was embodied in Leo Baeck. His Jewishness never could be doubted; nor could the fact that he was German.

In his student days Baeck had been attracted to the University of Berlin by its *Glanz*, the brilliance of its faculty. And the brilliance shining most strongly on him in those formative years came from a professor of philosophy named Wilhelm Dilthey, whose approach to scholarship was a continuation of the humanistic approach offered by Amos Comenius's gymnasium in Lissa. Dilthey was among those scholars who threw off the fixation with dates and battles and attempted to offer some understanding of what had happened in the story of humanity and of where people's past would lead them. Why do some civilizations fail and others rise? Can any factor in society be ignored as having no importance?

Some scholars—Nietzsche, for example—found answers in the emergence of a superior race. Toynbee, who followed, saw a rhythm in civilization. In contrast to them, Dilthey believed that ideas are the strengths of civilization, that there is no "superior" people. He taught, wrote, and advocated a universalistic approach to history that was concerned not only with events, dates, and personalities but with the whole panoply of emotions, ambitions, thoughts, and ideas that produced the events. Dilthey stressed that one should sympathize with these elements of the past—empathize with them, feel them, understand them, attempt to know them as the men and women who had experienced them knew them. History was not only a study but a revelation, a constantly unfolding and expanding source for the study of man's mind. Martin Buber, a contemporary of Leo Baeck's, also had Dilthey as a teacher and described him as the founder of "the history of philosophical anthropology."[16]

Years later, when Leo Baeck was famous for his writings on Judaism and the meaning of Jewish experience, students of his works attempted to trace the impact of Dilthey, the son of a Lutheran theologian, on the rabbinical student from Lissa. That there was an impact is obvious. Dilthey impressed his students through his intellectualism; none ever knew him well personally or could say that Dilthey was a friend. But this intellectualism produced an image of history—*Geisteswissenschaften*, a German phrase perhaps best compared to the English academic phrase "the humanities" which embodies a whole concept of learning. It was this spirit of *Geisteswissenschaften* that Baeck brought to his study of the Jews.

There were other influences also. Leo Baeck was a German and, in his study of philosophy, could not escape Immanuel Kant. A hundred years earlier Kant had announced not that God was dead but that faith was. One did not "believe" in God, but one understood that God existed, that He was a rational necessity. The moral law had not originated with God; reason dictated that God must exist to assure that people were rewarded with happiness exactly as the morality of their lives indicated they should be, said Kant. Traditional Judaism comes from the other direction: The moral law does originate with God; ethics is grounded in religion, and not religion in ethics. Despite the conflict between traditional Judaism and Kantian philosophy, Kant was popular among the German Jews in the nineteenth century. Like him, they were suspicious of faith, a word conjuring up a life behind the ghetto walls and across the eastern border. With him, they preferred this new "rational" approach, the avenue of reason. That Leo Baeck, at the end of his life, would be far different in his approach to religion from this Kantian approach is a tribute to his own sensitivity as well as to the strength of Judaism.

A third influence was Hermann Cohen. As a student Baeck knew Cohen through his writings only; later they became personally acquainted. Cohen was the son of a cantor and, like Baeck, had studied for the rabbinate at the Jewish Theological Seminary in Breslau. He gave up his plans to be a rabbi, however, and became a philosopher. Much of his writing dealt with Kant, and he accepted Kant's thesis of religion coming from ethics rather than ethics originating in religion. In the later years of his life, in a change presaging Leo Baeck's own development, Cohen came to realize that not all questions can be answered by a religion built only on a rational system of ethics.

Cohen, who died in 1918, had a large following among German Jews; this was due not only to his message but also to the force of his personality. Years after Cohen had died, Leo Baeck was asked by a friend if he believed himself influenced by Cohen's writings. Baeck answered that the influence came not so much from the writings as from Cohen's personality. Baeck then recalled having Sabbath dinner at Cohen's home and experiencing the rapture with which Cohen, the rationalist, chanted the blessing over the wine.

Before his death Cohen had seen Baeck as part disciple, part successor, and potential leader. There is a story that when Cohen was dying, his friends voiced their grief at the prospect of German Jewry losing its most honored spokesman. To this Cohen is supposed to have replied: "Be of good cheer; when I go, Leo Baeck will still be with you."[17]

Given the Bäck family circumstances, Leo always was short of funds during his student days. He attended the University of Berlin with financial help from the Mendelssohn Foundation; it was Dilthey who reported to the university faculty that Leo Baeck had passed the examination for a foundation fellowship magna cum laude. At times Baeck envied those students with sufficient financial resources to buy the books they wanted while he had to wait until the books became available at libraries. The Berlin coffeehouses then were liberal with their rolls, and these became a staple of Baeck's diet. Candles were the customary illumination in the coffeehouses then, and Leo would "liberate"—his description—the drippings from them to use in making his own candles.

Those were the stories he told in the later years of his rabbinical and university education. Obviously, it had been difficult for him, living in the cold and strange cities of Breslau and Berlin as a poor student; neither city is known for its warmth. But he never spoke of those years with regret. Rather, if he dwelt on the poverty, the hunger, and the cold, it was only with amusement. Leo Baeck understood that achievement comes with education; if that meant being hungry and cold, one paid the price willingly.[18]

In the 1890s the custom was (and continues) that rabbinical students conduct services on the Jewish High Holy Days for congregations without rabbis. Baeck led such services with a cantorial student, Magnus Davidsohn, who later described Leo Baeck's early efforts as a preacher. While allowance must be made for Davidsohn having written this account many years after the event and also after Baeck had become a famous rabbinical personality, the account nevertheless may be considered reasonably accurate because Davidsohn followed Baeck's career so closely. Baeck, so Davidsohn said,

broke with the tradition of preachers as it existed up to that time. No pathos, no great distance between him and the community. There stood a young preacher, hiding nothing of himself, plain and speaking simply.... One observed that there stood a personality who tried to bring to the community all that was in his soul and in his deep knowledge which that personality felt itself.[19]

Baeck's doctoral thesis was published in 1895—*Spinozas erste Einwirkungen auf Deutschland*, Spinoza's First Influences on Germany. It was dedicated to his parents, and on the title page Leo's last name is spelled Bäck. The ninety-one-page volume is a typical doctoral dissertation. If it was written under Dilthey's supervision, as is most likely because Baeck's school records show Dilthey was his most frequent instructor in philosophy, the work shows none of Dilthey's sweeping view of history. Rather, it is a carefully researched study of Spinoza's imprint on the German philosophers. The technique used is to quote from Spinoza and then to cite a similar statement from the German, or to relate a developing German philosophical position to one of Spinoza's stances. The purpose of a dissertation is to show that the doctoral candidate has the capacity for original research. Baeck's did that. It also is dull and unemotional, but perhaps of value to someone writing in later years about the German philosophers. The volume represents Leo Baeck, the scholar, at work, though occasionally he steps out of that role. Spinoza is referred to as a "courageous thinker." Lutheranism is criticized for bowing to temporal authority. Baeck understood German Lutheranism as having surrendered what he considered a proper role for a religious body—to offer a moral criticism of the temporal government when such a criticism is deemed necessary. He would repeat this in the 1930s, when he saw and experienced the warped results of that subservience.

There is another element in this dissertation, a suggestion of something with which Leo Baeck himself would wrestle during the coming years. Speaking of Spinoza, Baeck wrote that he had seen his own religion, Judaism, through the spectacles of the *Kabbala* ("*durch die Brille der Kabbala*"), a reference to a form of Jewish mysticism. Reflecting an attitude prevalent among nineteenth-century Jews, especially those educated in German institutions, Leo Baeck then derided mysticism as a wide-ranging delusion among the Jews of the time ("*unter den Juden weit verbreiteten Irrwahn*").[20]

Leo Baeck was ordained a rabbi in May 1897, the month he turned twenty-four years of age.[21] His academic education was completed, according to the terms of his upbringing. For the work that lay before him it was an efficient education. From his father and his family's rabbinical heritage he had gained a love of his religion. It would be for him not a fact of his life but *the* fact, controlling every other aspect of his life. From the gymnasium came an enjoyment of learning that would keep him constantly expanding his intellectual prowess. In later years, for example, he awoke at five in the morning to study Greek or Latin for an hour. In the Nazi years, when his responsibilities did not allow sufficient time for his studies, he changed his waking hour from five o'clock to four, so that he would still have time for his hour of study.

From the Breslau seminary, the Hochschule, and the Beth Hamidrash —a traditional school in Berlin that he also had attended "in order to become acquainted with the different theological tendencies"—he had acquired a vast knowledge of his religion. This, coupled with his emotional attachment to Judaism, was his weapon for counterattack when, in a few years, he saw Judaism threatened by an intellectual assault from Christianity.

From the universities of Breslau and Berlin, from his studies of Kant, his exposure to Graetz, and his more prolonged experiences with Dilthey, and from his studies of the writings of Cohen, Baeck had become first acquainted with and then a master of German philosophical studies and style. When he began speaking to Christians as well as Jews about Judaism, he would be expressing himself in a manner that the German Christians could not ignore; it was their style, their references. He was one of them.

3 RABBI

LEO BAECK first, however, had to find a job. Rabbis just out of seminary found jobs then the way most people did; they wrote letters of application. On December 13, 1896, Leo Baeck wrote to the "very honored" board of the Jewish community of Koenigsberg in Prussia, describing his educational background and adding that he would be ordained shortly. "For three years I have officiated at the High Holy Days in synagogues operated by the Jewish community," he said. "Also I held religious services for young people. I gave religious instruction in a high school for girls and at a school for young women."

For further information, he suggested in his neat and formal handwriting that they contact Herr Rabbi Dr. Maybaum who lived in Berlin on the street "behind the Catholic Church." With his application was a certificate announcing that he had officiated as rabbi in 1894, 1895, and 1896 in Berlin on the High Holy Days in different parts of the community. "His sermons were deeply thought out and demonstrated great knowledge," said the certificate.

Koenigsberg chose, rather than the recent graduate, a more experienced rabbi—one from Oppeln, leaving that community without a rabbi. Oppeln, not deterred by Baeck's inexperience, hired him, and it was there that Leo Baeck began his career as rabbi, teacher, leader, and *seelsorger*.[1]

Oppeln was in Silesia, near Breslau and only several hours journey from Lissa. The early history of its Jewish community is similar to that of other Jewish communities in Europe during the Middle Ages. The first Jews arrived before the fourteenth century, attracted to Oppeln because it "was an important commercial center; the great highways from Hungary and Little Poland to Breslau crossing the Oder at that point," explained Baeck in one account. In the fifteenth century the first Jew was killed there by Christians. In the next century, in the year 1565, all Jews were expelled from the city.

In 1813 five Jewish families began the modern Jewish community in Oppeln. By 1861 there were 590 Jewish individuals. By the second half of the nineteenth century Christians had come to accept the Jews, and the restrictions against them gradually fell. The most dramatic incident was the granting of the "freedom of the city" by the Christians to the community rabbi on his eightieth birthday, meaning that Jews no longer were barred from some parts of the city. At the time of Leo Baeck's arrival, the total population of Oppeln was 30,000, of which about 750 were Jews.[2]

These Jews enjoyed their life in Oppeln. A woman in Leo Baeck's congregation recalled years later that although the city was as "gray as the cement which was manufactured in its factories" and its ugliness "must be granted even by the most affectionate look back," in Oppeln

there still was the imposing market place with its decorated houses, of which not a few rose above the skyline with their swirling Baroque gables. In the middle rose the town hall, of which we tended to say with pride that it was built in the style of the Palazzo Vecchio in Florence, which it unmistakably resembled, in fact. And then there was the Oder with its still unspoiled brush-covered banks from which we, in the spring, cut branches. With a little canal there was created in the middle of the city an island with fine homes named Wilhelmsthal, with a castle, a castle park and a pond, which we used in the winter for ice skating. From one corner of the castle pond the ice house enticed us to a warm rest, and, if our money would reach, probably also to a cup of hot chocolate.

In addition to being pleasant, life there for Jews was prosperous. Traditionally on their High Holy Days the Jews have given to the poor of their community. In Oppeln, however, they had to find the poor outside their city limits; there were no poor Jews in Oppeln.

This community had been led for almost four decades by Rabbi Adolf Wiener. His successor briefly was Hermann Vogelstein, Baeck's colleague at Breslau. Vogelstein arrived in Oppeln while Rabbi Wiener was alive, assumed some of his duties, and then became the community's spiritual leader in 1895 when the elderly man died. After two years Vogelstein left to become rabbi in Koenigsberg, and Baeck came to Oppeln. While Rabbi Vogelstein was in Oppeln, the Jewish community had begun to build a new synagogue. With 600 members then, the community believed it was of a size to have a larger synagogue. The new synagogue was located on Wilhelmsthal Island, considered the loveliest part of Oppeln. Surrounded by fine homes, and "ruling over this idyllic scene [on the island] was the red-brick synagogue towering in the background, which had been built in the then common Moorish style. It was a tranquil, dignified structure, so much in harmony with the tranquil, dignified people . . ."[3]

One of Leo Baeck's first tasks in Oppeln was officiating at the synagogue's dedication on June 22, 1897. At the ceremony, in addition to the Jewish residents of the city, there were many non-Jews and many out-of-town guests, including Leo's father, Rabbi Samuel Bäck, who had traveled from Lissa to see his son enter for the first time the synagogue that would house his congregation.

Leo Baeck led the procession of the Oppeln Jews and their guests to the western gate of the synagogue. There, before receiving the key to the building from the architect, he led in prayer: "Dear God, you are our protection forever and ever. Before the mountains came and the earth and the world were created, you were God eternally and eternally." As the rabbi received the key, he continued the prayer, stressing that more magnificent than the new building and its adornments was the spirit existing within it to shape great and powerful things. Baeck led the congregation in saying that before them was not only a new building but "a new life with fresh strength" to dedicate to God's service. The prayer concluded with a plea for the congregants, "In everything which we think, work and strive for—to hate always the false appearance of lies, to love always the honest ways of the truth," and for the congregants always to remember the "Holy word spoken in a holy room . . . as the richest seed of virtue." Then the congregation, led by Rabbi Leo Baeck, advanced to the synagogue door and said:

So open up, you holy door, to the pious crowd of dedicated believers who receive consolation and refreshment from the meaningful words of the priest always. May a blessing come from this place, from the holy altar of this holy temple. May God crown our work with his blessing! May He be with us on all our days!

Leo Baeck stepped to the synagogue threshold, inserted the key into the lock, opened the door, and led his congregation into the sanctuary. Filing in, the members sang the hymn "How goodly are your tents, O, Jacob." The hymn tells of Balaam, a pagan, who had come to the

Israelites in biblical times to curse them, but on seeing the tents of Jacob, had been moved, instead, to speak of the beauty of the people and of their encampment. The hymn is a tribute to the Israelites' love of peace, a hope that peace might always surround them; the hymn also is a mark of their humility. It says, may they also live so that all strangers will say to them, "How goodly are your tents, O, Jacob, your dwelling places, O, Israel. Through the richness of your mercy, I enter this house, bend myself in your holy temple in respect for you."

The next step in the dedication of the Oppeln synagogue was the lighting of the Eternal Light. This is one of the two elements basic to a synagogue. Burning in front of the Holy Ark, never to be extinguished, it represents the eternality of God, the eternality of the love for God and of God's teaching. It is a reminder of the Temple candelabrum. When Judas Maccabeus, in the second pre-Christian century, reclaimed the Jewish Temple in Jerusalem from its defilers and sought to reconsecrate it, his first challenge was to find oil for the candelabrum. A new supply of oil took eight days to produce, and the candelabrum held oil sufficient for only one day. Yet, so the tradition says, that one day's supply of oil survived, miraculously, for eight days until the new oil was produced. The story symbolizes the Jews' belief that neither God nor the Jews' relationship with God can be extinguished.

After lighting the Eternal Light, Leo Baeck opened the Holy Ark in preparation for it to receive the Torah scrolls. Whether the synagogue imitates in its structure the great Christian cathedrals of the Middle Ages or the New England Protestant church, whether it is located in a second-floor room in a New York slum or on a plain in Poland, it houses a Torah.

The history of the Torah is 3,000 years old and begins, according to tradition, when Moses received the tablets of the law from God on Mount Sinai and carried them down to the waiting Hebrew people. Then, as the Hebrews traveled through the desert, they carried the tablets before them in a wooden Ark. This Holy Ark became the most important object to the Hebrew people. King David led them in a war to recapture it. His son, King Solomon, built the Temple in Jerusalem to house it.

The Holy Ark with the tablets from Sinai symbolized for the Jews the law of God. The word attached to this law was Torah—literally, teaching or instruction. Originally, Torah referred to the five books of Moses. The word constantly grew in meaning, however, to the point where a Jew speaking of Torah might be referring to the first five books of the Bible alone or to the totality of Jewish learning included in the Talmud and later writings as well.

The Torah scroll containing the five books of Moses is a sacred symbol. Jews are instructed to read it through each year so that they constantly learn from it and cannot claim to be unaware of the responsibilities the Torah places on them. To ensure that this instruction is fulfilled, those five books are divided into sections, one of which is read each week in the synagogue. To remind the Jews of the antiquity of their tradition, the Torah used in the modern service is prepared as it was in ancient times: It is written on parchment scrolls by a scribe who may not use any metal in his pens—metal is used in warfare and for killing, and nothing that can take a life may be used in the preparation of the Torah. For that reason, although David had rescued the Ark, it was Solomon, rather than David, who built the Temple in Jerusalem to house the Holy Ark. In First Chronicles 22:6-10 David tells his son Solomon that the Lord had forbidden him, David, to build the Temple because, said the Lord: "You have shed much blood in my sight and waged great wars; for this reason you shall not build a house in honor of my name. But you shall have a son who shall be a man of peace."

The Torah is holy, but it is not beyond the reach of the people. On joyous occasions having to do with the Torah, the scrolls are carried around the sanctuary so that all can either touch them or be near them. This was the next step in the Oppeln synagogue dedication, and Leo Baeck lead the procession.

The dedication ended with final prayers for the Kaiser and for the German Reich; the synagogue of Oppeln had become a house of prayer, a religious edifice, a center for the Jews of that community, and, as a description of the time had it, "an ornament for the city." It remained so for forty-one years, until 1938 when the Nazis burned it down.[4]

In 1897 when Leo Baeck had arrived in Oppeln, he was twenty-four years old. He had spent the previous six years in Breslau and Berlin with their universities, libraries, and theaters, their sophisticated and cultured people, their centers for intellectual debate and cultural opportunity. In contrast, the Oppeln he found was a middle-class manufacturing town lacking the stimulation of Berlin and Breslau. He did find, however, in Oppeln a community that offered him stability and support. Because of this security, perhaps, Leo Baeck was able to devote the time and the energy during the ten years he stayed in Oppeln toward his own intellectual and spiritual development. It was in Oppeln that Leo Baeck set out on the path that would take him to the point where he was one of the leading Jewish teachers and writers of the twentieth century, one of the most articulate spokesmen of that faith in its dialogue with Christianity, and the unanimous choice of the German Jews when the times compelled them to settle on a leader.

Also at Oppeln he found time for romance. There he met and married Natalie Hamburger, who became his greatest support, his most stabilizing influence.

The role that Natalie Baeck played in her husband's life was typical for a Jewish woman at that time; she was his helpmate, the partner in his endeavors, *die Rabbinerfrau*, the perfect rabbi's wife. Those who knew Leo and Natalie Baeck in the four decades of their marriage spoke of her kindness, her shyness, of the happiness Leo had with her. During their married life she made certain their house was open to his students, provided the peace and quiet for his studies. She was his secretary, often writing his letters and keeping his material in order; and his greatest follower, always attending his sermons and his lectures, and—from the audience if it were a lecture and from the women's section if it were a sermon in a synagogue—giving him a nod of approval when he finished.

For many Jewish women the role of helpmate that Natalie filled— figuratively, if not literally, ten paces behind her husband—was not sufficient. Throughout Jewish history there have been examples of women warriors, scholars, and merchants. When Natalie was beginning her married life, many Jewish women were receiving university degrees, entering careers, and establishing their own identities. When these career women married, many of them took as their last names hyphenated combinations of their family names and the husbands' family names to symbolize their intention of not being subordinate family members. These women were part of the society in which Leo Baeck was active in the later years of his life, and he had no difficulty accepting them as professional and cultural equals. Natalie also had no difficulty dealing with women who sought status equal with men. It was just that this was not her life, not her choice. Hers was to be *die Rabbinerfrau*.

Natalie's home was Oppeln; her grandfather was Rabbi Adolf Wiener, leader of the Jewish community until his death in 1895. Like Samuel Bäck, Rabbi Wiener had a doctorate in philosophy, but he was more of a reformer than Bäck. Chief among the reforms Adolf Wiener advocated was changing the Jewish Sabbath from sundown Friday to sundown

Saturday to coincide with the Christian Sabbath on Sunday. He also supported a prayerbook revision and did not object to Jews traveling on the Sabbath. He never forced his recommendations on the people of Oppeln, however, and they were tolerant of his liberalism.[5]

Natalie Hamburger was an attractive woman with dark hair, almost as tall as Leo Baeck and with regular features. She was on occasion mistaken for a Gentile, a mistake that gave Leo Baeck one of his favorite stories, one that he told for many years. While he was engaged to Natalie, according to this story, the two of them, properly chaperoned, vacationed at a resort together. As was the custom then, the couple promenaded around the village square each morning and afternoon. The mood was conservative. She wore a long, dark dress and a hat, as befitted a woman engaged to a rabbi. He wore a dark suit with vest, tie, and hat. She held his arm demurely. He tipped his hat to the ladies he knew, while she nodded her head. On one morning promenade, Leo Baeck saw one of his fellow students from the Hochschule and waved to him. Baeck was certain that his friend had heard of his engagement and was anxious to introduce his betrothed. But something was wrong. The friend, seeing Leo and Natalie together, immediately turned and left. The incident was repeated that afternoon. A surprised and hurt Leo Baeck, not understanding his friend's reaction, sought him out. "What is wrong?" he asked his friend. "How have I offended you?" The friend replied: "Here you are engaged to the daughter of one of the finest Jewish families in Germany, and you're with some *shikse*."[6]

Leo Baeck and Natalie Hamburger were married in 1897. The marriage was, of course, a major social occasion for the Oppeln Jewish community, which presented the young couple with a monogrammed silver chest. Friends who visited the couple in those years spoke of the "young married happiness" and "their simple beautiful married life." That description never has been disputed. Their only child, Ruth, was born in 1900.[7]

Baeck's arrival in Oppeln was at a time when the controversy over how much Jewish tradition should be retained in services and how much of the Christian services should be borrowed was at a flashpoint in many communities. The movement away from Hebrew in the services coupled with such proposals as changing the day of the Sabbath had brought on this controversy, which always was an emotional one. Rabbi Wiener, in one of his first pulpits, for example, had instituted the practice of giving sermons in German. Since many Jews in his community considered sermons a Christian practice, they became so incensed that Rabbi Wiener could deliver the sermons only with police protection.

In this controversy Leo Baeck demonstrated his ability as an arbiter in Oppeln, the conciliator between factions. He continued many traditional practices. In his services he wore the long robes of the rabbi, a head covering, and the prayer shawl called the *tallith* with its four fringed corners to remind the Jews of God's command in Numbers 15:39–40 that they wear tassels on their garments to "remember all the Lord's commands and obey them, and not go on your wanton ways." In the mornings he said his prayers and "laid *tefillin*," a process by which the Jew, with leather straps, attaches to his forehead and left arm leather boxes containing biblical passages, including that from Deuteronomy 6:4, beginning: "Hear, O Israel, the Lord is our God, one Lord, and you must love the Lord your God with all your heart and soul and strength." This is to remind the Jews that God led them from Egyptian bondage—"You shall have the record of it as a sign upon your hand and upon your forehead as a reminder" (Exodus 13:9).

However, Baeck also made some changes in Oppeln. The services were in Hebrew for the most part, but there was a limited use of German as a bow to the trend of the times, an acknowledgment that many German Jews could not understand Hebrew, and also as a recognition that the prayers said for the Kaiser and the Reich should be recited in German. Separation of sexes during the services was continued. There was a mixed choir, however, and the change that remained the most controversial in the German-Jewish services for years afterward was instituted here early in Leo Baeck's rabbinate— an organ was installed. Jewish services always had been melodic, but the music had come from chanting by readers or cantors. In the nineteenth century this ritual music had been collected, arranged, and stylized. This development led to a greater exploitation of the music's richness, and then to the installation of a choir followed by the argument over whether an organ should be installed in the synagogue. The opponents claimed not only that an organ was not traditional but that it made the synagogue resemble the Christian church too closely.

Those who opposed a mixed choir or the installation of the organ nevertheless supported Baeck because of his use of Hebrew in the services and because of his own personal traditional habits. Those who objected to the amount of Hebrew in the service or to Baeck's own traditional habits supported him because of the choir and the organ.

By the end of his decade in Oppeln there was no opposition there to Leo Baeck.[8]

For Leo Baeck life in Oppeln was pleasant. His wife Natalie, because of her origins there and her own charm, was one of the most popular women in the town, and their daughter Ruth was loved as the "community child." When, after a Friday-evening service, Leo, Natalie, and Ruth joined a local family for Sabbath dinner of fish from the nearby Oder River and Hungarian wine, they were welcomed as friends rather than as participants in an obligatory ritual of courtesy. On the table were the Sabbath candles, lit at sundown by the woman of the house to symbolize God's light.

Children who had grown up in Oppeln when Leo Baeck was rabbi there recalled that they were not forced to attend services—they went willingly. They listened to Rabbi Baeck speak "so solemn," as the children described it; as one recalled many years later, "the world around him disappeared." Leo Baeck actually was not that good a speaker, and his sermons never moved anyone so emotionally as that quotation suggests. He avoided emotional appeals, seeking instead to offer intellectual challenges. Still, the statement suggests something of the warmth that the people came to feel for their rabbi. "From the earliest days of my life," said one of his young students, "I was filled with an enthusiasm for Judaism because I saw it bound up in such a Jewish aristocrat."[9]

Children enjoyed this "aristocrat." He was kind to them and treated them with respect. He taught them religion in the secular school and was not above increasing their grades if they needed better marks to graduate, a practice he had learned from his father. On Saturday afternoons, beginning a custom that lasted through most of his life, Leo Baeck invited a few students over for lively and philosophical discussions about current events, chiefly Jewish questions—the liturgy, the music, the role of the Jew in German society, orthodoxy versus liberalism; all were thrashed out by rabbi and students while munching on Sabbath cakes and sipping tea. One student, unable to persuade the rabbi, concluded a discussion with a quotation from Friedrich the Great: "Therefore, each will finally be able to attain salvation after his own fashion."

Leo Baeck kept up private relationships with his students, writing to them when they were away at school, maintaining a camaraderie with them and demonstrating a respect for them as individuals. In 1904 he sent a note to one of his former students, Fritz Muhr, in

Breslau. The Muhr family had been particularly kind to Leo Baeck in Oppeln, and Baeck had encouraged Fritz in his studies. It was July, a time when Leo Baeck usually vacationed, but this summer, so he wrote, he stayed home during the "dog days in order to do some of my private work." The month was very hot, showing that "sweat does not only come before virtue." After thanking Fritz Muhr for writing from Breslau, Baeck said, "Your letter has brought me a little bit of academic air and memories of my own beautiful time as a student. Much nicer memories there cannot be . . ." The letter had the tone of one between equals. That was an important part of Leo Baeck's relationships; he never condescended.

The friendship between Leo Baeck and the Muhr family lasted for half a century, and it was typical of his friendships with many families. It ended, as many of them did, in the early 1940s when these families were destroyed by the Nazis.

He also felt certain obligations as a representative of Jewry in the city. In later years Baeck recalled that he gave his rabbinic successor in Oppeln this advice: "My dear friend, you must never forget that you represent not only Judaism here but also Jewry." Then Rabbi Baeck explained that once a week the leading citizens of the town of Oppeln gathered in the local tavern. There were members of the town council, the clergymen of the Protestant and Catholic faiths, and Leo Baeck. How did Leo Baeck represent Jewry in Oppeln with such a tavern crowd? "I always made certain," he said, "that I was the last one to leave the table."[10]

Very early in his career Leo Baeck discovered something that all clergymen eventually come to know—belonging to a community can reduce their independence. How far ahead of their congregations can they move? How independent of their fellow rabbis should they dare to be? Must they hold their personal inclinations in check to keep in line with their community and environment? When faced with these kinds of questions, Leo Baeck's tendency was to arbitrate—but never at the cost of his integrity. He wanted to be a point where all factions could meet, but he also knew that sometimes he must be, for some at least, a stopping point, a final word. That he did not abuse this position, nor enter into it lightly, made more powerful those occasions during his rabbinical career when he moved from being the great arbiter to become the man who could not be swayed.

This willingness to make himself the stopping point showed first at a rabbinical association meeting in Berlin in June 1898. Baeck, twenty-five years old, had been at his Oppeln post only one year. There were ninety-four rabbis at the Berlin meeting from various parts of Germany, representing the three trends in Judaism—liberal, conservative, and orthodox. The question being debated was which schools should be allowed to bestow rabbinical diplomas. The debate, growing more heated, jumped to the question of whether a student could transfer from one seminary to another, from a "liberal" to a "conservative" or to an "orthodox" school and back again. The lines between the divisions in Judaism were sharply drawn, and members of each movement argued vociferously against the "pollution" that would occur if one of its students went to another movement's seminary. Said one opponent: "I oppose with all firmness our recommending two years at [the orthodox seminary], two years at the Breslau seminary or the Berlin Lehranstalt. . . . That would be a great mistake; to the theology belongs knowledge and religious conviction . . ."

The young Leo Baeck rose. He was uniquely competent to speak to the question because he had, in fact, attended all three seminaries. Although his studies at the orthodox school in Berlin had been relatively brief compared to the time he spent at the Hochschule and in Breslau, he had attended the orthodox school deliberately to acquaint himself with the differing trends in Judaism. "It would be good," he argued, "if the young people go from the Lehranstalt to the orthodox seminary." The recently ordained rabbi paused and then asked his more experienced peers: "Why should men have only one direction?"

The question apparently provoked laughter from the other rabbis, who considered crossing divisional lines one step from heresy. "You must allow me to finish," said Baeck, and when the audience had quieted, he continued: "I believe a man should not be instructed merely in one direction. There could be a wish expressed by the rabbinical association that the institutions cooperate in this respect. The result could be a mutual toleration among the different groups." He suggested that rabbinical students attend all three schools as a matter of routine to "make unnecessary all the considerations which are being brought forth by the lecturers." No action was taken on Baeck's suggestion. It represented not victory but courage in opposing his peers, almost all of whom were older and more established in their careers.[11]

At the same meeting Baeck again opposed his fellow rabbis—as well as his own community in Oppeln. This second incident involved Zionism, a movement that had swept through European Jewry when a journalist, Theodor Herzl, witnessed the ugliness of anti-Semitism in

France and wrote *Der Judenstaat*, a call for the Jews to develop their own homeland so there would be a land for them free of hatred. Most German Jews considered the call ridiculous; after all, they were Germans who practiced Judaism, just as there were other Germans practicing the Protestant or Catholic religions. The German Jews already had a homeland and felt no need for another. It was known in advance that Zionism would be debated at the rabbinical meeting, and this had produced a larger turnout than had been anticipated. The session had to be moved from the regular site, the meeting hall of the Jewish community headquarters on Oranienburgerstrasse, to a larger room, the *Geselligen Vereins der Freunde*—the Club of Friends on Potsdamerstrasse—which was more well known among German Jews as a site for weddings rather than for acrimonious debates.

Herzl's Zionist call was only a year old, but already there had been a Zionist congress in Basel. The choice of that city in Switzerland was a reluctant one, a result of German animosity toward Zionism. Originally the meeting was scheduled for Munich because the Russian Jews coming to the session didn't want a Swiss site and also because Munich had kosher restaurants. But the Munich Jewish community refused to act as hosts to the meeting, and the Basel site was selected. This congress was derided by the members of the executive board of the German rabbinical association, who earned for themselves the title "Protest Rabbis" by calling Zionism contrary to the messianic promise of the Bible.

Now, at the meeting on Potsdamerstrasse, the members of the executive board wanted all the rabbis in the association to endorse their protest. The question was an emotional one, and debate was shut off abruptly before the pro-Zionists were allowed to speak. When the vote was taken, only three of the ninety-four rabbis present refused to support the executive board's protest against the Zionist congresses. One of those three actually said he too was against the Congresses, but he objected to the cutting off of debate. Only two of the rabbis were publicly willing to dare the wrath of their executive board by voting against it. One was a rabbi named Saul Katz. The other was Leo Baeck.

Baeck was not a Zionist, but he believed that the reawakening of a national Jewish consciousness, as represented by Zionism, could be valuable. There was another reason for his vote, one he spoke about years later. He was particularly proud of his vote, he said, because the executive board had tried to brand the Zionist supporters as heretics. Baeck considered this unfair and had to speak out against it.[12]

The 1898 incident reflected the emotionalism that surrounded Zionism among German Jews, who considered themselves Germans, an identity for which they had long struggled. One rabbi's comments on that meeting, although referring specifically to the liberal movement among German Jews, describe well the prevailing opinion. The rabbi said that the German Jews "understood Judaism to be pure religion and therefore [that it required] opposition to, or at least abstention from, those concerns, involvements, and tasks which Palestine as a national and cultural center of the Jewish people presented. The reformers in Berlin . . . considered themselves Jews by religion only . . ."[13] They would adhere to that position until Adolf Hitler and his Nazis disabused them of the notion.

In 1907 Rabbi Baeck, still in Oppeln, again felt compelled to speak out against the actions of his peers in another incident involving Zionism. A Berlin rabbi named Emil Bernhard-Cohn was in difficulties with the Berlin Jewish community because of his Zionist stance. Rabbis in Berlin were employed not by individual congregations but by the Berlin Jewish community, which assigned them to synagogues. This community could hire or fire untenured rabbis, and Rabbi Cohn was fired.

The charge against him was that he had used his pulpit and his teacher's lecturn to propagandize for Zionism. This he denied. "I have only presented Zionism in an objective and very formal way to the students in a two-hour lesson," he said, "and, to be sure, it was so objective, that after my presentation, a student confronted me with the question: 'So you are not a Zionist, Herr Doktor?' " Cohn also denied having propagandized for Zionism from the pulpit and charged the community had fired him because he would not promise to refrain from speaking in favor of Zionism at public meetings. "I can give no promise and would not bind myself," he said. Refusing to deny his feelings, he acknowledged that "I am a Zionist with all my heart . . ."

Cohn was an outcast; he had gone against not only the leadership of the community but also the wishes of the majority of his community —German Judaism never embraced Zionism. The retaliation had been cruel. Cohn was denied the right to make a living as a rabbi in Berlin because his political opinions differed from those of his lay superiors, and the Berlin Jewish community was denied his rabbinate. Hoping to gain both sympathy and support for his position, Rabbi Cohn sent a number of newspaper clippings to rabbis throughout Germany. One recipient was Leo Baeck.

Unlike most others, Baeck responded. "You were so thoughtful to

send me the little clippings with the reports about your suspension,"
began Leo Baeck's letter. "I have not had the honor of knowing you
personally. . . . However, the growing interest and involvement with
which I have followed your experience, as you describe it, has moved
me so personally that it has become an honest need for me to speak
to you a word of heartfelt sympathy." An "honest" need is the kind of
emotion Leo Baeck could not resist, even when he realized that his
action could become public and incur the wrath of the leading Jewish
community in the nation. He did not restrain himself.

"What happened to you," he continued in his letter, "is so illiterate,
so unreligious and so un-Jewish that one can scarcely understand how
it could have happened in the name of a Jewish religious community
which calls itself liberal. It is just as incomprehensible to me that the
Berlin Rabbi's council could be silent about it; but perhaps the council
has merely not yet spoken." The council had not spoken and did not
speak. "I myself want, as far as I can," said Baeck, "to work on having
the rabbinical association deal with the matter; I cannot imagine that
the last word has already been said. Allow me also to express my
heartiest wish that you may be able to remain in your profession."
Baeck continued that he did not believe the rabbis in Germany were so
rich in "men of individuality and steady attitudes" that they could
allow *"ein Mann über Bord!"*—"a man overboard." Although Cohn continued as a rabbi in Germany, finding congregations in other cities, he
did not serve again in Berlin for many years.[14]

Leo Baeck's position in Oppeln was not harmed by his public stands.
His role as a conciliator in the community, the person to whom all sides
in a dispute could come, the warmth of the relationships he and his
family had built there, all combined to create a tolerance for him when
he did become involved in controversy. With this tolerance there also
was pride as he began the role that would be one of the most important
throughout his life: to be a leading participant in his faith's dialogue
with Christianity.

He realized that anti-Semitism—no matter how hard the German
Jews worked to pretend it did not exist—was a factor in the dialogue. "I
always admonish our people to forget that there is anti-Semitism and
to live in a natural way without leering incessantly at their Christian
fellow-citizens," he once told a friend. At the same time Baeck was not
naive, understanding the problems of a minority member in a society,
particularly a society with institutionalized anti-Semitism as Germany
was. When one of his students wanted to become a linguistics professor,

for example, Baeck advised him to become, instead, a physician, explaining that anti-Semitism blocked a Jew from receiving a tenured university appointment.[15]

Baeck's struggle against anti-Semitism was primarily on the philosophical and theological levels. In taking on this responsibility he was well armed. His German education in the Gymnasium and at the universities of Breslau and Berlin had prepared him to speak to a Gentile audience with as broad an understanding of non-Jewish scholarship as most Christian writers had.

This dialogue with Christianity would occupy much of Leo Baeck's life for four decades. At the end he would be recognized as one of the great commentators on the Jewish religion in the modern world. His opponents largely would be forgotten, except as those with whom he had debated. In all these years, despite some rather unusual pressures on him and despite circumstances that might have pushed other men beyond reasonable limits, Leo Baeck always wrote with respect and often with affection for Christianity. He argued with it, challenged it, and disputed it, but he never insulted it.

His involvement began as a response to a slim volume written by Adolf von Harnack, one of the most famous of Christian scholars at the end of the nineteenth century. His book, *Das Wesen des Christentums* (The Essence of Christianity),* comprised a series of lectures that he had delivered to some college students to deal with a situation that Christians found alternately disturbing and challenging. Research was questioning the literal truth of the New Testament. Had Jesus actually lived? Had the authors of the Gospels actually witnessed what they wrote, or had they grafted some legends of the time onto the life of Jesus, obscuring the essential man? Could Christianity be richer, perhaps, if people understood that Jesus represented more than he was? *Das Wesen des Christentums*, in which von Harnack responded to those questions, was enormously successful, being in print for many years and selling many copies.

A device von Harnack used in extolling Christianity was name-calling directed at Judaism. "[T]he literal interpretation of God's revealed will proved that [the Jews] had been forsaken by God and had fallen under the sway of the devil," he wrote. "The Old Testament from cover to cover has really nothing whatever to do with the Jews. Illegally and

---

* This book is available in an English translation with the title *What Is Christianity?*

insolently the Jews had seized upon it, they had confiscated it and tried
to claim it as their own property. It would be a sin for Christians to
say: 'The book belongs to us and the Jews.' No, the book belongs now
and ever more to none but Christians."

Judaism, von Harnack continued, was "a religion of miserabilism!"
Christianity had developed "amid the wreck of the Jewish religion."
Other scholars saw the teachings of the Jewish prophets repeated in the
teachings of Jesus, but von Harnack saw threats—"There was always a
danger of an inferior and obsolete principle forcing its way into Christianity through the Old Testament . . ."

Despite his reputation as a scholar von Harnack demonstrated a lack
of knowledge and understanding of Judaism. He insisted that the Christian concept of the messiah—"effectively setting the man who knew
that he was the Son of God, and was doing the work of God, on the
throne of history"—was the Jewish concept. When Judaism had accomplished this, "its mission was exhausted." He denigrated the Jews'
love for the way of God as "particularistic and statutory regulations of
the law" and said that the disciple of Jesus called Paul had done away
with these regulations by claiming they were "to be understood in a
purely spiritual sense and to be interpreted as symbols." He charged
that Judaism had been "freed from its limitations by a process of philosophical interpretation." He spoke of a path "upon which a deliverance
from historical Judaism and its outworn ordinances was capable of
gradual attainment."

The Christianity he conjured up was the product of a nineteenth-century approach to religion, which placed religion on a Sunday shelf
where it was not to be touched the other six days of the week. To
Adolf von Harnack, Christianity existed in a world without relationship
to people. Christianity, he said, "is no ethical or social arcanum for the
preservation or improvement of things generally. To make what it has
done for civilisation and human progress the main question, and to determine its value by the answer, is to do it violence at the start . . ." He
ridiculed man's labor as "a valuable safety-valve and useful in keeping
off greater ills," but said, "it is not in itself an absolute good, and we
cannot include it amongst our ideals. The same may be said of the progress of civilisation. It is of course to be welcomed; but the piece of
progress in which we delight today becomes something mechanical by tomorrow, and leaves us cold . . ."

His view of Christianity was the popular romantic view of the time.
"Jesus," he wrote, "like all truly religious minds, was firmly convinced

that in the end God will do justice. If He does not do it here, He will do it in the Beyond, and that is the main point . . ."[16]

From the original contention that Judaism's only role had been as a predecessor of Christianity, this argument widened. A recent Catholic critic of this school described its development this way:

This view also penetrated to the liberals' understanding of Christianity, leading them to deny that Christianity and Jesus were in any way intrinsically "Jewish." Christianity was seen as the universal religion of nature or reason, which arose as the antithesis and negation of Judaism . . . what was hated in biblical revealed religion was stereotyped as "Jewish," while all positive values of spirituality, rationality, and universality were the characteristics of Christianity or philosophy that were antithetical to "Judaism."[17]

Von Harnack and the school he represented had a major impact on Christian thought in the twentieth century, an impact from which Christianity did not begin to recover for at least fifty years, and then only when it began examining its role in the Nazi attack on the Jews.

Leo Baeck long had been interested in writing; his articles began appearing in the 1890s, on religious subjects and often in the form of book reviews. In what is apparently his first published article, in 1895, he called for a greater understanding between religions, not so much in the spirit of tolerance toward one's fellows, but for the purpose of strengthening one's own religious convictions by learning about other religions. Baeck wrote:

Where the disciples of different beliefs are sharply separated from one another, scarcely a demand for a deeper understanding of religious ideas exists. Man is so complacent, so satisfied with himself, that he can feel no need to give any account to himself about what he believes. Suppressing a different belief is an act which shrinks to a very high degree any impulse to philosophical treatment of religion. The victor believes he is right because he has the power.

Armed with this power, the victor meets no opposition, Baeck wrote, because other men are afraid to oppose him. To this victor, said Baeck, "the suppression of the opposition stands in his eyes as being good in itself, just, and virtuous; because, after all, he is in possession of the truth. That his opponent and his opponent's religion are without morality, is self-evident to him—they are to be tortured by him and to become his servants . . ." In another article, in 1896, he asserted that Judaism is a religion without dogma, without a central authority. He restated that point throughout much of his writing career. Judaism, he insisted, is a religion of individual responsibility.[18]

Baeck first responded directly to von Harnack in a review of his book that appeared in the *Monatsschrift für Geschichte und Wissenschaft des Judentums,* then considered the most scholarly Jewish journal in the world. Baeck's review is thirteen pages long, and in many respects is a typical book review, beginning with a homage to von Harnack's position as a scholar and religious thinker and then tearing apart his thinking processes as well as his scholarship. Baeck challenged von Harnack not only on his knowledge of Judaism but also on his knowledge of Christianity.[19]

The matter might have ended there except that the same year the review appeared, the *Monatsschrift* was taken over by a newly organized group known as the Gesellschaft zur Förderung der Wissenschaft des Judentums—the Society for the Advancement of the Science of Judaism, which brought together Jewish scholars and published their writings. The society's first published book was Leo Baeck's *Das Wesen des Judentums* in 1905. More than seven decades later this book—greatly revised and expanded—continues in print in many languages. An American edition, published in 1961, had sold 25,000 copies in fifteen years. This book remains a comprehensive and persuasive statement of what its title intended for it, *The Essence of Judaism.*[20]

It is, in its first edition, 167 pages, of which 161 are text. The author's name is listed as "Dr. Leo Bäck, Rabbiner in Oppeln." The book, although an obvious response to von Harnack, alludes neither to him nor to his book. Also, the author's tone is more that of a German than a Jew. This book, Leo Baeck's *The Essence of Judaism,* became the great Jewish work only as it was worked on over the years by its author who constantly grew in his own knowledge, understanding, and emotional attachment to his religion. *The Essence of Judaism* definitely *became* a Jewish book—in the first edition it was not.

The first edition of *The Essence of Judaism* is an ideal representation of the German Jewish thought of the late nineteenth century. It was a product of the mind, not of the heart. Not only did it show how much Jewish scholarship had absorbed German philosophical technique in the single century since the Jews had emerged from the ghetto, it also demonstrated how much the German Jews had abandoned the trappings of traditional Judaism. The Germans did not wish to be reminded of their eastern European counterparts who still believed in the mystical quality of Judaism and understood that, with all Judaism's stress on the moral deed, there still remained an element of faith.

Leo Baeck had written of the Kantian ethical imperative, that men must do good if they are to exist in society and if society is to exist around them. If Baeck had not accepted Kant's thesis that moral law stems from reason rather than from God, he had accepted the Kantian approach—the emphasis on the rational, on what can be explained, and the de-emphasis on belief. Baeck wrote that Judaism had received its direction from the teaching of the prophets, and this source had withdrawn it from all mysticism and esoteric practice. Reflecting an attitude that had surfaced in his doctoral dissertation ten years earlier, Baeck wrote that Judaism is free from any alien matter such as "*naturphilosophischen, metaphysichen* [or] *mystischen*."

According to a rabbi who was a contemporary of Leo Baeck's, this first edition of the *The Essence of Judaism* "is not really intended as a theological book." Another rabbi, who followed Leo Baeck by several years, described it as "enlightenment, not Judaism." It was almost as if the Sabbath had been moved from Saturday to Sunday.[21]

But this kind of criticism came only decades after the book's appearance in 1905, when the book could be seen in perspective and also when it could be compared to later editions that Leo Baeck prepared. When first published, *The Essence of Judaism* was popular among German Jews. It was the work of a scholar whose research, analysis, and writing abilities were the equivalent of the most respected non-Jew's. Leo Baeck effectively had demonstrated that the Jew, not only in his dress but in his thought, had emerged from the ghetto. One of his students recalled later that Leo Baeck "was a believable representative." Leo Baeck was the representative the Jews wanted to have.

There was much in the book that was Jewish, of course. Primarily it was an argument against a religion of faith, the concept of religion that von Harnack had enunciated and that characterized German Protestantism at the time. In contrast to a concept of faith—a promise, in von Harnack's words, that "in the end God will do justice. If He does not do it here, He will do it in the Beyond, and that is the main point"—Leo Baeck argued that Judaism stressed the deed. However others defined the word *faith*, Baeck said that the Jewish definition was the commandment to do God's will on earth now. One seeks not the reward in heaven, but one performs the obligation on earth. To the followers of a religion of belief Baeck countered with a religion of life. To those who spoke of a religion with a "revelation" coming at a moment in time Baeck spoke of a religious experience constantly being revealed. To those who worshipped Jesus, Leo Baeck spoke of those who, rather than worship, practiced religion. In a world still wedded to the concept of hereditary rights, a world in which the circumstance of one's birth often was the most fortunate thing that could happen to a person, Leo Baeck countered that to the Jew, "what gives our life its worth, is what we become, not which family we come from."[22]

His book was a polemic. Challenging the claim that Judaism had died and that Christianity had superseded it, Leo Baeck had shown not only that Judaism still lived and thrived, but that perhaps it actually offered more to the world than did Christianity.

Leo Baeck's great achievement was not the slim volume that appeared in 1905, but his own growth. Eventually Leo Baeck would openly confront the Jews' embarrassment with their background and become the symbol of the Jews' willingness to grasp their religion in its entirety, to state with pride: "I am a Jew."

Two years after publication of *The Essence of Judaism*, Leo Baeck was invited to become rabbi in Duesseldorf. "He was then widely known to the public through his book," reported a history of the Jewish community there, "with which he had entered the prominent rank of representatives and heralds of our religion in the spiritual struggle of our day." The city was larger than Oppeln and the Jewish community was larger, too. The move was an obvious step up in his career.

His final day as rabbi in Oppeln was October 3, 1907. Two days before his departure he delivered his last sermon before the congregation he had led for a decade. "I never saw so many handkerchiefs," said a member of that congregation. "There was so much crying."[23]

He stood above his congregants on the pulpit—the Hebrew word is *bimah*—dressed in his long robe, with his small pointed beard, looking very much the promising young rabbi. Perhaps the importance of the move he was about to make is the reason he chose the subject he did that day. Speaking less for the benefit of his congregants than for himself, Leo Baeck advised that the true rabbinical role should never be forgotten. Judaism, he said, "does not know the difference between priest and layman . . . it does not give a higher position to anyone in God's house." The rabbi remains "only a member of the community," and the Jewish "ideal" is that all members of the community are "God's scholars—each one becomes his own teacher of religion and each gives to himself God's words."

Until the time when this ideal is achieved, however, and all do become God's scholars, there is a role for the rabbi. "It is the necessary division of the work which places this law in front of us," he said. The obligation on the rabbi is "to dedicate his whole strength, the whole profession of his life" to the teachings of Judaism, "and to explain them so that others can receive them."

This necessary division, this bestowing a title upon an individual, Baeck continued, "also brings dangers." Many people believe that religion is satisfied "if there is somebody who dedicates his days to its tasks and its teachings." But this is a misunderstanding of the rabbi's role, he insisted. Rather, the rabbi "who has the office in God's house, can only point out and suggest but he cannot replace or take away that which the religious ideal asks from everyone."

If there is a danger to the community, said Baeck, then also there is a danger for the rabbi, who must not allow himself to feel he is in a position above his congregants. "Steps lead to the pulpit, yet they are only steps of wood or stone," he said. "They do not lead above the community." How easily can the rabbi "surrender to a feeling of superiority because he is talking at a higher level and because no one opposes him . . ." Baeck asked if it were not insolent and pretentious to describe the rabbi's words "as God's words" because, after all, the rabbi's words are "only narrow human speech, human words." The rabbi can be successful, but "only where honest thinking and honest conviction strive for expression, where the spiritual way works which our wise people called the reverence before the community." Only then can words "have an everlasting success."

Standing before the people whose Sabbath dinners he had shared, whose children he had educated, and at whose marriages he had officiated, Rabbi Baeck wondered if there had been such success in the red-brick, Moorish-style synagogue he had dedicated ten years earlier. "This hour of saying goodby is accompanied by doubts and thoughts, accompanied by the knowledge that the achievement is so far behind the desire," he said. If some words "have penetrated the soul," then it has happened because "the souls have opened themselves, because the hearts were ready to receive and to understand." He then reminded his congregation that never in his years on the *bimah* before them had he used the word *I*. This was a characteristic of Baeck, in both his preaching and his writing; he never spoke of himself in the first person. At this moment he explained that "the one who talks here should forget the 'I' and should only have before his eyes that for which he speaks." This time, however, he wanted to make an exception because the thankfulness he felt can be expressed only "in a personal way."

Then he said farewell to the community in which he had fulfilled his duties with happiness and satisfaction, "in which I, accompanied by an always growing benevolence, was listened to with openness." He reminded the people that he was saying goodby "to God's house where I once said the words of dedication and which has become my house of God." He said farewell to the young people of the community "who were my youth." He said farewell "to the heritage which my predecessors prepared for me, above all to the man who worked here for more than half a century and gave to the community its character and teaching"—this was Rabbi Wiener, Natalie's grandfather. Leo Baeck then said he would be leaving a richer person because he had learned much while teaching others.

He closed by saying that he as an individual meant very little, "the single person must step back behind the duty which continues from generation to generation." Then: "Men come, men go, but duty remains, the duty that gives the answer to all questions and doubts of life. It is the remaining and the certain thing in the change of the days and the situations. If the loyalty to duty and the thought that the joyful, ready loyalty to our religion are alive in the hearts of the old and young, then the word, which has been spoken in this house and to this community, has become a blessing and benefit. Amen."[24]

In that sermon Leo Baeck had set a standard against which he expected to be measured. He would never be above his congregation. He recognized that the rabbi alone could not satisfy the religious responsibilities of any of his congregants; rather, people must fulfill their own responsibilities. As he left for Duesseldorf and the next phase of his career, Leo Baeck understood that with dedication the rabbi also must have humility.

Duesseldorf was quite different from Oppeln. In Oppeln, as in Baeck's native city of Lissa, the insecurity of a Jewish community caught between east and west still lingered. Many of the Oppeln Jews, if content within the confines of their own community, were embarrassed by the orthodoxy of their neighboring Polish Jews. In part this may have been because the Oppeln Jews traced their roots in that city through generations, while their Christian neighbors traced theirs through centuries. In contrast the Jews in Duesseldorf, on the western border of Germany, had been neither influenced nor concerned about their fellows in Poland. Jews first came to Duesseldorf in 1418, but were expelled twenty years later. In 1582 one Jew received permission to settle in the city. Two hundred years later there were twenty-four families, and the Jewish community of Duesseldorf was firmly established, growing in the nineteenth century along with the city. In 1816 there were

303 Jews in the city with a total population of 22,653; by 1905, shortly before Leo Baeck arrived, there were 2,877 Jews in a total population of 253,274. This increase among both Jews and non-Jews did not come from an increase in the birthrate but from persons moving from a rural to an urban area. This movement was more pronounced for the Jews because they were denied the right to own land in many rural areas; in addition, their interest in religious study made large communities with their educational opportunities more attractive.

For the Jews, Duesseldorf was particularly pleasant. They had civil liberties as well as opportunities for education, to enter the business world, and to prosper. The city, in contrast to the surrounding areas and to many other cities, generally was free of anti-Semitism. The daughter of a man who was a minister in Duesseldorf while Leo Baeck was rabbi there recalled years later that no difficulties ever existed between the Jews and her father's church. Or as another Protestant resident of the area put it: "In the time of the Emperor we didn't know anti-Semitism; only in the time of Adolf Hitler."[25]

The Jewish community had decided in 1899 to build a new synagogue on Kasernenstrasse; it opened in 1904, to become a landmark not only of Judaism but also of the city. If one observed Duesseldorf from a distance, according to a report at the time, the synagogue's tower, covered with green copper, rose commandingly above the other city buildings. The services copied those of the liberal Oranienburgerstrasse Synagogue in Berlin, and the Hebrew used was known as "approved," meaning that no eastern European pronunciations were allowed to creep in. The struggle over whether to have an organ, the test for the liberality of a synagogue in Germany, had been waged prior to Baeck's arrival. Forty-eight members had signed a petition against having an organ, but they lost. The synagogue had its organ as well as a mixed choir when Baeck arrived.[26]

Baeck probably was the community's first liberal rabbi; his nearest rabbinical colleague was in Duisburg, about twenty-five kilometers away. The situation gave Baeck a great deal of authority and also placed heavy responsibilities on him. A reticent person himself, not given to showing emotion, an intellectual whose sermons still appealed more to the head than to the heart, Baeck often was surprised by the emotionalism of his congregants, who adopted the cheerfulness and the extroversion of their fellow Rhinelanders. "One day I saw myself exposed for the first time," he once said, "to the emotional outburst of a stranger which I had great difficulties in restraining and redirecting into objective channels."[27]

One of his chief responsibilities, as it had been in Oppeln, was teaching. Students learned their religion in the gymnasium in the Kosterstrasse during two sessions a week. There were three groups—lower, middle, and upper. The first was taught by a teacher, while the rabbi taught the upper two groups; his subjects were Bible and Jewish history and ethics and the philosophy of Judaism. At first Baeck had problems. The previous rabbi, Samuel Hochfeld, had been well liked by the students, and they were skeptical of anyone trying to replace him. When Baeck arrived in the late fall of 1907, it seemed their skepticism might have a basis. Said one student:

The new rabbi, Dr. Leo Baeck, was unintelligible to us, not only what he said but how he said it. His language, his tone, the melody of his language distinguished itself in a grotesque way from the Rheinish style of speaking familiar to us, so much so that we could not refrain from laughing in the first hours. It was inconceivable to us that the community leaders could have selected such a dreadful speaker—and he must also be just as bad a preacher —as the successor of the rhetorically brilliant Dr. Hochfeld.

The students abandoned their skepticism "with astonishing rapidity," recalled this student. Baeck was innovative; he instituted a question-and-answer session in the second week of instruction. "We students were encouraged to place questions of any kind and from every area to Dr. Baeck, and he was ready to answer either immediately or in the next hour. . . . So there was something in Duesseldorf that was not like any place else."

These question-and-answer sessions were important not only because of the information that the students gained, but also because of the attitude of respect toward students that Leo Baeck had developed in Oppeln. "We entered this new experience with real spirit," reported the student many years later. "That we students, who had been handled up to that time and long after with condescension, could here determine, freely and without constraint, what we wished to speak about, had an importance which will be scarcely clear to the students of our day."

Those question-and-answer sessions were enjoyed more than any other classes and the students were anxious to attend. But they were not Baeck's only innovation. The teaching technique then in vogue had the instructor present a lecture for an hour, collect the assigned homework from the students, and then spend the second hour questioning students about the material. "Not so with Dr. Baeck," said the student, ". . . [he] led each following hour with a repetition in an abbreviated form of that which he had explained in the previous hour. His regular question was: 'Is it totally clear to you?' " And when a student asked a question, the rabbi called it "important" or "good." There was no embarrassment on the students' part. Sensing their positive response, Leo Baeck quickly moved his classes to another level, developing special courses in the Talmud and in Rashi, a Jewish commentator of the Middle Ages.

Leo Baeck did not neglect the education of Jewish women. He was one of the leaders in German Jewry in insisting that women achieve the same rights within the religion as did men. In Duesseldorf he introduced the process of confirmation for girls. This was a graduation ceremony from religious instruction, and it came with the traditional present for accomplishment in a Jewish religious program—a book, usually a volume of German prayers for Jewish girls, and inscribed by Baeck—*"Meiner lieben Schuelerin Sophia Pineas zur Erinnerung an Ihren Konfirmationstag!"* is a typical inscription.[28]

Baeck was a frequent lecturer in the community, and a talk he gave in 1911 under the auspices of a German-Jewish organization shows somewhat how his concept of the uniqueness of the Jewish people was developing. Against the backdrop of German Jews trying to present themselves as no different from other Germans, Baeck argued that minority status placed the Jews in a position that did indeed make them different. They were members of a moral order, united across borders by a commandment of God. In contrast to others who would unite politically, economically, or socially, the Jews united around the goal of fulfilling an ethical responsibility.

"The question of the position of Judaism among the religions can be answered at first statistically," he began. "There are on the earth about one billion six hundred million people, and among those are some ten million Jews. So each Jew sees himself surrounded by those of different beliefs; however, only the 160th among them sees a Jew. Perhaps that is why, therefore, we are still the great unknown people on the earth."

He conceded people charged Jews with having "the strange characteristic of multiplying ourselves; if there might be twenty of us, one would think there were two hundred of us." Although there may be some truth to that, Baeck said, it probably was due to "our small number [giving] us a high ability to move around." He insisted that this "does not change the fact that it is our fate, and will always remain so, everywhere to be a minority," not only a minority, he said, but *the* minority." He added that "We have always been the few. We have never had the calmness that comes from the knowledge that our views are those of the men with power, and we have never found the proof of our convictions in that the people around us think and believe as we." In the parliaments of the world Jews have always been on the left, representing "the most loyal opposition of our God." Jews, "according to God's will . . . always have stood in opposition to the views which rule the world and which [are] dressed in the gloss of the success and the power . . . [The Jews] have always been . . . the great nonconformists, the great 'different' group which wanted to retain its beliefs." Leo Baeck insisted: "We do not merely exist, but we are something. We represent our own style in mankind . . ."

That difference was only rarely appreciated. People who stand against the view of the men with power risk the enmity of those who worship the gloss of success and power. Baeck believed that to be the fate of the Jews: chosen to live as a conscience to the world's people, many of whom preferred not to hear from their conscience.[29]

Baeck, Natalie, and Ruth lived in an apartment on Kasernenstrasse near the synagogue. On Sabbath afternoons the three of them often walked along the Rhine, many times accompanied by a member of the ever-growing group of nieces and nephews who used the home in Duesseldorf as a way station during their growing-up years, going to school in the city, acquiring some sophistication, and perhaps even meeting a promising young man or woman. Natalie—ever *die Rabbinerfrau* —made certain her husband's clothes were cleaned and pressed, that he ate properly, that he had the serenity needed for his studies, his sermon preparation, and his increasing writing interests. She was a "Zauber," one of those nieces recalled; the word is German for magic and enchantment. It meant that Natalie Baeck was a beautiful woman, kind to friends and relatives, gracious to those who came into her house, and sensitive to her role as Leo Baeck's wife. In the way she kept the apartment clean she also reflected something of the eastern Jew's concern in the face of sophisticated western neighbors—"So no one should say that people from Posen aren't neat."

The apartment held the accumulation of a decade of marriage and housekeeping. The Baecks had brought with them the monogrammed silver chest the Oppeln congregation had given them when they married in 1897; ten years later, when the Baecks left, the congregation also had presented them with two three-armed silver candleholders, which now stood on the dining room table of their Duesseldorf apartment. There were other furnishings that also represented the love of friends and the heritage of family: Rabbi Adolf Wiener's silver walking stick, which had passed first to Natalie's mother and then to Natalie and Leo Baeck. Among the paintings there was an engraving of a Rembrandt self-portrait, done by a well-known copper engraver of the eighteenth century named Schmid and given to Baeck by a family in Oppeln as a token of affection. To this, Baeck also added in 1910 an original Rembrandt engraving, another self-portrait, which he purchased in Duesseldorf. There was music in the apartment. Natalie played the piano and taught the nieces and nephews who lived with her. A favorite composer of hers was Felix Mendelssohn, the grandson of Moses Mendelssohn, who had begun the Jews' move from the German ghettos.

Their apartment was across the street from a theater where a famous German actress of the time, Louise Dumont, starred. In one of the few things Leo Baeck ever did reflecting vanity, he took voice lessons from the actress. As his Duesseldorf students had learned, he was not a good speaker in those years, delivering his sermons in a singsong chant. Despite the voice lessons he never succeeded in becoming a dramatic speaker. Eventually his voice deepened and developed a guttural quality that, particularly in later years, was interesting to his audience. But Baeck's effectiveness always depended more upon content than upon delivery.[30]

After staying in Duesseldorf five years, Leo Baeck took another step on his career—to Berlin, the premier city in Germany, a leading city of Europe, and—intellectually—the giant among Jewish communities in the world. It seemed appropriate that this modern rabbi—he used the spelling Baeck now, the modern German style, rather than the family spelling of Bäck—should move to this city where he would have the opportunity to develop himself into a Jewish scholar of world renown.

The custom of German Jewish communities in recruiting rabbis was to ask the candidates to give a trial sermon, the ordeal of the *Probepredigt*. This Baeck refused to do. He believed himself capable of meeting any test but also believed the *Probepredigt* beneath the dignity of the rabbinic office. He received the Berlin appointment anyway. His reputation both as a rabbi in Oppeln and Duesseldorf and as the author of *Das Wesen des Judentums* allowed him this independence.[31]

He arrived late in 1912 to replace a senior rabbi, Sigmund Maybaum, who had been one of his teachers at the Hochschule fifteen years earlier and now was retiring because of illness. In Berlin, Leo Baeck was an employee of the Berlin Jewish community, not of any particular synagogue or division within Judaism. The Jewish community had a democratically elected board representing almost all the Jews in Berlin. The Berlin Jews operated—in addition to houses of worship—hospitals, orphanages, homes for the elderly, a cemetery, and social and welfare agencies.

A rabbi was assigned to a synagogue by the community officials. Although, during his thirty-year career in Berlin, Leo Baeck came to be identified with particular synagogues, he, like the other rabbis, could be and often was assigned to conduct services at any synagogue. The rabbis' schedules were published in the Jewish community newspaper, and those interested in hearing a particular rabbi followed his schedule. The rabbis usually kept office hours at home which also were listed in the newspaper. They earned life tenure after five years, and this theoretically gave them independence in religious matters from the lay people who were elected by their fellow Jews to govern the community. In later years Baeck used this independence far beyond its religious implications, as he struggled with those lay leaders to unite the German Jews against the Nazi threat.

The Berlin Jewish community was financed by taxes: every taxpayer reported whether he was Catholic, Protestant, or Jewish, and part of his tax payment automatically went to support that religion. With large sums of money from these tax collections, the Jews rushed to catch up with their Christian neighbors, who had been erecting huge churches for hundreds of years.[32] They built houses of worship that, in some cases, were grander, larger, and more ornate, if possible, than the Christian churches. The new Jewish houses of worship were cathedral-like, seating hundreds of people, sometimes thousands. The problem was not that the Jews adopted the architectural style from Christians; lacking an architectural style of its own, the synagogue always has reflected its environment. Nor was the problem that the Jewish houses of worship in Germany had been dependent for their construction on the ignorance and poverty of the masses, nor that they had been financed by the thievery of the nobility, nor that they represented a class-conscious and feudalistic society.

Rather, the problem was that in those cathedral-like sanctuaries the Jews allowed a priestlike figure to come between themselves and their

God. Leo Baeck had reminded his congregation in Oppeln that the Jewish religion knows no difference between priest and layman. The steps to the *bimah*, he had said, do not lead above the community. In Berlin, however, the rabbi was a distant figure, above the community. Not having a single congregation, he never developed a close relationship with those who came into the synagogue. "The Jewish Community of Berlin . . . owned and operated all synagogues of all denominations except those of the ultra-orthodox and separatist Adass Israel," said Max Nussbaum, who had been a rabbi in Berlin. He continued:

Each one of us was therefore not the rabbi of a specific temple but the rabbi of the entire Jewish community. In a congregation of 170,000 members, as it were, the relationship between rabbi and congregants differed in many ways from the personal, pastoral relationship we find in the smaller closely-knit congregations in the United States. In the large metropolis of Berlin over which the thousands of member families were spread, the rabbi could not possibly attempt to visit all the sick or even call on the mourners after each funeral, unless they were personal friends.

The rabbi dealt with most families only at ceremonies commemorating birth, the bar mitzvah, confirmation, marriage, and death, said Rabbi Nussbaum.[33]

It was not only the size of the congregation that had produced a change in the status of the rabbi from a teacher among his fellow Jews to the priestlike figure seen almost exclusively standing atop the *bimah*, dressed in a long robe, his head covered, and with the *tallith* draped over his shoulders; a person apart from those who sat beneath him. In days past he had been called by affectionate, respectful, and spiritual titles—rabbi, rav, rabban—but now, with all of his degrees, he was called *Doktor*. A well-known satirical barb at the time went that once rabbis had become doctors, Judaism had become sick.[34]

Rabbi Leo Baeck was among the most impressive and dignified of the German rabbis. A year shy of his fortieth birthday when he arrived in Berlin, he had maintained a trim, athletic build through brisk walks and summer vacations mountain climbing in Switzerland. He wore his rabbinical robes well, and his face was long and thin, outlined by his short, pointed beard.

He first preached in the Luetzowstrasse Synagogue. *Strasse* is the German word for street, and it was common practice to name the synagogues by their street locations. The same year Leo Baeck came to Berlin, 1912, the Fasanenstrasse Synagogue was opened, and this soon became the site where he preached most frequently. Built in a Moorish style, this synagogue, with its three domes, was described as an architectural beauty and was featured in several art magazines when first opened. Not only did it represent the new affluence of the German Jewish community, it also represented the Jews' growing status as citizens of Germany. Many prominent non-Jews attended the formal opening, including members of the military and a personal representative of the Kaiser. Even the synagogue's location was significant, on Fasanenstrasse near Kurfürstendamm, the main avenue of the elegant new western section of Berlin. Affluent Jews were moving into this area now, and the Fasanenstrasse Synagogue was regarded as a fashionable place of worship. Those who came most often were the upper-middle-class Jews who lived nearby in the Kurfürstendamm area. On High Holy Days they arrived for services dressed in swallowtail morning coats, striped trousers, and high hats. These people liked the rabbi from Lissa. He looked like a German and spoke like one. More and more of the services were in German rather than Hebrew.*

The chief cantor at the Fasanenstrasse Synagogue was Magnus Davidsohn, a friend of Baeck's from his Hochschule days. Baeck as a student rabbi and Davidsohn as a student cantor had led services together in Berlin in the 1890s before their ordinations. Years later Davidsohn recalled Baeck's first sermon at the Fasanenstrasse Synagogue on December 28, 1912: "With a stroke the entire scholarly and cultural life of our great community was activated . . . [Baeck] was not only the great Rabbi, not only the scholar, but literally the founder of a new era." The statement probably is a better reflection of what Baeck later became in Berlin rather than of what he achieved in that first sermon.[35]

While in Oppeln and Duesseldorf, Baeck had maintained contacts with the Hochschule and was a contributor of both money and books. His return to Berlin coincided with the Hochschule's losing one of its principal teachers, and he was asked to fill the opening. Generally the Berlin rabbis were expected to teach religion to young Jewish children attending the gymnasiums in the city. Baeck was excused from this duty because of his past at the Hochschule, with one exception.

The exception involved a German school known as the Emperor Wilhelm Gymnasium but dubbed "the Patent Leather Gymnasium" because it was located in a fashionable neighborhood. Children of a num-

* The Fasanenstrasse Synagogue site now is the site of the Berlin Jewish community building. The doorway to the synagogue is used as the doorway of the building. The synagogue itself was destroyed by the Nazis in 1938.

ber of wealthy Jewish families attended, and the job of instructing them in their religion was considered an important one. Shortly before Baeck's arrival in Berlin, one of the students had used an umbrella to strike a teacher who had failed him. The incident was a scandal, and the Jewish community was appalled. Students in Imperial Germany did not strike teachers, nor did teachers provoke such behavior. Baeck was asked to take over the teaching responsibilities in the Patent Leather school for a short time. His method of teaching children without condescension succeeded, and within three months decorum was restored, and the scandal was forgotten.[36]

When Leo Baeck had been a student at the Hochschule in the 1890s, his fellow students had complained that the dirty rooms on Unter den Linden were a disgrace to the Jewish community. The Hochschule building to which Baeck returned as a teacher, in contrast, was a disgrace to no one. In the 1890s a wealthy Jew had donated a plot of land at Artilleriestrasse 14 as a site for a building. The building was opened on October 22, 1907, and, like the large synagogues, represented the new affluence of the Berlin Jews. The stone arch above the entrance was crowned with a lion and had horns of plenty on each side. The building had five floors—the street level, three floors, and an attic—a marble entry hall, and a spiral staircase. The entry hall floor was of inlaid stone; the ceiling was paneled wood. Two doors led off each landing into bright and spacious lecture and reading rooms. The school was around the corner from Oranienburgerstrasse, where the Jewish community had its main office and where one of the most attractive of Berlin's synagogues was located.

The Hochschule building lasted as a Jewish school until 1942, when the Nazis closed its doors.* In its time hundreds of young men and women were trained to carry on an ancient tradition, dedicated to independence of thought. Judaism, Leo Baeck had argued, has no dogma. One learns Judaism and one practices Judaism when one studies it, challenges it, argues with it, and finally comes to understand the responsibilities it places upon the individual. The role of the Hochschule was to encourage that Jewish independence of thought.

But between the aims and achievements of the Hochschule lay a great

---

* The building still stands in East Berlin. Its street name and number have been changed (Tucholskistrasse 9), and the front has been resurfaced to cover the bullet and shell hole scars from the Second World War, but there is no mistaking the arch, still regal. There is a nursery on the first floor and apartments on the upper floors. (Author's visit to the building, June 11, 1976.)

distance. Baeck covered that distance by combining both history and religion in his teaching. He realized also that the work of Christian scholars indirectly offered inspiration; the more they ignored the Jewish sources of Christianity, the more he felt compelled to challenge that ignorance. He became an authority on the Jewish origins of the New Testament and eventually claimed—long before Christian scholars in Germany accepted the premise—that the Christian Bible cannot be understood without understanding the Hebrew writings preceding it and of its time. Baeck viewed Judaism as being constantly revealed through its history. To him Judaism and its history, the religion and the process of its existence—its past, its present, and its future—were one. This concept would become the basis of his most complex book, *Dieses Volk—This People Israel,* which he began under the threat of Nazism and the pressure of Theresienstadt.

Baeck articulated the beginnings of this concept in his inaugural lecture at the Hochschule, May 4, 1913. Entitled "Greek and Jewish Preaching," the lecture was a tour de force of scholarship demonstrating Baeck's command of Greek, both the language and history of the people, and also his knowledge of religious cults and sects developing at the time of the Greek civilization.

On one level the lecture was a history of the development of the sermon from its Greek origins to its use by the Jews in modern times. On a second level it was a study of how Judaism adapted the Greek concept of the sermon and transformed it into something intrinsically Jewish. On a third level it was a call for the rabbinical students to exert themselves to the utmost in their profession.

Baeck began with a definition of the Greek and Roman religions as state religions. "A passage in a speech against Andocides, ascribed to Lysias," he said, "characteristically describes an offense against the state shrines as a real crime only if it is perpetrated by a native." Because one only had to participate superficially in these state religions without having any sincere belief in them, they were not enough for those with religious needs. These individuals had to turn to the mystery cults, which promised redemption, or to the philosophical religions.

Baeck traced the historical development of the sermon through the philosophical religions, which used it as a device to appeal to reason. The sermon's home, he noted, was principally in the Cynico-Stoic religions, which advocated virtue and self-control. Citing many of these old texts, he said there had been a widespread need for the sermon "because each of the various schools, convinced it possessed the truth,

was anxious to propagate it." The sermon ultimately acquired a democratic feature because of Socrates, who declared that "virtue and piety
could be learned . . . were accessible to everyone and therefore could and
should be preached." This democratic feature, Baeck said, also characterized modern Judaism—"here, too, we have the postulate that religion can be learned. It is the Torah, the 'teaching.' "

Baeck continued with this blending of history and religion. "The
Torah," he declared, "is thus opposed to the Gnosis, the knowledge derived through the sacraments." He defined "Gnosis" as the knowledge
"which man acquires not by his own efforts but receives only if he is
among the initiated and redeemed; as the science that cannot be taught
but only attested"; as that which "needs the herald more than the
preacher."

The lecture was history, it was philosophy, and it was Judaism. Further stressing the democratic feature of Judaism, Baeck said the Greeks
had used the word *icon*, image, when speaking of the likeness of God,
but they used it to mean something exclusive. "The term belonged to
the cult of the ruler and heroes prevailing in the Greco-Roman world,"
said Baeck. To be in the image of God, according to the Greeks, was
possible only for the elect, "who were raised up to the level of the
Gods." In Judaism, however, use of the word denoted man, any man,
all men. "Man is given the attribute that elsewhere is given only to the
elect of the elect, be it the emperor or god incarnate; here man as such
is the icon of God."

Baeck said that the Greeks' brilliance and "elegance of style" were
advantages for them but were also dangers. Their search for eloquence
and beauty of form, he said, "often resulted in the sacrifice of real
content and conviction. . . . It has justly been said that Hellenism died
in the cult of beautiful form." In contrast, Jewish sermons from the
same period show "an almost studied indifference to artistic form." With
this indifference, however, there was also a coherence. The Jews had a
unity of religion compared to the variety of Greek schools. Judaism survived, said Baeck, while the Greek religions did not, because Judaism
dedicated itself to exploration and not to intellectual and religious sub-
jugation. And the Jews had an oral tradition. In the absence of dogma,
in the absence of "rigid texts," they had the obligation to study ideas.
"All this can still be followed in the ancient Hebrew sermons," he
said, "and it shows that the Jews of that time did not try to evade the
spiritual issues of their day."

Baeck commented wryly that "Judaism seldom remained in a state of intellectual quiescence; it lacked the necessary consummated religious system that has been proved and proclaimed once and for all." Lacking this "consummated religious system," the Jews had in its place the "consciousness of conviction."

Knowledge, he insisted, did not mean knowledge acquired but "knowledge in the sense of a constant searching, which one knows can never reach its end." To the future rabbis who heard him that day Baeck offered the constant search. "The history of Jewish preaching, too," he said, "shows how we can remain faithful to what is best and most characteristic in Judaism . . . To preach means 'to learn and to teach.' "[37]

This lecture was given in the ornate Hochschule building, then only six years old. Like its neighbor, the cathedral-like Oranienburgerstrasse Synagogue, it was a physical sign of the Jews' apparent acceptance in Berlin. The middle-class life they had begun to lead in Imperial Germany had an impact on the Jews in Berlin. They were becoming burghers. They studied, sipped coffee and read the newspapers in the outdoor cafes, and looked almost indistinguishable from their non-Jewish neighbors. After a history of expulsions and returns, slaughters and deprivation of rights, perhaps the place and time finally had come when they could live in peace.

4 FELDRABBINER

THE FIRST REFERENCE to the Jews in Berlin is in the year 1295 of the Christian era; an ordinance prohibited the weavers in the city from buying yarn from Jews. During the next hundred years or so the Jews in Berlin lived in isolation, partly from their own desires and partly from social pressures. By the middle of the sixteenth century they seemed safely ensconced in Berlin, having gained the protection of the city government. This legal protection was granted not because it was an individual's right but by the power of the state and was withdrawn by that same power in the year 1571. There was a pogrom that year in Berlin, and those Jews not killed were subsequently driven from the city, leaving Berlin without any identifiable Jewish residents.

Despite that history Berlin was no worse a home for the Jews than other European cities. Centrally located on trade routes, it offered them an opportunity for a livelihood. In 1671 a few families drifted into the city to begin the modern history of Jews there. At first the tolerance shown them was minimal. In 1712, for example, city officials were sitting in on Jewish services to make certain Jews did not include any questionable references to Christianity. The officials especially watched for the *Alenu* prayer, which Jews say at the end of their service to express reverence for God, to hope for the time when God's name "shall be worshipped in all the earth," and to denounce idolatry. The Christian overseers believed that some of the Hebrew words, in the critical reference to idolatry, were code for Jesus, and they weren't going to allow any of that.

The Jewish community in Berlin grew slowly. In the decades that followed their return the increase in their numbers can be counted in tens. In the beginning of the eighteenth century there were perhaps a hundred Jewish families in the city. In subsequent years, whenever the Jewish population showed signs of increasing, edicts were issued to restrict marriages, limit immigration, or, as happened in some instances, force Jewish residents to leave. During this century Jews represented approximately 2 percent of the city's total population, and by the end of the century that percentage had decreased slightly. The Jews in Berlin were confined to certain areas of the city, denied admission to the craft guilds, and had no civil rights. Traveling between communities required payment of a travel tax. Any Gentile, even a child, could order a Jew to bow and doff his hat.

Still, through the cracks created by the grudging tolerance of Germans, the Jews began moving into the mainstream of German life. This movement gained considerable momentum in the late 1700s when Moses Mendelssohn began translating the Bible from Hebrew into German. The Jewish Free School was established, where Jews were taught in German rather than in Hebrew. Slowly, educated Germans and educated Jews inched closer together, attracted by each other's intellect and by what each culture could offer the other. The followers of Mendelssohn sought to separate the Jewish religion from Jewish culture. Why could not the Jews live with a set of religious principles that would not prevent them from living lives similar to those of the German Protestants or Catholics? One non-Jewish observer commented in the 1780s: "It seems that where you live the Jews are still orthodox; here, with the exception of the lower classes, they are so by no means. They buy and sell on Saturdays, eat all forbidden foods, keep no fast days." One follower of Mendelssohn described the Berlin Jews in 1793 as belonging to four groups. The first he called the "true believers"—those remaining in the ghetto—and said they were "fossilized and unable to assimilate" and that they were dying out. The second group was the "libertines," Jews who called themselves Christians but still were shunned by their Christian neighbors. The third and fourth groups were the "educated" and "partly educated"—those upon whom it was hoped a "pure" religion could be established.

Those Jews emerging from the ghetto gradually gained their civil rights. This was partially due to examples of other nations; the United States, France and other European countries were granting full citizenship to their minorities. It was also due to the sweep of Napoleon and his armies through Europe, leaving in the wake of their military victories a new spirit of enlightenment, which had been developing in

France. And it was also due to the Jews themselves demonstrating that the German nation was foolish to deny itself their contributions.

Travel restrictions were lifted, and the Jewish population of Berlin grew. Along with many other Germans, Jews moved from the country-side to the city with its opportunities for intellectual stimulation and economic gain. By the end of the nineteenth century Berlin was swollen by an industrial expansion. The city had a total population of almost 1.9 million, of whom 92,000, or almost 5 percent, were Jews. Ten years later, when the old town of Berlin annexed its suburbs to become the modern city of Berlin, the Jewish population was slightly less than 4 percent. Many of these Jews had moved to Berlin from Posen, where the Jewish population dropped from 62,000 in 1871 to 30,000 in 1905. Many of those Posen Jews had been taught by Samuel Bäck. This was one reason for Leo Baeck's popularity among the Jews in Berlin—he was known to them and their families.

As they became full citizens, the Jews were perplexed about how to deal with their Judaism. The proposal to move the Sabbath from Satur-day to Sunday, advocated by Natalie Baeck's grandfather among others, was one example of the kinds of solutions offered, all characterized by the elimination of elements that made Jews appear different from non-Jews. Hermann Cohen was one of those who called for the Jews to make Sunday the Sabbath. According to him the change would make the Jews masters of the Sabbath rather than its servants. Read-ing some of Cohen's writings at the time, a question arises as to whether a Jew really is the author. For example:

Our Israelite religion, as it exists in our midst today, has already begun in fact a cultural, historical union with Protestantism. Not only that we have more or less definitely and openly thrown off the tradition of the Talmud as binding just as they have [discarded] the tradition of the Church. But in a much deeper sense, in all spiritual questions we think and feel in accord with the Protestant spirit. Thus this common good in religion is in truth the most powerful and effective and unifying force for a genuine national fusion.

Such statements were extreme; they represented the far end of a popular movement to combine Judaism with Germanic tradition. As part of this movement so many Jews welcomed Leo Baeck's *The Essence of Judaism*—it combined the two cultures so well.

Once the emancipation process had begun, the German Jews became devoted to the fatherland. In statements and letters and even from the *bimah*, they attempted to demonstrate as great a loyalty to the fatherland —if not a greater one—as that of the German Gentile. In 1812 a typical statement by a leading Jewish layman called for prayers for "blessing and success for my kind, for my fellow citizens, for myself and for my family—and not for a return to Jerusalem, not for a restoration of the Temple and the sacrifices." There were no such wishes for return and restoration in his heart, said this Jew, adding: "Their fulfillment would not make me happy. My mouth shall not utter them."

"Put us to the acid test of danger," cried a young German Jew to his Gentile countrymen. "You will find us clean of residues of egoism and without the indecency of over-refinement. Allow us the fatherland to which we belong by birth, custom, and love and we shall gladly lay down our lives and our possessions on its altar." This young man pleaded for the crumbling of "the dark wall of division between us."

A prominent spokesman for liberal Judaism in Germany delivered a speech at the Hochschule in the 1870s, asking, "What are we then?" He answered: "Germans! We are, wish to be, and can be nothing else." Not only because the Jews used the German language, but because of "the land we inhabit, the state we serve, the law we obey, the scholarship which informs us, the art which inspires us . . . the beginning and the need of our lives is here."

Throughout the nineteenth century Jewish leaders vied with each other to demonstrate devotion and loyalty to the fatherland and to prove that being Jewish did not hinder that devotion and loyalty. Occasionally there were doubts. Some believed, as a non-Jew had said in 1807, that the "more westernized the Jew became, the more he was hated; the average Christian preferred the 'dirtiest orthodox to the cultured man.'" A Jewish writer, Berthold Auerbach, found this to be true. During his career he moved away from Jewish themes. At its end, however, he realized that he still had not been accepted by his non-Jewish contemporaries, saying in 1880 that "I have lived and worked in vain."

In the 1880s a group of Jewish students in Breslau called for an association of Jewish students to "rekindle the consciousness that we are Jews, which has nearly disappeared, and that we are part of a great unity of historical and cultural significance." The students were prescient when they said what the objections from other Jews would be: "You should not set yourselves off, should not stress your differences, but rather should try to obliterate them and assimilate yourselves." In the face of such objections, they insisted, "simultaneously, we can be Jews and Germans in the best sense of the word."

These doubters were, however, the unusual ones. Most German Jews took the position, as one phrased it, that ". . . a religious community that constitutes only a small fraction of the population must carefully avoid all outward, public practices of its ritual commandments and must strive mightily to adapt itself in its external life to the general customs of the society." During the closing years of the nineteenth century the German Jews were shaken somewhat by the Dreyfus case in neighboring France. The French military needed a scapegoat in a spy case, and Captain Alfred Dreyfus was an ideal candidate for sacrifice—he was Jewish. This case led Herzl to announce his call for a return to Zion, but German Jews did not heed that call. Hannah Arendt has written that many of the emancipated Jews in Germany did not understand that "The case of the unfortunate Captain Dreyfus had shown the world that in every Jewish nobleman and multimillionaire there still remained something of the old-time pariah, who has no country, for whom human rights do not exist, and whom society would gladly exclude from its privileges."

Those German Jews who feared the outcast's fate believed, many of them, that the way to deal with that prospect was to hide their Jewishness. In the early 1900s a young woman named Jeannette Wolff, becoming active in Jewish social causes, was warned by her rabbi against too much involvement. "Pogroms," he said, "could be the result of the Jews being too visible."[1]

This trend toward assimilation was formalized in 1893 when the Jews founded the Central-Verein deutscher Staatsbürger jüdischen Glaubens—The Central Association of German Citizens of the Jewish Religion. These Jews formally disassociated themselves from Jews of any other nation. As one of its founders wrote, "We are not German Jews but German citizens of the Jewish faith. We are anchored in the ground of our German nationality. We have no more in common with Jews of other countries than have German Catholics or Protestants with Catholics and Protestants of other countries." One of the most honored Jewish spiritual leaders in Germany during the nineteenth century was Abraham Geiger. He called Jerusalem "an honored memory of the past . . . not a hope for the future." He said Jerusalem should be honored as "you would the great dead, but do not disturb its peace."

Jews first were elected to the German parliament in the middle of the nineteenth century. By that time every German state had granted them civil rights. The Jews did not believe those rights could or would be revoked; Germany would remain a country of laws, and all of its citizens would have equality before its courts. They had proof. In 1900 there had been a perjury trial involving a ritual murder charge. This charge —that the Jews murdered Christian youths and used their blood for the making of Passover matzos—had menaced the Jews for a thousand years. Leveling of the charge usually had been followed by an obscene burst of violence against the Jews, which civil and church authorities ignored until after the attacks against the Jews had ended. This time, however, troops stopped the riots before the damage was done. The anti-Semitic accusers were charged with perjury, tried, and convicted, and an editor of an anti-Semitic newspaper was convicted of slander.[2]

Jews had entered German life fully. "To become a literary critic or the editor of a civilized periodical was, for a German Jew, to gratify both his traditional yearning for excellence in the world of words and his more recent, but no less exigent, love for the country of Goethe and Schiller," one commentator has said. In addition to entering the world of arts, Jews also made great strides in the world of business. Albert Ballin, born in 1857, became associated with the Hamburg-American shipping line before he was thirty, and under his leadership it became the outstanding shipping business in Germany and perhaps the finest transoceanic line in the world. He was a friend of political leaders and passionately devoted to his country. Another famous Jew who enjoyed success in the business world was Walther Rathenau, who had inherited a large industrial concern from his father and expanded and improved it. Born a Jew and always identified as a Jew, Rathenau had difficulties living with that identification. His solution to the "Jewish problem" was for Jews to rid themselves of practices their German neighbors found objectionable or did not understand. Like Ballin, he was passionately devoted to Germany and became a government official.[3]

In 1914 an event allowed the Jews to prove their devotion to their fatherland and also set in motion the shaking of their status, although they did not realize it at the time. Perhaps the First World War was an inevitable outgrowth of the nationalistic tendencies that had been developing since the consolidation of the cities into states. Perhaps it was really a cover for the struggle for trade routes. Or perhaps it was, as D. H. Lawrence described it, "sensational delight posing as pious idealism." The thousands of studies never can explain what it is that causes men to kill each other and to destroy each other's homes and lands in such a systematic way.

For the German Jews, however, the war offered another meaning. Since Moses Mendelssohn had led them out of the ghetto 130 years earlier, they had been waiting for the opportunity to prove their loyalty to their fatherland. "Put us to the acid test of danger," young German Jews had demanded. Now their demand could be met.

"All Germans must do their duty," proclaimed one Jewish association when the war began, "but the German Jews must do more than their duty." And so they did. The youngest of all German volunteers was Joseph Zippes, a thirteen-year-old Jew who lost both his legs at the front. The first Reichstag deputy to enlist was Ludwig Frank, a Jew. "I have the greatest desire to live through the war in order to help construct the inner foundations of the Reich. At the moment, however," he wrote, "my place is at the front in the line with the others . . ." He joked about whether the French bullets had been advised of his "parliamentary immunity." They had not. He was killed in 1914.

These Jews were no different from any other Germans fighting for Germany. Their loneliness, their dreams, their dangers, their longings were the same. One seventeen-year-old wrote home from the front about missing school and the chance to exult with his fellow students over the German victories. The time of his letter was the Jewish festival of Chanukah, and he said he missed the holiday treats— raisins, mandarin oranges, white and brown cakes. He wanted his family to send him a package of those sweets and added that he wanted some books, too, "for it's the mind that builds the body." This youth was Walter Oppenheim, one of a large troop of young men who in March 1915 advanced, singing, against the British at Flanders. Along with 60,000 of these troops Oppenheim was killed by British machine guns. The bullets had not been marked for Catholics or Protestants or Jews, only for Germans.

Walter Oppenheim was buried in his home town of Hamburg in a special enclosure at the cemetery honoring the war dead. His family and friends followed his coffin to its grave while the military played with muffled drums, *"Ich hatt' einem Kameraden, einen bessern find'st du nicht"*—"I had a comrade; you cannot find a better one." Walter was the only son of Berta Oppenheim, and she devoted the remainder of her life to helping soldiers who had been injured in the war. For years she read books to blind veterans, translated works into Braille for them, wrote letters for them, devoted all of her time to helping them. It was her labor of love.* [4]

Statistics also tell a story of loyalty and sacrifice. Before the war there were 3,500 Jews in the German military. Commissioned ranks were barred to them. During the four years of the First World War 100,000 Jews served in the German army, approximately one-sixth of all Jews in Germany at the time and almost all Jewish males of military age. Of this number 80,000 were in combat; 35,000 were decorated for bravery; 23,000 earned noncommissioned rank, and more than 2,000 became commissioned officers once those ranks were opened to them. In all, 12,000 Jews lost their lives fighting for Germany. By any measure the Jews in Germany had been put to the "acid test" and had met it with their blood.[5]

Hermann Cohen, the philosopher, then having enveloped himself in Judaism, appealed to the American Jews to support Germany in the war. He argued that much of the intellectual rebirth of Judaism had been "a German reform and from Germany and through Germans it migrated to you [in America]." He called on the American Jew to support Germany as the "basic esthetic force and center of his cultural sentiments—and this is Germany which he must honour and love." The American Jew, Cohen continued, should at least be neutral in the conflict, rather than favor England and the other Allies, but he added that the American Jew "must envy us German Jews who can battle for our Fatherland, borne at the same time by the pious conviction that we will obtain human rights for the greater part of our co-religionists."[6]

There was no question where the Jews of Germany had placed their loyalty. They were Germans. They would prove it on the battlefield, and on the battlefield they would require chaplains—*Feldrabbiner*.

The German military automatically provided chaplains for its Protestant and Catholic soldiers, but not for its Jews. There had been one exception, in 1870 in the Franco-Prussian War. The government at first had refused to provide Jewish chaplains, explaining that the few Jewish soldiers were too widely dispersed for effective coverage. After the High Holy Days in 1870, however, the military relented before the visible presence of the Jews in the German army, 7,000 of them. Jewish chaplains were then provided with food, transportation, and quarters but not with other benefits given to the ministers and priests. The rabbis

* In 1941 Berta Oppenheim was expelled from the association through which she had done this work because she was Jewish. She died in 1942, committing suicide rather than go to a concentration camp.

were not commissioned and were not paid by the military. When the Franco-Prussian war ended, the Jewish chaplains were not invited to participate in the official thanksgiving services with the Protestant and Catholic chaplains.

That situation prevailed when the First World War began in 1914. The Army provided chaplains for the Catholic and Protestant soldiers but not for the Jewish. *Feldrabbiner* were supplied by the local Jewish communities, which also gave prayer books for use in the field. The *Feldrabbiner* wore military uniforms, had the benefits of officers' status in terms of eating and shelter, but had no actual rank. Leo Baeck at this time was forty-one years old, with a wife and a teenage daughter. He had been a rabbi for almost two decades and was now beginning, in Berlin, the most prominent part of his career. Still, he was one of the first to volunteer as a *Feldrabbiner*.

Baeck believed in the German cause. He "was a German patriot but not for a moment a chauvinist," said Ernst Simon, who had known him well. War would not have been his choice, but faced with war, Baeck did what any loyal German did. He gave it his support.[7]

He left Berlin for the front on September 13, 1914, bound for the headquarters of the First Army in France. More than a week's traveling by train and wagon was required. "During this time," he said, "the most sleep I had was five hours one night." He began his duties September 20, drawing up a work plan after meetings with military officers and the Catholic and Protestant chaplains. Each day he moved to a new location as he visited field hospitals and headquarters of different army sections; the schedule kept him moving from seven in the morning until seven at night. It was grueling, but he enjoyed it. "I become known in the army very rapidly," he said, "in what was rather a widely spread area, and I myself gained an overview of my work."

His greatest problem was the distances between the Jewish soldiers. "The lines of the area which the Jewish field rabbi must administer officially, stretch in different directions over forty to seventy kilometers," he reported. Not only were the travel routes between stops difficult, but almost all the troops were positioned in trenches, "and it is not possible everywhere to get to them." He considered visiting hospitals his most important job and had visited nine in his first seven days on duty. "I have met Jewish wounded soldiers in almost all of them," he said, "to whom it was obviously a great benefit to be visited." To each wounded soldier's family he sent a letter describing the man's condition.

At first Baeck was not able to hold any religious services because he had not found a large enough group. When he moved to Chauny, however, where there was a hospital with a large number of Jewish wounded as well as Jewish soldiers and medical personnel, Baeck arranged to hold a Yom Kippur service. At his request the German commander authorized the freeing of Jewish soldiers from their duties —if the war permitted—to attend services.

Services were held on a Tuesday evening and on the following day in a small room in the Church of Notre Dame in the town of Chauny; all the other large rooms in the town were being used as hospitals or as barracks for soldiers. Prayer books supplied by the Berlin Jewish community were distributed. Between thirty-five and forty soldiers attended, and Baeck was pleased to recognize in the candlelight the faces of some Berlin friends.

The service for the holy day of Yom Kippur—the Day of Atonement —comes at the close of what are called the Awesome Days, the ten-day period that begins with Rosh Hashanah, the Jewish new year. This is a solemn period having no relationship to the festive New Year's celebration of the secular world. In this period Jews examine their lives, seek out their failings, vow to correct them, and build a stronger relationship with their God. In this period their object is to achieve holiness, to live as God's laws command the individual to live. In this period, too, according to the Jewish tradition, God opens the book of life and records each individual's future year. Knowing this, individuals must ask how they should be motivated—by goodness or evil, by honesty or deceit? Will they live in a holy way or not? Then the book is sealed on Yom Kippur, the Day of Atonement. This day is the symbol of the Jews' salvation, that through the deeds in their lives they can achieve holiness and can come close to God. This is the most awesome day of the Jewish religion. And so it was that Tuesday evening in the corner of the Church of Notre Dame in the town of Chauny.

"I had the feeling," Baeck said, "that everyone was touched by this day."

He was intrigued by the curé of the church who, knowing a little German, had asked to sit in on the service. Baeck had agreed, of course, and was pleased when, after the service, the curé asked for a prayer book as a remembrance.[8]

During the war Baeck had several occasions to introduce Judaism to Catholic priests. Once, just before Passover, he needed some parsley for the Seder. In this Passover meal the parsley represents the coming of spring and the joyfulness of a new life in freedom. Before the Jews eat the parsley, they dip it in salt water as a reminder of the time when the Hebrews were slaves and of their exodus from Egypt—this is the story traditionally told at the Passover meal—and of their opportunity for a new life in the promised land.

After searching for the parsley, Baeck finally saw some growing in a small French churchyard. Dressed in his German uniform, he presented himself at the church door and asked the curé if he could have parsley from the churchyard. The curé looked at him skeptically, more because of the request than because of the enemy uniform.

"It's for Passover," Baeck explained.

Still skeptical, the curé took Rabbi Baeck into his study and showed him a reproduction of Leonardo da Vinci's The Last Supper. Asked the curé, "Do you mean they still do this?"

Baeck said the custom had not died out and invited the curé to attend. Baeck always enjoyed telling the remainder of that story. The curé did attend, sitting quietly in the back of the room while the Jews went through the Passover service—reading the Exodus story, eating the traditional foods to commemorate events in that story, and drinking four cups of wine to symbolize the four terms used for redemption. At one point in the service there is a call for all those who are hungry to come forward. When the chanting of the service that night came to that point, the curé pulled his chair forward to the table and joined the Jews in their meal.[9]

During the remaining war years Baeck held services in other churches, both Protestant and Catholic, in open fields, in rooms of vacated houses, wherever Jews could be gathered. "I have been able to observe how the Jewish soldiers are elevated by the mere awareness that a rabbi is with them," said Baeck.

"We were all very, very moved by this overpowering hour," commented one soldier in a letter home after a service Baeck had conducted at the front. "[It] will never escape from our memory." The service to which this soldier referred was for the Sabbath and took place in December 1914 in a military hospital at Chauny. There were only a dozen Jews attending, plus a non-Jewish soldier "who had asked to sit with us and who was completely overpowered" by the service. They met in the front room of the hospital, crowding on a bench. Baeck's sermon lasted three quarters of an hour, and in it he insisted that the soldiers not lose their patience but trust in God to guide them. The distinguishing mark of the service, as this particular soldier remembered it, was Baeck's prayers for the Kaiser and the fatherland.[10]

Baeck saw his chaplain's role as a traditional one. He visited soldiers in the trenches, often bringing them small packages of food. He spent much of his time in the military hospitals, writing letters to the families of the wounded soldiers. "These visits to the hospitals were the most important part of my work. The wounded were reminded of a bit of home and their hopes were lifted; they felt, as I often noted, elevated that a minister came to them as one came to the members of the other religions . . . I had to write a lot of letters on some days," he reported.

"At the funerals where the dead are mostly buried in a common grave," Baeck said, "I have spoken at the gravesite together with the Protestant and Catholic ministers, after which I joined them in the funeral procession. I have always informed the families of the time and place of the funerals and of the time of the death."

Leo Baeck believed it was important that he as a rabbi be visible. "Only in that way," he said, "is it possible to give the soldiers—if not all of them, at least many of them—the personal impression and assurance that a rabbi is among them." Then he added: "It is very essential that the Jewish soldiers learn that, and also that the members of the other religions know it. It is important for the acceptance of Judaism . . . It also is important for the position of the Jewish soldiers that their religion stands visibly next to the others."

Stressing loyalty to the fatherland was a standard part of the field service. A soldier who attended a 1915 Rosh Hashanah service wrote home of the man at his side saying the solemn prayers "with a rifle next to him." The soldier continued: "When Rabbi Dr. Baeck in his prayer asked for the blessing for our homeland for those who were far away from us and dear to us, many a tear would creep down the eyes of those who never before had been seen to cry." Another soldier wrote to his family of a service in which Baeck called for loyalty to the Kaiser, and the soldier continued: "To enact this word as Germans and Jews will be our goal. We have learnt what loyalty up to the death means. We will be true to the belief of our forefathers up to our last breath." The German Jews had been told by their leaders that they must do more than their duty, and that they tried.[11]

In addition to the chaplain's traditional exhortation to be loyal to the fatherland, there was another element in Baeck's sermons. "The hard course of war," he said one Sabbath, "is that destruction is our guide. Here we see around us what must be destroyed in our drive for victory.

However, we know something else also: When there is again quiet ... gratitude can remain everywhere we will go in the service of arms." He told the young Jewish soldiers that the honor of the fatherland required not only that they be victorious on the battlefield, but that they also show "friendliness and kindness" to the defeated enemy. Many of the enemy, he said, "have endured difficulties, their hearts have been ploughed and tilled through, they have become susceptible to any kernel of good, so that it can grow as fruit of the future." To those called on to kill and to maim, Rabbi Baeck cautioned, "To each of us here in this place has come the opportunity to do justly. It makes us, if we use it, richer inwardly." The responsibility of German soldiers, he said, was a victory allowing them "to work and create in the years of peace." Then shall victory be truly won—when men use their victory to create a spirit of friendliness, decency, and justice. Leo Baeck wore a military uniform, but he remained a rabbi.[12]

Baeck served almost the entire war, on both the western and eastern fronts. On the eastern front particularly he traveled a great deal by horseback. He had two favorite stories about his riding. Once he stopped at a waterhole for a drink, but his horse refused to touch the water. Baeck, being cautious, also refrained from drinking even though he was very thirsty. Later he learned that the Russians had poisoned the water. "That horse saved my life," said Baeck.

Eventually his horse died, but the army could not spare another. There was a small Jewish community in a nearby village, and Baeck was certain that its members were horse traders. When he visited them, however, the Jews professed to have no horses. They were Polish, afraid of the Germans, and were hiding their horses from the German army. Leo Baeck understood this, but he needed a horse. "Do you want your rabbi to go on foot?" he demanded of his fellow Jews. The next day the villagers brought him a horse.[13]

His experiences on the eastern front brought him into close contact with many eastern European Jews in ways he had not experienced before. They often attended his services, and sometimes he was a guest in their homes. In later years he would not look on his coreligionists from this area with the disdain felt by his fellow Berliners.

Baeck was also chaplain for a prison camp that housed Russian Jews. During the war, and particularly after the Russian Revolution, he helped many of the Russian Jews who were fleeing the Communists to settle in Germany. There also were several incidents recorded during the First World War of German Catholics dying without the presence of a priest to administer the last rites of their faith. Many rabbis learned these prayers and said them over the soldiers who were so near death that they were unaware their helper was not a priest. Friends of Leo Baeck's from the war credit him with having said these prayers over a dying Catholic soldier at least once.[14]

There also was the opportunity in Baeck's travels along the front to visit with old friends and relatives. One of his nephews, Kurt Fischer, was working with the Red Cross, transporting the wounded from Wilna to Koenigsberg, when he was called out by an officer and told that the *Feldrabbiner* of the Tenth Army wanted to see him. That was rather impressive for an ambulance driver. Fischer was pleasantly surprised to see his Uncle Leo. They had dinner together, and the young Kurt Fischer enjoyed his sudden prominence.

Kurt Boehm, who had known Leo Baeck in Oppeln, met him again in 1916 at a Yom Kippur service on the Russian front. The service was held in an open field with seats made from tree trunks in the style of a Greek temple. Although he had not heard Baeck preach for fourteen years, Boehm immediately recognized his deep, guttural voice. Baeck remembered Boehm from Oppeln and invited Boehm to sit with him at the end of the holy day and share "a great coffee board with white bread and marmalade."

Coincidentally, a few days later Boehm was sent to the town where Baeck had his headquarters. "Baeck lived very typically in one of the Russian village houses," recalled Boehm, "with an orderly who opened the door for me and invited me in. There were hearty greetings, coffee and sandwich bread and a wonderful exchange of thoughts." That particular meeting was interrupted, as many were for the rabbi and his Jewish soldiers, by the sudden sound of shells shrieking overhead. "But the shells, by good fortune," Boehm said, "did not reach the city but it went into a nearby lake." The attack meant that Boehm had to leave immediately, but he saw Baeck one more time during the war. Again it was at a service, not in an open field but in a destroyed church without a roof —"In the truest sense of the word under the open skies."[15]

Despite his heavy involvement as a *Feldrabbiner*, Baeck continued an active interest in the Hochschule via the mails. There were long letters between him and school officials about its progress. Baeck's advice was sought, and given, on faculty appointments and about the affairs within the Berlin rabbinate. He was particularly concerned about the Hochschule teachers and their finances. In 1917 the faculty members were suffering because one source of their income, a collection of funds during the High Holy Days, had not produced as much money as it ordinarily did. Baeck offered a solution. There was a vacancy at the Hochschule in a position known as the Mendelssohn chair, with funds for the appointment of a scholar to give a series of lectures. Baeck recommended having the regular members of the Hochschule faculty give the lectures and divide the money for the appointment among themselves to augment their salaries. "First you have to live," he said, "then you can be a philosopher."[16]

Those remaining at home were caught up at the beginning of the war in the jubilation of seeing their Germany on the march. Then as the weeks and months stretched out to years, as the lists of dead and wounded lengthened, and as supplies of food and other necessities decreased, they surrendered their jubilation to despair. When the United States entered the war in 1917 on the side of the Allies, the people at home knew, as did the soldiers at the front, that defeat had become only a matter of time.

The Jews in Berlin responded to the war much like their non-Jewish neighbors. They held concerts in their synagogues to raise money for the relatives of those killed in the war, conducted special services in honor of Kaiser Wilhelm's birthday, eagerly read the newspapers for some hints of a victory, put up as best as they could with the increasing deprivations as the war effort took more and more of the German resources, and waited for news from the battlefield of husbands, brothers, and friends.

Natalie Baeck, of course, was very proud of her husband. When Leo was attached to General von Kluck's First Army, she enjoyed describing how popular her husband had become through his travels, saying, "In the entire First Army only two people are acquainted with all its units, Kluck and Baeck."

Natalie maintained an informal open house for her husband's students; as they passed through Berlin, they always could stop by the Baeck home for coffee and cake. Rationing meant a minimum of meat, which Natalie and Ruth gave to the house servants; they became virtual vegetarians during the war.[17]

Ruth then was in her teens, and her education was important to her father. Before the war Baeck had supervised it himself. While he was away, he had one of the faculty members at the Hochschule watch over Ruth's schooling for him. Leo wrote often to his daughter. "I celebrate your birthday this year from far away," he said in a 1915 letter, "but still with you after one year during which you also have experienced many things." He told her to hope the universal hope, "that soon quiet and peaceful times will come back and will lead us to home from far away."

In the birthday greetings to his daughter Leo Baeck was no different from any other father. "Above all what I wish for your birthday," he said, "is that you may always remain healthy and happy. That is best of all. You now are one year older and also one year wiser. Now you can help your dear mother more and be better at her side. You can talk with her better and take good care of her." Leo Baeck did not forget that a birthday also is a time for presents. Natalie had given Ruth presents from both parents, but the father had his own special presents. "One I have chosen for you," he wrote, "is a flower vase made out of a French cartridge shell." He wanted to send it, but it weighed too much, so he would bring it on his next furlough. "Yesterday," he added, "I sent you chocolate for your birthday table . . . Have a good day on your birthday and may you enjoy all the good things the day brings to you." The letter was saved by Ruth and then by her daughter, becoming creased and yellowed, a memento of a father's love for his daughter.[18]

For those Jews participating in the war there was little sign of anti-Semitism on the part of their fellow soldiers. One of Leo Baeck's students from Duesseldorf remembered an officer once referring to a street in Berlin as having "too many crooked noses." But this was an exception, the student said, and, actually, "Most of the officers were gentry and did not engage in overt anti-Semitism."

Other Jews also met only isolated problems. Georg Salzberger, a *Feldrabbiner* from Frankfurt am Main, recalled heading for the front in a car carrying a German civilian and a high-ranking army officer. They seemed happy to have his company and the conversation was pleasant until they asked him of which church in Frankfurt was he pastor. "No church," he replied, "I am rabbi." For the remainder of the trip the other two passengers did not speak to him. "I was not present for them," he said. He told that story more than a half-century later, not with bitterness but to demonstrate the uniqueness of the anti-Semitism he encountered during the war's early years. Actually, he continued, he made many friends among the German officers; many attended the services he conducted.

By Leo Baeck's own accounts of his activities and by those of men who observed him, he ran into no difficulties of that nature. He was well liked, received the necessary support from the German high command in his efforts to conduct Jewish services, and was welcomed wherever he traveled. He often ate in the officers' clubs and joined freely in the conversations, and the only notice given him was that the gambling in high-stakes card games was sometimes stopped out of deference to his clerical position. He was friendly with the other chaplains of the Protestant and Catholic faiths. A photograph taken of Baeck with a Protestant and a Catholic chaplain, all three of them in military uniform, was referred to as "the Old and the New Testament."

Yet the situation was not as placid as those anecdotes suggest. The Jews were coming into contact, many of them for the first time, with non-Jews in informal and close situations. German soldiers came from all parts of the empire, from the large cities where Jews had lived as their neighbors for decades and from the small towns and the farmlands where a Jew never had been seen. Rabbi Salzberger commented on this at the time in a Jewish publication. "With all our ability to think and to judge, we Jews too have not always seen our environment with unclouded vision," he said. "This we now begin to understand in our close and intimate living with people of other faiths. We too are not free of errors which so often were committed against us, namely, considering the exception the rule." He considered it natural that the majority in which the Jewish minority lived had less knowledge about the Jews than the Jews had about the majority of Germans.

Just as I have experienced it, so doubtlessly have many others in their conversations with Christian troops and officers. Even among people who are otherwise well educated we discovered an amazing ignorance of the history and the nature of Judaism. Hardly anyone knows how many Jews live in Germany. The number was generally overestimated by six or eight times. Even well-meaning people are convinced that it is the purpose of Judaism to conquer the world economically and spiritually, to say nothing of other oft repeated fairy tales.[19]

Those last few sentences of Salzberger's describe a latent anti-Semitism among the Germans. In the security of the prewar years the Jews had hoped it was lessening and looked to the time when it might disappear entirely—but it was too much a part of the German *gestalt* to be eliminated in a few years. Then, as the German military victories turned to defeats, anti-Semitic grumbling became louder. Although the word itself was a relatively recent one, only coming into use at the end of the nineteenth century, what it represented—a deep, abiding hatred of the Jews—had its origins much earlier, at least 2,000 ye

This hatred of the Jews had begun as a political weapon
Jews and early Christians were competing for proselytes. The c
of the Christian church realized they would have difficulty app\
the Romans to convert while acknowledging that Jesus had been killed
by the Romans. So they shifted responsibility for the death of Jesus
onto the Jews. As one Catholic commentator recently wrote:

It is important to note that the shift is not merely from Roman to Jewish
authority, but from *political* to *religious* authority. It is important to the
Gospel tradition to throw the blame for the deaths of Jesus and his disciples
not merely upon Jewish . . . political authorities, but specifically upon the head
of the Jewish *religious* tradition and its authority . . . The word *Jews* in the
New Testament tradition has an important resonance. The term *the Jews*
is used as a constantly repeated hostile formula in Acts and John particularly.[20]

Explained another Christian commentator: "The primary source of
Jewish-Christian tensions, a development that permanently alienated
all Jews and resulted in the charge of deicide, was the transformation
of a historical event into a theological principle."

The history of the Catholic Church in the early centuries of the
Christian era is filled with virulent anti-Jewish statements. Anti-Semitism was not something the Church merely allowed to happen; it was
encouraged, nurtured, and propagated by the Church. Said St. Justin to
a rabbi: "[T]ribulations were justly imposed upon you, for you have
murdered the Just One." A Catholic priest, Edward H. Flannery, wrote
in the 1960s: "More ominous was the emergence of a teaching not yet
fully formulated but clearly enunciated in St. Hippolytus and Origen:
that Jews are a people punished for their deicide who can never hope
to escape their misfortunes, which are willed of God. This thesis
formed the first seeds of an attitude that would dominate Christian
thinking in the fourth century and greatly contribute thereafter to the
course of anti-Semitism."[21]

Again, however, this anti-Semitism was clearly a political weapon.
Jews had continued their proselytizing work through the fifth century
of the Christian era. Their arguments to the potential converts were that
men must live moral lives and work to bring the messianic age when
justice and love shall triumph. To achieve these ends, the Jews argued,
individuals must abide by strict laws of conduct toward themselves and
their neighbors. In competing with early Christians for converts, the
Jews argued that Jesus was a Jew and his preaching was in the Jewish

tradition. Christians countered by saying that one should not become Jewish because Judaism was marked by harsh and petty laws, Jews had killed Jesus, and that the only purpose of Judaism had been to prepare for the coming of Jesus—the same position that Adolf von Harnack enunciated 1900 years later.

The proselytizing movement in Judaism began to fade, however. In Christian societies there often was a legal prohibition against Jews seeking converts, and the Jews came to accept their seclusion as a way of life. Still, the attacks on the Jews did not cease. Over the centuries some members of the Catholic Church burned synagogues, murdered Jews, raped Jewish women, and stole Jewish property. Eventually this kind of "sufferance" was transformed into a policy of almost open attack. In the Fourth Lateran Council of 1215, the Church ordered all Jews and Saracens to distinguish themselves from Christians by some mark of their dress. The Nazis repeated that policy in 1941 by ordering all Jews to wear a yellow star on their clothes.

Rosemary R. Ruether, a Catholic and a student of the anti-Semitism in Catholic theology, has written: "The Church . . . proved incapable of understanding that the mob merely acted out, in practice, a hatred which the Church taught in theory and enforced in social degradation whenever possible." As for the Crusades, they produced "a compensatory wave of new anti-Judaic myths to justify this gratuitous slaughter of an unoffending group of people. The myths of ritual murder, well poisoning, and host profanation arose in the wake of Crusader violence to provide an image of the Jew as an insidious plotter against Christianity and to justify fanaticism. These libels had not existed before. They arose as a reaction and an attempt to justify the violence of the Crusades, after the fact." She then pointed out another fact the Crusades had demonstrated—the vulnerability of the Jews. Christian communities, she said, "saw that this prosperous group, seemingly under the protection of powerful princes, actually could be attacked by any mob with impunity. The weak forces of law and order were helpless against such mob violence. After this lesson had been learned, the pogroms never ceased for many centuries." Anti-Semitism, born in a political struggle, had become cemented into the Catholic Church.[22]

In contrast to this history there have been individual Christians who, in acts that would be repeated during the Nazi period, risked their positions, their reputations, and their lives to protect their fellow human beings. During the Second World War, when Pope Pius XII hid Jewish children in the Vatican to save them from the Nazis, he was following a tradition established by a few Catholic clergymen in the Middle Ages who hid Jews in their churches to save them from the marauding Crusaders.

But it was not the tradition of those few individuals that was handed down to the German Catholics; rather, it was the inbred anti-Semitism. For generations German families had attended weekly masses and heard the denunciation of the Jews, just as their fathers and their grandfathers had heard the anti-Semitic charges. One of these Germans was Adolf Hitler. In the comprehensive biography of Adolf Hitler by John Toland, the impact on Hitler of this church attitude toward the Jews is described this way: "Still a member in good standing of the Church of Rome despite detestation of its hierarchy ('I am now as before a Catholic and will always remain so'), he carried within him its teaching that the Jew was the killer of God. The extermination, therefore, could be done without a twinge of conscience since he was merely acting as the avenging hand of God . . ."[23] And Hitler's understanding was not unique to the German Catholics.

Many non-Catholic German Christians were followers of Martin Luther, who led the Protestant reformation. When Luther left the Catholic Church in the sixteenth century, he had strong sympathies toward Jews. However, there was a political motivation. His hope was that the Jews, who never as a group had embraced Catholicism, would join his religious movement. Not only would such conversions increase the size of Luther's following, but they also would demonstrate to the world his movement's superiority over Catholicism. As Luther wrote,

I hope that, if the Jews are treated friendly and are instructed kindly through the Bible, many of them will become real Christians and come back to the ancestral faith of the prophets and patriarchs . . . I would advise and beg everybody to deal kindly with the Jews and to instruct them to come over to us. If, however, we use brute force and slander them, saying that they need the blood of Christians to get rid of their stench and I know not what other nonsense of that kind, and treat them like dogs, what good can we expect of them? . . . If we wish to make them better, we must deal with them not according to the law of the pope, but according to the law of Christian charity.

Luther's Christian charity toward the Jews lasted only twenty years, until it became apparent that the Jews would not succumb to his blandishments. For Luther, the Jews' refusal to join him was a defeat he did not accept graciously. Two decades after inviting the Jews to join his movement he wrote: "Their synagogues or churches should be set on fire, and whatever does not burn up should be covered or spread with dirt so that no one may ever be able to see a cinder or stone of it. And this ought to be done for the honor of God and of Christianity in order that God may see that we are Christians . . ." He also wanted the Jews stripped of their property, deprived of their prayer books, and their rabbis forbidden to teach. The comments were in an essay of his written in 1543 and entitled, "Concerning the Jews and Their Lies." It was included in the standard collections of Luther's works available in Germany.

Lutheranism was dominant among the Protestant sects in Germany. In 1817 the Lutherans and the Calvinists (officially known in Germany as the Reformed Church) united to form the Evangelical Church in Prussia. Although Calvinism rejected anti-Semitism, Lutheranism did not; since it was the stronger of the two, anti-Semitism became virtually a religious tenet among German Protestants.

As pervasive as this anti-Semitism was within the churches of Germany, it alone was not responsible for the modern hostility toward the Jews. If there had been no other factors contributing toward this hostility, the Jews might never have been singled out over so many years as the enemy of the Germans. The Scandinavian nations, for example, were heavily Lutheran; but, as they were to demonstrate during the Second World War, they were not anti-Semitic. Italy was almost entirely Catholic; yet, during much of the Second World War it resisted the efforts of the Hitler government, its partner in the war effort, to attack its Jews.

Heinrich Heine, the German Jew who converted but always maintained a kinship to his original religion, writing almost a century earlier, offered another reason for the virulence of German actions against the Jews. Heine thought that a love for violence twisted into excesses passions that many others might control. He wrote:

Christianity has to a certain degree moderated that brutal lust of battle such as we find among the ancient Germanic races who fought not to destroy, nor yet to conquer, but merely from a fierce, demoniac love of battle itself; but it could not altogether eradicate it. And when once that restraining talisman, the Cross, is broken, then the smouldering ferocity of those ancient warriors will again blaze up, then will once more be heard the deadly clank of that berserk wrath of which the Norse poets say and sing so much. The talisman is rotten with decay, and the day will surely come when it will crumble and fall. The ancient stone gods will arise from out of the ashes of dismantled ruins and rub their eyes; and finally Thor with his colossal hammer will leap up, and with it shatter into fragments Gothic cathedrals . . . A drama will be enacted in Germany in comparison with which the French Revolution will appear a harmless idyl.[24]

That "berserk wrath" was set loose by the First World War and its aftermath. Germany began the war with an image of itself as a military colossus astride the world. The German people had had a love affair with the soldier, perhaps for eons, as Heine had said, but certainly for decades. When the Reich was formed in 1871, Kaiser Wilhelm I was primarily—almost solely—a military man, having earned fame in 1848 by advocating force against the revolutionaries and receiving the nickname *Kartätschenprinz*—prince of grapeshot. A painting of his coronation shows him surrounded by men in military uniforms, not one in civilian clothes. During his reign, the brief rule of his son Friedrich, and that of his grandson Wilhelm II, which began in 1888 and ended with the First World War, the glorification of the soldier continued. Every man served in the army. His social and professional activities included marching and military maneuvers. He understood that a military role would be part of his adult life. There is a photograph of Kaiser Wilhelm II's ten-year-old son wearing a military uniform. In other countries the picture would be of a boy playing soldier. In Germany the photograph was of the child being made a lieutenant in the First Guard Regiment. War was reality for the German people.[25]

They believed they were chosen for greatness. "Our Lord God would never have taken so much trouble over our German nation," proclaimed Wilhelm I, "if he had not intended us for such great things. We are the salt of the earth."[26]

As German men had marched in military maneuvers, they understood their direction was Germany's "place in the sun," a place befitting a great empire. The German writer Erich Maria Remarque caught that spirit in his novel of the First World War, *All Quiet on the Western Front*. When that novel's soldier-narrator is on leave from the trenches, he hears his former schoolteacher insist that Germany should have "at least the whole of Belgium, the coal areas of France, and a slice of Russia." The teacher exhorts the young soldier to "smash through the Johnnies." When the soldier, drawing on his personal experiences at the front, replies that a breakthrough may not be possible, the teacher "dismisses the idea loftily and informs me I know nothing about it." The euphoria the Germans felt when the war began in 1914 was not dispelled. One may argue over who began that war or what caused it, but there is no argument about the mood of the German people at the prospect of war. They were great soldiers ready to march across Europe in spiked helmets. They welcomed the war's coming. They rejoiced when it began. On August 2, 1914, when the war between Germany and Russia was declared, in a scene repeated in many other cities in Germany that day, thousands of Germans jammed the Odeonsplatz in Munich. A face in that Munich crowd well represented that German mood. Adolf Hitler then was a thin, handsome young man with dark hair and a neatly trimmed moustache. The expression on his face in a photograph of that Munich scene is one of ecstasy. This is what he had hoped for. "The struggle of the year 1914 was not forced on the masses," he wrote later. "No, by the living God—it was desired by the whole people." The only worry that "tormented" him at the time "as so many others," he said, was "would we not reach the front too late?"[27]

Two years later Germany was losing the war, but Adolf Hitler and many other Germans could not accept the impotence of the German military. They were "the salt of the earth," chosen by God to conquer the world, or at least Europe; they could not understand why God had forsaken them. There must be another reason. In grasping for that alternative the Germans turned to those they had been taught in their churches to hate. They turned to the Jews.

When Erich Ludendorff was appointed German military commander in 1916, he saw his role not as protecting Germany, not as saving Germany from as much damage as possible, not even as securing an honorable peace, but as protecting the image of the virile German as the mighty conqueror. One of the first acts of the war ministry after Ludendorff took command was a statistical inquiry into the religious affiliations of people working in defense industries at home, in the military service in the front lines, and behind the lines. Whatever Ludendorff's motive in seeking the inquiry, his record as an anti-Semite indicated the inquiry's purpose was to provide ammunition for an attack on the Jews. At one point, for example, when the Kaiser spoke about negotiating with the enemy, Ludendorff replied that there was still a chance for victory if, among other things, there was a greater sacrifice on the home front. Specifically, he advocated "more vigorous conscription of the young Jews, hitherto left pretty much alone." The survey he ordered of participation in the war effort by religious affiliation was not published; its results would have destroyed any charges that German Jews were not contributing to the war effort.

At home, attacks leveled against Jews increased. Walther Rathenau, whose industrial and financial genius was responsible for so much of Germany's ability to wage war, was a favorite target. Rathenau was a thief! He had filled up the war industries with his Jewish friends, who were using the war to make unconscionable profits. Germany was losing the war only because the Jews found it to their advantage that their brothers in other countries earn profits.

Soldiers in the trenches joined with military commanders and business leaders to denounce the Jew. Adolf Hitler, who emerged from the war a corporal, wrote in *Mein Kampf* that "The offices were filled with Jews. Nearly every clerk was a Jew and nearly every Jew was a clerk. I was amazed at this plethora of warriors of the chosen people and could not help but compare them with their rare representatives at the front." This accusation became known in Germany as *Dolchstoss*—a stab in the back. The word became shorthand in postwar Germany for the charge that Germany had not lost the war but had been sabotaged from within by the Jew.[28]

For some Jews, those killed fighting, what their fellow Germans believed of them no longer mattered. Some had been Baeck's students at the Hochschule, and he conducted a memorial service for them—in the same way that clergymen of other faiths conducted similar services for their young friends, perhaps using many of the same words.

"We see Alfred Salomon before us as we knew him," said Baeck of one rabbinical student, "the young, the tender, the almost girl-like face, the *verträumten* eyes under the smooth blond hair." Baeck recalled the young Salomon's first sermon—"The peacefulness of the day caused him to open up his heart, and in his quiet voice he told of his childhood in the quiet Wittenberg, where he, at an early age, had lost his father; of the years here in Berlin, where his mother and sister had followed him; and at last of his hopes, his wishes for his life." When the war began, young Salomon had been one of the first to volunteer "against the pleas of his mother." He died at Flanders. "We will never forget him," said Baeck.

Nor would they forget Alfred Salomon's friend, Max Lichtenstein, who had "the physique of a man, with a delightful glance as if he were looking out at the world with the eyes of a poet, full of belief in himself and his future." The community had placed much confidence in him, Baeck said, because he was equipped with all the talents that make a person a preacher and a teacher—"the sense for experiencing the soul, the fine psychological feelings were part of him." Rabbi Baeck recalled that Max had written him from the eastern front about his first impressions of Polish Jewry. "He had entered enthusiastically into all the problems of the Jewish youth and so spoke of all that lay before him on his way," said Baeck, "including his most inner feelings and desires." Young Max, an artilleryman, was standing by his cannon when he was killed. In his memorial sermon Baeck lamented the death of Max Lichtenstein with words from the Talmud: "Oh, the beauty which has gone from the earth."

Another pupil Baeck recalled in that memorial sermon was Siegfried Schemel, who apparently had come to the Hochschule too early, before he was ready to make a career decision. He changed his plans. But then Siegfried, with the help of his fiancée, realized what his real goal was, Baeck said. He returned to the Hochschule, convinced his former teachers there of his dedication, and was reenrolled for a semester before the war began. He died in a French prison camp.[29]

There were 12,000 young men like Alfred, Max, and Siegfried; young German Jews—or, as they would have called themselves, young Germans of the Jewish faith—who died in that war. In the postwar years those dead Germans of the Jewish faith were betrayed—as were the hundreds of thousands of other young Germans of the Catholic and Protestant faiths—by their political leaders. When the war ended in 1918, the Germans had a choice. Either they could delude themselves with their past glory, imaginary as it was, or struggle for their future. The Germans over the coming years refused to admit that Germany had lost the war and insisted that victory had been stolen from them. Declining to accept the reality of their present, in effect they surrendered any real hope for their future.

Leo Baeck returned to civilian life a few months before the armistice in June 1918, after almost four years as a chaplain. At his first service on June 28 in the Fasanenstrasse Synagogue the leadership of the Berlin Jewish community turned out to welcome him. Community leaders stepped to the *bimah* to praise Baeck. One said that the community "now will willingly trust [him] twice as much in his education and leadership" because his war experiences had given him a greater capability "to give to others from a higher strength that comes from the treasure of his religious experience, education, and edification."

Another speaker referred to the Torah reading for the next morning's service—Numbers 25:10-30:1. It told of the priesthood given the grandson of Aaron, describing the true priest as the one who creates peace and helps to regain the peace that has been lost. Then the speaker used that selection to describe Leo Baeck's chaplain role:

To give peace a home on this earth, to protect it when the powers of hate and destruction fight against it is the most noble task of the priestly office. In this most noble priestly duty, Rabbiner Dr. Baeck has proved himself in the middle of the war when he was preaching to our sons about a higher world of love where the brutal force of earthly happening is not valid and when he lived himself as a host at the festival table and as a consoler in the rooms of the sick at the hospital.

In his response Leo Baeck said he was "thankful," understanding that word to mean a willingness to assume "the duties that come to us for the future, for the future we seek does not come as a gift to us." He reminded his audience that once Jews had "the enthusiasm, the ability to put their inner strength into something, that is the condition of our future." Then he said to them: "In the recent years the small and the petty had come to occupy us more and more, had become the victor." Leo Baeck had gone away four years earlier as the essential German. He returned, no less a German, but more a Jew. "Today," he told the congregation, "it seems as if we have too much history and too little enthusiasm, too much defense and too little of that eagerness that we must possess for our future. We have to see God in front of us, our God, the God of our children." The use of the word *defense* by Baeck is interesting. Until then the movement among Jews in modern Germany had been a defensive one, one of denying their heritage or at least of defending themselves against too obvious a manifestation of that heritage. No more, said Baeck.

Jews coming home from the war, he insisted, "need this belief that has not only a 'no,' not only an 'if' and a 'but,' but which has the cheerful and proud 'yes' of enthusiasm." Leo Baeck was almost a revivalist as he concluded: "We need this eagerness for our Judaism. It connects us to the spirit to which our future belongs. It should be the bond with God, the bond of peace, about which our Biblical word speaks."[30]

Clearly the war had changed Leo Baeck. He had not been captured by the nationalistic spirit that encouraged war at any price and called for Germany's victory over any foe. He had the greatest loyalty to his country, the loyalty demanding recognition of its faults and acknowledgment of its failures. If he had not realized those faults and failures in 1914, he realized them in 1918 after seeing most of the western world

—including England, France, and the United States—oppose Germany. He realized that Germany had not worked for peace.

He placed working for peace, which is a Jewish commandment, in the framework of a community endeavor. "Our Jewish community has not become a church," he said after the war; "it is a community in a special sense . . . a community of blood and spirit; to a certain extent, a great family in which the children of the same forefathers and the same beliefs are together." He had grown up a German Jew, one of those who looked skeptically at the orthodox Jews of Poland and Russia with their strange ways so alien to the German burgher. Then he had spent four years away from Germany, dealing with Jews in France, Poland, and Russia. These Jews had befriended him, and he had conducted services for them. Leo Baeck had seen their needs, particularly those Russians fleeing the Revolution. He had said prayers in Hebrew so the Poles and the Russians could join in saying them. Now he was preaching to his fellow Jews in Berlin that it was not the Berlin Jews who were chosen but all Jews. Jewish history, "previously a mere chronicle," was "the chronicle of a single group of men." And this community, this chosen people, was bound together uniquely as a spiritual community. The Jews were chosen not only to receive God's blessing—God's blessing can come to any individual. Rather, they had been chosen for a spiritual responsibility, to seek peace and to act justly. It was this responsibility that pulled them together into a community.[31]

Baeck's conviction that one cannot be Jewish and be only an observer had deepened. A few months after his return from the war, in a letter to Martin Buber, he jotted down some ideas he had been thinking about and had been hearing from others: "We have to say something about the questions which now are standing in the struggle of the spirit. The questions about war and peace, the questions about politics and morals." By "we" he meant the Jews. "Judaism," he declared, "cannot very well abdicate and hide." With that letter Baeck attached some notes further amplifying how he construed man's responsibility. The theme in those lines was repeated often in his writing; the identical lines appeared formally in a Hochschule lecture of his the next year. "Times are changing," he scrawled, "and so many times have their new earth; but man, the same man, always stands on it. The man remains and therefore the duty remains. To work and to look forward is therefore the command for us. An earth goes, an earth comes, but the man remains. The man and his duty. With this word we think of the past, and with that word we greet the future."[32]

Erich Ludendorff, Adolf Hitler, and other Germans might take refuge in the past, cry *"Dolchstoss!"* and complain that their land had been denied its victory, but Leo Baeck would insist that the Germans should seek their future and do their duty.

Duty is a word Baeck often used to describe being Jewish. He had emerged from the First World War knowing that to be a Jew means to do one's duty. "Judaism cannot very well abdicate and hide," he had declared to Martin Buber. That was because Judaism is the religion of the deed; to be a Jew means to act.

5 COMMUNITY

As LEO BAECK SPOKE of duty and of the Jew's obligation to act, Adolf Hitler was meeting with his followers in the cellars of Munich, beginning a political career that would alter the history of the world. For Hitler there was no question that the Jews of Germany, and the Jews of the world, were the enemy:

If the threat with which Jewry faces our people has given rise to undeniable hostility on the part of a large section of our people, the cause of this hostility must not be sought in the clear recognition that Jewry as such is deliberately or unwittingly having a pernicious effect on our nation, but mostly in personal intercourse, in the poor impression the Jew makes as an individual . . .

To begin with, the Jews are unquestionably a race, not a religious community . . .

All this results in that mental attitude and that quest for money and the power to protect it which allow the Jew to become so unscrupulous in his choice of means, so merciless in his use for his own ends. In autocratic states he cringes before the "majesty" of the princes and misuses their favours to become a leech on their people.

In a democracy he vies for the favours of the masses, grovels before "the majesty of the people", but only recognizes the majesty of money . . .

And this had the following consequences: purely emotional antisemitism finds its expression in the form of pogroms. Rational antisemitism, by contrast, must lead to a systematic and legal struggle against, and eradication of, what privileges the Jews enjoy over other foreigners living among us . . . Its final objective, however, must be the total removal of all Jews from our midst. Both objectives can only be achieved by a government of national strength, never by a government of national impotence . . .[1]

In September 1919 Adolf Hitler, then still an obscure army corporal, was calling for a government of national strength, one that would rid Germany of its Jews, make it *Judenrein*. In Munich he had joined a workers' party made up largely of roughnecks, disgruntled soldiers, and misfits, men united by their failures and linked by one other element, their anti-Semitism. At this time they, not the Jews, were the apparent outcasts. The Weimar Republic had come to postwar Germany, bringing democracy with it and outlawing religious discrimination. The state gave its Jewish citizens the same support it gave to its Christian citizens; the Constitution of 1919 terminated second-class status. There was proof, then, that the Constitutional mandate was working.

In 1911 a study had listed some of the ways in which Jews were discriminated against despite the Prussian constitution outlawing such behavior. The study noted that it was obligatory for elementary schools to provide religious instruction to Catholic and Protestant children, but for Jewish children it was voluntary on the part of the local community—this much had been the result of the labors of men like Samuel Bäck in the latter half of the nineteenth century. The study also noted that the state provided training in religious education for teachers of the Christian faith, but Jews provided for their own. In addition, the state maintained Christian theological faculties at the universities and subsidized seminaries, but there was not a single chair of Jewish theology in any of the universities within Prussia.

In contrast to this prewar discrimination, in the early postwar years money poured into the schools for Jewish education at the same rate as for Christian religious education. Germans of the Jewish faith were welcomed into public life too. Yet, none of the Jews could forget the anti-Semitism they had known before Weimar or the *Dolchstoss* charge that erupted at the war's end. Some were concerned by roughnecks like Adolf Hitler, too, but all of this began to fade before the apparent equality and excitement of the Weimar Republic.[2]

Actually, the Weimar Republic never was as much as its memory. Still, it was very much. "Unbelievable cultural glamour," recalled one who had spent his twenties in Berlin in the days of the Republic. It was an unleashing of intellect and artistic emotions that had been suppressed for dozens of years. And it was undeniably brilliant. The motion picture, a young medium, never had been so creative and rarely has been since. New trends began in architecture, art, music, and in relations between the sexes. A half-century later these trends still influence the lives of men and women almost everywhere.

Berlin was the focal point of the Weimar Republic, and Berlin was the home of the German Jews. From the very founding of the republic in the city of Weimar in 1919, Jews had been active participants. A Jew actually had been a major author of the new constitution with its emphasis, unusual for a European nation, on religious freedom. Of the 423 delegates attending the constitutional convention nine were Jews and four had Jewish family backgrounds. The success of Walther Rathenau and Albert Ballin had shown that Jews could make their way in the business world. Now they moved into the artistic world. Max Reinhardt's brilliant theatrical staging, Elisabeth Bergner's radiant acting, Arnold Schönberg's music with its revolutionary twelve-tone scale, Lion Feuchtwanger's and Stefan Zweig's writings—these Jews were part of the Weimar culture as were Albert Einstein and many other scientists, bankers, and journalists.

They were visible. Lutherans and Catholics were active in these fields, too, but they rarely were identified as Lutherans and Catholics; Jews almost always were identified by their religious affiliation. Leo Baeck had commented on this in his 1911 lecture in Duesseldorf, that the Jews have "the strange characteristic to multiply ourselves; if there might be twenty of us, one would think there were two hundred of us." One historian of the Weimar Republic has written: "Indeed there were far more Jewish tailors than writers and journalists." But few were interested in seeing the tailors as well as the journalists. What that attitude connoted largely was ignored by the Jews. "Yes, there was always anti-Semitism in Austria, but not in Berlin, not until much later," was a typical reaction to the situation of the Jews in Berlin during Weimar.[3]

A strength of the Jews in Berlin was the status of the *Gemeinde,* their community. There is no equivalent in English. In most other countries Jews join congregations on a voluntary basis. Contributions to those congregations are voluntary, as are contributions to support hospitals, homes for the elderly, schools, and social services. The German Gemeinde was based on an entirely different concept, which had begun in the Middle Ages, not for the best of purposes. Special privileges and authorities were given to favored Jews by the monarchs. Through these favored Jews—"court Jews," they often were called— the intention was to control the Jewish community and to pull from it as much as possible in taxes. That motivation had disappeared by the middle of the nineteenth century, but the concept of a corporate entity had been given legal status, and so the Gemeinde came into existence.

All Jews except those who formally had converted to Christianity —atheism and agnosticism were officially unknown in Germany until the closing quarter of the nineteenth century—belonged to the Gemeinde of the city in which they lived. They paid taxes to that Gemeinde, usually collected by the state with the regular taxes. Toward the end of the nineteenth century, when the cleavage between the interpretations of Judaism intensified, individuals were allowed to separate from these Gemeindes as a matter of conscience. That meant usually that orthodox members of the community were allowed to establish their own Gemeinde with the same legal status as the parent from which they had split.

Almost from the beginning, the Berlin Gemeinde was the largest Jewish community in Germany. By the early 1900s it represented approximately one-third of all German Jews. There were several reasons for this. The Jews were primarily city dwellers because of the centuries-old restrictive laws that had prevented them from owning farmland and forced them into urban areas. Also, the Jews practiced their religion as part of a community—they required a *minyan*, a Hebrew word meaning the minimum of ten adult males necessary before a service could begin—and so had sought the city where they could find this community. Berlin particularly was attractive as an urban center because it had the intellectual excitement of Berlin University, a developing commerce, and a growing culture.

There also was an arrogance, a feeling held by Jew and non-Jew alike, that to be a Berliner was to be perhaps somewhat better than to be only a German; it was to live in the center of things, where the action and power were.[4]

After the First World War these changes accelerated. "The political upheaval . . ." wrote Leo Baeck about this period, "brought for the Jews of Germany essential changes both in structure as well as in the spiritual attitudes with it." The structural changes of which Baeck spoke dealt with the land in which he had been born. The cities where he had grown up, been educated, and first practiced as a rabbi no longer were German. The peace treaty ending the war called for a plebiscite to determine whether that area of eastern Germany, under international control since the war's end, would be returned to Germany or become part of Poland. About 99 percent of the Jews in those areas voted for resuming political ties with Germany; they had always felt closer to the Berlin area than to their Polish neighbors. Those Jews who had been born in eastern Germany and moved away, like young Ruth

Baeck, returned to vote for continued ties with Germany. (Ruth later was fond of recalling that she was feted by many old family friends in her native Oppeln. "I survived there," she recalled, "because I had goose liver paté every morning.") But the Jews were a minority, and Poland won the territories in the plebiscite. Baeck said the Jews in those areas "who considered themselves tied to the German culture both by language as well as by a spiritual affinity, gave up their homes, each and every one of them, and moved to a different part of Germany." For many of those who moved after the plebiscite Berlin was the natural choice for a new home. There were economic opportunities in the city as well as fellow Jews with whom to form *minyans*.[5]

Financially, the members of the *Jüdische Gemeinde* in Berlin had done well. Widening of economic opportunities had paralleled the nineteenth-century increase in civil liberties. Because government and academic-tenured positions still were denied them in that century, however, the Jews entered industry and commerce just at a time when there was an expansion in these areas—the industrial revolution had arrived. The financial success of the Jews soon became evident. The income of the Berlin *Gemeinde* from taxes on its members increased by 50 percent during one decade in the second half of the nineteenth century, and by that much again in the next decade. This money enabled the Jews to carry on their tradition of taking care of the less fortunate members of their community. They had both the will and the means to provide all the social services their community needed.

This prosperity showed in another way. The Jews in Berlin earned more money, or at least paid more in civil taxes, than did their non-Jewish neighbors. A study made early in the 1900s showed that the average Jewish taxpayer paid 357 marks in civil taxes, the Protestant paid 132 marks, and the Catholic paid 111 marks; the "dissenter," the individual without a religious affiliation, paid an average of 270 marks. This higher earning power of the Jews was a factor—despite the facade of the "good" relations between Jews and other Germans in the 1920s—goading the non-Jew into being envious of the Jew's success.

In addition to economic progress there also was opportunity for the Jews to develop their religious practices. Through the Hochschule and other seminaries German Judaism was producing scholars who stood equal to those in any other area. A student of German-Jewish history, Jacob R. Marcus, at the beginning of the 1930s applauded the German Jew as "the first to emerge a 'modern.'" Although conceding that the German Jew had failed to produce a "blending of Hebraism and Westernism," Marcus said the German Jew "did achieve something else which was to make him unique among the Jewries of the world."

German Jewry modernized its religious practices, introduced decorum into its worship, evolved great communal, educational, social, and philanthropic institutions which served as models to Jewry everywhere, applied the scientific method to Jewish studies and emerged in a position of undisputed academic leadership in world Jewry—all the more remarkable because it never, during this entire period, constituted more than five percent of the Jewish population of the world.[6]

While accomplishing that, German Jewry paid a high price. It was not only the cathedral-like synagogues and the distance between the Jew and the rabbi above him on the *bimah*. Rather, it was the attitude toward Judaism that the German Jews showed. On a Friday night there might be only two dozen persons attending a service in one of the cavernous Berlin synagogues. Although the move to make the Jewish Sabbath coincide with the Christian one never gained wide support—Leo Baeck would not countenance it, nor would most rabbis—the fact that even a minority did was a unique development in the history of Judaism. An example of the rationale for switching the day of the Sabbath was given in this story told by a writer named Emil Herz. In the 1920s he met a Berlin rabbi who had been prepared for the rabbinate by Herz's grandfather. "I fancy," Herz reported saying to the young rabbi, "my grandfather would turn in his grave if he knew that his favorite pupil was celebrating divine service on Sunday instead of Saturday." The young rabbi contradicted Herz "vehemently":

I'm convinced that your grandfather would have realized the need for innovation, even if he didn't approve of it. In the old days it was easy for the Jews to keep their shops shut on Saturday, but later they were forced by law to observe the Sunday rest. Two rest days in the week is more than most people can afford in these days of commercial competition. Your grandfather didn't live to see this turn of events, he was spared these struggles with his conscience. What are we to do? Take a look at the synagogues in Berlin, they're empty except for a few old men, women and children. Must the majority of our professionally employed co-religionists be deprived of their religious devotions? Must their Judaism be confined to the New Year and the Day of Atonement, two days in a year?[7]

Being Jewish has always been difficult. Adhering to traditions that others did not hold always was a challenge. It was much easier to change the traditions or to surrender Judaism entirely, which many of the German Jews had done even before the coming of the Weimar Republic. This trend first became visible in the nineteenth century. Heinrich Heine converted from Judaism to Christianity in hopes of being able to practice law, which he then decided not to do, becoming a poet and critic instead. Karl Marx usually is described as a Jew. One of his recent biographers has pointed out that although the family members were "thoroughly Jewish in their origins," they were "Protestant by necessity." Conversion was necessary for entry into certain professional areas in nineteenth-century Germany. "It is like a miracle!" claimed one converted in 1818. Moses Mendelssohn, who had led the Jews from the ghetto in the late eighteenth century, had said that Jews should never barter their essential religion for citizenship. His descendants became Christians.

If the conversions were not massive in number—perhaps several hundred a year during the decades before the First World War—they were steady. One recollection is that in the typical Berlin Jewish family at the beginning of the twentieth century the son interested in a university career converted as did the daughter who was about to marry a Christian. If there was another child, one entering business or industry, he or she remained a Jew. The story is told of a German rabbi who saw seven of his grandchildren converted by 1907. The intermarriage rate was high: Between one-fourth and one-third of all marriages involving Jews had a non-Jew as a partner. Jews who married out of the faith did not cease to be Jewish, but in Germany intermarriages acted as a pull toward Christianity. If the Jewish partner did not become a practicing Christian, in many cases the children or the grandchildren of the marriage did. The figures so frightened some Jewish scholars that they anticipated the disappearance of the Jews in Germany within several decades. One book written in 1911, *Der Untergang der deutschen Juden*—The Decline of the German Jews—predicted Germany would have no Jews by the end of the century because of the growing number of conversions and mixed marriages.[8]

A shadow followed those Jews who stayed with their faith, one they could not eliminate from their lives. Peter Gay, a historian of Weimar, has quoted a prominent Jew after the First World War: *"Stiefkinder müssen doppelt artig sein"*—Stepchildren must be doubly good. There was an awareness that German society judged a Protestant or a Catholic as an individual without regard to religious affiliation, but it judged a Jew as a Jew. One of the reasons for the industriousness of the Berlin *Gemeinde* was to raise the cultural and educational standards of all Jews, so that none could be criticized; all would be "doubly good."[9]

For sensitive Jews there was a dichotomy between their hope to be both German and Jewish and the lack of total acceptance they gained as either one. One who had grown to manhood in the 1920s commented many years later: "I felt I was a good German and a good Jew. My friends went to church, and I went to synagogue." The speaker paused for a moment, then added: "I wasn't prepared for Hitler." Franz Rosenzweig, one of the most brilliant philosophers to emerge from the First World War, was asked in 1923 which he would stress, his being German or his being Jewish. "I refused to answer," he said. "If it should happen that life should put me on the rack and tear me into pieces, I would get to know with which of the two halves the heart would go, as the heart is placed in the body in a non-symmetrical way." Then Rosenzweig added: "But I would also get to know something else, that I would not survive this operation."

Rosenzweig's love for Germany led him, with Martin Buber, to begin a new translation of the Hebrew Bible into German. Unlike Moses Mendelssohn's translation more than a century earlier, this translation was not intended to teach Jewish youth pure German. Rather, the intention was to retain the original Hebrew flavor of the Bible and the spirit it expressed. The translation, which was not finished for decades, was intended as a *Gastgeschenk*, a symbolic act of gratitude by the Jews to their fellow Germans for so welcoming them into their hearts as friends and neighbors.

Martin Buber had described the problem in 1916. The German Jews, he said, "assure the Germans that they are not different in order not to be treated as aliens. But we are different and, yet, in very truth and plainly stated, we are not foreign."[10] He was summing up the plight of the minority; his words can refer not only to the Jews in Germany but of any minority anywhere. Can any minority, religious or ethnic, survive in a majority state? Can it retain its dignity and its values, can it contribute its values to the majority? Can the majority likewise act with tolerance and intelligence to allow the minority to survive? Is assimilation, the loss of individuality and character, the price that must be paid for survival?

To this last question Leo Baeck in the 1920s answered again and again, "No." The Jew cannot surrender individuality and character. Although Baeck had said many times that Judaism has no dogma and that tradition and practices may change or be altered, he never forgot that such changes should strengthen the religion, not weaken or hide it. He insisted that the Jews take pride in their religion. Because Baeck was so German in his writing and his preaching, he was ideally suited for the role of making such demands upon his fellow Jews. A woman whose family had been close to Baeck's in this period recalled many years later, "Although Leo Baeck was an observant Jew, soaked with Judaism, on the outside he was a *goy*." She continued: "Whenever the Jews of Berlin wanted to be represented by a particularly dignified person, they called on Leo Baeck. He was very popular with assimilated Jews; they liked to have him officiate at weddings because he looked so good before all the non-Jews." The woman added of Baeck: "He was so much a pastor."

In looks this was true. In the 1920s Baeck was in his fifties, and certain habits of appearance were integral to his personality. He dressed formally; the suit was dark with a vest, and he never was seen without a suit jacket. Tall, with his hair and beard now graying, he looked like an aristocrat. And he walked like one; his body bent forward, his arms swinging in wide arcs at his side, his eyes staring straight ahead and rarely looking to either side. He also was, as a fellow rabbi said of him, a "man who commanded distance." This was due partly to the habits of the German society in which he lived, partly to his own personal reticence—he still did not use "I" in his sermons or writings. W. Gunther Plaut, whose family had known Baeck closely, exclaimed years later, "The idea of calling him 'Leo'!" Plaut then added that although one never seemed close to Baeck, "he had a way of treating you as if he respected you, not as if you were a child."[11]

This man, aloof, dignified, Gentile in manner, a Jew who had become a German, now was the German who was a Jew. This man would call other German Jews back to their Jewishness. He would do this through his preaching, his teaching, his community activities, and his writing.

About Leo Baeck's preaching there were two descriptions popular in Berlin. One said that his sermons were "private conversations with God." Another described Baeck on the *bimah* delivering his sermon as *der Fahrstuhl*—the elevator—a reference to his pushing himself up physically as he made a point. Although both were intended as criticisms, there was another side. Listening to Baeck demanded that one follow the development of the sermon theme carefully, ponder its significance, and stretch one's intellect to its utmost. Listening to a sermon by Leo Baeck was an exercise of the mind.

Baeck refused to help his listener through dramatics. "It was beneath his dignity to use techniques," said Joachim Prinz, a fellow rabbi in Berlin. "There was no performance." Fritz Bamberger, one of Baeck's pupils, said of him, "His rabbinical bag did not contain a well-assorted collection of Jewish tales labeled for various occasions." By the 1920s Baeck's voice was "very husky, a whisper really; it had a haunting quality," said one who heard him speak many times. "It was a very effective method of presentation, especially in Germany," continued this observer, adding, "The average German is trained to listen rather than to speak." Another who had heard Baeck many times described the impression made by Baeck through his sermons—"It was something different from what one was accustomed to by men such as Maybaum, Rosenzweig, Weisse; Baeck would not and could not compete with their theatrical talent."

"The high point of the synagogue experience was the regular preaching of Dr. Leo Baeck . . ." recalled another. "The structure of his sermons had a highly developed classical beauty and was exemplary. The fullness of his insight of the spirit overrode all which the liberal rabbinical tradition had to offer. Although clearly not interested in attending the synagogue, as a student I was regularly in the synagogue—at least, during the semesters I spent in Berlin—if Dr. Leo Baeck was preaching."[12]

Second to Baeck's importance in Berlin as a preacher was his importance as a teacher of other rabbis. Martin Buber once said that for a teacher "you do need a man who is wholly alive and able to communicate himself directly to his fellow beings." Such a teacher was Leo Baeck. Few responsibilities in his life were as heavy upon him as that of teaching. He taught with compassion, with all the strength of his intellect, and with all the openness of a dedicated heart. In a 1926 lecture he described educating a person "the most artistic accomplishment of man." His German background showed through in that lecture when he did not use the word *Erziehung*—education—but used *Bildung*—bringing someone to self-realization. It is not educating people but helping them to educate themselves. Leo Baeck considered being a teacher a religious task. "Religion," he said, "wants to educate and form; it wants to give a certain thing a substance, a meaning, and a sense; it wants to realize and to fulfill . . . The religious man is driven to educate."

Baeck taught two subjects at the Hochschule during his career there. The first was Midrash. This includes the early commentaries written on the Bible, the remarks rabbis have made about the Bible's contents, and their interpretations of what the Biblical passages mean and how they can be adapted to contemporary life. He also taught homiletics, the technique of sermon presentation. Baeck's approach to this subject was in line with a description of the course offered by Hochschule officials when Baeck had first arrived there as a teacher in 1913. Homiletics, they said, is education for rabbis "who are called to plant the word of God in the hearts of their listeners."[13]

One of his former pupils, Fritz Bamberger, recalled years later that Baeck did not teach philosophy at the Hochschule. "He taught theology but he was reluctant to call it that," said Bamberger. "He was very cool, speaking as he wrote—in an idiomatic German; the idiom was his own. There was little change in speed and tempo. The verbs were underplayed. Nouns were overplayed. It was a march of ideas." Bamberger added, "That was true even when Baeck talked about simple things, but then he rarely talked about simple things."

Rabbinical students from the United States coming to study at the Hochschule in the 1920s—"America still was a cultural frontier," said one, "and if you wanted to learn anything about Judaism you went to the Hochschule"—found Baeck's lectures difficult to follow. "He was abstract and philosophical," explained one of those Americans many years later. The American paused for a moment and said: "I guess it was fifty percent my fault."

Leo Baeck also was remembered by his pupils as a stern taskmaster. The homiletics class was at eight o'clock in the morning, and Baeck began it at eight—"bitter early," recalled one student—no matter how many pupils were absent. Formality marked the sessions, with the students wearing dark suits and ties and addressing Baeck as *Herr Doktor*. He replied to them with *Herr Kollege*. One student said of the distinguished rabbi addressing the student as an equal, "That was his kindness."

He urged brevity upon his students. "You may speak about anything," he once said to his class, "but for not more than twenty minutes." It was difficult for his students to stand before him and give a practice sermon. Said one of those students: "Only God could possibly have known how the heart of a 23-24-25-year-old student would pound in anticipation of presenting a practice sermon before Baeck." Each student, it seemed, had his version of a devastating review by Leo Baeck.

One remembered Baeck commenting, "Much of what you said was good and much of what you said was new. But unfortunately"—there would be a heavy sigh and perhaps even the trace of a smile—"what was good wasn't new and what was new wasn't good." Another: 'Your sermon is very good, except for some details. The introduction should have some connection with the text and the body of the sermon, and the language could be simpler, and the sermon would be twice as good if it were half as long; but otherwise, it is a fine sermon."[14]

Despite the severity of the reprimands there was a closeness between Baeck and his students. Those who went through his classes never forgot him. He was in the tradition of the German university professor; he came into the classroom a few minutes before his lecture was to begin, hung up his hat and coat in the professor's room, gave his lecture, put on his hat and coat, and went home. "Universities were not constructed for any other kind of relationship," one student recalled. Still, given the coldness of the format, Leo Baeck often broke through. Constantly he sought to help his students. Many received scholarships with his assistance, particularly after he became president in the 1920s of the German order of B'nai B'rith, the Jewish fraternal association, which had scholarship funds available. And there were other forms of assistance. "When he learned that I needed to recuperate after an operation," another student reported, "he persuaded a family with whom he was friendly to invite me to their estate near Berlin for several weeks." For another student, Wolli Kaelter, the relationship became even more personal. Kaelter's father had been a rabbi and died when the son was only twelve years old. Baeck had been a friend of the elder Kaelter and assumed a father-role for the young man, encouraging him to enter the rabbinate and assisting him financially.

Many of his students, away from their own homes while studying in Berlin, found a family warmth at his house. These visits of the students to the rabbi took place on Saturday, the Sabbath, and Natalie served tea and cake. "Professor Baeck always allowed every visitor to talk at length about his problems," one student recalled. Sometimes during the week Baeck, in walks around the Tiergarten, would discuss with the students philosophy or current events. "Leo Baeck had an encyclopedic mind and a memory unparalleled," said one who enjoyed those walks. "When quoting Plato, Leo Baeck always had the citation correct." In these personal gatherings Baeck tended to be less formal in his advice on how to construct the proper sermon: "Only if you are leaving for Africa should you give your congregation everything you know."

As a matter of course Baeck said hello before a student could greet him. "For the two and one-half years I was at the Hochschule," said one student, "Leo Baeck and I used to approach the building from opposite sides. Only once did I manage to tip my hat before he did." Said another student: "Leo Baeck was a man of surpassing politeness." Baeck once forgot to reply when this student sent him a paper he had written on Kant. When Baeck finally remembered, he wrote to the student, "In the joy of reading it, I forgot to reply."

Joachim Prinz, a student at both the Hochschule and the University of Berlin in the 1920s, has a favorite story of Leo Baeck's politeness. Baeck had invited him to Saturday dinner, and Prinz—anxious to make a good impression—dressed in his Sabbath best and brought flowers for Mrs. Baeck. He arrived at the proper hour, and Baeck invited him into the library. The two men began to chat. They chatted and they chatted. Every few minutes, Prinz remembered, a maid opened the library door, thrust her head into the room, only to be motioned away by Baeck. Baeck did not discuss these interruptions, nor did Prinz. They sat in the library like that, each man a study in courtesy until finally Prinz's hunger overrode his politeness. "Forgive me," he asked, "am I not invited to dinner with you?" Baeck smiled as politely as possible and answered: "Forgive me, but you were invited for next week." Prinz, although certain Baeck had erred on the dates, did not feel he could contradict the professor and apologized profusely as Baeck led him down the stairs.[15]

Leo Baeck's attitude toward women as students in the Hochschule was unusual for the time. Even in liberal synagogues women were seated in a separate section, and the prospect of a woman becoming a rabbi was totally unacceptable to the Jewish community. However, Baeck did encourage women to attend the school with the object of becoming teachers. Ellen Littmann, who said she believed herself to be the first woman to complete the academic program at the Hochschule, recalled that she began speaking with Baeck about attending the school when she was twelve. She had just read the first edition of his *The Essence of Judaism*, was enthralled by it, and began immersing herself in Judaism. Eventually this led her to attend the Hochschule. When her parents opposed her studies there, Baeck won their approval by saying that a teaching position would be available to their daughter after she graduated from the Hochschule.

Another woman, Perle Haskel, came to the Hochschule from Lithuania at the age of seventeen. Most of the male students were ten to fifteen years older and had had what appeared to be a more thorough religious training. However, she had received adequate training in a Jewish school and later recalled that "Professor Baeck always was remarking that I knew the Bible much better than all the other students." She may or may not have known the Bible so well, but certainly she did not feel alienated from what was traditionally a male domain after Baeck's comments. In addition to her academic accomplishments Perle Haskel was very attractive. Once Baeck came into the school and found a number of the male students paying court to her. "Now," he said, smiling, "I understand why little Perle is coming to our school."[16]

Many of Baeck's students in the years following the First World War came from nonobserving Jewish families. But the war, very much a part of their memories in the 1920s, and the havoc of the postwar years sweeping through Berlin like sudden storms—the revolution in 1919, inflation in 1922—had stirred within them thoughts and questions about their religion. Judaism still was close enough to them that they sought an answer in the faith of their fathers. Baeck's lectures transcended pedagogy to reach their faith.

A series of lectures that intrigued the students was on Midrash. Fritz Bamberger recalled that the traditional way of dealing with Midrash at the time was to treat these rabbinic commentaries as a source of legends, as examples of morals and religious points. Baeck, however, approached the Midrash as a historian would, examining it as a source of ideas. Against Berlin in 1922—"a drab, unhappy city flooded with inflation money of which most of the students had none"—a Baeck lecture shone, wrote Bamberger, "brilliantly for all the glory that scholarship can have."

A particular lecture revolved around a Midrash written in the early days of Christianity as an answer to a Christian interpretation of the first sentence in the Bible—"In the beginning God created Heaven and Earth." There had been several translations of the original Hebrew, but Jews had not seen in any of them reason to deny God's unique responsibility for the creation of the world. Baeck showed that the early rabbis had argued in the Midrash against the Christian commentary that God had created the world through an intermediary. Said Bamberger:

And as the lecture progressed, the men who had preached the opposite sermons receded and so did the time in which they lived and the circumstances which shaped their special ways, and the conflict became an eternal conflict between two great ideas on which two great religions were built: Judaism believing in the immediate confrontation of man and God; Christianity believing that man needs an intermediary to bridge the gap between him and God.

Baeck had "set his sights on the ideas which remain changeless in the ever-changing procession of men."

Another aspect of Leo Baeck that emerged in these lectures was his attitude toward the rabbinate. Part was his own life-style, personally rigorous. "An orderly mind," he told his students, "is not a matter of intellect but of character." He would quote to them that "He who is not disciplined is not educated." With the reticence and the discipline, however, the individual still must emerge; the rabbi cannot hide. "A sermon is not to be delivered," a student recalled Baeck saying, "it is the person who must deliver himself . . . The greatest message one can preach is one's life."[17]

Another important part of Baeck's attitude toward the rabbinate was his belief that the rabbi should be available to all members of the community. His habit of not using the word *I* in his sermons or his writings was a manifestation of his belief that the rabbi should restrain himself so that, in the end, he could be available to all who sought him. This led to the impression that Baeck was a compromiser, one who would not take a stand. Many stories deal with this impression. A Berlin rabbi recalled once telling Leo Baeck: "It's a good thing you're not younger; you can't say no." According to another story: "Leo Baeck was a great *jeinsager*; he couldn't say *Ja* or *Nein* but always said yes and no combined." Baeck frequently was made the subject of an old Jewish story in which a rabbi is approached by an individual seeking support in a dispute. "You are absolutely right," the rabbi tells the man. Then the second party to the same dispute comes and is advised by the rabbi: "You are absolutely right." An outsider later says to the rabbi, "How can two people taking opposite points of view in the same dispute be right? That's not possible." The rabbi replies: "You also are absolutely right."

These stories illustrate an essential point about Leo Baeck. He was reluctant to disappoint or to hurt people unnecessarily by responding negatively to a request. As Baeck's student critiques showed, he could be direct and even painfully blunt as a teacher. But he believed that a rabbi should not become so identified with one cause that the advocates of the other side would not turn to him. Many years after this period one of his students confronted Baeck in London. "I told him," said the student, "that in his homiletics seminars we sometimes gained the impression that he wanted to dissuade us from taking a clear position on actual questions, as, for example, socialism." Baeck looked at the student thoughtfully and said finally: "You misunderstood me. I wanted to educate you for your task as a rabbi who must be careful and hold himself back on the pulpit." Leo Baeck—like his father before him—belonged to no party, but to Judaism.[18]

Beginning in the 1920s Leo Baeck frequently was referred to as the "Chief Rabbi of Berlin." The title was incorrect. Although many European communities bestowed the "Chief Rabbi" title on an individual, the Berlin Gemeinde did not. The Gemeinde members feared that singling out one rabbi for such a title would offend the others, producing more friction than the title warranted. But the activities Baeck assumed in this period were such as to make him chief rabbi in responsibility if not in title. Because of his experience as a *Feldrabbiner*, he was particularly interested in the Reichsbund jüdischer Frontsoldaten, an organization of Jewish war veterans; frequently he volunteered as a speaker for the organization in an effort to raise funds and to attract attention to the plight of the Jewish victims of the First World War.

He also became president of the Zentralwohlfahrtsstelle der deutschen Juden, an organization formed after the war combining all Jewish social welfare agencies. This position was particularly significant in the early 1920s, when inflation ripped apart the financial sinews of both public agencies and private individuals. The Berliners needed wheelbarrows filled with mark notes to purchase a loaf of bread. They rushed with their salaries to stores to purchase goods, hoping that saving only a few moments would enable them to buy goods before the inflationary spiral carried them out of their reach.

The Berlin Jews, caught with the other Berliners in this spiral, in 1922 sent Ismar Elbogen, a Hochschule teacher, to ask help from the Jewish community in the United States. He managed to raise a substantial sum, and Baeck received it the morning of December 14 in Berlin. After turning the check over to the Zentralwohlfahrtsstelle, Baeck reported to Elbogen, "I felt like the men from Kohn's *Prague Ghetto Tales* who took two policemen with him to make certain that he and his money arrived safely. Because I didn't have any policemen, I at least looked around very suspiciously." He added: "The rich gifts will help many people over the winter."

In 1922 Leo Baeck was elected president of the Allgemeiner Rabbinerverbandes in Deutschland, the association of both Liberal and Orthodox rabbis. He also was a member of the executive committee of the Central-Verein deutscher Staatsbürger jüdischen Glaubens, the association of German citizens of the Jewish faith. "His strong and influential position in the organization rested on the fact," said one of Baeck's contemporaries, "that he identified himself in each case with those sections of their program that corresponded to his own views, without expressly disassociating himself from those tendencies to which he did not subscribe."[19]

In 1924 Baeck was elected grand president of the B'nai B'rith lodges in Germany; there were 103 lodges with 13,000 members. The words *b'nai b'rith* mean sons of the covenant in Hebrew, a reference to the relationship between the Jews and God. The order was a fraternal one in which Jews of different persuasions, Orthodox and Liberal, Zionist and non-Zionist, could come together. "Money alone couldn't buy you in," recalled one member. "One could only belong if he made contributions to continuing Jewish life. There were social halls, large libraries of Jewish literature, summer camps."

Much of what the B'nai B'rith lodges did came under the heading of community affairs—providing scholarships, funding hospitals, supporting other charitable activities. But there was also a conscious effort to hold Jews to their faith; conversion and intermarriage were taking their toll and causing considerable concern among leaders of the Jewish community. In 1928 the B'nai B'rith grand lodge, which was made up of representatives from other lodges, urged all members to keep the Jewish spirit alive by discouraging marriages between Jew and non-Jew. The individual lodges were requested to take "appropriate measures," which were not specified. In the same vote the lodge determined that "For a brother who withdraws his children from the Jewish community, there is no place in the order." Leo Baeck is not recorded as speaking to that harsh stricture; never did he indicate in his personal life reluctance or discourtesy in dealing with Jews involved in mixed marriages, with the Christian offspring of such marriages, or with Jews who had converted. Still, some remarks he made at the Lodge meeting that year indicated his sympathy at least with the emotions leading to the adoption of that stricture. His remarks dealt with *Menschheitsideal*—the human ideal—and his message was that people could serve humanity only if they were true to themselves and to their community. "We experience human society as our Jewish society . . ." said Baeck. "Not away from Judaism, but through our Judaism does the way lead to the fulfillment of our idea of humanity."[20]

Unlike in Oppeln, Baeck had little contact with the clergymen of other faiths in Berlin. "They lived in splendid isolation—the Jews, the

Catholics, and the Lutherans," recalled one Berlin rabbi. The ghetto walls had come down, but only the actual physical walls. The intellectual, spiritual, and emotional walls still stood. One modest effort to break down those walls in the 1920s was made by a German nobleman, Count Hermann Keyserling, in Darmstadt. He established what he called a *Schule der Weisheit*—a School of Wisdom. It was in effect what a later generation might call a think tank. Prominent persons with different backgrounds were invited to participate by giving lectures. Baeck was the Jew invited in 1922, 1923, and 1924. The lectures he gave those three years—"Commandment and Mystery," "Greek and Jewish Thought," and "Death and Rebirth"—were efforts to explain the essential differences between Judaism and Christianity. As Krister Stendahl, dean of the Harvard Divinity School, has pointed out, "Most of what Baeck wrote . . . had Christianity as a partner in the dialogue." But the dialogue was more a monologue in those years when Catholics and Protestants saw the Jews only from a distance.[21]

Baeck engaged in many other activities, too, some of a more personal nature. One of the most luminous personalities of this period was Franz Rosenzweig—luminous not only for the philosophy that came from his pen while he lived an active life, but also for the courage he showed as he slowly died from a debilitating disease. Rosenzweig, who lived in Frankfurt am Main, knew he was dying and wished to bequeath something to his son more tangible than property. His hope was to be ordained a rabbi so that after his death the son would know that the father had held a position of importance in the Jewish religion. Rosenzweig's own rabbi had agreed to ordain him, but then died. Baeck stepped in and ordained Rosenzweig, although there was a question of whether Rosenzweig's studies were sufficient for ordination.

The written instrument conferring ordination is known in Hebrew as the *semicha*, the laying on of hands. Traditionally it authorizes the recipient to teach, to decide on matters of ritual, and to be a judge in matters of religion. The *semicha* granted by Baeck to Rosenzweig did not include those authorizations. It was, however, more than honorary. Entitled the "Crown of the Torah," the *semicha* called attention to Rosenzweig's contribution to Judaism: "He increased the message. He gave it a scholarly tongue, and he cried in the ears of the one people the words of freedom and comfort . . ." And it closed with the "testimony before the community of Israel, that his strength is suitable to stand in the halls of the Temple and to guard the custody of the holy shrines." Rarely had a dying man's wishes been so well carried out.[22]

Because of his position in the community Baeck was called upon to speak on many occasions and to officiate at many services. Speaking the eulogy at the grave of a prominent teacher, Baeck said of the man: ". . . *aufgewachsen* . . . *emporgewachsen* . . . *hinausgewachsen* . . ."—not only had the man grown himself and achieved personal success, he also had given of himself to others. Baeck also officiated at many Bar Mitzvah ceremonies. One young man, Conrad Rosenstein, years later remembered his Bar Mitzvah ceremony and how Baeck had explained that when a Jewish youth goes through the ceremony, he is called to the law, accepting restrictions on his life. Although to the world such restrictions are looked upon as unpleasant, even if necessary, Baeck continued, to the Jews they are a matter of joy. The Jews, Baeck said, understood that only the law and self-control offer true freedom and raise man above the common creatures. Conrad Rosenstein remembered Baeck praying that this joy, this freedom, would come to the "Bar Mitzvah boy."

A friend recalled Baeck addressing a non-Jewish audience of philosophy teachers in the late 1920s. He began with a quotation from Aristotle—in Greek—and then said that man's highest level is achieved through poetry and that the responsibility of instruction in philosophy is to lead the student to an appropriate summit of experience. The friend remembered that the audience gave Baeck "long and warmhearted applause" when he had finished, an especially exciting climax since Baeck's wife had been concerned that "the climate for us, i.e., for the Jews" in the auditorium had not been favorable.[23]

Baeck also was knowledgeable about the artistic world. On one occasion he offered a severe critique of a production by Max Reinhardt, the reigning impressario of the German theater. "To my surprise," said a family friend who heard this story from Natalie, "I learned that Dr. Baeck charged Max Reinhardt with cheap sensationalism. It was not easy for me to digest this. Like all members of my generation, I was brought up to admire Max Reinhardt." Another friend, a person whose career was music, had many conversations about classical music with Baeck and found he had a refined taste. In the field of art Baeck was an admirer of the work of Kathe Kollwitz, a German artist whose drawings of the poor and downtrodden of the 1920s were a bitter social commentary. He also was a student of more traditional art, once saying:

One can write a history of art—and it has been written like this—showing how painting evolved from one kind of painting, then an opposite approach, then both combined; the whole of Italian painting has often been presented in this way. Then, however, the genius Rembrandt came who painted quite differently: It was light that fascinated him, not the outlines of figures, but the reflection of light on them was what he wanted. Or to mention another aspect of his genius: Up to his time, splendour and glamour had been predominant in painting—God the Father in His Majesty, Jesus in his glory, the Virgin Mary in her beauty and radiance, and likewise on earth the noblemen, the great and wealthy, kings, patricians, the popes and the magnates. Rembrandt was not impressed by these. He had a deep compassion for the human being, and he painted the humble, the poor, the ailing, the lame, hunchbacks and cripples. It was a revolution.

Although Baeck's knowledge encompassed many spheres, he led a compartmentalized life. To the rabbi with whom he discussed services there was no talk of the theatrical world. To the student of music there would be little talk of religious services. The energy required for the task at hand was available to him because he did not waste his energy. He had preached discipline to his students, and discipline is what he practiced.

Most of those who knew him only from a distance were not aware that beneath the exterior there was an incisive person, sometimes a caustic one. Baeck criticized those who "read the reviews of books instead of the books only in order to be able to chatter about them." Of a rabbinical colleague who enjoyed hearing himself described as scholarly, profound, and brilliant, Baeck offered only the description: "He is a well-tailored man." Once, after hearing an overly long lecture, Baeck told the speaker: "You might have done better to give one lecture instead of three combined in one." As one of Leo Baeck's associates put it, "If Baeck had a deep and abiding faith in humanity, he also did not like some individuals."[24]

As the 1920s were ending, Baeck was one of the most prominent people in the Berlin Jewish community. When Jews graduated from the Berlin gymnasiums, the standard present for them from the Jüdische Gemeinde was Baeck's *Das Wesen des Judentums*. But the man who disliked using "I" in his sermons was not impressed by the accouterments of success. When he visited the United States in 1925 and 1930, he traveled on a tramp steamer. To an inquiring nephew he explained that this mode of travel was preferable to him, first, because the captain's wife was the cook, meaning the food was very good; and, second, there would be few other passengers, and he had privacy for his work. When he traveled within Germany by train, he went third class and sat up reading all night in the compartment.

Leo Baeck always sought to be helpful. In the late 1920s a young Jew named Ernst Simon took a teaching job in Haifa, in what was then Palestine. Without telling Simon, Baeck wrote a letter to the school director to introduce Simon and to help ease the way for him. "That was quite typical of Leo Baeck," said Simon years later. He had learned of the letter by chance, and said, "If Baeck could do a thing indirectly, he would do it that way, so the beneficiary would not know." Another time Baeck donated a large number of frames for a young artist, Else Mediner, who was having her first showing in Berlin. "It wasn't so much the deed which influenced me," she said, "as the way he gave them. Because he showed his thankfulness for one having turned to him, that never allowed any embarrassment of the beggar to arise. Never did he ask any questions. Never did a donor help so kindly and so fast."

The young rabbis who worked with Baeck found themselves, to their surprise, addressed as his students had been, as *Herr Kollege*, although they might not yet be ordained. "Leo Baeck could relate well to people of different levels," said one of those young rabbis. "He set the stage, knowing intuitively at which level to operate." His courtesy, usually a grace, also could be a tactic. "It was sometimes his best weapon," said Ernst Simon, who worked with Baeck in the 1930s, "in order to let the other people know he didn't think anything of him."[25]

His learning process never ceased. "I never saw Leo Baeck without a book, often one in Greek," said Joachim Prinz. Baeck continued rising every morning at five o'clock for an hour's study. He was fluent in Hebrew, Latin, and Greek, in addition to his native German. During the First World War, when he was stationed on the eastern front, he learned enough Russian to converse with the Jews he met there. Later he also learned English because, said a close associate, "He always had felt a close affinity to the Anglo-Saxon world." He was knowledgeable about American history, especially admired Abraham Lincoln, and was fond of quoting the Gettysburg Address.

His ability to function efficiently on so many levels was due to his boundless energy and to his home life. "He would sit back with his hands clasped behind the chair's back or under his legs, as if he were holding himself down; he had such explosive energy," recalled one associate.[26]

Natalie, still *die Rabbinerfrau* after twenty-five years of marriage, had gained some weight but continued to be an attractive and imposing woman. "She had great dignity," said a family friend, "but did not shine in her own right. It was preordained. If you were the rabbi's wife, certain things were expected of you in dress, demeanor, appearance, and also it was expected that you support your husband." In the 1920s Count Hermann Keyserling, the founder of the School of Wisdom in Darmstadt, put together a book on marriage, asking a number of famous persons to write essays on the subject. Among those who contributed were Havelock Ellis, Thomas Mann, Rabindranath Tagore, C. G. Jung, Paul Ernst, and Leo Baeck.*

Called "Marriage as Mystery and Command," Baeck's essay showed that he brought to even the personal side of his life the same sense of discipline and personal responsibility that he did to the public side. Although a person had no control over the "fundamental fact of his life" —his birth—said Baeck, he did control the second most important fact, his marriage. "It is effected by man himself," Baeck wrote in the essay. "It belongs to his own will and to his own doing." This act of marriage "may mean the holiness of life, or it may become the triviality of existence." He scoffed at "the unfaithful one" as "he who lacks mystery." There was a danger in marriage: "Marriage is entered into on the flowery path of poetry, but is conducted in the realm of prose ... the dreariness of the everyday will too soon cling." To counter this danger the "command" was needed. For Baeck this was the command of religion, which exalts marriage "above craving and above depression." This, he continued, "is the great venture which piety accomplishes ... in that it brings religion into the everyday, seizes its hours, the hours of prose." So it was with the marriage between him and Natalie; the danger of dreariness had been countered.

Natalie "gave him the possibility to be Leo Baeck," said one of their relatives who was a frequent visitor in their house. She protected the privacy of his study. Humoring him, she accepted his rising at five o'clock in the morning to read Greek and his entertaining his students on Saturday afternoons. And, of course, when he preached, she was always in the women's section, listening intently, and when he had finished and turned to find her, ready to give him a nod of approval.[27]

The Baecks and their daughter Ruth vacationed every summer in the Alps, sometimes in Italy or Switzerland, but most often in the 1920s at Freiburg in southern Germany. There were walks along the trails and

---

* Among those who refused was George Bernard Shaw, who explained: "No man dare write the truth about marriage while his wife lives. Unless, that is, he hates her ..."

conviviality with friends. A family friend who vacationed with them in those years, Frederick J. Perlstein, described the Baeck family as being very close and very happy. Leo Baeck's demeanor during his vacations was one of perfect naturalness with nothing to suggest that he was a prominent rabbi. There was, perhaps, one exception to that. Perlstein then was in his teens, and when his family and the Baecks ate together in a kosher restaurant in Freiburg, he said the blessings in Hebrew over the food. This, he remembered, pleased Baeck considerably.

On his vacations Leo Baeck was like any other vacationer, allowing his letter-writing to slip occasionally. When Natalie wrote her mother a letter, Leo attached this postscript: "In the struggle between Nature and the desk, the desk is the loser this year . . . Especially Ruth and I walk a lot. This is what we did yesterday while Natalie stood by our apartment in the Green, but in the next letter I will write more."

Their style of living was not ostentatious, though marked by apparent formality. Even when hiking along the mountain trails, Baeck wore a suit with vest—one with knickers instead of long trousers and perhaps of a lighter color than the usual dark suits he wore in Berlin, but still a suit. "Informality is not my picture of Dr. Baeck," said one acquaintance.[28]

Ruth was an attractive young lady who soon found romance with Hermann Berlak, a certified accountant. The Berlaks and the Baecks had known each other for many years. In 1921 Hermann received his doctorate magna cum laude. Each member of the Baeck family wrote him a congratulatory letter—Leo, Natalie, and her mother Else Hamburger, who lived with her daughter and son-in-law. Ruth also wrote a letter. Despite their romance, it was formal according to the German custom. "Honorable Herr Berlak!" was the saluation. It read: "Also from me heartiest congratulations. May everything in your life come true with 'magna cum laude.' " It was signed: "Yours, Ruth Baeck."

The Baecks were like the parents of every other daughter; no man was quite good enough for their child. "No one could understand why Hermann and Ruth waited so long to marry; they were always together," said a person who was living at the Berlak house at the time.

Hermann and Ruth were married in 1923. A few weeks after the marriage, while they still were on their honeymoon, Leo Baeck wrote them a letter. While it was addressed to both of them, it was directed primarily at Ruth, his only child. It was her birthday, and the father began by recalling "the years of the birthday cakes and the birthday songs." He remembered the time in the army, "when I observed this day far from you." Leo had arranged with the mayor of Bruder, where

Samuel Bäck, Leo Baeck's father, was rabbi in Lissa, and an account of his rabbinate there described it as "graceful." When he died, the bells of the town hall and of the Christian churches rang out in sorrow. Leo Baeck said the prayer at his father's grave, describing Samuel Bäck as belonging to no party but to Judaism. As the father had been, so the son would be. (*Author's collection*)

Synagoge in Lissa.

The synagogue in Lissa where Rabbi Samuel Bäck officiated. Lissa, where Leo Baeck grew up, was one of the more influential factors in shaping Leo Baeck's life. Caught between the east and the west, between the ghetto and the world beyond, it produced a Jew who loved his tradition and, at the same time, desired to embrace the intellectuality of western scholarship. (*Author's collection*)

Leo and Natalie Baeck. When Leo married her, he was following a family tradition which had the son who became a rabbi marry the daughter of a rabbinical family. Until Natalie died in 1937, she was her husband's helpmate, the partner in his endeavors, "die Rabbinerfrau"— the perfect rabbi's wife. (*Author's collection*)

The Lissa synagogue building in 1974. It had not been used as a synagogue since 1938, when the Nazis destroyed some synagogues and desecrated others during Kristallnacht. (*Photo by Leonard Baker*)

The synagogue in Oppeln where Leo Baeck first served as rabbi. He dedicated the building in 1897, describing it then not only as a new building but as "a new life with fresh strength" to dedicate to God's service. The building was known as "an ornament for the city" until 1938, when the Nazis burned it down. All who saw the burning synagogue never forgot the sight. Forty-four years later, a Franciscan monk who had witnessed the scene rose from his chair as he described the flames rushing up the synagogue's tower, and he cried: "Die Turm! Die Turm!" (*Photos courtesy of the Leo Baeck Institute, New York*)

In 1905 Leo Baeck's *Das Wesen des Judentums* was published, and he quickly entered "the prominent rank of representatives and heralds of our religion." Two years later he became rabbi at the much larger synagogue in Duesseldorf, a significant step forward in his career. (*Photos courtesy of the Leo Baeck Institute, New York; and the Library of Congress*)

When the First World War began, the German Jews rushed to demonstrate their loyalty to the Fatherland. Feldrabbiner—military chaplains—were needed, and Leo Baeck, although in his forties and having just moved to Berlin, was one of the first to volunteer. (*Photo courtesy of the Leo Baeck Institute, New York*)

As a chaplain, Leo Baeck personally experienced little anti-Semitism. Here he is (in the center of the photograph) with the Catholic and the Protestant chaplains. This picture was jokingly referred to as "the Old and the New Testament." The Catholic and Protestant chaplains were members of the German army, but Baeck was not—the German army would not have a Jewish chaplain.(*Author's collection*)

Leo Baeck served almost four years as a Feldrabbiner, on both the western and eastern fronts. This photograph was taken in Lithuania in 1917; Baeck is the fifth from the left in the top row. He saw his Feldrabbiner role as a traditional one: conducting services, writing letters, visiting the wounded in the hospitals. These last, he said, "were the most important part of my work. The wounded were reminded of a bit of home and their hopes were lifted." (*Photo courtesy of the American Jewish Archives*)

Leo Baeck in the 1920s. (*Photo courtesy of the American Jewish Archives*)

The German Jews in Berlin had reached a level of living which Jews had not known for many centuries. Here they emerge from the Levetzowstrasse Synagogue after a High Holy Day service—a regular Sabbath service never brought out such crowds. The men are dressed in frock coats and tall hats, the women in long dresses. (*Photo courtesy of the Landesbildstelle Berlin*)

One of the most famous of the German synagogues was this one on Oranienburgerstrasse. It was more than ornate; it represented an elegance which lulled the Berlin Jews into believing they were secure in Germany. The building was burned during Kristallnacht in 1938 and then was further destroyed by Allied bombing. The facade still stands in East Berlin, however, maintained as a reminder of the fate of the German Jews. "Vergesst es nie"—It must never be forgotten—says a plaque placed on the building by the Jewish Community of Berlin. (*Photos courtesy of the Landesbildstelle Berlin*)

Teaching at the Hochschule für die Wissenschaft des Judentums was one of
Leo Baeck's most important activities. Here he urged a generation of rabbis to
give their sermons about any subject "but for not more than twenty minutes."
More than subject matter, Baeck offered himself, his attitude toward the
rabbinate, as an example. "A sermon is not to be delivered," he once said, "it
is the person who must deliver himself. . . . The greatest message one can
preach is one's life." The Hochschule building still stands in East Berlin, but
now is an apartment house. (*Photo courtesy of the Leo Baeck Institute, New
York*)

One of the innovations at the Hochschule was allowing women to become students. There also were non-Jews among the student body. This photograph was taken in the 1930s; Baeck is sitting in the first row in the right of the photograph. Standing at his left is Ismar Elbogen, a leading German-Jewish scholar. Most of the persons in this photograph did not survive the Nazi savagery. (*Photo courtesy of the Leo Baeck Institute, New York*)

Leo Baeck and Natalie enjoyed hiking; it was their traditional summer vacation. But whatever the time, summer or winter, vacation or work, Leo Baeck always wore a suit jacket and tie. He was a German burgher, and any other costume would have been out of keeping for him. (*Photo courtesy of the Leo Baeck Institute, New York*)

The Eastern European Jews who settled in Berlin with their living habits from the ghetto and their religious orthodoxy made the assimilated German Jews uncomfortable. Their presence was one of the reasons why some German Jews supported the Zionist cause, in hopes it would encourage Eastern European Jews to emigrate. One such group was a pro-Palestine committee formed in 1927 of prominent Jews. Albert Einstein is seated in the center of the first row, and Leo Baeck is the second person to his right. Baeck's own involvement with Zionism was mixed. At Theresienstadt, however, he acknowledged that he had become a Zionist. (*Photos courtesy of the National Archives and author's collection*)

One of Baeck's many activities in the 1920s was serving as president of the B'Nai B'Rith, the Jewish service agency. This painting of Baeck by Max Westfield hung in the B'Nai B'Rith lodge in Duesseldorf but did not survive the Nazi destruction during Kristallnacht. (*Photo courtesy of the Leo Baeck Institute, New York*)

When the Nazis came to power in 1933, anti-Semitism, which had been an integral part of their belief and of their election campaign, became part of their policy while governing. On April 1, 1933, the Nazis sponsored Boycott Day, during which "good" Germans were not to deal in Jewish stores. The sign on the store in the photograph reads: "Germans! Defend Yourselves! Do not buy from Jews." The Nazis launched "educational" campaigns to further turn the Germans against the Jews. The signs in the photos read "Inability and insolence are the marks of the Jewish race" and "The Jewish costume warned of racial dishonor." (*Photos courtesy of the National Archives*)

Unfähigkeit und Frechheit waren die Merkmale der von Juden gepriesenen Afterkunst.
Unfähigkeit und Frechheit sind die Merkmale der von Juden fabrizierten Aftermachwerke.
Unfähigkeit und Frechheit sind die Merkmale der jüdischen Rasse!

The Nazis forced the Jews more and more to educate their children, to arrange for the emigration of those fortunate enough to leave Germany, and to take care of their needy. The Jews formed the Reichsvertretung, headed by Baeck, which dealt with these problems. Here Baeck is opening a meeting in 1934 of the Jüdisches Winterhilfswerk, a Jewish social agency. (*Photo courtesy of Hans Pimm*)

Hermann and Ruth were honeymooning, to have the town band serenade Ruth on her birthday. After saying he hoped that had gone according to plan, he extended his "dearest wishes" to Ruth and her husband—"You know them even if I don't phrase them." And then Leo Baeck added the wish that every father holds for his daughter: "May your life keep for you, give to you, and fulfill for you everything which you possess now and are longing for ."[29]

Ruth and Hermann had one child, Marianne—nicknamed Janne—on whom the grandparents doted. As a toddler she first learned to run while her parents were vacationing. Natalie was the traditional grandmother when she heard the news—"Daily I had pictured in my thoughts what a surprise it would be for you if the child were to run toward you," she wrote. Leo Baeck, the somber, conservative, often cold-appearing clergyman, conceded that "the little one was a special joy for me." When the Berlaks vacationed in Vienna in 1928, Marianne stayed in Berlin with Hermann's parents. Baeck wrote Hermann and Ruth, "We talked one time with Janne. She is gaining great flexibility with the telephone. We only regret, at least for us, that the television has not been invented yet."

Marianne accepted having a famous grandfather with equanimity. She recalled years later, "I first noted the difference when as a little girl I was taken to one of the Berlin synagogues at which he was preaching, and I asked my mother in much too loud a whisper: 'Why is Grandpa wearing that long black dress and why is he talking that way?' "

Baeck was interested in children, fond of them, and could deal with them warmly. In the early 1920s, when inflation struck Berlin and some families were unable to buy food for their children, Baeck arranged for one thousand children to go to Vienna for between three and five months. There they were fed and cared for by various Jewish institutions and families. To his nieces and nephews he was very much the friendly and beneficent uncle. As very small children they played with his watch chain. When they were older, they explored his library, a high room with a ladder on wheels running along the bookshelves. When one of his grandnephews rode the ladder around the room, the relatives told him to stop; but Leo Baeck laughed and asked them not to interfere with the child's ride. "Maybe some day he'll want to look in the books," said Baeck.[30]

In the 1920s the Baeck family lived in a third-floor apartment at Burggrafenstrasse 19, an embassy neighborhood. The home was comfortable; the chairs were well upholstered and covered to protect them from wear, a practice common to frugal middle-class Germans. The windows were curtained. It could have been home to any German professor or professional person. Baeck had his office there. The community newspaper listed that Rabbi Baeck was at "Burggrafenstra. 19" between eleven o'clock and noon to anyone wishing to see him.

There was little, it seemed, that could disturb the equanimity of Baeck's life. He had his family, his career, and a confident attitude. Even a health problem requiring surgery could not upset him. In a memoir, the surgeon did not identify Baeck's specific problem but said that the operation was a difficult one, and that Baeck "agreed with a natural quietness and a natural submission to all the hospital procedures." Baeck told the doctor that his personal suffering was no longer his concern but that of the doctor. "Therefore, he didn't have the right to worry about my action," the doctor said. He credited Baeck's positive attitude with hastening recovery.[31]

Although a leading rabbi of the liberal movement in German Judaism, a movement that had dropped many traditional Jewish practices, Leo Baeck was very much a traditionalist in his personal living habits. He placed *tefillin* upon his arm and forehead every morning. He covered his head inside a synagogue. (Years later Ilse Blumenthal-Weiss, who had attended many Berlin services conducted by Baeck, saw him in New York City attending an American Reform service. According to the American Reform custom, he was bareheaded. "That was something for me," she said, "to see him without a hat.") While conducting services, he also wore a rabbinical robe. "Always wear a robe," he said to his students. "Then you will know that you are properly dressed." He considered the Sabbath sacred. For him it was also a day for intellectual recharging, not only a day to meet with students and friends, but also a time for returning to religious studies. People did not smoke in his presence on the Sabbath because striking a match was considered a violation of the injunction against working on the Sabbath. He and Natalie maintained a kosher house. The meat they ate was slaughtered and prepared according to a carefully prescribed ritual. They refrained from eating all meats from certain animals and carefully avoided mixing meat and milk dishes. They also followed other eating practices in minute detail. Although there is no specific explanation for the origin of the kosher laws in the Jewish religion, there are many opinions, most deriving from the commandment of God that the Jews be a holy people. One path toward holiness was through proper eating habits—abstinence and discipline.

Another rabbi, who came to the United States and dropped most of these practices, spoke many years later of Baeck and tradition. "Why tradition?" speculated this rabbi of Baeck. "Did he need a fence, something to hold him together?" No, tradition was not a crutch. Tradition was a badge of Jewishness which Leo Baeck wore proudly. It was his inheritance. He had grown up in a traditional household. He had learned the mechanics of wrapping the leather straps, the *tefillin*, on his body from his father, who undoubtedly had learned them from his father. His mother had kept a kosher kitchen. The ritual was part of Leo Baeck's life; it was a comfortable sense of order, a pleasant memory, a way for him to pass on the joy of his own youth to his child and grandchild. When Leo Baeck was very old, he talked about those symbolic rituals with a friend. "The rituals," he said, "have a poetic quality and observing them gave a life a new sense of beauty."[32]

In the synagogue, however, he accepted—as he had in Oppeln and in Duesseldorf—many changes. These included the use of an organ, a choir of males and females, a shortening of services, and the greater use of German. When the Prinzregentenstrasse Synagogue opened in 1930 to become the first in Berlin allowing men and women to sit together, Baeck had no difficulty in preaching and officiating there. In addition to encouraging women to attend the Hochschule, he also was instrumental in Berlin in making the Bat Mitzvah ceremony available to women. Jeannette Wolff, who lived in Westphalia, brought three of her daughters to Berlin for the ceremony; rabbis in Westphalia would not officiate at the ceremony for women. Baeck not only officiated at these ceremonies but wrote personal notes to each of Frau Wolff's daughters, advising them always to be optimistic, to understand that however difficult their problems were, others still had more serious ones.

Those changes within the synagogue and in the services were part of a formal split between the Liberal and the Orthodox rabbis. Baeck, because of his appreciation of the ritual and because of his own experience of growing up in a traditional home, often bridged the gap between the two groups. This split had developed in the nineteenth century and been formalized in 1908 with the organization of the Vereinigung für das liberale Judentum in Deutschland—the Association for Liberal Judaism in Germany. Its constitution, approved by 301 German Jews from all walks of life, began with what always had been a truism in the Jewish religion, that the religion "is capable of development in accordance with changing times, without thereby changing its nature . . . A conflict between law and life is foreign to Judaism. While reverently maintaining the cords which tie them to the past, German Jews must bring their secular life into agreement with their inner convictions. They must not lay emphasis on the maintenance of antiquated statutes, customs and dead mores." This association, in effect, ratified for a group of Jews the transformation that had been developing within German Judaism for more than a century.

This ratification was carried further in 1912 by a conference of sixty-one Liberal rabbis at a meeting called by the Association for Liberal Judaism. They produced a document at that 1912 meeting known as *Richtlinien zu einem Programm für das liberale Judentum*—Principles of a Program for Liberal Judaism. This document recognized the increasing role of women in the Jewish ceremony—"The participation of women in religious and communal life is indispensable." However, there were limits to the liberalism of these rabbis; they did not allow mixed seating in services. That 1912 document also sanctioned changes in religious practice. Were Jews unable to refrain from working on Saturday, the Sabbath? Observances on Friday night only became acceptable. "Rest at home, attendance at services and the celebration of Friday nights and the eves of holy days are to be given increased attention. Sacred customs like the kindling of lights, the blessing by parents of their children, the prayers over wine and bread, the celebration of Seder and Chanukah should be surrounded with new sanctity." Was it inconvenient to begin the Sabbath at the time of sundown on Friday as tradition commanded? "The beginning of the evening observance shall be fixed by each community in accordance with its needs, without reference to calendaric calculation." Had music—the organ and the choir—become more prevalent, as well as the use of the German language? Perfectly acceptable, said the rabbis.

In addition, this 1912 statement dealt with difficulties the Liberals had found in the Jewish liturgy. "The services on Sabbaths and holy days, with the exception of Yom Kippur, should be shortened considerably. If possible, the repetition of prayers should be avoided . . . Those prayers which are not truth in our hearts should be eliminated." These sections of the statement reflected the rabbis' desire to accommodate Judaism to German secular life while at the same time strengthening their ties with what they maintained to be the essential Judaism. The rabbis said that Liberal Judaism "rejects the evaluation of piety by measuring its outward observances. It recognizes as worthwhile only that which, for the individual, has the power to elicit pious sentiment, to advance moral action, and to recall religious truths and experiences vividly."

Orthodox rabbis reacted violently to this 1912 statement, threatening to strip rabbis who had prepared it of their rabbinical authority and challenging the Jewishness of individuals who subscribed to the statement. The Liberals responded that "nobody has the right forthwith to debar a rabbi who received proper ordination . . ." and "nobody can disallow the Jewishness of a Jew who through birth or declaration belongs to Judaism, or mark him as an inferior member of the religious community of Israel simply because he belongs to a certain religious party."

In the 1920s some Orthodox rabbis refused even to belong to the Jüdische Gemeinde, so concerned were they at being contaminated by the Liberal movement. Those Orthodox Jews who stayed in the Gemeinde engaged in constant disputes about how to implement policy within the Jewish tradition. In this area Baeck's practice of holding himself back in public confrontations seemed to be successful. He was the rabbi the Liberals turned to when negotiations with the Orthodox community were necessary. Given the hostility between the two groups, the position of conciliator between them was a difficult one. Baeck managed it because he had the respect of both groups. Personally he adhered generally to traditional practices and respected such practices. But, given his understanding of Judaism, it was natural for the Liberals to consider him one of their own.[33]

The dispute between Liberals and Orthodox often surfaced in the World Union for Progressive Judaism, which was organized by Jews from all over the world in the late 1920s. One of the Union's founders, Lily H. Montagu, recalled that during a meeting one year a group of German Orthodox rabbis planned to introduce a resolution "quite contrary to the spirit of Progressive Judaism." Afraid of a floor fight at the meeting but uncertain what to do, Lily Montagu and her friends went to see Leo Baeck. "Never mind," he told them, "I will explain to the rabbis and no resolution will be introduced." His visitors believed he did not understand the strength behind the resolution. "But," they told him, "this resolution is supported by the whole group and it is to be brought forward tomorrow." Baeck smiled. "There will be no resolution," he said. And there wasn't.

The secret of Baeck's success with the Orthodox rabbis was that he never was so critical of them in public that they were unwilling to meet with him and consider what he had to say. Also, he respected the Orthodox rabbis and did not treat them frivolously, as some did. Baeck's attitude was recalled by a man who was working with youth groups and who asked Baeck what to do about some problems he had encountered with the Orthodox community. "If you can give in without violating your conscience, do so," Baeck replied. "If you can't, tell them. They'll come up with a Halakic decision. It will take them one week." The Halaka is the body of Jewish law found in the Talmud; Baeck was saying that even the traditionalists were not so locked into past practices that they wouldn't be accommodating when called upon.[34]

There was to be no permanent solution, however, no resolution of the dispute between the Liberal and Orthodox communities in Germany, between those who believed Judaism was strengthened by change and those who believed that it was eroded by change. Although perhaps neither side would have agreed, Judaism was and is able to live with this dispute. Judaism historically has thrived on internal disputes.*

The Orthodox/Liberal split was not the only important issue facing German Jews. There were three others—the dispute between the Zionists and the anti-Zionists, the anti-Semitism in Germany, and the growing German nationalism.

The struggle between the Zionists and the anti-Zionists was a continuation of the one that had begun before World War One. Although Leo Baeck embodied the qualities of German Jewry and was thought of as the outstanding representative of that group, he did not share the antagonism that most German Jews felt toward Zionism, coming very close at times to embracing the cause himself. His earlier support of Zionist causes—the refusal to support the German rabbis in their protest resolution in 1898, the defense of Rabbi Cohn's rabbinical rights in 1907—had motivations other than a desire to see the Jews develop their own homeland. But Leo Baeck realized, particularly during and after World War One, that Jews never could separate their religion from their ethnic background. The German Jews, who wanted to be like the Protestants and Catholics, often turned to Leo Baeck when they wanted a religious leader because he looked more German than Jewish. But Baeck understood, more than they, that he was both German and

---

* Liberal Judaism in Germany had an impact on the development of American Reform Judaism, particularly in the modernizing of the services, the greater use of the vernacular in the services, and in theological exploration. The two, however, are not identical. Liberal Judaism in Germany, to cite one example, adhered much more closely to Jewish traditions than did American Reform groups.

Jew. He became publicly involved in this dispute in 1916 while serving as a *Feldrabbiner*. Hermann Cohen had written a pamphlet attacking Zionism, and Martin Buber replied sharply. Baeck, in his usual way, had tried to conciliate the differences between the two men. In one article he wrote that "Judaism is a unique happening in the history of mankind, a word of the Creator's which may no longer be repeated ... Neither the element of religion nor that of peoplehood can be removed from the Jewish existence." Although there is an obvious effort at conciliation in that statement, it does not ignore the Zionist claim that Judaism has a nationalistic quality. At the time it was a daring statement. Yet Baeck's position as a leader of German Jewry was not weakened for the same reason that he had survived any difficulty after his 1898 vote and his 1907 support of Emil Cohn; he was so highly regarded by his peers that they would not challenge him.

During the 1920s his support for the Zionist movement increased. Partly it was due to an understanding that a national home in Palestine would be an alternative for the eastern European Jews who, chased from their homelands by anti-Semitic violence, had sought refuge in Berlin in their self-made ghettos on Dragonerstrasse and Grenadierstrasse to the discomfort of the Berlin Jews. Partly it was due to the fact that even if he could not embrace Zionism's ultimate goal, he believed it did much to develop an interest among Jews in their faith and their heritage. And partly it was his desire to serve Judaism by being a conduit between the Zionists and anti-Zionists.

On January 6, 1927, the *Israelitisches Familienblatt* ran a photograph of the Die Berliner Gründungsversammlung des Pro Palästina-Kommittees—The Founding Congress of the Pro-Palestine Committee. Among those in the photograph were Albert Einstein and Leo Baeck. He also became involved with the Keren Hayesod, an organization collecting funds for the development of Palestine as a Jewish homeland, although this was opposed by the Central-Verein, the association of Germans of the Jewish faith. They believed that financial contributions could be better spent for Jews in Germany rather than in Palestine and had passed resolutions opposing the Keren Hayesod in 1921 and 1926. Baeck was a member of the Central-Verein board, but he formally joined the Keren Hayesod in 1929.

Did these activities mean that Leo Baeck was becoming a Zionist? In the late 1920s Martin Rosenbluth was executive vice president of the German Zionist Federation, working in its offices at Meinekestrasse 10 in Berlin. In his memoirs he listed Leo Baeck, along with Albert

Einstein, as "among our new supporters." In the early 1930s Gershom Scholem, the Jewish writer and philosopher, discussed Zionism at length with Baeck. Scholem had come to Berlin from Palestine and was under the impression that Baeck was an anti-Zionist. "But in our talk," said Scholem, "I found him to be very sympathetic." Scholem later discussed this with Robert Weltsch, editor of the Zionist *Jüdische Rundschau* newspaper. Weltsch was not surprised. "Baeck has been with us a long time," he said to Scholem.

Rather than being a Zionist, it is more likely Baeck believed that with conditions in Germany as they were, even the German Jews might need Palestine in the future. He spoke of this point in the early 1930s at a meeting of the Keren Hayesod in Koenigsberg. Adolf Hitler had not yet come to power, but the rumblings of Nazism could not be ignored. At the start Leo Baeck conceded, "Who of us is not sure that the thought he represents is the strongest?" Moving quickly to the question frequently posed by German Jews, he asked why the German Jews shouldn't spend their money in their homeland to support their cultural institutions there and "leave the sacrifices for Palestine to our brothers in happier countries until, on a better day, the time will come when we will be able to participate?" He rejected any affirmative answer to that question, saying: "Giving is learned with giving. Who begins to sacrifice for one thing gains the ability to sacrifice for something else."

Then Baeck argued that the Jews of Germany might someday need Palestine. "What will be, we cannot know. We cannot know what will be in Palestine, and we cannot know what will be here in Germany. We are not able to know it." He insisted to his audience that supporting Palestine was to benefit future generations as much as the Jews then living in Germany. "Who will say that perhaps at some point the grandsons of those who stand here today in security will not have to leave the land of their fathers?" He reminded his audience, "Also in Spain, where the Jews had lived for hundreds of years in security, the days of wandering came." Then he asked the gathering: "How will we answer when our grandchildren reproach us by asking why the father, the one who stood before, did not help with the work of the son, for the grandchild?" He continued: "Which judgment will the people on this Earth make about us Jews if the opportunity that is there . . . has not been used in this hour because of indifference, narrowmindedness, obstinacy; and, therefore, this opportunity has been lost." To lose that opportunity, Baeck charged, would be *hillul hashem*—in his words, "a desecration of the Godly name before the eyes of the world." Years later, when Baeck recalled having given that talk, he said his audience was "startled and incredulous."[35]

Baeck did not see the future horror for Jews in Germany; no one did. But he was sensitive to events and understood that the potential for danger existed. During the Weimar Republic in the 1920s there was the resurgence of anti-Semitism. Although the Jews had joined in the general prosperity and the excitement of Weimar that had come in the mid-1920s, they had never been totally accepted. As the decade ended, they were met with more hostility than they had known before.

Throughout the 1920s the examples of anti-Semitism multiplied. Perle Gold, a young Jewish woman living with her aunt in Berlin in the 1920s, dated a non-Jew. When she told him she was Jewish, he replied: "Oh, I know. Because of the Jews there was a world war." In this decade an anti-Semitic book entitled *Sünde wider das Blut*—Sin Against the Blood—was published. It was a book of hate, of violence, and of vileness. It was also a bestseller. A newspaper editor, Dietrich Eckart, offered to pay 1,000 marks for proof that a single Jewish family had sent three sons to the trenches during the First World War for a minimum of three weeks. The names of dozens of families were supplied to him, and the courts forced him to make good his offer when he at first ignored the evidence. Although the Jews had won a victory in the courts, they achieved little in overcoming injustice born of irrationality. Said one German scholar, a non-Jew: ". . . hatred for Jews is today the only point of reference common to all value judgments. It replaces religion for many—and we must bow our heads in shame in admitting this truth."

Anti-Semitism in Germany during the 1920s, despite all gains the Jews believed they had made, was pervasive. Jewish newspapers printed lists of those vacation resorts welcoming Jews; it was understood that resorts not on the list did not admit Jews. In 1927 a Protestant theologian expressed the strong attitude of his fellow church members when he said: "The Church must have eyes and words for the threat that Jewry poses to German folkdom." In the universities education did not enlighten. Jewish students were physically attacked by their non-Jewish fellow students in the years after the war. Student fraternities refused to admit Jews and expelled any member who married a Jew. A Jew was defined not as a person who adhered to Judaism, but as any person with at least one Jewish grandparent. This definition was an echo of Adolf Hitler's 1919 statement that "the Jews are unquestionably a race, not a religious community."

Throughout the history of the hatred the Jews had known, they could escape the animosity of their neighbors by surrendering their religion through conversion. But in Germany anti-Semitism had developed another way, as Adolf Hitler and the students demonstrated. No longer was the target Judaism; now it was the Jews. The object had become a people rather than a religion. The question that had disturbed the German Jews so much during the nineteenth century, whether they were members of a race or of a religion, had been answered for them by the Germans. They were a race; if one-fourth of their family heritage was Jewish—one grandparent only—they were the target.

The legal system moved the same way. In 1922 Walther Rathenau, the German industrialist who had worked so hard for the cause of his homeland during and after the war, the Jew who never had been quite comfortable with his Jewishness, was assassinated. His murderers virtually were declared heroes. The courts had become political instruments, weapons along with the guns of the murderers—especially when the victims were Jewish.

The business world was not better. It became so difficult, for example, for a Jew to obtain a job from a non-Jew that one Jewish publication stated in 1928: "A non-Jewish employer for a Jewish employee is as good as out of the question any more." In the late 1920s widespread boycotts were organized of Jewish businesses. "Buy German, not Jewish" was the slogan.[36]

Along with this resurging anti-Semitism returned the German vision of the imperial warrior, destined to rule other peoples and other nations. The Germans embraced this new nationalism with a religious passion. Leo Baeck did not see it as a new religion but as a continuation of the old religion that had developed from German Lutheranism. "The all-controlling police state," he said, "is in a direct line from Lutheranism." That line is so strong, Baeck believed, "that one of the historians of Protestantism dared to speak of a 'Prussian religion.'" Luther won political support for his sect by adopting a policy of hands off the government. What the German state considered to belong to Caesar would remain with Caesar, and what the Lutherans understood to be God's would stay God's.

According to Baeck, German Lutheranism lacked "the social, messianic urgings, the pressures, as they exist in our Bible, to shape and improve the world." The rabbi was concerned by this lack in Lutheranism because his understanding of religion was directly the opposite. Baeck believed the religious man was a constant challenge to the state, a moral gadfly. To Baeck, possessing that spirit of resistance meant that man "as a mirror image of God" was "able to overcome everything harsh, able to shape everything and to build" so that man did not have to be "resigned in front of anything."[37]

The Catholic Church in Germany also did not present a challenge to the state. As part of its medieval heritage, it was itself a political entity. It dealt with the German government, bargained with it, and refrained from criticizing it. In return it operated without fear of attack from the state.

For the Germans the result was to confuse their state with their religion. Perhaps no other modern country deified itself quite as much. The Germans mistook the grandeur of power for the religious ideal, believing the full attainment of power to be a religious crusade. They did not question the morality of that crusade; they had been taught by their religions not to question the state.

The German concept of chosenness was pervasive. Each group within Germany was so impressed with its own self that it chose not to meet with any other group, refusing to expose itself to any outside influence. "The old aristocracy met the lesser nobility and the captains of industry and banking only with reluctance," said Walter Laqueur, the Weimar historian. "It ignored those who were not of true blood and was only dimly aware of the existence of artists and intellectuals." The same was true, on the other side, of the intellectuals. They had their own newspapers, their own clubs, their own favorites in the world of art. This entrenchment in the familiar economic, social, and intellectual circles obscured the fact that Germans were thrashing around in the confusion following the First World War, trying to understand why, if they truly had been chosen for military victory, they had failed on the battlefield and had been degraded at the peace table.[38]

Germany in the 1920s was paying for a tragic history, one in which the state rather than the individual had been exalted, in which the individual's sense of responsibility never had been nurtured, in which institutions—especially the organized churches—had existed without an objective that was more than merely self-perpetuation. Germany was paying for having ignored the Kantian imperative—personal responsibility built upon rational decision. Germans were developing —in Leo Baeck's phrase—"the religious sentimentality that goes so well with brutality."[39]

Why did other German Jews not see the coming threat? Hans J. Morgenthau, who was born in Germany and educated there in the 1920s, offered one reason.

The very conception of German Jews as Germans of a minority religion and of the Jewish religion as one religion among many made it impossible for German Jewry to recognize the precariousness of their position and the possibility of a catastrophic separation from Germany. If they were Germans like any other Germans and if Judaism was just a religion like any other religion, why should a Gentile German, except a small minority of prejudiced bigots, treat them as anything else?

For the German Jews to have acknowledged their predicament, to have recognized the danger of a violent separation, would have meant a complete denial of an entire way of life. They had fought hard to demonstrate themselves to be Germans of the Jewish faith. They had no way of recognizing the future without acknowledging that their struggles had been for nothing.

Georg Salzberger, a rabbi in Frankfurt am Main and a *Feldrabbiner* with Baeck during the First World War, said, many years after the Nazi period: "There were indications, yes. But not an expressed anti-Semitism. One could lead a normal life until 1933 when Hitler came to power, then everything changed. None of us could guess what his coming to power meant." Salzberger paused for a moment and added: "Not even the greatest pessimist."

Yet some Jews did perceive the danger. Emil Herz, a publisher, reported a conversation he had with the writer Arnold Zweig, who was visiting Berlin before returning to Palestine. Herz considered the decision to surrender German citizenship for a home in Palestine to be hasty. "In Palestine," he said, "a state of war exists between Jews and Arabs." He admitted the situation in Germany had problems, and "if the Nazis really come to power we shall have to suffer painful setbacks, but even so our personal safety will not be in question." Zweig, in response, laughed. "Personal safety for the Jews in Germany! I tell you, the lives of all of you are in danger here, in greater danger than in strife-torn Palestine. Over there we have at least got arms; here we are defenseless."

When Albert Einstein lived in Germany, he once said: "If my theory of relativity is accepted, then will the Germans say, 'Einstein is a German,' and the French, 'Einstein is a Jew.' If, however, it is not accepted, the Germans will say, 'Einstein is a Jew,' and the French will say, 'Einstein is a German.' "[40]

By the mid-1920s the return of Germany's rampant nationalism was obvious. In 1925 the German people for the first time elected a president (Friedrich Ebert, the first Weimar president, had come to the office as a result of a parliamentary vote rather than a popular vote). The Germans chose a man with no political experience, Paul von Hindenburg, the 77-year-old military hero. Three years earlier Hitler had attempted a putsch in Munich. It failed, and he was given only a mild sentence; he was treated in jail more as a hero than as a revolutionary.

With this German return to nationalism and militarism evident, Baeck summed up his own thoughts in a 1926 letter to a friend. He wrote that the thinking person discovers "two basics of our essence in ourselves" —loyalty to the state and individual morality. Kant already had pointed out those two basics when he said "that each man is a citizen of two worlds, and," added Baeck, "it is true in a greater sense than he intended." Because of this dual existence in the two worlds each man faces "task and conflict. All martyrdom comes from that. Humanity belongs to the realm of the state and the realm of God. Which laws shall men obey if conflict is involved?" He cited then the conflicts facing "the most honest pacifist in war . . . [and] so many honest social democrats." Describing the conflict as one of the soul, he said that when it appears, "then can the hour come when it is commanded to choose—for the earthly or the eternal." Baeck argued that the moral course, not the way of militarism and nationalism, was actually the one to follow, even if ultimately it meant martyrdom. He cited the line in Genesis 12:1: "*Lech lecha me-Arzecha*," in which God commands Abraham to go out to a country. Baeck took this line to mean that "The choice commands one to be ready to become a martyr, to accept the primacy of religion and its command; its primacy above all."

He cited examples from Jewish history, in Spain and Palestine, in which Jews had chosen the primacy of religion over the state. Then Baeck turned to the non-Jews in Germany. "It is an intellectual and moral misfortune of Germany that many leaders for so long a time have known nothing of the two realms, that one has made from German nationalism a religion. Instead of believing in God, they believe —above all the Lutheran ministers—in Germanism . . ."

Said Baeck: "Where one is a stranger to the world of God, then one remains also a stranger to martyrdom . . ." Jews could not be strangers to martyrdom because of their insistence on taking the moral course. "We Jews root more deeply than all the others in the spiritual world, in the religion . . . We are the people of God to whom the conflict has fastened more deeply and more often, not only occasionally but constantly . . . Especially the last years have led us more strongly to what is typical for us. We have learned even more deeply that we are rooted in the realm of God." The letter was a commentary on current events, written specifically in reference to Germany in the mid-1920s. However, it was more—it was a call to those who believed in God or who described themselves as moral to face their challenge and, if necessary, to accept their martyrdom. The true calling of religion, of any religion, demands no less.[41]

6 FIGHTER

Leo Baeck's chief weapon in the struggle to renew Jews' interest in their religion—more significant than his sermons, his leadership role, his teaching, and his many other activities—was his writing. During the 1920s he produced a steady stream of essays and articles. More important, in this decade he revised *The Essence of Judaism*. It is this second version that is still read more than a half-century later.

In his writings of the 1920s Baeck did something almost unique, even daring, for a prominent Jewish theologian: He made his adversary Christianity. Usually Jews did not respond to attacks on their religion by Christians; in the second as well as the first edition of *The Essence of Judaism* Baeck did not refer by name to Adolf von Harnack, the Christian theologian whose derogatory remarks about Judaism had provoked him to write the book. More important, Jews rarely had written critically of another religion. Baeck believed, however, that there must be a change if the Jews truly were to regain an appreciation and understanding of their religion.

The Jews and their religion were "in unbridgeable opposition" to Christianity, according to the apostle Paul, and Baeck further interpreted Paul as saying that the Jews "are the evil principle" and that "all redemption signifies redemption from this world of Judaism. And for this reason the Jews as such [to Paul] are the real enemies of the Christ and of the true God. They are the only ones who—all of them together, their patriarchs, their prophets and their teachers—never will be redeemed." That Pauline concept is what Baeck determined to struggle against.[1]

The adversary was not Jesus. Leo Baeck had respect for the figure of

Jesus; many commentators on Baeck's writings use the word love to describe his attitude toward the central figure in Christianity. Of Jesus, Baeck wrote, "In the old Gospel which is thus opened up before us, we encounter a man with noble features who lived in the land of the Jews in tense and excited times and helped and labored and suffered and died, a man out of the Jewish people who walked on Jewish paths with Jewish faith and hopes. His spirit was at home in the Holy Scriptures, and his imagination and thought were anchored there . . ." This man was particularly Jewish "in every feature and trait of his character, manifesting in every particular what is pure and good in Judaism." Baeck insisted that "This man could have developed as he came to be only on the soil of Judaism . . ."[2]

Nor was the adversary Christian religious beliefs. Baeck would confront Christianity and make his points against it philosophically and theologically, as he would expect a Christian scholar to challenge Judaism. "Positive neutrality demands that the ultimate and innermost questions be raised honestly," argued Baeck. "Open and not concealed, complete and unqualified, they must gain room for themselves with all their opposition—the understanding for that which unifies and binds them together does not come in spite of opposition but through it."[3]

Baeck's arguments, instead, were with what he considered the distortion of the Jesus figure by those who had exerted a Grecian influence on the young religious movement 2,000 years earlier and also with the denigration of Judaism by Christianity.

How had Jesus become the focal point of another religion? Baeck argued that the term *messiah* as used in the Hebrew Bible served as "a parable, as testimony of vision." But in the Gospels, he continued, it "has received a new sense . . . and has become a very specific term. It is no longer the ancient apocalyptic image that appears in it; it has become an independent theological concept." Jesus began as a teacher, but,

The man whose life and words the tradition wanted to report had early ceased, in his disciples' faith, to be a mere teacher—and when they believed in him, he eventually came to believe himself to be the messiah, the Christos. The Christian community was firmly convinced that he had been the messiah.

Ultimately the image of Jesus

had to be embellished to an even greater extent with everything that the Bible and the reflection of centuries had seen in the anointed of the Lord, the son of David, upon whom the spirit of God will rest, the helper and liberator—

and with everything that had been prophesized concerning him. Out of the suffering of the time a poem of his passion had developed, and out of its longing and ideals a vision of his power and his deeds—and all this, too, had to become part of his image. Moreover, unfaltering faith had long raised the figure of the messiah beyond all human limitations into a supra-historical, supra-terrestrial sphere. He was endowed with the radiance of the heavens and transfigured above the earth. The apocalypses in particular had related how he had been chosen by God from the beginning and dwelt in another world, from which he would eventually descend when his time came. His growth was surrounded by miracles. Of all this the people felt sure. And this meant that the tradition of Jesus' life had to be fitted into this mysterious image in which the world beneath and the world above were blended. It was this image which supplied the outlines and the texture.[4]

Baeck argued specifically with attacks leveled at Judaism by Christians, who were saying that it was an inferior and outdated religion, that it had stagnated for 2,000 years and was better forgotten. From a sense of pride Baeck began by idealizing Judaism as the religion of the deed, stressing the imperative that the individual act in a moral way. Baeck wrote that Christianity, by contrast, was a romantic religion, a passive religion of faith. Judaism commands one to act; in Christianity, one is acted upon. Judaism seeks questions; Christianity seeks answers.

To Baeck "before religious understanding there stands religious deed." He believed that "thinking rightly is dependent on doing rightly." As he cited from chapter 24, verse 7 of Exodus—"All that the Lord has spoken, let us do and hear"—he emphasized that the doing preceded the hearing. "Thus," said Baeck, "the commandment stands foremost, and the commandment does not take man up to God that he be united with God, but places man facing God that he may listen to Him and serve Him."

To Baeck, Christianity invited the negation of individual responsibility. "The salvation that comes through faith," Baeck wrote of Christianity, "is in no sense earned, but wholly received; and it comes only to those for whom it was destined from the beginning . . . Man is no more than the mere object of God's activity, of grace or of damnation; he does not recognize God, God merely recognizes him. . . . He is the object of virtue and of sin—not its producer, its subject. One feels like saying: man does not live but is lived . . ."

The quotation is from one of Baeck's most famous essays of the 1920s, "Romantic Religion," in which he declared that Judaism is a "classical religion [in which] man is to become free through the commandment; [while] in romantic religion"—Baeck's name for organized Christianity—"he had become free through grace."

"The ideal here [in Christianity] is no longer the ethical personality which man should embody as he strives and struggles," continued Baeck, "but the superhuman and thus after all mystical personality; the saint, the hero, the god-man. Enraptured, one feels seized by him—and has satisfied oneself as well as him. And because the ideal here is 'over-holy' and 'tremendous,' people like to praise all this as a heroic ethic." Rather than being a heroic ethic, Christianity was "merely a heroic landscape with a castle built right up into rosy clouds where phantasy loves to alight from time to time without obligation."[5]

At its most obvious level the essay "Romantic Religion" is a polemic against Christianity, a defense of Judaism against 2,000 years of attacks. Still, there are two other levels on which the essay should be understood. Written when the signs of the Weimar Republic's failure were beginning to show, the essay is a call to members of all faiths to acknowledge that religion demands morality. The purpose of religion is not the individual's personal salvation but, rather, the individual's impact on the salvation of others.

At a second level the essay was Baeck's call to his fellow Jews to rid themselves of their apologetic air: Do not be embarrassed by your religion, particularly when it is compared to Christianity. Judaism is the superior of the two, and the central fact of Christianity—the presence of Jesus—is actually a Jewish presence.

Leo Baeck delivered this message forcefully to the German Jews because he himself had come to terms with his religion. The significant difference in Baeck's attitude toward his religion between his early years out of the seminary and the post–World War One years was his acceptance of Judaism as a religion and not only as a cult of reason. Judaism included both the moral imperative and the mystical, the incomprehensible, the faith he had denied two decades earlier when he had written that the Jewish religion is free from "naturphilosophischen, metaphysichen [or] mystischen."

However, the mystical qualities Baeck found in Judaism were not related to those he had found in Christianity. In Christianity the mystical, the unseen, the faith he had criticized, was a replacement for the deed. In Judaism mysticism compelled the Jew more powerfully toward the fulfillment of the deed.

Baeck's life does not include a single dramatic incident or moment of blinding revelation that led him to his acceptance of the mystical.

The process of acceptance was a slow one for him, a continuously building process that began when he emerged from the formal part of his education and became a practicing rabbi and also began a process of self-education, rising at an early hour to study Greek and refusing to limit his intellectual horizons.

To a man with self-confidence and an inquiring mind, once freed from the shibboleths of a traditional education, an understanding of the role of mysticism in Judaism must take shape. Mysticism had been the center of great movements within the religion for a thousand years and could not be dismissed. While at its worst, it was the ennobling of superstition and the denigration of learning—the faith that Baeck saw in Christianity—it also could be a celebration of the joy of life and the opening of the religion to all with faith; that was the message of the Baal Shem Tov, the mystical leader of the east European Jews in the early eighteenth century.

Baeck's work in the area of mysticism has been appraised by Rabbi Alexander Altmann, who commented that his "chief merit lies in his effort as a theologian to integrate an awareness of our mystical tradition —at least some of its strata—into the very fabric of modern Jewish thought." Along with the study of the Talmud and the rational approach to Jewish philosophy was the element of mysticism, this willingness to believe. In his writings Baeck brought the three of them together; they all were part of Judaism. "No other Jewish theologian among his contemporaries—liberal or orthodox—has a comparable achievement to his credit," said Rabbi Altmann.[6]

Baeck approached this mystical presence in Judaism in a scholarly way. How did it originate? What contribution did it make? What purpose did it serve contemporaneously? He first wrote about the positive role mysticism plays in Judaism only six years after he had denied its presence in the 1905 edition of *The Essence of Judaism*, in an article entitled "Die Parteien im gegenwärtigen Judentum in ihrer geschichtlichen Grundlage"—The Parties in Modern Judaism and their Historical Basis—which appeared in a Protestant publication, *Religion und Geisteskultur*. He began this article almost as if he were talking about the man who had written *The Essence of Judaism:* "In the terra incognita which the history of the Jewish spirit unfortunately is for so many people, mysticism is probably the least known." This was unfortunate, he insisted, because "mysticism occupies an important place in Judaism; its history covers more than one thousand years, and it is hardly possible to grasp all of its facets." How had it originated? "Within the Jewish community," Baeck wrote, "mysticism arose out of the spontaneous yearning of the human heart. It grew especially out of the times of distress, when there was a need for that hope and optimism which can only be fulfilled through faith in the omnipresent and omnipotent Mystery." Although this is an historical analysis by Leo Baeck, it also is a statement of the heart. It was for Baeck his own Rubicon crossing, his recognition that life includes not only the intellectual but also the emotional; religion, if it is to be truly meaningful, must encompass both.[7]

Three times a day the observant Jew says a prayer called *Shema Yisrael*. The prayer is simple, brief: "Hear, O Israel, the Lord our God, the Lord is One." The concept embodied is monotheism. For the Jew monotheism is the concept of a single supreme force, and the law emanating from that force is the supreme law. The commandment of God against murder, for example, cannot be compromised. There are no other gods to mitigate the impact of that directive. "To make the ethical the center of religion," wrote Baeck, "is the special characteristic of monotheism." Also, if there is only one God and all men and women on earth are created in His image, then all are equally deserving and equally worthwhile. Baeck stated that Leviticus 19:18, which "Akiba called the determining sentence of the Bible, and which usually is rendered, 'Love thy neighbor as thyself,' means in its truest sense, love your neighbor for he is as you. This 'as you' is the essence of the sentence." So, if one has faith, if one believes in this God of morality, then one cannot seek to harm another human being; more, one must seek always to do the good deed—that is the moral imperative in Judaism.[8]

Leo Baeck explained that acknowledging the mystery is the first step; the next is to follow the commandment. "All religious experience in Judaism is a two-part thing," he said in 1922. "It is first the consciousness to be created, or, what is the same thing, the knowledge of the mystery, the hidden, the irrational of life, of the basis of all being. And then it is the knowledge of that which man should create, the knowledge of the determining, the creating, the idea of his life, of the way which is shown to him." Seventeen years earlier, he had dismissed mystery as not being a part of Judaism; now he insisted that Judaism's "special quality" is that "those two religious experiences have in Judaism their absolute unity, that one can only be understood in the other one."[9]

This became the theme of his writing, the mystery and the commandment embodied in Judaism, the source of life and the direction one gives to that life. It was, for Baeck, the formula for the truly free person. Only those who understand that life comes from God and then control the direction of that life by exercising discipline and living at peace with their neighbors are truly free. This was Baeck's message, this is what he taught his fellow Jews, that the essence of Judaism is individual responsibility. Man can choose the life he wishes, but, if mankind is to survive, each individual must choose the religious life, which means "love thy neighbor, for he is as thou."

When the revised edition of *The Essence of Judaism* appeared in 1922, it was very much like Baeck himself. As he said in the foreword to the new edition, *"Es ist ein altes Buch . . . und es ist ein neues Buch"* —it was both old and new. The length had increased from 167 to 327 pages. The three-part organization remained the same: the character of Judaism, the idea of Judaism, and the preservation of Judaism. Most of the book's growth was in the second section, the idea of Judaism, which went from eighty-eight pages in the first version to 202 pages in the second. It is in this section that Baeck wrote of faith in God, in man—in one's self, in one's fellow man, and in mankind. It is in this section that the acknowledgment of mystery is entwined. "Whenever the hidden and unfathomable is experienced, man can react either with the devoutness of silence, that most intimate feeling of the living God, or with poetry and prayer which sings of the ineffable," wrote Baeck. "That is why mysticism, in which this urge to express the inexpressible finds its sometimes too exuberant outlet, is usually so rich in words, so bathed in the ecstacy of poetic eloquence." Mysticism "unifies man with God."

There also is an acknowledgment that the claim the German Jews had developed over the past hundred years, that they had no connection with Jews outside of Germany's geographic borders, was not acceptable. In the first edition, when Baeck wrote that only in Israel did an ethical monotheism exist, he uses the phrase, *"und Israel war damit eines der Völker geworden"*—"and Israel became then one of the peoples." In the second edition he revised the phrase to acknowledge that Jews are united across geographic borders in a moral community: *"und Israel war damit eine der Nationen geworden"*—"and Israel then became one of the nations." He continued: "This is what is meant by the election of Israel. Hence this word primarily expresses a historical fact: there was assigned to this people a peculiar position in the world by which it is distinguished from all other peoples."[10]

Had Baeck written a completely new book? No, but in revising the book he had improved upon it significantly, adding to it, allowing the experiences of his life as a scholar, rabbi, and chaplain to pour out. He was not afraid to admit he had changed as he had grown in his profession. For him it was a development process, something of which he would be proud.

For more than half a century *The Essence of Judaism* has been a beacon to the Jewish people. It is both a traditional and a modern analysis of the Jewish religion—traditional in that it acknowledges the emotion the Jews feel for their religion as well as the responsibility it places upon them to lead ethical lives; modern in that it was produced by a scholar using scientific research methods and writing with a verve and a mastery of his subject. Contemporary Jews feel comfortable with this second edition. It exalts their heritage rather than denying it, as did the first version.

Baeck's book became a standard reading assignment for German Jews. It was the book young people received when they were confirmed. For the Jews who had ignored their religion it became the first book to read on the road of return. For the Jew or the non-Jew seeking a succinct statement about the meaning of Judaism, this book is, perhaps more than any other, a statement that is both comprehensive and eloquent.

Some of the lines at the end, in a section entitled "The Right to Be Different," offer a definition of what is meant by being Jewish, of the Jewish understanding of the word *election*. Baeck wrote: "By its mere existence Judaism is a never silent protest against the assumption of the multitude that force is superior to truth. So long as Judaism exists, nobody will be able to say that the soul of man has surrendered. Its very existence through the ages is proof that conviction cannot be mastered by numbers."

Baeck believed that "just because it was always a minority, Judaism has become a standard of measurement of the level of morality. How the Jewish community has been treated by the nations among which it has lived is always a measure of the extent to which right and justice have prevailed; for the measure of justice is always its application to the few." Baeck conceded that the extent to which right and justice prevail often was not very great, so that "It requires religious courage to belong to a minority such as Judaism always has been and always will be; for many days will come and go before the messianic time arrives."

The final paragraph of the book begins with a plea by Leo Baeck to his Christian neighbors. "Judaism," he told them, "lies open for all to see. We acknowledge the treasures possessed by other religions, especially by those sprung from our midst. He who holds conviction will respect the convictions of others."[11]

Those words coming in the 1920s, when Nazism was finding adherents in Germany, say that in the coming decades Judaism would bear witness. The Germans would be tested on their ability to tolerate a dissenting minority within their midst. The Jews would be their cross to bear.

7 ENEMY

In the 1920s Germany was rife with small fascistic parties. Almost any ex-soldier with a few friends as "party members" claimed a political organization. In a time of discontent and uncertainty the "soldier-on-horseback" is very appealing, even if he needs a shave and has holes in his shoes. Adolf Hitler surpassed them all to become the most effective politician of the twentieth century. He persuaded a modern, civilized nation to follow him to degradation, defeat, and despair—and to support him enthusiastically almost to the very end. For no other politician can such a claim be made. He did this by using several tools; one was anti-Semitism.

Hitler frequently has been quoted as saying that "If the Jew did not exist, we would have had to invent him." That is what he did. The Jew he attacked never existed. This is the Jew who had refused to fight for Germany in the First World War, the Jew who had robbed the nation, the Jew who was in league with Jews in other countries to control the world, the Jew who corrupted the Christian. This Jew never had been a reality. Yet this was the Jew whom Adolf Hitler presented to the German people as their enemy. That he succeeded so easily in convincing the Germans that the Jew was their enemy is a reflection of Hitler's brilliance and the prevalence of anti-Semitism among the German people.

The English word "slogan" translates into German as *Schlagwort*. But the best translation of *Schlagwort* into English is not "slogan" but "hitting word." Hitler intuitively understood this; no one used propaganda as effectively as he used the *Schlagwort*. Janet Flanner, the *New Yorker* writer, reported in the 1930s, "Where most newcomer autocrats in history have rushed into rule by *coup d'etat*, Hitler rose slowly to Reichsführer by fifteen years of lecturing."

It was not only lecturing. It was enticing people with words in speeches, on billboards, and in the newspapers. He coaxed the Germans more and more until they bent, their minds and their bodies, under the persistent and persuasive Nazi propaganda. The potential effectiveness of propaganda had impressed Hitler before the First World War. "Propaganda, only propaganda is necessary," he had said. "There is no end of stupid people." In *Mein Kampf* he spelled his attitude out clearly. "All propaganda," he wrote, "must be popular and its intellectual level must be adjusted to the most limited intelligence among those it is addressed to . . . But the most brilliant propagandistic technique will yield no success unless one fundamental principle is borne in mind constantly and with unflagging attention." The propagandist must confine himself "to a few points and repeat them over and over."[1]

Hitler knew how to use the tools of propaganda. The Nazi newspapers were filled with hitting words about the Jews and with vile caricatures of Jews preying on Christians. In the 1920s radio was only beginning, but Hitler made effective use of it, as he would of the movie camera in the 1930s. With airplanes he often managed to appear at several places in Germany in a single day.

When he spoke, his words—particularly his attacks on the Jews—fell on receptive audiences. Not only had the Germans' religions taught them that Jews were to be despised and destroyed, but their political tradition likewise made abuse of Jews acceptable. Prior to Hitler the most famous of Germany's political leaders was Otto von Bismarck, chancellor in the latter half of the nineteenth century. At first he had sought and received the support of liberal political movements, which included many Jews among their members. He publicly applauded the efforts of Jews to assist their German fatherland. But then later, for various political reasons, he joined forces with the conservatives, including anti-Semites, and jettisoned his one-time Jewish supporters and friends. He condoned attacks upon them, not as individuals but as Jews. Under Otto von Bismarck, anti-Semitism became a political weapon that was used at the highest level.

While all nations have had anti-Semites in public life, Germany had the distinction of being the only modern western nation before World War One with a political party built on the premise of anti-Semitism. In the 1893 election for the Reichstag the anti-Semites gained a total of 263,000 votes and had sixteen representatives in a parliamentary body of 377. In 1903 the anti-Semites had nine Reichstag members; six in 1908. In 1911 there were twenty-two announced anti-Semites in the Reichstag; thirteen, the next year. Small in number, the anti-Semites were an ineffectual group in terms of legislation and were considered an annoyance by many of the German Jews. Their real significance, however, was not seen then; they were the beginning of the formalization of anti-Semitism into an organized movement; irrational hatred had become a political tenet.

Adolf Hitler realized the depth of anti-Semitism among the German people. The Jew was the one "enemy" which the German people accepted. Other political leaders of the time might shout against conquering foreign states and past opponents, but Hitler gave the German people an enemy they could see, touch, and conquer.

In 1920, the National Socialist Party—the Nazis—adopted a twenty-five-point program. Many of these points had little to do with politics and were, instead, attacks on Jews: point 4 declared that a Jew should not be a German citizen; point 6 denied public office to Jews; other sections called for the expulsion of the Jews from jobs in times of high unemployment and for their removal from positions in the news media.[2]

While the Jews of Berlin were basking in their new emancipation—becoming active in the theater, winning election to the Reichstag, forgetting to attend their synagogues on Friday nights—Adolf Hitler understood what they did not: Jews had not really been accepted as Germans. The religious and political traditions of attacking the Jew had not been erased. The anti-Semitism of the Nazis was not an extraordinary development—anti-Semitism among German people was not extraordinary. Adolf Hitler led the German people only where they wished to go.

Hitler's use of anti-Semitism as a political weapon should not obscure his own pathological hatred of Jews. In Vienna, where he lived before the First World War, eking out a subsistence living while trying to develop as an artist, anti-Semitism was popular not only among the poor and uneducated but also among the cultured and financially well off. There were many newspapers dedicated to anti-Semitism, and it was a popular subject at club meetings, in taverns, and at lectures. As this hatred emanated from the professors, lawyers, and doctors, it had an impact on people like Adolf Hitler. Hitler has told of the beginnings of his anti-Semitism, as he would have it known, in a well-known scene from *Mein Kampf*. He wrote:

Once, as I was strolling through the Inner City, I suddenly encountered an apparition in a black caftan and black hair locks. Is this a Jew? was my first thought.

For, to be sure, they had not looked like that in Linz. I observed the man furtively and cautiously, but the longer I stared at this foreign face, scrutinizing feature for feature, the more my first question assumed a new form:

Is this a German?

As always in such cases, I now began to try to relieve my doubts by books. For a few hellers I bought the first anti-Semitic pamphlets of my life . . .

He then wrote that he concluded, after his reading, "that the Jew was no German," and, "Gradually I began to hate them."

His anti-Semitism was part of his belief in the purity of the German race. "In blood alone," he declared, "resides the strength as well as the weakness of man." And, "The folkish state must . . . set race in the center of all life. It must take care to keep it pure." He wanted this to be the touchstone of the new Germany he would lead. He said:

The crown of the folkish state's entire work of education and training must be to burn the racial sense and racial feeling into the instinct and the intellect, the heart and brain of the youth entrusted to it. No boy and no girl must leave school without having been led to an ultimate realization of the necessity and essence of blood purity.

His blood-purity concept turned him not only against Jews but against all who did not meet his racial standards. "It is a scarcely conceivable fallacy of thought to believe that a Negro or a Chinese, let us say, will turn into a German because he learns German and is willing to speak the German language in the future and perhaps even give his vote to a German political party," said Hitler.

But his venom against other groups could not match that against the Jews. "Indeed," he scoffed, "things can go so far that large parts of the host people will end by seriously believing that the Jew is really a Frenchman or an Englishman, a German or an Italian, though of a special religious faith." He conjured up for the German people the specter of "international Jewish world finances" forging "a coalition . . . now on the march and prepared to attack the horny Siegfried at last." At another time he said: "While the idiotic bourgeoisie looks with amazement at such miracles of education, full of respect for this marvelous result of modern educational skill, the Jew shrewdly draws from it a new proof for the soundness of his theory about the equality of men that he is trying to funnel into the minds of the nations."[3]

Hitler was correct. While he preached the superiority of a group of people whose ancestors had lived in a particular geographic region for a long period of time, the Jews preached the brotherhood of man— your neighbor is as thou, said Baeck. While Hitler tried to create a concept of racial purity, the Jews taught that all men are created in the image of God and are therefore equal before God. While Hitler spoke of the ignorance of man, Jews like Leo Baeck spoke of the decency of man; even in the years to come, as Leo Baeck watched his world destroyed at the hands of his German neighbors, he demanded that each man be judged as an individual. While Hitler preached that government and law were to be used for the advancement of a particular state, to be bent if the needs of that state demanded, the Jews taught that basically the ultimate law is God's law.[4]

The Nazis made clear what they thought of the Jews in the 1920s and early 1930s, before they came to power. During this period they were involved in the desecration of more than 120 Jewish cemeteries and fifty synagogues. In 1930 they mounted one attack in which eight Jews were killed and a second attack later that year in which seventy-eight Jews were injured. In that same year they advocated legislation that echoed their 1920 program: "Whoever contributes to the debasement and disintegration of the German race by mixing with members of the Jewish blood community or with colored races is guilty of racial treason."[5]

Hitler's biographers frequently speak of Hitler as a Christlike figure. They do not mean to compare Hitler with Jesus but to say that the German people came to believe in Hitler as a messianic figure almost above life. Not only did the Germans vote for him, they worshipped him. "This is not a revolution," said an American of the German infatuation with Hitler. "It's a revival. They think Hitler is God." A German recalled: "Our neighbor's wife had a whole row of Hitler photos one next to the other. And when Hitler spoke she said, 'I could almost hug the radio.' " A churchwarden said: "Christ has come to us through Adolf Hitler." Prominent Germans, even those with education and sophistication, began to speak of him as "the only human being who never erred" and "as solitary as the Lord God." Said another: "The intense will of the man, the passion of his sincerity seemed to flow from him into me. I experienced an exaltation that could be likened only to religious conversion." Hitler capitalized on this. Saying that Jesus had initial responsibility for the destruction of the Jews, Hitler declared: "The work that Christ started, but could not finish, I—Adolf Hitler—will conclude." He encouraged his subordinates to adopt the attitude stated by one: "Our program can be expressed in two words: 'Adolf Hitler.'"

Part of this exploitation was mechanical. Joachim Fest, a German biographer of his, wrote of an introductory speech being prolonged so that Hitler did not appear until the precise moment when the sun broke through the clouds, framing the Führer in a blaze of light. But it was more than mechanics and more than propaganda. Hitler knew the German condition. The people had been through a war that had devastated them and their land as well as their virile image of themselves. Then they had undergone a revolution that had changed their form of government to a democracy—a form for which they had not wished, were not prepared, and could not understand. Then they had experienced inflation and unemployment. They ached for someone they could trust to solve their problems. Adolf Hitler presented himself as the messiah figure they had been taught to trust.[6]

Hitler knew that the road to success was not in creating a political party but in creating a military movement and calling it a political party. The Germans had loved uniforms and martial music; they had long honored their military men. They had welcomed the First World War, rejected their defeat in the field, and claimed rather they had been defeated by *Dolchstoss*. War remained a national crusade, and Hitler played on this. Even when his party could not afford uniforms, it had a symbol in the swastika on armbands and flags. As the party grew, it developed the brown uniforms, songs, badges, a military walk and salute, and all the trappings of a military machine. Nazism did not appeal to reason; it demanded that people march. Hitler did not ask people to join him in a political crusade; he insisted that they fight with him in a battle. He spoke in the language of the military and organized his Nazis into military units. One did not vote for Adolf Hitler; one campaigned for him and fought alongside him.

In 1932 an assistant military attaché at the American embassy in Berlin, Major John H. Hinemon, Jr., attended what was billed as a political meeting of the Nazi party. The meeting was held in the Deutsches Stadium in Grunewald, about eight kilometers from the center of Berlin. The seating capacity was 65,000. At three o'clock in the afternoon the stadium was one-fourth filled. By seven o'clock all seats were taken and several thousand people were standing in the aisles. "All roads leading to the entrances of the stadium were lined with Nazis, in uniform, formed in a line on each side of the roads, and spaced about four feet apart." Major Hinemon described the events at the meeting:

The program started at 5:00 P.M. with a band concert, given by a Nazi band of some 100 pieces, which was concluded at 7:00 P.M. [when] a large group of Nazis, dressed only in shorts, filed into the stadium at a trot and went through a series of setting-up exercises. The participants in the setting-up exercises made their exit at 7:30 P.M. and at 7:35 P.M. the marching in of the Nazi troops, the S.A. (Storm detachments), began. Marching with the precision of trained soldiers to the music of the Nazi band, the companies, or detachments, entered the arena of the stadium through two entrances. The detachments, headed by their officers, marched in the column of squads, each squad consisting of six men, three each in the front and rear ranks. It required about forty minutes for all of the detachments to march in, and it is reported that there were 20,000 Nazi troops present in uniform. The troops formed a solid rectangle, and were faced toward the side of the stadium in which the speaker's stand is located. In appearance, bearing, and discipline, they seemed to be up to the standards of well trained military units.

Joseph Goebbels, the party propagandist, then repeated the Nazi litany of wrongs done to Germany. When he finished, Nazis carrying torches entered the stadium in single file, "the two lines marching in opposite directions around the arena. When the parade was completed, the stadium was completely encircled with Nazis, about a yard apart, each holding in his right hand a lighted torch." Finally, at 9:45, Adolf Hitler,

dressed in the Nazi uniform and without head dress, entered the stadium in his automobile. He sat on the back of the front seat as he was driven around the stadium, and acknowledged the "Heils" of the group in the stands with the Nazi salute. All Nazis in uniform stood at a rigid attention while his automobile circled the arena. Hitler then walked to the speaker's stand . . . There he stood for fully 15 minutes, surveying his troops, while the Nazi band played and the audience acclaimed him as their leader.

Hitler then spoke, calling upon Germans to forget the old political parties and unite behind "one great national movement to re-establish Germany in the high position she once held among the nations." Major Hinemon thought Hitler's speech was received "almost with reverence." At its end "all troops stood at attention, and all others in the stadium stood, with the right hand raised in the Nazi salute, while the band played the national anthem."

What the American major described was not so much a political meeting as a religious revival, a dramatic production, a military tour de force. "It was interesting to study the make-up, the quality, of the thousands of people assembled in the stadium," said Major Hinemon.

The great majority, in appearance, conduct, and bearing, seemed to belong to the middle class; that is, they seemed to be substantial, thinking citizens, who feel that they are supporting a worthy cause, and a leader who will bring them out of the depression through which Germany is passing. There was no evidence of that stratum of humanity which goes in for mob violence and which is opposed to all organized government. Unquestionably the assemblage was made up of men of all political leanings, from the extreme right to the extreme left, but all seemed to be satisfied to join together in the great movement which Hitler, by his personality, leadership, and spell-binding speech making ability, has so successfully developed.[7]

One of Hitler's German biographers said of the way Hitler affected his audiences that he "delivered one of his passionate speeches that whipped the audience into a kind of collective orgy, all waiting tensely for the moment of release, the orgasm that manifested itself in a wild outcry. The parallel is too patent to be passed over."

Hitler's success in gaining converts moved Baeck to warn that almost everywhere the infatuation with the state increases and works "to level all individuals." In a society that has been ignoring its own laws, Baeck asserted, "It is no accident that all forms of Constitutions are directed to the overpowering might of the state, from the Platonic state to the states of modern times." Standing against this overpowering might Baeck saw the family. "In the individual life of the family, the ability to stand against the power of the state and against the parties who are fighting for the power, has its strongest roots. The important question of family life is today the important question of human individuality, of human character." Baeck commented that "the historical guilt of nationalism" is the emphasis it placed upon a "one-sided romanticism" and upon Darwinism "with its overstressing on breeding and the power of the bestial feelings."[8]

Presaging concerns that would become common in the later nuclear age, Baeck cautioned, "One thing cannot be forgotten. The closer people and human communities become, the more they need—in order to live side by side—a true equality. Between undeveloped areas in the emptiness of the woods there can be a lasting war situation but between nations that are not divided by a binding distance, weapons cannot stay directed against each other."[9]

But Baeck and others who recognized the danger of Adolf Hitler and his fascist movement were not strong enough to persuade the Germans to put aside their infatuation with a man on horseback. When the Depression first struck the world in 1929, the German government was incapable of coping and incapable of pulling strength from the people, who preferred a messiah in military uniform more than the hard work necessary to regain economic stability. In a democracy, which Weimar was intended to be, politics is a system by which individuals control their lives in relation to the state; and in the democracies in the United States and England, for example, individuals did begin to move toward economic stability without surrendering their rights as citizens and without destroying the rights of other citizens. But the Germans chose to revert to a system of politics in which the state controls the individual.

In 1932 Leo Baeck told a friend that he doubted the government intended to be an effective instrument for reform or an effective leader in "the struggle against the economic crisis in Germany." Rather, he suspected that the government was "only a sliding wall being closed" so that, in secret, "a scenery or a theatrical effect can be created" to usher in a new government.

Historians have argued whether the coming to power of Adolf Hitler was something that could only have happened in Germany at the time, a result of a unique history and an unusual series of events; or—more frightening—whether an Adolf Hitler could come to power in any nation. Historians argue whether the rise of Nazism was inevitable because of the conditions of the Versailles Treaty, or, whether, as Walter Laqueur, a Weimar historian, said, "There was nothing inevitable about the advance of the catastrophe" and that Weimar failed not because of circumstances beyond human control but "to a large extent [was] the outcome of loss of nerve, of political failure and economic error."

Whatever the cause, on January 30, 1933, Adolf Hitler became Chancellor of Germany; he assumed the position legally. Whatever the historical argument to this point, there is none with the historian's observation two decades later: "The world was now ready for the massacre."[10]

8 STRUGGLE

"Das Ende des deutschen Judentums ist gekommen."

Leo Baeck spoke those words—"The end of German Jewry has arrived"—shortly after Adolf Hitler came to power in 1933. They were not generally believed by the German Jews, who could not conceive of being ripped from German society as, for example, the Jews had been expelled from Spain in 1492. "Many Jews in Germany met the events of the year 1933 inwardly unprepared," said Baeck. "These events overtook them with a certain suddenness; one could say that to the enemies, who stood back themselves, the key to the fortress, which should have been guarded, was handed over."[1]

"Suddenly people were actually reading those ridiculous newspapers published by the Nazi party, instead of just making fun of them," recalled Lilli Palmer, the actress, who grew up in Berlin as a German Jew. "My father," she continued, "with his love of Germany, refused to believe that his country would ever allow itself to be represented by 'that kind of man.'" When Hitler came to power, her father assumed he would drop his "mad ideas" and "behave decently." Lilli Palmer remembered that "It never occurred to my father to emigrate. As chief of surgery at Berlin's biggest Jewish hospital, he was irreplaceable anyway."

Irreplaceability was a quality on which the Jews prided themselves. The biographer of Max Warburg, the Hamburg banker, wrote that Warburg was convinced he would never be a Nazi target because he was "the German patriot of World War I, the friend of the Kaiser, the man who refused to sign the financial clauses of the infamous Treaty of Versailles, the uncrowned financial king of Hamburg, close to Schacht, the president of the Reichsbank, soon to become economics minister in Hitler's government, the man in fact who was a German before he was a Jew."

Warburg's was almost a universal feeling. After all, how could one have a Berlin without the chief surgeon of an important hospital, a Germany without the most prestigious banker in Hamburg, a theatrical world without Max Reinhardt and Elisabeth Bergner? Could one really sever a person like Albert Einstein from Germany?

Early in 1933 Martin Buber told his fellow Jews, "Today we need not disassociate from Germanism, with which we have an inner relationship which nothing that Germans do can change."

One German Jew, who made a study of the Jewish emigration under the Nazis, commented later, *"Hinterher ist es leicht, weise zu erscheinen"*—"In hindsight it is easy to appear wise," but added, "In the year 1933 no one could know whether the optimist or the pessimist would be correct." There were many optimists who felt that the Hitler reign would neither be long nor effective in its anti-Semitism. Martin Rosenbluth reported a conversation he had with a Cologne businessman shortly before Hitler came to power. Rosenbluth, a Zionist official, had been speaking of the need for a Jewish homeland if the Nazis took over in Germany. The businessman, a Jew, replied: "Look here! Even if Hitler should be successful, he could hold his position for only a very short period of time. As for the Jew, maybe during the first few days there might be some minor incidents in your Berlin. But even there the police would soon enforce order." The businessman continued: "Certainly nothing untoward will happen here in the Rhineland, where our Jewish communities have existed for more than a thousand years. Why, some of them even go back to the Roman period."[2]

Implicit in those remarks was reliance by the Jews on the law. That this reliance was naive in Nazi Germany was not apparent in 1933. Even Baeck, in later years, recalled regretfully the missed legal opportunities. During the 1920s he had enjoyed congenial working relationships with Prussian government officials, especially in connection with questions and problems of educating Jews in the state schools. Working with these Prussian officials, Baeck hoped to develop a concordat between Prussia and the Jüdische Gemeinde similar to those developed by the Catholic and the Protestant churches strengthening their positions as legal entities. A bill for such a concordat was prepared in 1932, and it was to come before the state parliament in 1933. Baeck called it a plan "which promised much" but which "came to nothing" after Hitler was appointed Chancellor. If the bill had been enacted, however, it would have made no difference, given the perversion of law about to take place.[3]

Another reason why there was a general feeling of disbelief in the destructive intentions of the Nazis is that during Weimar the German Jews had dwindled to a smaller group than in the days of the Emperor. Exact figures are difficult to ascertain because there is a dispute over who exactly was a Jew. Were professed Protestants in reality Jewish if their parents or grandparents, or even only one of them, were Jewish?

There is general agreement, however, that by 1933 there were between 500,000 and 600,000 Jews in Germany, representing less than one percent of the total German population of 65,000,000, down from the 1875 high of 1.25 percent. The Jews were highly visible because of their concentration in the cities—one-third of German Jews lived in Berlin, and one-half of all German Jews lived in six cities—Berlin, Frankfurt am Main, Breslau, Hamburg, Cologne, and Leipzig. This urban concentration had resulted from a movement away from the smaller communities where the Jewish presence was shrinking. It disappeared entirely from 566 small communities between 1900 and 1933.

Despite the charges of Hitler's propaganda, Jews were not all that active in business and banking fields. Although concentrated in urban occupations such as commerce, banking, industry, and trade, and the professions, they controlled none of them. In Prussia, which included Berlin, there were 2,239 Jewish lawyers, 4,055 medical doctors, and 778 dentists. This was a high level of achievement but not indicative of domination. The Jews had a long tradition as bankers, one that had begun when almost the only occupation open to them was moneylending. But even this involvement had begun to decline. By 1925, of the 236,000 Germans identified as bankers or brokers, only slightly more than 3 percent were Jews. One reason for the decline was the hiring practices of the banking institutions controlled by non-Jews. They would not hire a Jew, certainly never for a position of importance, unless the individual converted from Judaism and, in addition, became a pronounced anti-Semite; banks controlled by Jews hired without regard to religious affiliation.

In business, too, Jews were not as influential as the Nazi propaganda claimed. Almost all Jews active in retail businesses were involved in family-owned concerns. "The number of Jews active in industry, who are not employed in clearly Jewish operations, is relatively small. It may be between ten thousand and fifteen thousand, or about five percent of the total . . ." according to a Jewish study made at the time.

Jews as well as non-Jews had been struck by the Depression. One in every three Jewish taxpayers then had an annual income of less than 2,400 marks; almost one in five Berlin Jews received charity. The Jews had done well in Germany professionally and financially, but they did not dominate the German economy.[4]

During this time the Jews' loss of interest in their religion was evident in many ways. One was the decline in the number of children attending Jewish schools. By the early 1930s generally the only Jews sending their children to Jewish schools were those still living in rural communities, extreme Orthodox Jews, and Jews who had recently emigrated from eastern Europe. The Jewish middle class in the large cities did not send their children to Jewish schools, preferring to send them to state schools, hoping this would enhance their chances of entering the universities in later years. They were avoiding Jewish tradition; they did not want their children to associate with the children of the Orthodox and of the eastern European Jews.

The experiences of Lilli Palmer, growing up as the child of an assimilated family in Berlin, are typical. Almost the only time she knew she was Jewish was on the High Holy Days when her father "made concessions and took us to dinner at his parents' house . . . for these things were important to his father." Lilli Palmer "hated those gatherings" because, "I had to sit still for hours on end, listening to my grandfather chanting Hebrew of which I understood neither words nor meaning."[5]

These assimilated Jews believed they would be supported by their fellow citizens—the "circle with whom one had been connected in common work and in common political spheres through decades," as Baeck described them. The press in the 1920s had reported and commented negatively on anti-Semitic outbursts, and the Jews looked for similar reporting and commentary in the 1930s. But the press was quiet. It would not anger advertisers, feared physical abuse by Nazi supporters, and would not challenge the authority of the Nazi government.

Industrialists also were passive before the Nazi anti-Semitism, attracted to Adolf Hitler and his promises to suppress Communists, labor-union agitators, and others who threatened corporate profits. Those profits became more significant under Hitler; a war economy is a profitable one for industry, and the owners of German industries knew that.

Those who were presumed to have some intelligence, to be "liberal" in the sense of having an open and unbiased outlook, also accepted anti-Semitism as a price to pay for the new order. University professors continued their opposition to Jews; no education and no experience could change that attitude. An American woman studying in Germany at the time was advised by a German university professor that her dissertation would be more acceptable if she "grouped all Jewish authors together." She didn't, but the acceptance of anti-Semitism at the university level in Germany impressed her so deeply that she spoke of it years later.

Scientists, trained to weigh facts dispassionately, ignored the moral implications of their work. "The Versailles Treaty hadn't placed any restrictions on rockets, and the army was desperate to get back on its feet," Wernher von Braun recalled. "We didn't care much about that, one way or the other, but we needed money, and the army seemed willing to help us. In 1932, the idea of war seemed to us an absurdity. The Nazis weren't yet in power. We felt no moral scruples about the possible future abuse of our brainchild. We were interested solely in exploring outer space. It was simply a question with us of how the golden cow would be milked most successfully."

The artist also turned away from the Jews. "If you could listen to our work here and see how good it is," wrote Richard Strauss, the composer, to a friend, "you would abandon all worries about race, with which you trouble your rich artistic brain quite unnecessarily, and would rather write for me as much as possible." Strauss was president of the Reichsmusikkammer, an organization of musicians in Germany officially sanctioned by the Nazis. He insisted that politics and art should not be mixed, that they could be kept separate. Strauss apparently held that attitude until the Gestapo found a letter written by him disavowing any personal feelings of anti-Semitism—"To me there are but two categories of men: those who have talent and those who have not." For such heresy the Nazis dismissed him as head of the Reichsmusikkammer.

Politicians were willing to accept, overlook, or discount Nazi anti-Semitism. Franz von Papen, a leader in the 1932–1933 government, conceded that "for years anti-Semitism had been one of the basic tenets of the Nazi Party programme. The loss of the war, the Versailles Treaty, the inflation, and the financial crisis of the early thirties were all ascribed to Jewish influences. The whole party was permeated by the atmosphere of these accusations." Despite this background von Papen and others were willing to accept Hitler's assurances that anti-Semitism would be curbed. Von Papen said he frequently discussed with fellow cabinet members, "men whose personal integrity and character were above suspicion, how we were to reconcile Hitler's assurances with actual developments. We all agreed that there was no reason to doubt Hitler's intentions, and hoped that experience in the Cabinet would have a beneficial effect on him."

The average person also tolerated Adolf Hitler's anti-Semitism. Lilli Palmer, after losing her first theatrical contract because she was Jewish, was joined for a cup of coffee by her landlady, who had been friendly toward her and sympathetic with her aspirations. "It's really a shame," said the landlady, "because you can't deny that Hitler is a good man. You bet your life he'll make Germany great again. Too bad he has this . . . this thing about the Jews."

John Toland reported in his biography of Hitler: "By mid-1933 the majority of Germans supported Hitler. The bourgeoisie and the workers, the military and the civil service, the racists and some of the best brains in the country swelled the Nazi ranks. It has long been a political principle that power corrupts. It can also sanctify." This support of Hitler grew. Werner Maser, one of Hitler's German biographers, explained Hitler's widespread popular support when war broke out in 1939:

Six years and six months prior to 1939 there had been no autobahns, no marriage grants or child allowances, no tours sponsored by *Kraft durch Freude*, no really favourable opportunities for aspiring farmers. There had been no Adolf Hitler schools, no National-Political Education Centres, or pre-military training for the young, no *Arbeitsdienst* or "reconciliation of the social classes." Nor had there been a Greater German Reich, a (pervertedly) proud national consciousness among the people, nor yet food and work for everyone. To many all this spelled "National Socialism," the achievement of one man alone, Adolf Hitler.

The Jews thought they could rely on their neighbors. But their neighbors turned to suck at the golden cow. Said Robert Weltsch, editor of the *Jüdische Rundschau, "Ich verstehe die Welt nicht mehr"*—"I understand the world no more."[6]

There were exceptions. A Christian friend of Baeck's, Baron H. H. von Veltheim-Ostrau, refused to succumb to the Nazi virulence. A few months before Hitler came to power von Veltheim discussed with Baeck a recent spate of Nazi desecrations of Jewish cemeteries. To von Veltheim the acts revealed "the hopeless decadence of our sad people." He understood the acts "not only as the excrescences of political passion . . . but as an outburst of lawlessness against everything that is spiritual." Even with people like von Veltheim, however, there was a naivete when dealing with Nazi anti-Semitism. In March 1933 the Nazis staged a raid on the offices of a Jewish organization and reported they had found an illegal manuscript. Baron von Veltheim wrote Baeck about the incident, saying that "Very sad it would be if illegal manuscripts were really found in the office of the Central-Verein." He then hastened to assure his friend Baeck, "I can never, never believe that any German would do anything to somebody who, like you, dear Herr Doktor, lives so much as an example for every person, works and is such a factor in the German intellectual life, who stood and stands high above all party biases."

Would anyone else have acted differently than did those who supported Hitler? Lilli Palmer wondered about this when, years after the war, she returned to Germany and a friend said to her, "Let me ask you a question. If you hadn't happened to be Jewish, would you have left Germany?" Miss Palmer said she didn't know, that she had often wondered.

"And?"

"Maybe . . . not. I loved my life in Germany. I'm afraid . . . I'd have stayed."

"You see?"

"But I would have never joined the Party or—or even paid lip service to that insane racial business, or renounced other people."

"Naturally not. But you'd have stayed! And most of the people that you're looking at in this room . . . just stayed."

That the Germans were succumbing to the temptations to stay and enjoy the life they loved in Germany was something Leo Baeck realized. But he searched for those Germans who would protest; he sought a life built around the brotherhood that was so much a part of his Jewishness. "Of myself and my wife I can tell you the usual," wrote Baeck to a friend. "In this time of nervousness we are searching to maintain our way of life and to be happy in the light hours which the sun gives us in these weeks." To his friends and visitors from abroad, Baeck "breathed cheerfulness and faith, and maintained the same serenity of spirit."[7]

There was more than cheerfulness. In the weeks and months after the Nazis came to power Baeck began to plan his course as a leader of the German Jews. His role could not be a passive one. His writings and his preaching, his civic activities, his stance as one above the temporary movements, had marked him as the one to whom the Jews could turn for leadership. He had no inclination to shirk that responsibility now.

Formulating the proper approach would not be easy, given that his fellow Jews did not believe that their time in Germany had ended. Many argued that if Adolf Hitler lasted as Germany's ruler only for a few years, then those Jews who had left would have been in error.

Baeck operated on several levels. As a rabbi he believed his proper role was to exhort his fellow Jews to maintain faith in the ultimate triumph of justice. Through sermons from the *bimahs* in the Berlin synagogues and articles in Jewish community newspapers during this period, he insisted to the German Jews they remember that the "sense and the essence of justice . . . is that it exists, that it is not woven onto the wheel of happenings, that it stands there firm and independent from whatever happens and from whatever pulls it in the other direction. Fate comes and fate goes, but justice remains." Baeck reacted to a system growing more totalitarian by writing that "The freedom of *man* . . . is based on what man experiences in himself as being beyond all men and all events; it is not as the freedom I described before, something rational; but it means something irrational. It consists in the knowing about that alone which is real, and that is the connection of man with the godly . . ." His acquaintances who spoke out against the Nazis and against the anti-Semitism often received a telephone call or a message from Baeck congratulating them on their courage and assuring them that their efforts were appreciated.[8]

In March 1933 Leo Baeck met with the leaders of the Central-Verein, the association of Germans of the Jewish faith, to tell them not to expect the National Socialist regime to end shortly. "The two other European dictators, Mussolini and Stalin," he said, "have lasted much longer than most people had predicted." A Nazi-ruled Germany for many years was a probability the Jews had to face. It was at this meeting that Baeck announced that the history of Jews in Germany had ended. He proposed a two-part plan—emigration of the young and a strengthened cultural and spiritual life for those Jews who remained. This was his theme during the next decade. It was concerned not only with the survival of individuals but also with the survival of the religion. The young people would carry the religion abroad, adhere to it, and, with their enthusiasm and energy, nurture it so that it would grow stronger. This became the policy of the German Jews—save the young and succor the old.[9]

Frederick J. Perlstein, whose family had vacationed with Baeck's family in earlier years, was an agronomist and had established agricultural communities for miners who, victims of black lung disease, needed to learn a new way to earn a living. Perlstein was a Jew whose family claimed it could trace its background in Germany back to the time of Alexander the Great. When Hitler came to power, however, Perlstein believed he had no future in Germany and planned to leave. With his bags almost completely packed and his tickets in hand, he stopped by the Baeck apartment. "I have my visa, and I am going," he said. Baeck replied that he also had the opportunity to leave, to accept a teaching position at Oxford University in England. He had decided to reject the position, although he knew many German rabbis were leaving.

Then, looking directly at Perlstein, Leo Baeck said: "And they need you." Baeck argued that Perlstein had a moral obligation to stay because he was uniquely qualified to teach agriculture to the Jews who had spent many generations in the cities and ghettos, far from farmland. The training was necessary, Baeck said, for three reasons: farmers could get visas more easily than members of other professions; the most likely place for the Jews to emigrate would be Palestine, which needed more farmers than anyone else; and, if schools were closed to the Jewish youth, then farm schools would help those young people.

"I unpacked my bags," Perlstein recalled. "If you stay," he remembered saying to the rabbi, "I stay."[10]

According to Truman Smith, a military attaché at the American embassy in Berlin, "the Nazi anti-Semitic actions at this time were mild." That viewpoint, however, was against an expectation that Hitler intended "to perform ultimately a radical surgical operation on the Jews and remove them totally from German political, intellectual and commercial life and ultimately, if possible, from the German soil." The Jews saw things somewhat differently. In the weeks following Hitler's coming to power they were assailed and beaten by Nazis in occasional street attacks. Nothing was done to protect them. A few Jews were arrested on fabricated charges. One German Jew, Ernst Herzfeld, recalled an ominous note. "The leading commentaries of the Nazis," he said, "had the tone: You German Jews are our hostages; we will hold on to you."

This "hostage" view received support at a meeting, Saturday, March 25, between a group of German Jewish leaders and the Nazi official Hermann Goering. Baeck, not yet holding a formal position, had not been invited. Present were Julius Brodnitz, chairman of the Central-Verein; Heinrich Stahl, president of the Berlin Jüdische Gemeinde; and Max Nauman, leader of the small Verband National-Deutscher Juden, an association of German Jews opposed to Zionism. Also present was

Martin Rosenbluth, the Zionist official, who was not invited into the actual meeting (the Zionists were represented in the session by Kurt Blumenfeld). Goering berated the German Jews for the bad press that Germany was receiving in newspapers around the world, which were reporting Nazi violence against the Jews. Goering wanted some of the German Jews to travel to the United States and England and stop the press from printing these accounts. In the Nazis' framework his request was not unusual; to them the press was another element controlled by the government.

The Jews answered that they had no control over the foreign press, were not responsible for the stories appearing in the newspapers, and could not influence Jews living in other nations. Blumenfeld said he would take the trip but only with the understanding that he would tell the full truth of the Jews' situation in Germany. "What is there to tell?" shouted Goering. "You know perfectly well that there has been no change in the situation of the Jews, and that nothing untoward has happened to them." Max Nauman became equally incensed. Goering, he said, must be aware of the incidents in which Jews had been subjected to physical abuse. Goering dismissed the incidents with *"Wo man hobelt, fallen Spähne"*—"Where one planes, shavings will fall." The meeting ended inconclusively. Actually there was no way the issue could be resolved; acts against the Jews were being intensified.[11]

On April 7, 1933, the Law for the Re-establishment of the Professional Civil Service was enacted, under which Jews, or non-Jews with at least one Jewish parent or grandparent, would be ineligible for the civil service. Those already in civil service would be forced to retire. Exempted were those in the civil service prior to 1914, those who had fought in the First World War, or people who lost a father or son in that war. The same day a similar law was enacted prohibiting Jews from practicing as lawyers. The same exemptions applied, but they were not very effective; no persons who hoped to win a case hired a Jewish lawyer to represent them before a court where judges wore swastika armbands. In the same month students classified as Jewish by the Nazi definition were limited to 1.5 percent of the student body. Before the year was over the ritual of kosher slaughtering was prohibited within Germany; kosher meat had to be imported from other countries at great expense.[12]

There were two other events in those early Nazi years that—in retrospect—indicated the future course for the Hitler regime much more clearly than did the denial of the Jews' civil service status. The first was the boycott on April 1, 1933, a few days before the law prohibiting civil service status to Jews. Using the foreign press criticism of his regime as an excuse, Hitler declared a one-day boycott of Jewish stores; Germans were not to shop in Jewish stores that day or purchase any services from a Jew. Storm troopers were posted in front of the Jewish stores, placards directed Germans to stay away, and store windows were soaped with the word *Jude* or the six-pointed star of David. Offices of Jewish lawyers and doctors were similarly marked. Many Germans ignored the order, passing by the German soldiers or laughing at the signs in the windows; actually, because the boycott was on Saturday, those shops owned by Orthodox Jews were closed.

Still, the order had shaken the German Jews. From sporadic violence the Nazis had escalated their anti-Semitism to an organized campaign. "Because of the mistakes of a few, for which we were never responsible at any time, the German Jews—who feel themselves bound to their German homeland with all their heart—shall have to undergo an economic disaster," said a letter to Adolf Hitler from the executive board of the Berlin Gemeinde. The letter, after recounting the statistics of the Jews who had fought and died for Germany, concluded:

The charges which have harmed our people touch most deeply our honor. For the sake of both our honor and truth we solemnly raise our guard against this attack. We trust that the *Reichspräsident* and the Reich government will not allow our legal rights and livelihood to be seized in the German fatherland. We stress again in this hour the acknowledgement of our relationship to the German people, our holiest duty, our obligation and most passionate wish is working for its renewal and strengthening.

The subsequent attendance at religious services revealed, even more than that letter, the depth to which German Jews were moved. Many who virtually had given up attending Friday night services, who were living as if they were not Jews, returned to their religion. In the 1920s, when Baeck and the other religious leaders had fought to lead the German Jews in such a return, it seemed they had failed as more and more the Jews enjoyed the pleasures of a secular, assimilated life. But the speed and the enthusiasm with which the Jews sought out their Jewish institutions in the Nazi period indicate that beneath the surface, Baeck and the others had sown rich seeds.

On the Friday evening before the boycott day, Joachim Prinz, a Berlin rabbi, recalled that all seats in his synagogue were filled one hour before the service started. In addition, he said, "many people stood in the aisles, leaned against the walls and sat on the steps which led to the altar." That night the rabbi saw famous Jewish actors, writers, and other prominent people "who had come for the first time to pray with Jews." To him the most touching experience was the moment when all stood to sing the *Shema*, the statement of monotheism, the affirmation of the Jews' faith. "The choir and the organist were drowned out," said Prinz. "As a matter of fact, the organist who was a Jew was so overwhelmed that he could not continue to play. At that time the organ and every other trapping of the synagogue were proved to be artificial and superfluous. They revealed their Protestant character and seemed no longer to fit the new atmosphere of daily peril."

A writer at the time caught the flavor of what was happening. Robert Weltsch, editor of the *Jüdische Rundschau*, a Zionist newspaper in Berlin, wrote in an editorial a few days after the boycott:

The mark of the Jew was pressed upon all Jews of Germany on the first of April. Everyone knows who is a Jew, evasion or hiding are no longer possible. The Jewish answer is clear—it is the short sentence which the prophet Jonah spoke: *Ivri anochi.* Yes, a Jew! To say "Yes" to being Jewish, that is the moral sense of the present events. The times are too agitated to allow for argumentation. Let us hope that quieter times will come. We Jews, we can defend our honour. We think of all those who for five thousand years were called Jews and were stigmatized as such. We say "Yes" and wear the yellow badge with pride.

There was, however, another reaction to boycott day. "One speaks of the day when Jewish businesses were boycotted," said Leo Baeck. "In truth, justice was boycotted. The Jewish business community overcame that day a long time ago; the concept of justice has not overcome that day . . ." He wrote those comments two decades after boycott day, when the Nazi virulence was history. Baeck then continued: "Each retreat begins with a great cowardice. We have experienced it. The first of April 1933 speaks of that. The universities were silent, the courts were silent; the president of the Reich, who had taken the oath on the Constitution, was silent." To Baeck boycott day was "in history the day of the greatest cowardice. Without that cowardice, all that followed would not have happened."[13]

Baeck was speaking of the real reason for the success of the Nazi attacks on the Jews. Hitler's order for a boycott of Jewish businesses was a tentative step, almost as if he were feeling his way. How far would the German people allow him to go? How much pressure could he bring to bear? Would the religious, social, and business institutions protest his blatant anti-Semitic act? When there was no resistance by the institutions and organizations through which the German people spoke, Hitler realized he was free to go on to the next step. This continued part of the Nazi experience—an outrage against a minority—would be met with neither criticism nor resistance by the nation's institutions. Each step from boycott day in 1933 to the attempt at the physical destruction of the Jewish people in the 1940s was met by this reaction—the absence of protest from the responsible organizations of the community.

But if the institutions failed, many individuals did not. "The little people in Germany remained good," said Leo Baeck. "The workers shared their breakfast rolls with their Jewish workers; the little people made possible the life of the Jews in these years, the little people of Germany." He remembered individuals who had walked into the Jewish shops on boycott day under the eyes of Nazi storm troopers while the heads of the institutions to which they belonged remained silent. "As regards character," said Leo Baeck, "the cultural pyramid stood on its point; the highest, ordinarily over the least, this time were under the greatest."[14]

After boycott day, the second event indicating the future trend of Nazism was one of Hitler's most extreme actions during his first years in power, the Röhm affair. Ernst Röhm had been a loyal supporter of Adolf Hitler in the 1920s. In 1934, however, for political reasons, Hitler decided to have Röhm and dozens of his supporters killed. The acceptance by the German nation of Hitler's action showed its willingness to grant him absolute authority. When Hitler later determined to remove the Jews, there would be no challenge to his actions.

In retrospect one again wonders why the Jews could not visualize the future. Given Hitler's demoniac hatred for them plus the German nation's willingness to allow him authority over who lived or died, why could the Jews not have anticipated the events of the next decade? Given also the Jews' history of persecution, exile, ghettos, and pogroms, why could they not recognize that the "security" they had was an illusion? Amos Elon, in his 1970s study *The Israelis*, tried to place in perspective the Jews' understanding of the kind of violence to which anti-Semitism could lead. "Modern readers, versed in the details of concentration camps, death factories, and nuclear weapons," he wrote, "are frequently left unmoved by contemporary accounts of pogroms in Kishinev or Homel, Zhitomir, Odessa, and Kiev, or tales of smaller outbursts of violence and arson at the turn of the century in hundreds of towns and hamlets throughout White Russia and the Ukraine." He continued: "In the quieter days of 1890 and 1900 the sudden slaughter of forty or fifty innocent men, women, and children, innocent except for their being Jewish, was so traumatic a shock that everywhere in Eastern Europe Jews began to change their entire outlook on life."[15]

Pogroms in which forty or fifty people were killed were, in 1933, not far from the Jews' experience. In a decade that figure would multiply by the tens, the hundreds, the thousands, the hundreds of thousands. No one could visualize that, not even, in Georg Salzberger's phrase, the greatest pessimist.

The scattered organizational structure of German Jewry was not adequate to stand against Nazi anti-Semitism. Who could speak for the Jews? counter the charges? demand legal rights? There were more than 1,300 jüdische gemeindes in Germany, of which the one in Berlin was the largest, and which were affiliated with landesverbändes, state associations. There also was the Central-Verein—the Germans of the Jewish faith—with perhaps 70,000 members. The anti-Zionist Central-Verein was several times larger than the Zionistische Vereinigung für Deutschland, the Zionist organization. In addition there was the association of Jewish veterans of the German army from the First World War and a variety of smaller groups, offshoots from the larger ones. Each group had its political purpose, its leaders who did not wish to surrender power, its members who looked at the German situation differently. In short, the German Jews were exactly like any other group of people facing a need to organize.

In previous decades there had been efforts at developing a national organization of Jews primarily to counter anti-Semitism. These efforts never had taken hold, however, because most Jews had not seen the need for such an organization. Interest increased somewhat following the First World War. "The trend of the new post-1918 Germany was to overcome the old particularism and to create a united, homogeneous state," explained Baeck. "The Jews of Germany were inspired by the same desire for unification." Some of the provincial state associations had joined together, drawing financial support from the wealthy communities. "Much valuable work was done by the Landesverbände as such, as well as by their cooperation," said Baeck. "Special stress must be laid on the assistance rendered to the smaller communities which were weakened by the departure of many of their members, particularly the wealthier members." If conditions in Germany had not changed, said Baeck, this somewhat casual organization probably would have been sufficient. "When the rise of Nazism increasingly threatened the position of the Jews in Germany," he said, "the demand became insistent for a representative body of the whole of German Jewry, provided with adequate funds and powers."[16]

In the summer of 1932 a group of seven Jews, representing a wide variety of backgrounds except for Zionism, met in Berlin. They realized that the Nazis might come to power, and they wanted to develop an "umbrella" organization that would confine itself to a political role. By the time the Nazis took over at the end of January 1933, the concept had developed into a widely based movement among German Jews. Formally organized in April, it was called the Reichsvertretung der Landesverbände—the National Council of the Land Associations. Leo Baeck and Leo Wolff, a lawyer, were named cochairmen.

The Reichsvertretung position toward the Nazis was one Baeck had been urging upon all German Jews. The decision had been made to request a meeting with Adolf Hitler to discuss the Jewish situation. The request, signed by Baeck and Wolff, was sent June 6, 1933, but was never acted upon. With it was a statement drafted by Baeck:

The German-Jewish question demands a clear word for the German Jews.

The German Jews face the possibility of being outlawed in their German fatherland. Deeply hurt, the German Jews cannot defend themselves because they are in the minority; but they cannot be denied the opportunity to speak openly and honestly about their feelings.

The German Jews refused to accept accusations they are either followers or originators of some kind of a "system," while in truth they always have demonstrated and now are ready to demonstrate their willingness to adjust to every order of the state, willingly, if one leaves to them their decency, work, and freedom.

The German Jews refuse to constantly point out their centuries-old German culture, their permanent connection with the German land and spirit. The reality of history speaks for them, speaks of their work, of their loyalty, and of their ties to the German people.

We may expect, also, that the German-Jewish question will be solved on a legal basis and with the weapons of nobility, that there will be created an honest understanding about our place and way . . .

The well-being of Germany, as well as the well-being of the German Jews, insists on that.

The statement showed there would be no apologies for being Jewish, only a call for legal rights. A small minority, under attack, was standing erect, demanding decent treatment as citizens of Germany.

This council did not last very long. Since it represented only the land associations and not the other Jewish groups, its effectiveness as a spokesman for German Jewry was severely limited. Baeck saw this council as dominated by the Berlin Jüdische Gemeinde and Heinrich Stahl, its recently elected leader. Five years Leo Baeck's senior, Stahl was a Berlin native—*ein Urberliner*. His friends were fond of him, saying that he was perhaps "impulsive" but that "he had a kindly way in which he effected a reconciliation." Said another: "From his selection to the leadership [of the Berlin Gemeinde] in May 1933 . . . he had served his community actively, untiringly and fearlessly. He was a goodly and sympathetic personality. No one, even among those who disagreed with him, could ever stay angry with him."

Baeck had no personal argument with Stahl at that time, but he did not believe that Stahl recognized the precariousness of the Jews' situation. Baeck left the Reichsvertretung in the summer of 1933. With his departure he was saying: Bring in all the Jewish organizations, so that there will be an organization truly representing the German Jews and not dominated by any one group.[17]

Without Baeck's leadership the Reichsvertretung quickly floundered, and the need for its replacement by a stronger organization became obvious. One of the leaders in this movement was a prominent Jew from Essen, Ernst Herzfeld. In later years he recalled problems the Jews faced the summer of 1933: "How to set up a legal administrative institution to be recognized by all? Who would be capable of rallying all the forces and guiding them?" He knew that the land associations, the basis of the failed Reichsvertretung, had to be included in any new organization. So the question became first how to bring them into a new organization, then how to keep these large land associations, especially the Prussian group which was controlled by the Berlin organization, from dominating and angering the other Jewish interests. "The solution of the first question was easy," Herzfeld recalled. "The other was very difficult."

Herzfeld was faced with the same difficulty that had felled the first Reichsvertretung. The Jüdische Gemeinde of Berlin, representing one-third of all German Jews, would dominate the new association financially and politically; it had shown itself unwilling to surrender any of its power. Herzfeld also had strong doubts about the efficacy of a new Reichsvertretung dominated by the Berlin group. "Party conflicts after the First World War had left their mark on the shape of the Berlin community more than on any other," he said. "I would not dare to venture an opinion on whether this exaggerated party strife resulted from the inability of the community's leaders to curb it, or whether it was the methods of factional contest that repelled all those who might have been capable of assuming the leadership." Whichever it was, the leadership of the Berlin Jewish community was a mass of political strife. Sometimes the Zionists were in power; sometimes they were out. The "liberals" dominated at times, and then they receded. "When Hitler rose to power," Herzfeld said, "party strife receded, but the Gemeinde committee and its council did not change." Those members, Herzfeld said, "lacked a sense of proportion and diplomatic skill."

Herzfeld began planning an approach along with two other Essen Jews, Georg Hirschland, chairman of the Essen Jewish community, and Rabbi Hugo Hahn. Their first plan was to enlist the support of a number of the Jewish communities in Germany to form an organization with built-in safeguards against domination by any one community and then present it to the Berlin community leaders as an accomplished fact. If they rejected the proposal, "it would have to be clear that the responsibility for the failure would rest on Berlin exclusively."

The first question dealt with by the three Essen Jews was who should be asked to lead what was intended to be truly a national organization of Jews. There never was any other person discussed for the position except Leo Baeck.

There were several reasons for the unanimous choice of Baeck. He "was farsighted and endowed with great diplomatic skill," said Herzfeld. Also, his activities read like a list of the major Jewish organizations in Germany. He was president of the B'nai B'rith, chairman of the rabbinical association, a member of the executive board of the Central-Verein, a leader of the Jewish veterans' group. Although not a Zionist, he had supported the development of Palestine for Jewish settlers. In addition, Herzfeld said, there was another factor, a more political one. The plan still was to lure the Berlin community into the association, and "it was not . . . thought an excessive demand that the Berlin community should agree to their own elected spiritual leader being made chairman."

There also were other reasons. At this time in his life, as Leo Baeck passed his sixtieth birthday, he was the acknowledged intellectual and spiritual leader of the German Jews. Traditionally, they selected men with that kind of stature to lead them rather than the businessman or lawyer. Friedrich Brodnitz, who worked with Baeck during these years, commented much later, sitting in his New York City office, that Leo

Baeck was chosen because of his reputation. "His name meant something to every Jew in Germany." As the Zionist newspaper *Jüdische Rundschau* said in 1933, Baeck was "a man who cannot be tied to any party, because his unique personality and his great Jewish ethos, his great Jewish knowledge and experiences and his ability to judge elevate him above the usual divisions."

In addition, although Leo Baeck had lived his life as a rabbi and as a scholar, he had gained a political shrewdness as a result of serving on the boards of organizations with tens of thousands of members. He understood budgets. He knew how to effect his will in groups, the maneuverings necessary to bring together people with conflicting viewpoints. He was a politician.

There was perhaps one final reason. Joachim Prinz, a young rabbi in Berlin in the 1930s, years later explained it this way: "Why select Leo Baeck to head the national Jewish organization? The Gestapo officials could not talk to Leo Baeck the way they talked to me. He represented the dignity, the history of the Jewish people. He represented that which in Jewish existence is eternal. He was a prophetic figure, not a prophet, but a prophetic figure. He commanded respect, even from the Gestapo."

The three Essen organizers began sending out cautious feelers to the leaders of other communities, not giving all the details but generally outlining the problems and giving some indications of the proposed organization's structure. In these private meetings the commitment given was that Leo Baeck would be asked to assume the leadership of the new organization. Baeck was unaware of these maneuverings, but when finally approached, he was responsive to the plan and offered to surrender some of his other administrative responsibilities to have time for the new position. "We thought it a matter of prime concern to promote the emigration of the youth," said Herzfeld of his discussions with Baeck. "We considered it axiomatic that the young people want a future and have a right to one—and that they would not find it in Germany." The two men estimated that 6,000 to 10,000 Jewish youngsters completed schooling in Germany every year. "Our first concern," Herzfeld recalled, "would therefore be to give them vocational training and to help them to emigrate."

With Baeck's agreement adding to their strength, the Essen group then met with Julius Brodnitz, leader of the Central-Verein. His reaction was positive, and he suggested that the developing organization's base of support be widened to include the large organizations not connected with the landesverbände, such as the Central-Verein, the Zionists and the others. This suggestion was in line with Baeck's thinking, and the Essen trio quickly agreed. The rationale was obvious —there would be one organization instead of many. "The joining of these organizations and their constant cooperation was likely to place the authority of the new organization on a wide basis," said Herzfeld, with his concern for the potential dominance by the Berlin community still evident. "It was an additional point of our scheme to make all the important groups and all those who would take part in our practical work, subordinate to a central supreme leadership, a 'cabinet of personalities.' "

Julius Brodnitz then began to move in on the organizational process. From his background in the Central-Verein he had developed the contacts and the organizational ability to bring the concept to fruition. In August he invited a number of prominent Jews, including Stahl from the Berlin community, to meet with him in Essen. They found an organization already in the process of development—as the Essen triumvirate had planned. Stahl realized that the planning had gone too far to be stopped and so made little protest at that time. "No personal matters whatsoever were mentioned at the official conference," Herzfeld recalled. "Only the overall organizational structure of the proposed body was discussed and even this without any details, but after about four hours of negotiation, the chairman was able to state that full agreement had been reached among all participants."

Actually, it was not quite that smooth. Stahl voiced concern about Baeck becoming head of the new organization. Although the Berlin Gemeinde, which Stahl headed, was Baeck's employer, it never had been able to dominate him. Nor could it threaten him; he had tenure as well as reputation. When the others insisted upon Baeck as president, Stahl bowed before an accomplished fact.

There were other difficulties. Chief among them was persuading the Zionists to join the organization. Rabbi Hahn wrote Baeck, who had not attended the August meeting, for his advice on how to deal with the Zionists, the Jewish veterans, and the liberals—all of whom had balked at joining. Baeck correctly understood this letter to mean he should begin politicking among his acquaintances in these groups, asking for their support of the new organization.

Another decision made at the meeting was to ask Otto Hirsch to join the new association as executive director. Born in Stuttgart in 1885, Hirsch had become a lawyer and then joined the civil service in

Wuerttemberg, where he was active in Jewish organizations, serving on the board of the Central-Verein. The *Jüdische Rundschau* said of him that he belonged "to one of the old south German families that have grown in a very natural way into connections with the German surroundings. He has retained for himself a clear feeling and an open view for the necessities of Jewish existence. Within the Central-Verein, Hirsch belonged to that group which recognized at a very early time the significance of the settlement work in Palestine for all Jews, and he had worked with all his strength." He had been chosen for his administrative ability and also for his robust manner. Ernst Simon, who knew both Hirsch and Baeck, described their working relationship this way: "The two men complemented each other. There were some differences between them which they could exploit with the Nazi leadership. Otto Hirsch was the old-soldier type, the sportsman who couldn't be terrified. Leo Baeck was the religious stoic, the man of great cultural background. Each had a bearing that impressed the Nazis." Years later, as Simon sat in his study in Jerusalem, he added of Otto Hirsch: "He postponed the worst."

At first Hirsch had not wanted the job. "He was absolutely unwilling and persisted in his refusal," said Herzfeld. Finally he changed his mind, said a friend, even though "Otto Hirsch knew that it [the new Reichsvertretung] wouldn't succeed . . . But he also knew that the half-million German Jews were unprepared, in the large part, for the Nazi terror, that they needed a unified representation and a leadership, whether they chose to emigrate or chose to stay . . . He undertook that responsibility as an officer who goes into a seemingly hopeless battle, out of loyalty and a consciousness of duty." Hirsch would pay the price of the loyal officer who leads his troops into the hopeless battle.

In the years they worked together as leaders of the Reichsvertretung, Leo Baeck and Otto Hirsch became close friends, often visiting each other's homes. In visits to Hirsch's home Baeck met an anti-Nazi Gentile German named Theodor Heuss. Hirsch and Heuss had been students together and enjoyed a warm friendship, which they shared with Baeck. Years later, after the destruction of Nazism, that friendship between Baeck and Heuss took on a significant political dimension in the efforts to rebuild relations between the Germans and the Jews.

A meeting to formally establish the new Reichsvertretung was set for September 3 in Berlin. At that session the Berlin community made another effort to control the new organization. Stahl explained that members of his board had objected to his actions supporting the new Reichsvertretung.

"I regret to say," explained Stahl, "that the decisions to which I assented reluctantly in order to achieve a practical result have run into serious and well-reasoned objections . . . it appears above all impossible to give power of attorney to an organization which has no satisfactory program"—his description of the new Reichsvertretung. He then said that the Berlin Gemeinde "has to take these matters into its own hands." Citing that community's large number of members and its financial strength, Stahl said that only it was capable of giving "the necessary authority to the presidium."

Said one participant: "They quite openly proposed as a solution that the management of affairs be handed over to the Berlin community."

Showdown day was Sunday, September 17. Stahl had called a meeting for that morning of the executive committee of the Berlin Gemeinde, which he hoped would formally back his position that the Berlin community should control the new Reichsvertretung. He said in a note to the committee members that the proposed Reichsvertretung lacked sufficient standing with both officialdom and individual Jews. To the Berlin community, "which alone includes a third of the Jewish souls in Germany," along with other large communities, he said, must fall the responsibility "to create by this time a final authoritative representative body."

Baeck called a meeting for Tuesday, September 12, with some of prominent Berlin Jews, including several with influence in the Berlin Gemeinde's executive committee. At that meeting he offered more authority for the Berlin Gemeinde in the proposed Reichsvertretung, but stopping short of control. This had to be accepted by the Gemeinde, Baeck insisted, because the German Jews needed a single organization to represent them; a Reichsvertretung controlled by a few large organizations had been tried and failed. Also, since that failure, the Zionists had become more adamant in their refusal to enter into a group dominated by the Berlin Gemeinde. This was a strategic point. Although the Zionist organizations in Germany had only a small membership prior to 1933, they had attracted more adherents after Hitler came to power and now could not be ignored. For the leaders of the Berlin Gemeinde it was take it or leave it.

They decided to take it. Following the September 12 meeting Leo Baeck wrote to Georg Hirschland in Essen: "This essential discussion led to a complete agreement; the personal close contact shows the possibility—even guaranteeing with confidence—of a fruitful working together." He suggested that Hirschland schedule an organizational meeting in Berlin the afternoon of September 17, a few hours after the meeting called by Stahl, "because then we will have the results, or at least the directions, of the meeting called by Herr Stahl."

On September 13 there was "a long confrontation" between several persons who had met with Baeck the previous day on one side and the leadership of the Berlin Gemeinde on the other. The result was clear: The Berlin Jews would go along with the new Reichsvertretung; if Stahl asked for a vote on Sunday morning to push the Gemeinde in another direction, he would lose. This message was understood. Invitations to the organizational meeting of the Reichsvertretung for Sunday afternoon were sent out. Baeck himself not only wrote the announcement of the Reichsvertretung's founding but also distributed it to the press in advance of the meeting.

The meeting went without surprise. When it ended, there was a new Reichsvertretung with Leo Baeck as its president. Baeck went home and quickly wrote a short note to Georg Hirschland in Essen. Now that the work was completed and the organization formed, Baeck said he wished to express his heartiest thanks to the *Autor und Meister*" of the plan. Within the following weeks all German Jewish organizations joined the new Reichsvertretung; it was a representative group with no one group or faction dominating it. Stahl was on the executive committee, as were people appointed by the other groups or land associations, but the committee was an independent group. However, the dispute between the Berlin Gemeinde, headed by Stahl, and the Reichsvertretung, headed by Baeck, did not end; it smouldered, to erupt at a later time.[18]

In assuming the presidency of the organization, which became officially the Reichsvertretung der deutschen Juden—the National Council of the German Jews—Leo Baeck risked a great deal personally. He became the leader of a people under attack by a powerful opponent. Although he realized much of the danger for Jews living under the Nazis—no one could anticipate the full danger—he understood that many of his fellow German Jews did not, meaning they would resist his leadership efforts. He knew, from the dispute with the Stahl group, that the organization he now headed would have its internal administrative difficulties. Also, as the individual who stood between the Nazis and his fellow Jews, he would be pushed by the Nazis if he stood too erect and by the Jews if he did not stand erect enough. In his new role there was more potential for failure than for success. There were other roles opened to him in the coming years. Why not leave Germany and become a spokesman outside of her borders against Nazism? Why not emigrate and organize help from outside? These were honorable choices, and many Jews made them. Why did Leo Baeck take on the personal risk of dealing with the Nazis?

Baeck knew as well as anyone that he was the natural choice, the only choice, to lead the Reichsvertretung. There were many other famous scholars—Martin Buber, for example. But none had the contacts, both with the Jews and with other Germans, the experience with the various groups of Jews, the prestige that Leo Baeck had. He knew it was his task. Baeck once had quoted the philosopher Spinoza that "Happiness is not the reward of virtue but virtue itself." This, Baeck said, is only another version of an ancient Jewish saying—"The reward of a duty is the duty and the punishment of sin is the sin." He connected the two phrases that way in the second edition of *The Essence of Judaism*. There was another line in that book, written more than a decade earlier, that could also be applied to his situation in 1933: "The history of thought and commandment is always the history of those who sacrifice themselves, who accept ingratitude and expulsion, who pay with their days for the souls of others. Suffering too has its messianic quality."

That is how he understood his Jewishness. It commanded him to accept the tasks placed before him despite the consequences. After the First World War he had commented to Martin Buber that Judaism could not shirk its responsibilities. And in 1933, when asked to become the president of the Reichsvertretung, he accepted because, "The life of man can and should be more than just a sequence of days, more than a fate that has come to be and is coming to be. When man chooses his life, when he makes it the task which God sets for him, the commandment that God has given him; then even amidst the flux of the immediate, his life will have its share of what is coming to be . . ." Leo Baeck's Jewishness gave him an accepting attitude about the responsibilities that come to the individual. "A life goes astray when it does not find the possibilities which are innate in it," he wrote. "A life fulfills itself when it understands and accepts that which is sent to it."[19]

Leo Baeck now began to deal with what had been sent to him.

9 RESISTANCE

On September 21, 1933—which was Rosh Hashanah, the Jewish New Year—the Reichsvertretung announced its formation, representing the Landesverbände and "all the great organizations of the German Jews." The Reichsvertretung asked Jews to forget differences among themselves and unite "with all passion for Judaism." The declared hope was that "the government will support us by not depriving us of our political rights, and we expect that the Jews in foreign countries will assist with their rich financial means as the German Jews in better times have always given readily to Jewish people outside the German borders who needed help."

As a plea for unity the declaration went far toward including the different compass points of German Judaism. There was an appeal to those "who have kept themselves away from Jewish life." Opening up the "holy ground of Palestine" for German Jews was endorsed. Emigration of those "who do not find a place to live in Germany" was encouraged. Maintaining the education of Jewish youth and adults in the "values of the German culture" was also endorsed. But at the end the declaration returned to its basic point: "It is right to make Judaism alive in us. Let us stand together and with trust in God work together for the honor of the Jewish name."

Despite that declaration there were still many differences within the Reichsvertretung. Some members wanted more emphasis upon emigration. Others believed the better course was holding on in Germany until conditions improved. Should funds for education be spent on training young Jews to become farmers (in anticipation of their emigrating) or would the money be better spent on religious education?

If emigration were the proper course, how would one make this clear to families that traced back their ancestors in Germany for hundreds of years? How could one petition the government to stop the attacks by Germans on Jews when the government itself encouraged such attacks? A friend of Baeck's from the Hochschule looked back on the work of the Reichsvertretung many years later and concluded: "It was a hopeless struggle which the National Committee had to wage under tragic conditions."[1]

Eventually the Reichsvertretung developed into an organization of more than a hundred people. It supervised all the welfare problems of the German Jews, their education, and emigration, and was their emissary in dealing with the Nazi government. It raised funds from the separate Landesverbändes and other member Jewish organizations, and received donations from Jewish organizations abroad. It also sought the help of Jews abroad in welcoming Jews into new lands. One of Baeck's first letters as president of the Reichsvertretung was to Chaim Weizmann in London: "Allow me to express myself ... how very thankful I am that you have undertaken the leadership of the Palestine work for the German Jews."

Baeck's responsibility was primarily a political one, both inside and outside of the Reichsvertretung. At the board meetings he was the one who had to resolve the conflicting opinions; outside he was the one who gave a picture of a united Jewry that was in the contradictory position of conciliating a hostile government while not surrendering anything of itself—at the same time trying to save as much of itself as it could. Baeck presided at board meetings, sitting at the head of the table with about a dozen of the directors. "Baeck would begin by saying we had a particular problem to discuss," said one participant. "He would spend about two minutes discussing the problem, and then call on the others. When the others had finished after talking, perhaps, for a couple of hours, Baeck summed up in about two minutes; everyone agreeing with his summation. Only later did they realize that his final summation was the same as his introductory remarks."

There were approximately two of those board meetings each month at the Reichsvertretung offices, Kantstrasse 158, which was about halfway between Baeck's home in Schoeneberg and the Hochschule. At these meetings Baeck addressed the directors by their titles, and he always was addressed as "Herr Doktor Baeck"; this formality reflected their German upbringing. He succeeded in these sessions because, as Joachim Prinz said of him: "He was a leader of the people without

being of the people. He never danced or laughed with the people."
Said one who worked with Baeck at this time: "Leo Baeck's success was
due to language. He was a typical German intellectual, and he spoke as
an intellectual."

In the Reichsvertretung, said a participant, "Everything had to be
considered over and over again. Leo Baeck was very careful, always
trying to gauge the reaction of the Germans." That point emerges again
and again from those associated with the Reichsvertretung: the pressure
of working in an openly hostile environment, the Gestapo constantly
looking over the shoulders of the Reichsvertretung workers. Gestapo
officials frequently attended board meetings and also demanded to know
what took place at the other sessions. The Jews were trying to save
themselves from drowning in a sea in which every wave pulled them
down.[2]

Through all of this Baeck remained calm. Adolf Leschnitzer, a Reichsvertretung worker, came into the offices one morning and asked: "Is the
cardinal here?" The nickname, although never used to Baeck's face,
stuck. He did have something about him of a prince of the church. In
his calmness he demonstrated austerity and discipline, an attitude of
being above ordinary quarrels. Leschnitzer later wrote that the "cardinal" title was only half-correct. "There was still something else to
his essence: an honored leadership, the strength, the hardness with
which he drove himself above all but sometimes showed against others,"
said Leschnitzer. He pictured Baeck, when "in a narrow circle," as
being hard in his judgments about individuals. "When he was angered
by human frailties," said Leschnitzer of Baeck, "then all diplomatic
niceties could fall from him, and he expressed his opinion frankly,
making his criticisms without restraint. He expressed his harsh judgments then mostly in polished form, showing that what he said did
not spring from the irritation of the moment—that it had been merely
released by it."

Even after Baeck took on his new position, he continued to rise
before dawn for his hour of translating Greek. When the workers at
the Reichsvertretung arrived there at about ten o'clock, he was already
there and obviously had been for some hours. He usually stayed at
the Kantstrasse office until about noon, when he went on to the Hochschule.[3]

In operating the Reichsvertretung, Baeck relied heavily upon Otto
Hirsch and Julius L. Seligsohn, whose family, said Baeck, "belonged to
the aristocracy of Jewish Berlin, an aristocracy which had already dem-

onstrated itself distinctive above all else in spirit and in participation in Jewish life." Seligsohn, a lawyer, was born in Berlin in 1890 and had fought for Germany in the First World War. He had been decorated many times, receiving among his medals the Iron Cross, First Class. He was discharged as a first lieutenant and after the war became active in Jewish organizations. He was a handsome man who, said Baeck, "had all the good characteristics of the Berliners, and especially the Jewish Berliners." Baeck defined these as "a sharp understanding, a biting wit, a sense for reality and, finally, what not many had, a sense of humor, as did Otto Hirsch." Seligsohn used these attributes effectively. "He was the mediator, who fostered the necessary connections to the representatives of the existing community apparatus and who cleared away many difficulties and also many hindrances," said Baeck.

Another prominent person in the Reichsvertretung was Cora Berliner. Until the Nazi takeover she had been a Prussian government official. Denied her civil service status, she went to work for the Reichsvertretung, where she used her statistical and analytical abilities to marshal facts and figures about the economic plight of the Jews. Cora Berliner was a beautiful woman, then in her mid-forties and perhaps at her loveliest. Unmarried, she had maintained for many years a relationship with a German Jew, a married man who had been a cabinet officer in the Prussian government before the Nazi takeover. The relationship had been a private one; no one was certain of its details other than Cora Berliner, her friend, and perhaps some of their acquaintances. Leo Baeck never indicated publicly whether he knew the details of the friendship, except once when—after the man had died—he referred to the man's "beautiful" relationship with Cora Berliner.[4]

With all the activities of the Reichsvertretung, the essence of its approach was to follow the law. There would be no activity by the Reichsvertretung officials not consistent with the law. In particular, the Reichsvertretung would do nothing to offer the Nazis the opportunity to accuse the Jews of lawlessness. This attitude was demonstrated in January 1934 when the Reichsvertretung made its most significant formal effort to obtain legal treatment of the German Jews from the Nazi government.

A lengthy memorandum signed by Baeck was sent by the Reichsvertretung to every member of the German cabinet. It was a detailed, documented account of the abuses against Jews during the previous year. "Allow us to present you a memorandum," said a covering note to each minister. "We are always at your disposal for a meeting." The memorandum began: "While the entire German people is called on by the government to the cause of the renovation of the fatherland, there is a psychological and actual threat to the German Jews who are rooted in Germany and its culture." Intentional in that sentence is the tone that the German Jews were being blocked from contributing to the strengthening of Germany because of attacks against them; the Jews were not yet willing to publicly divorce themselves from the land of their birth. "To speak out," said the memorandum, "becomes a duty ... if our religious communities are about to break down, if measures taken against the German Jews work not only against the Jews but also against the well-being of Germany." With all the political strife in the Reichsvertretung, with all the personal and political differences between its leaders, they all were reasonable men who believed in the reasoned way as the proper way. If they took that approach, they anticipated—hoped, at least—they would find a reasoned response.

The first part of the memorandum dealt with the legal restrictions enacted in the previous year excluding Jews "basically from the practice of law and offices in federal government, state and community, and other public legal bodies ... [and] the part of the Jews in all academic professions was essentially restricted or even eliminated." If these restrictions were carried over to other spheres in which the Jews earned their livelihood, the Reichsvertretung memorandum said, this "would not only take away the possibility of existence for the German Jews, also it would take away benefits from the German economy." Trade connections would be harmed as well as individual employer-employee relations. "Misery, not only poverty, must be the result of these interferences in the economy," said the memorandum, asserting, "This development has already started. The tax potential of the German Jews is dwindling. The Jewish communities are not able to handle their religious, social, or cultural tasks which come to them today even more than before." Then the Reichsvertretung called for an end to the economic restrictions against the Jews.

The second part of the memorandum dealt with Jews who were unemployed because of legislation barring them from certain jobs or because they were young and—prohibited from attending German schools—could neither find nor be trained for work. The Reichsvertretung said: "We are conscious of the fact that the job levels among the German Jews overwhelmingly within the academic professions and in the large cities were unhealthy." The Jews, Baeck among them, with that sentence accepted a piece of Nazi propaganda, even though they added that the "unhealthy" result was "an historical development." Again, however, the intention was to travel a reasoned way. "The desire of the Jewish youths for physical work of every kind is there," said the Reichsvertretung, but the youths could not find jobs outside the city. They could not upset that "unhealthy" balance unless they were welcomed into the craft and agricultural jobs—which they were blocked from entering by the Nazis. The Reichsvertretung then asked that no job be closed to a person because of his religion and that Jews have the opportunity for vocational training and job experience in crafts, agriculture, and forestry.

In the third part, the Reichsvertretung said that even if the restrictions are lifted, as requested in the first two sections, many Jews still would have to emigrate. This was an obvious appeal to those Nazi officials who believed that emigration was a proper solution to the "Jewish problem" in Germany. Statistics were placed at this point in the memorandum to ridicule the charge that Germany had been dominated by Jews and that the domination was growing. These statistics showed that the Jews in Germany never had represented a significantly large part of the population and that this percentage had been steadily decreasing.

In Prussia, in the year 1816, 1.2 percent of the population was Jewish; in 1925, only 1.06 percent. In Bavaria, in 1818, the percentage was 1.45 percent; in 1925, the figure was 0.66 percent. Even in the large cities the trend was similar. In 1895, 5.14 percent of Berlin's population was Jewish; in 1925, the figure was 4.29 percent. In 1866 in Hamburg, Jews represented 4.4 percent of the population; in 1925, only 1.73 percent. Since then the number of Jews has decreased further.

The Reichsvertretung then asked that the Nazi government help in the training of Jews and in their migration.

"Even harder than all the economic deprivation," said the Reichsvertretung in its final point, "is the psychological pressure." To be described as worthless was something "no community can accept if it wants to maintain its honor and decency." The Jews said they objected to discussing the point because of pride and because of concern for their children. But there was a deep pain, they said, more so because it was "not something occasional in the eagerness of an election campaign, but . . . it is premeditated and repeated." They pointed out that the harassment of the Jews by the Nazi government had a political result: "Jews live in the countries with which Germany is struggling for world respect. They personally feel defamed as they read in German newspapers that members of their people and belief are being defamed." The argument concluded with the request that "In the future every defamation of the Jewish community and faith be terminated."

The document, appearing four months after the organization of the Reichsvertretung, was an attempt to appeal to the Nazis on the basis of restraint, law, and reasonableness. By how many officials and at what rank in the German government it was read is not known. There was, however, little interest in it. Most officials who saw it commented, as did an underling in the foreign affairs ministry: "It presents a detailed, short statement—four pages, worth reading—about the discriminatory measures against the Jews in Germany . . . The ideas are reasonable." The official added: "An answer is hardly necessary."[5]

Again and again the Jews, calling on the German government for legal and civil rights, were rebuffed. They were caught in a trap: Trained to believe in law and reason, they were surrounded by those who perverted law and laughed at reason. Only a few months after that memorandum, in May 1934, Joseph Goebbels, head of the propaganda ministry, charged in a speech that German Jews were responsible for an economic boycott against Germany by foreign nations. In the name of the Reichsvertretung, Baeck and Hirsch protested. If that protest meant nothing to the Nazis, it meant something to the Jews as Baeck and Hirsch spoke with pride. "We, as the representatives of the German Jews, cannot keep silent in the face of that charge," they said. Rather than promoting the boycott, the Jews had been encouraging trade between Germany and other nations. "How little is this recognized in Germany itself. How much—despite explanations of important officials from the business field—the Jews are rejected, excluded and, what is worse, are treated with contempt in all areas of Germany."[6]

At this time there was a sporadic boycott against German goods organized by some militant Jewish and non-Jewish groups outside of Germany. It was not supported by the leading Jewish organizations and was not encouraged by Jews in Germany, and was not very effective. Even if it had been, however, it would have made no difference to the Nazis. In a choice between harassment of Jews on one side and growth and economic stability on the other, the Nazis generally preferred harassment of Jews, a choice that some German government officials— including Hjalmar Schacht, president of the Reichsbank—constantly complained about.[7]

For the Jews in Germany there was a new reality. The Nazis must be resisted; education was the Jews' first weapon.

"It was becoming clear," said Leo Baeck of the 1933–34 events, "that the Jewish schoolchildren had to be removed from the public schools and that Jewish schools had to be provided for them." Not only was there the problem of an increasing number of restrictions on the Jews in public schools, there also was the developing anti-Semitism on the part of Gentile students and teachers. It was a particularly difficult situation for the young Jewish children, who did not have either the perspective to understand that abuse was part of their history or the education, secular and religious, to give them at least a psychological protection against anti-Semitism. In developing what was in effect a new educational system, there were two problems: finding the funds needed to construct the physical plant and to operate the program, and locating adequate teachers among the German Jews.

For all peoples education is a joy and a source of strength, but this is particularly true of the Jews. Traditionally the Jewish youth begins his formal education when he learns to read the Torah—a drop of honey is placed on the page where he begins as a symbol of the sweetness of the process that now opens before him. His religion then commands him not only to read the Torah but to constantly reread it and study it, always learning from it. Education in Judaism is a central point; for the Jews this reverence for education carries over to the secular side of their lives. If education were denied to young Jews, they would lose an important strength. As Martin Buber expressed it, "What was at stake in the work performed under such great difficulties was to oppose Hitler's wish to wear down Jewry; to give the Jews, and especially the young people, an unshakable support."

Any education program for German Jews, by necessity, had to include Martin Buber. A contemporary of Baeck's (he was born in 1878, five years after Baeck), Buber had taught Judaism and comparative religion at the University of Frankfurt for a decade prior to 1933, when he and other Jews were ordered dismissed from their university posts by the Nazis. For three decades he had written about Judaism, delving into Hasidism and espousing Zionism. He considered himself German. "I was brought up on German culture and literature. If I have a mother tongue, it is certainly German, although I speak several other languages. Yes, I am very German in many ways," he once told a friend. In Frankfurt am Main in the early 1920s he had organized with Franz Rosenzweig, the Freies Jüdisches Lehrhaus, which brought together prominent Jews for lectures and discussions. Leo Baeck was a frequent participant. It was this Lehrhaus, Buber's writings, and his professional reputation that made him the focal point of Jewish education under the Nazis.[8]

Leo Baeck and Martin Buber had known each other for many years. It was a relationship of mutual respect, if one marked occasionally by the usual difficulties created when two strong personalities meet. A student of Baeck's, Max Vogelstein, recalled being invited to have Sabbath dinner with Baeck and his family one Friday evening. When he arrived, the student found the only other guest was Martin Buber. Any fear Vogelstein might have had at not being able to converse adequately with two such leaders of German Jewry's intellectual world was quickly dispelled. When together, Baeck and Buber did not speak to others, nor did they speak to each other. Vogelstein reported that he sat and listened "to those two people holding monologues with each other" through most of the evening. Finally, Vogelstein interrupted and spoke briefly of himself, to be able to report he had participated in a conversation with Baeck and Buber. "The art of dialogue was not known that evening," he said.

Even with his own reputation at the time, Buber considered Leo Baeck the more esteemed. A mutual friend recalled being with Buber when he received an invitation to dine with Baeck. "Buber became very excited, as if he were an Englishman invited to dine with the queen," recalled the acquaintance. This friend also recalled Baeck not always returning that respect for Buber, accusing him of responding to popular fashion in his teaching. *"Was lehrt er jetzt?"*—"What is he teaching now?"—was Baeck's derogatory comment.

Except for those occasional private comments, Leo Baeck got along well with Buber, and there were frequent and friendly communications. In 1932 when Buber sent Baeck a copy of one of his books, Baeck replied: "For two weeks I have been with you now in each free hour and every hour has been a good one. I am a slow reader who reads many things twice, and so I am now in the first chapter which especially holds me."

Ernst Simon, who knew and worked with both men, reflected on the differences between them. Both "belonged among the outstanding and courageous leaders of German Jewry in its most critical hour," but Baeck "was forced to take responsibility for the organized Jewish community at the end of German-Jewish history, and thus faced the necessity imposed on men of action to make unavoidable compromises." Buber without that responsibility was free to teach "the meaning of spiritual resistance against identification with the aggressor ... he was and remained our teacher, not a leader of men."[9]

Very early in the Nazi regime Buber stressed the need for the revival of Jewish education; on May 21, 1933, he spoke in the large hall
of the First Elementary Boys' School of the Berlin Jewish Community,
the so-called Schule Kaiserstrasse. He began by stating that the period
before the First World War had been characterized by stability, but that
the current period was marked by the opposite, and the German Jews
were the passive objects of events. Then, turning to education, he said
that eras have accepted educational prototypes. In the Middle Ages it
was the ideal of the perfect Christian. In the nineteenth century the
image was less precise, the person of general knowledge. Currently, he
told his audience—and this was less than three months after the Nazis
had come to power—the image was of *"der völkische Mensch,"* the
extreme nationalistic type.

How could stability be achieved? With "the essential Jewish reality,"
he answered. This referred to the singularity of Israel's individuality,
which was expressed by its history in three ways: one, a history of the
obscure and the suffering; two, a history conceived as a dialogue between the deity and mankind; and, three, a history representing a reality
of faith imbuing the present with a feeling of eternity. Then he called
for an "essentially Jewish school" permeated with that spirit and in-
culcating that spirit within its students. In this school, he said, the
teaching of Judaism would not be limited to hours marked "religious
instruction." Rather, Judaism would be used to shed light on a variety
of subjects. A Jewish school, he insisted, must be more than a school
that merely replaces Christian religious instruction with Jewish religious instruction.

At the end of his talk he told his German-Jewish audience that the
hope of a permanent Jewish home in Germany was "an illusion." This
was similar to Baeck's remark made at the same time that the thousand-
year history of the Jews in Germany was at an end, and was just as
widely disbelieved. Buber continued to speak bluntly to German Jews.
"Let no one ask for which country we wish to educate people," he said.
"For Palestine if it may be so; for any foreign country if it must be so.
For Germany if it can be so."[10]

Buber saw the immediate task as educating the people who would
teach Jewish youth. This was in the early summer of 1933, when
the old Reichsvertretung was still in existence, with Leo Baeck at its
head. On June 13 there was a meeting in Berlin to discuss turning over
the responsibility for training the new teachers to an administrator who
would report to an advisory committee. At the meeting Baeck advocated

Buber's appointment as administrator. "He spoke very clearly for your getting the position," a friend reported to Buber, "saying you were the only person appropriate." The friend added: "Baeck very seldom does that, backs a person as being the only individual appropriate for a position." The friend, however, reported that no specific decision had been reached. "In spite of bowing before you"—*"Bücklinge vor Ihrer Persönlichkeit"*—"the liberals were doubting whether you would get the position . . . the orthodox said the same thing because they are afraid for their autonomy; they hope to protect themselves by having an administrator who is neutral."

On June 21 Baeck wrote to Buber that the administrator's position had been created, implying that Buber would be offered the position. He conceded there had been some sharp criticism of Buber but said it was without effect. "One should allow the crows to crow," Baeck wrote. "This time, I believe, no one has listened to them." Buber responded twice to that letter. First he wrote a formal letter to Baeck as president of the Reichsvertretung; then he wrote a personal note. In both he opposed a school run by an advisory committee, saying, "We don't have time at this period, and because we cannot wait for developments instead of acting. The presumptions under which we have to work are so difficult that we must, at the very beginning, establish it completely and properly . . ." Buber understood that the decision to have an advisory committee run the teachers' academy was a political one, to appease the various groups in the Reichsvertretung. However, he considered the decision a mistake. Baeck "has obviously handled the whole matter tactfully," he said to a friend, "but on this occasion tactfulness was not the right approach."

The proposal for a teachers' academy remained in somewhat haphazard form until December 1933, when Leo Baeck, as president of the new Reichsvertretung, wrote to Buber asking him to work without an advisory committee in developing a teachers' academy. Baeck was able to offer a budget of 40,000 marks for the first year and six rooms provided without charge by the Mannheim Jewish community, which also would handle administrative matters.

Buber spent almost three months attempting to establish the school before confessing failure to Baeck, explaining there were not enough people able or willing to travel to Mannheim for the program. As an alternative, he suggested establishing a resource center in Frankfurt, which would provide information by mail and would offer courses in the vacation periods, beginning in April. This program was worked out, and dozens of teachers received both educational training as well as instruction in Judaism under Buber's tutelage until 1938, when he went to Palestine.[11]

The program was important because teachers in Jewish schools prior to the coming of Nazism had varied in quality. In some small towns the teachers often officiated at religious services; they knew the communities, fitted into them well, and had personal relationships with students and their families. These teachers came primarily from the Orthodox end of the Jewish spectrum. Another kind of teacher, located in the larger communities, taught with a politicial purpose. It may have been to bring the east European Jew more into the mainstream of the assimilated society in Germany or to indoctrinate the youth into Zionism. Also, a limited number of German Jews were teaching in the secular elementary and secondary schools. Although these had the best formal education, usually university degrees, there was no measurement of their knowledge of Judaism.

Who was trained at Buber's center and at the other training sites that developed in the years after 1933? The first group consisted of those Jews who either had been teaching in the secular schools or preparing to teach but found themselves without jobs by the 1933 law that denied Jews civil service status. Then there were the leaders of the various Jewish youth movements. The problem with this disparate group was persuading them to overcome their political biases—each youth movement was tied to a particular political group within the Jewish circle— and to train them to become Jewish teachers rather than advocates of Zionism or anti-Zionism or of Liberal or Orthodox Judaism. The third group, a large one, included those people within the Jewish community —rabbis and others with previous experience teaching Judaism—who had been trained for a different need. A person who had been a marvelous Hebrew teacher while preparing a youth for the Bar Mitzvah ceremony might be less effective in teaching English. Jewish women who previously had stayed home now took training to assist at the growing number of schools. As the schools grew, more of these teachers were needed, and training became more important. Much of the money for this training was funneled to the Reichsvertretung from the American Joint Distribution Committee, and part of its report for 1937 gives some indication of the breadth of this work: "In order to overcome the shortage of Hebrew teachers for the instruction of adults, a second course for the training of such instructors was opened on June 15th. The course lasts half a year. The second course for the training of gymnastics and sports teachers was completed this year. All participants passed the state examination for sports and gymnastics teachers. A third course was opened with official permission on May 3rd." An army of teachers was recruited and trained in the five years between 1933 and 1938.

The reaction of Jewish parents varied at first. Most Zionists saw their worst fears realized with the coming of Hitler to power and immediately withdrew their children from secular schools and placed them in Jewish schools. They did this not only because of the Nazi laws restricting the number of Jewish students in the secular schools, they explained, but also to save their children from the constant harassment by anti-Semitic students and teachers. Other parents reflected another attitude prevalent among German Jews: Nazism is a passing thing, and Jews should not jeopardize their status in Germany, certain to be regained after Hitler's passing. Unfortunately, that attitude often resulted in the Jewish child's loss of self-respect as well as the child's experiencing severe emotional disturbances, if not physical abuse. As the dangers became more obvious, this second group diminished, and the pressures on the Reichsvertretung to establish even more schools increased.[12]

During the period from 1933 to the end of 1938 there also was a change in emphasis. At first Hebrew was the primary foreign language taught in the Jewish schools, with French second. This reflected the thought that Jews would remain in Germany, that Hebrew was the language of their religion and French the language of the cultured European gentleman. By 1936, however, a shift was noticeable. A new edition of the guide issued by the education department of the Reichsvertretung omitted references to a continuation of the German-Jewish life, replacing them with calls for the learning of a foreign language useful for emigration. English was considered important; the United States and England were the nations most desired as new homelands by Jews emigrating from Germany. Palestine also was a goal for the emigrants, and English was widely used there. This shift reflected Leo Baeck's steadfast conviction—despite the skepticism of his fellow Jews —that the Jews had no future in Germany. "The only thing to do," he told a visitor in August 1934, referring to the young German Jews, "is to get them out."[13]

Another factor reflecting the shift toward emigration was the vocational training offered in schools administered by the Reichsvertretung. With the universities shutting their doors to Jewish students and with many foreign nations being more receptive to emigrants with skills than to scholars, the need for vocational training became urgent. The German workers' associations, however, were not cooperative; they refused to assist in the training of young Jews, even when offered assurances that the youths would emigrate and not compete for jobs in Germany. As a result almost all vocational training of Jewish youth was done under the aegis of the Reichsvertretung, which generally paid two thirds of the costs while the community from which the youths came paid the other third. The training period lasted from several months to two years, depending upon the trade. Primarily the instruction dealt with the land—agriculture, forestry, irrigation, and the metal trades. A 1937 report by the Joint Distribution Committee described the scope of some of this training:

This year the metal workshop of the Jewish community in Berlin was opened. The Reichsvertretung participated in half of the costs, receiving in return the right to designate half of the pupils. Mostly young people from small communities have been sent to this workshop.

Early in May the artisan school of the Ort Society was opened with courses in woodwork, metals and installation. The Reichsvertretung did not participate in the courses, but has nevertheless designated a large number of pupils from all over the country, for whom it pays the tuition and maintenance fees, in so far as the pupils and their families are unable to do this. The Reichsvertretung has opened a home at Rosenthalerstra. 41, Berlin, for young people from out of town who attend training centres in Berlin. This home has room for 50 persons, who live there and are boarded and supervised. Two leaders of the youth movement take care of their spiritual development.

A course for welders, with 40 participants, was likewise opened this year. This course is the first that has opened in a long time for older men, who are usually over 35 years of age and married . . .

One observer commented that the training in these schools "was generally of a high standard, thanks to the cooperation of highly qualified Jewish and some non-Jewish experts and specialists."

A number of agricultural communities were established. The average number of young people in these training areas was about 3,000 at one time. "During the difficult time before their emigration," said an account of this work, "these centres also helped the young people psychologically by an intensive cultural and community life." One of these agricultural communities, at Halbe, was organized by Frederick Perlstein, the family friend who had remained in Germany for this purpose at the specific request of Leo Baeck. Perlstein had worked at several agricultural communities, helping them to get started, before beginning the one at Halbe in 1935 with eighty young men and women. The site, about an hour by train from Berlin, was frequently visited by Baeck. Although a city person, he enjoyed these forays into the country, watching Jewish youths doing such traditional farm chores as pitching hay and feeding animals. On occasion Baeck would judge challah baking contests.[14]

The academic education of the children continued, too, along with this vocational and agricultural education. According to the 1937 report by the American Joint Distribution Committee, there were 148 Jewish elementary schools in Germany, fourteen "higher" schools, and five intermediate schools. "The number of Jewish pupils in Germany may be placed at approximately 39,000," said the committee. "Of this number, 23,670, 61.27 percent, attend Jewish schools." The joint committee provided the funds to the Reichsvertretung, which also assessed its various member organizations for financial support and then distributed funds to these schools according to their needs. There was no conscious effort by the Reichsvertretung to favor a Zionist-oriented school over a non-Zionist one or a Liberal school over an Orthodox one. This was a result of the understanding by Baeck and the others at the time of the Reichsvertretung's founding that it must represent the broad spectrum of German Jewry, not just specific groups.

The accomplishment of the Reichsvertretung in developing a school system for the Jewish youth within five years was, by any measurement, significant. Still, it was not adequate; nothing could be. By 1937 even the most ardent assimilationist was willing to concede that a secular school run by the German state was no place for a Jewish child; a refuge was needed. "The streets had become," recalled a Jewish teacher in Berlin, "to an ever greater degree, no more than an unavoidable thoroughfare from which the Jewish children sought to escape as quickly as possible." There were no public playgrounds where Jewish children would be free from abuse. "As time went on, public parks, public baths, and even public benches were 'Prohibited to Jews.' And so the school had to fill this gap too," said the teacher. The Jewish youth then spent their free time in the yard of the Jewish schools. In the afternoons volunteers organized games, taught crafts, and began teaching languages —especially English—for the time the students would emigrate.

"But even the walled-in schoolyards between the school building and the synagogue were no longer safe," continued this report. Stones frequently were thrown over the wall where young children were playing.

When the culprits could be identified, police refused to interfere. Stores at which Jewish children purchased their pencils and papers were covered with anti-Semitic pictures. When the students went out, they frequently were attacked by members of the Hitler Youth. On one occasion a Danish teacher, a non-Jew, complained to the authorities about those Hitler Youth activities. "A few days following this incident," said the report, "his Danish passport was confiscated. When he contacted the Danish Consulate he was told that, of course, there was no question about his legal rights, and that these could be asserted; but that he had better leave the country immediately if he wanted to save his life." The Danish teacher left.

There were exceptions to this hostile environment in the secular schools. Leo Baeck's granddaughter, Marianne, attended a secular school until late 1938 and had little difficulty. And there were other similar examples. "In the early phase of the Nazi regime," according to a Jewish teacher's report, "there were still some state schools where conditions had not yet become unbearable for Jewish children. Much depended on the attitude of the heads of the schools, and even more on the influence of the individual teachers. Among them also could be found the just, the heroic, and the martyrs." But the number of "heroes" in the schools dwindled as it became increasingly difficult for the individual to stand against the crowd. Those who did so usually found themselves dismissed.[15]

Another aspect of Jewish education in Nazi Germany that continued important was the Hochschule. This academy for training rabbis had always been a significant part of Leo Baeck's life, from his student days to his years as a rabbi. Here he indoctrinated a generation of rabbis with his lectures and his personal example of how a rabbi should conduct himself and how an intellectual mind should approach history. During the Nazi period he continued as a teacher there. Rabbis always were needed.

The pressures on the Hochschule increased in the 1930s. Previously the students attended both the University of Berlin and the Hochschule, receiving their secular training and a degree from the first and their rabbinical authority from the second. Beginning in April 1937, however, the Nazi government prohibited the secular universities from granting degrees to Jews; in actuality, even before that date many Jews attending these universities had been forced to leave. For these students the Hochschule widened its program to offer the regular doctoral and rabbinical training. The Hochschule had been offering courses in Hebrew, the Bible, the Talmud, homiletics, Midrash (these last two continued to be Baeck's courses), and Jewish History and Literature—a program built around rabbinical training. By the 1935–1936 school year the courses included world history, philosophy, Latin and Greek, as well as psychology.

Although teachers had better-than-average chances to emigrate and the Hochschule faculty changed frequently, the quality of the Hochschule instructors remained high. Jews who no longer were allowed to teach at the state universities moved to the Hochschule. The faculty roster there at times included names such as Arnold Metzger, Hans Friedländer, Fritz Kaufman, Arnold Bernay, Hans Liebeschütz, and others who were well known in the academic field. Martin Buber frequently gave guest lectures. For overall excellence the Hochschule probably rated higher than any other educational institution at the time in Germany. "We had a university-Ersatz," said one faculty member.

This transformation of the Hochschule into a general university attracted a number of students. Not only was it a desirable place for those interested in Jewish history, culture, and religion, but other Jews interested in attaining a broad cultural education, despite the Nazi restrictions, realized that it was the only place for them. In the summer term of 1936 there were sixty-nine regular and thirty-six "external" students (those attending for general purposes rather than to become rabbis or Jewish teachers). By the next summer those figures had jumped to fifty-eight and eighty-three; this trend toward having more external than regular students continued until the Hochschule's closing. The quality of these students was high. A faculty report at the time said: "The number of inefficient students is infinitesimal. The majority of our students are gifted and industrious. The few untalented but industrious students cannot be called inefficient." (The students at the Hochschule were not unique among the Jews at the time. Despite the difficult living conditions in Nazi Germany, Jews continued to respect their educational opportunities and to use them well. A survey by the Reichsvertretung at the time showed that of 122 Jewish graduates of institutions of higher education, nine had passed their examinations with honors, fifty-six with a rating of good, and fifty-seven with a rating of fair.)

Although the Hochschule building had thick walls, the sounds of the outside world could not be eliminated. "Our Talmud discussions were often conducted to the accompaniment of the knocking sound of endless Nazi columns goose-stepping with clocklike precision," said a teacher. Before each class students and faculty congregated in the halls to discuss the government's latest anti-Semitic measure and to speculate on the future of the German Jews. Occasionally a Nazi official entered the building, usually in connection with the Monday lecture series given by the faculty members. Alexander Guttmann recalled giving his first Monday lecture as a young Hochschule faculty member. He was frightened when a man in civilian clothes suddenly stood up, announced he was a Gestapo official, and demanded to see Guttmann's identification papers. At another of those lectures a building attendant stopped a man who was smoking a cigar from entering the lecture hall; smoking was not permitted in the hall, the attendant explained. Some faculty members gasped, recognizing the smoker as a Gestapo official. But the Nazi dutifully put out his cigar before entering the hall.

Still, for the students the Hochschule was a refuge. "We were a small community in the midst of a hostile world which in every respect was entirely different from us," wrote one student. "Whatever our personal view on particular questions might have been, we belonged together, and were linked by bonds of affinity and mutual affection." The Hochschule was an island. The Nazis were content at this time to separate Jewish culture from the German and did not pay much attention to the inner workings of Jewish institutions except in a pro forma way, so that students found relief at the Hochschule from the tensions and ugliness outside. "For the following generations," a student conceded, "who are aware of the horrors which came later, this may hardly appear intelligible. Many of us were aware that we were surrounded by grave dangers. The whole work was based on infringements of Nazi laws and the discovery of this might have brought about a catastrophe for our institution and for ourselves. Still, we felt sheltered in our hearts . . . remote from the world of tyranny and barbarism." The student acknowledged, "This happiness in the face of dangers was irrational and, scrutinized by the intellect, almost absurd. Still, it was a reality for which we felt grateful and which we shall never forget."

One of the students reminisced about Leo Baeck's Friday morning lectures.

His remarks on the weekly Torah portions, his elucidations, interpretations, observations were always inspiring; what he said on Friday morning in a class was so often helpful for sermons scheduled for that evening or the next morning. When he lectured one could forget the world outside the classroom, the world of calumny and inspired hatred which slowly moved toward unspeakable actions of brutality and crime.

The student recalled that in one of Baeck's lectures,

he utilized a biblical text for an exposition of a sermon on democracy. He described the development of the democratic principle from the Greek city-state to the Swiss canton, to the democratic system under the British crown and the democratic ideal of the United States and the students forgot for that hour that they were living in a country whose leaders despised and hated that very ideal and were determined to destroy it wherever it was found as a way of life.

Another student at this time described Baeck's presence at the Hochschule as "a tremendous boost to our morale" because of his reputation. "Although he had the weight of German Jewry on his shoulders, I don't remember his ever missing a class."

Were these young Jews fiddling inside the building at Artilleriestrasse 14 while their world burned outside its doors? Two points can be made. First, they could not know there would be such a total conflagration of their world. Second, preservation of the religion was deemed important, and education was the means to preserve it. "Prior to 1933," recalled a student many years later, "being a rabbi was considered a lazy, safe, soft job. But after 1933 there was a growing belief in the need to re-vitalize the religion, and there was a different attitude in the Hochschule. The only response to the Nazis, according to this interpretation, was a renewal of Judaism."[16]

The Nazis changed the Hochschule's name again to Lehranstalt. The institution, which had opened sixty years earlier as a Hochschule, had been downgraded to the status of a Lehranstalt a decade later. In 1920, in the glow of the Weimar Republic's liberalism, it was again elevated to Hochschule status. In 1934, however, the Nazis insisted on its name being changed once more to Lehranstalt. In his opening address to the students in the first semester after the name change Leo Baeck said that university status, the Hochschule, had developed an "ominous ring" because of the way the Nazis had taken over all universities. He told the students: "Formerly we were a Hochschule; now we are a Lehranstalt, again! Gentlemen, the time will come when we shall be proud of having remained a theological college . . ." Although decades later the words seem almost bland, as a student who heard Baeck that day said, "in a dangerous and dramatic hour . . . those present will never forget the deep impression made by his words."[17]

Baeck was constantly aware of the pressures on his students. "Our students live in the *Gästementalität*—some will not be here tomorrow and none knows whether he or she will be here the next semester. In the

former days, during the semester one could use as a theme that the conclusion will follow, but not today . . ."

There were pressures on him, too. Most meetings of the Reichsvertretung were attended by Gestapo officials, and at these meetings funds
were allocated for the Hochschule—16,800 marks in 1937, for example.
That was acceptable to the Gestapo, but using the funds at the Hochschule to replace the university education denied the Jews, however, was
not. There was not much concern over the possibility of the Gestapo
inquiring into what was going on, but there had to be restraint involved
as far as publicly revealing the activities inside the building. The reports
to the Gestapo, for example, defined the work at the Hochschule as
being in two areas—lectures about Judaism and lectures of a "general
scholarly nature." Once the Gestapo inquired about this second category.
There was immediate fear that the inquiry presaged an attempt by the
Gestapo to close down the school. "We answered that its object was the
training of rabbis and of teachers of the Jewish religion," said one of
those involved. There was no follow-up.

At a meeting of the Reichsvertretung council a more serious confrontation occurred when a member stood up and denounced using funds
at the Hochschule to replace the educational opportunities lost because
Jewish attendance at universities was restricted; the funds, so this argument went, should have been used solely to train young Jews in trades
and agriculture, talents they would need for emigration. The argument
was a familiar one to the Jewish leaders. What made it unique this day
was that the two Gestapo officials looking bored in the corner of the
meeting room had heard it. Baeck immediately adjourned the session for
lunch. During the break the talkative official was reminded that he had
revealed much of the Reichsvertretung's activities before the enemy. "He
was shocked; he had overlooked [the Gestapo's] presence, and he
promised not to return to the subject," said one man present. After the
lunch break the meeting went on to other items, and the morning's
argument was not brought up again. The Gestapo officials did not make
any fuss. Apparently, and fortunately, they had been so bored in the
morning that they had not paid any attention to the discussion. "We had
passed through a rather trying hour," said one official.

By the late 1930s the Hochschule was the last of the rabbinical seminaries in Germany the Nazis allowed to remain open. Former students
of the Orthodox rabbinical seminary, with their own school closed,
began attending the Hochschule. This meant that the Nazis inadver-

tently had accomplished something the German Jews had been unable to accomplish on their own, a working relationship between the Orthodox and Liberal Jews. "This would have been inconceivable before," said Ernst Simon.

The Hochschule's last report appeared in 1938. "We must acknowledge the possibility that this is the last annual report . . ." it said. "The workers of the 'Lehranstalt' have had considerable difficulties to overcome in the past year. But it has been possible to enable lecturers and students to continue their work without interruption." Said Ernst Simon years later: "One can hardly imagine today how much worry, suffering and hardship lie behind those simple words, formulated with so much reserve and objectivity."[18]

In addition to educating their own, Jews have had a tradition of caring for their own who are in need. This was a responsibility German Jews had assumed prior to 1933, and one they continued under the Nazis. In Berlin the Jewish community agency handling the welfare work had been the Zentralwohlfahrtsstelle. In the 1920s it used funds from the German government and from American Jews to help those Jews hurt by the inflation that had struck Germany. Within its framework there were social and youth welfare departments, employment and vocational training sections. There was assistance to the aged, to the sick, to people in trouble with the law. There were day-care centers for children and recreation activities. The Zentralwohlfahrtsstelle also was an umbrella organization for a number of older Jewish welfare agencies. The oldest, founded in 1716, was the Brides Endowment Association. There were other associations to assist out-of-work members of trades, to finance the burial of indigent Jews, and to assist the families of deceased persons. There were also a dozen establishments throughout Berlin providing free meals for the indigent.

With the coming of Hitler a new organization was established— Zentralstelle für jüdische Wirtschaftshilfe—to meet the new responsibilities. "The welfare organizations were at once able to cope with these new tasks as they had at their disposal the machinery developed during the pre-Hitler period," said a study of these activities. In addition many accomplished administrators from the German bureaucracy were available to work for the Jewish welfare agencies once they had been excluded from the civil service because they were Jewish. The Zentralstelle ultimately assumed all relief and welfare responsibilities except those involving emigration. Much of its money came from foreign Jews. In

1934 it became part of the Reichsvertretung and centralized all fund-raising and disbursements.

Until the winter of 1935 the Jews in Germany joined other German citizens in a program known as the German Winter Relief, a nationwide charity into which all taxpayers and business concerns were assessed according to their incomes. The money went to provide necessities—food, clothing, fuel—to the needy in the winter months. Generally, Jews received assistance from the fund equal to what they had given to it. In the fall of 1935, however, Giora Lotan, who operated the welfare section of the Reichsvertretung, was called to the office of the German Winter Relief and informed that Jews could no longer participate in the relief program with other Germans. There would be no objection, however, if the Reichsvertretung operated its own program. The significant question then became whether the Jewish owners of large companies should contribute to the German or to the Jewish Winter Relief Fund. The director of the German fund argued that the contributions from Jewish firms should go to his group because the earnings were created by Christian employees. Lotan apparently won the contributions for the Jewish fund when he replied that such a rationale sounded Marxist.

Annual collections totaled four million reichsmarks. About 15 percent went to the central welfare office to assist small communities while the remainder was spent locally. A chief source of funds for the German fund had been the *Eintopfspende*—the one-pot donation. The theory was that one Sunday a month a family ate a frugal meal, something that could be cooked in one pot, and donated the money saved to the Winter Relief Fund. The Jewish fund continued this approach and tied it to the idea of a registration of the Jewish people. Modeled loosely after Exodus 30:11–16, beginning: "When you number the Israelites for the purpose of registration, each man shall give a ransom for his life to the Lord," this "registration" took place on February 27, 1938.

This kind of penchant for detail produced interesting statistics about the Jewish economic situation in Germany. Giora Lotan reported that in the winter of 1936–1937 one in five Jews—82,818—received assistance. In the Saar region the percentage was almost 40 percent; in Berlin it was 20 percent. The average family size was 2.17 persons; 40 percent of the welfare recipients were single, and one in three was between the ages of forty-five and sixty-five.

The Jewish Winter Relief Fund was caught in the same squeeze that struck all Jewish welfare work. There was demand for greater assistance, but the Jews in Germany had less money available as the Nazi economic restrictions upon them tightened. The American Joint Distribution Committee said that the figure of 82,000 receiving assistance in 1936–1937 was slightly below the previous year's number, but

the proportion of the Jewish population requiring the assistance of the Winter Relief increased, since there was a considerable decrease in the population due to emigration and excess of deaths. . . . The special conditions existing in the needy districts were expressed by the fact that the number of these districts increased and the grants from the equalization fund or through the system of equable distribution had to be given in a large measure.

For needy Jews a total of 3,630,353 reichsmarks was spent that winter, the committee reported.

The Joint Distribution Committee was concerned by what it termed "the disproportion between the possibilities of giving help and the requirement of the work." No longer was it possible, said the committee, to satisfy all requests for assistance. The welfare office at the Reichsvertretung in 1937 had received requests for increased assistance from all districts in Germany, but funds were such that all those requests had to be denied. Nor was there much possibility, said the committee, that the situation was going to improve. With "half of the needy people over forty-five years of age, the prospects for the future are indeed dark. At the same time the economic situation in the small communities is growing steadily worse."

The problem of the aged was severe—the demand for places in homes for the elderly was increasing, while the number of such places contracted. The problem of the children was even more serious. For the first six months of 1937, the Joint Distribution Committee reported that although the budget for the care of dependent children was exceeded by almost 50 percent, "applications were refused with a severity that was pitiful. There were a number of cases of children who could not be placed properly because the necessary few marks were not available . . ."[19]

In that same period, the first six months of 1937, the Reichsvertretung spent almost two million reichsmarks, of which about one-third came from within Germany and two-thirds came from abroad, primarily the American Joint Distribution Committee. The largest expenditure, more than 600,000 reichsmarks, went for "Economic aid, including training, retraining, credit aid" to help Jewish businesses survive and, more important, to train Jews for the careers that would help them emigrate. The second largest expenditure, almost 350,000 reichsmarks, went for emigration and repatriation. Schools ranked third in expenditures. Next were youth activities, and then relief. By this time there was no question that the emphasis had been placed on emigration and preparing people for new careers abroad, although there was no particular announcement that such a policy had taken precedence over other approaches.

A major problem the German Jews had in receiving financial help from abroad was that the Nazis confiscated much of the money as it passed through government channels. Reichsvertretung officials constantly sought ways to block the thievery. One popular system involved German families sending their children to school abroad. Rather than pay funds directly to a school in England, for example, the funds went to the Reichsvertretung. An English Jew wanting to contribute to the Reichsvertretung then paid the Jewish child's expenses in England. In that way cash never crossed borders.

Donations from abroad became increasingly important as the economic base of the Jews in Germany shrank because of the Nazi restrictions. At the end of 1934 Cora Berliner produced a report for the Reichsvertretung detailing those restrictions: Nazi party members could not enter into business deals with Jews or see Jewish doctors or lawyers; businessmen who wanted export licenses could not have Jewish representatives abroad; Christians were directed not to enter Jewish shops; the musicians' and actors' guilds refused to admit Jews; the list seemed endless.

By 1937 the number of Jewish unemployed had reached 10 percent, a level "never before known to the Jews in Germany, and the continuation of this tendency is anticipated." Jewish businesses found it virtually impossible to maintain their activity against the Nazi restrictive attitudes. Jewish publishers and bookstores offered one example. On August 1, 1937, a decree prohibited Jews from publishing or selling books without permission of the Ministry of Propaganda. Jewish publishers could deliver books only to authorized Jewish booksellers and Jewish organizations, and Jewish bookstores could sell only books on Jewish subjects to those identifying themselves as Jews.

As the jobs and the businesses disappeared, the Jewish communities throughout Germany also disappeared as their members emigrated either to a foreign country or, in many cases, to a larger community in hopes of finding a new way to survive—and thus adding to the number of workers chasing after the few jobs available to Jews in the larger communities. By 1937 this movement from the smaller communities was pronounced. In the Prussian state alone during that year 100 synagogue buildings, vacated in small communities, were put up for sale. Of the 800 Jewish communities in the Prussian association, one-half had populations of less than fifty people in that year.

The Reichsvertretung, by increasing its efforts and the pressures on its member groups and individuals, raised funds to meet the most urgent demands in 1937. This could not happen in 1938. Money became so scarce that homes for children and the needy had to be closed and the real estate sold. One of the problems, in addition to the tightening of the Nazi economic rules, was that the effects of emigration were beginning to be seen. Many of the most productive people were leaving or had left Germany. Those remaining had reduced incomes, could not contribute sufficiently to the Reichsvertretung's causes, and also needed more help. The Jews were caught in a vicious circle.[20]

Despite economic restrictions, growing unemployment, and the harassment of their children, the resurgent interest on the part of the Jews in their religion did not cease. Joachim Prinz was invited by the Berlin community to give a course in Jewish history. The biggest hall available seated only 3,500; the course was broken into two sections when 7,000 people applied. Prinz described the students as "young, old, converted, assimilated, pious, marginal . . . To be a Jew was now a new discovery, and to emphasize one's Jewishness in the face of danger and disgrace became the thing to do." Another German rabbi at that time reiterated that the renewed interest in their religion by Jews, produced ironically by Adolf Hitler, continued unabated. "Morning services produced large attendances," he said. "Sometimes it would be necessary to have two services."

The Jews turned to their religion as never before because Judaism, as Baeck had taught, was not a revealed religion but one that is constantly revealing; each generation finds its own story within Judaism's story. Prinz said:

Many of the prayers had been written in the medieval context of persecution, and even the Psalms spoke about "the table prepared in the presence of mine enemies." Many stories of the Bible began to make sense or had a new and different meaning for us. The story of David and Goliath became a story of hope. If he could slay the giant, so could we in the end be victorious over the giant people who called themselves supermen of a superrace.

Being Jewish, then, and observing the religion, became both an act of hope and of defiance. "Passover was now the great day of hope for delivery from our own Egypt," said Prinz. "The whips which beat the naked bodies of Jewish slaves in Egypt were the very same that struck our bodies. Slavery was no longer an abstract term, foreign to the world of the twentieth centry." Jews living as third-class citizens in Germany in the 1930s understood the concept much better than they had during the previous decade. The sudden disappearance of neighbors, the beatings, and the insults told the story of the Passover much more vividly than did any Haggadah, the book that recounts the story of the Jews' persecution in Egypt and their exodus from that country. Prinz, again:

The Passover slogan "From slavery unto freedom" became the song of our lives. If the slaves of Egypt could be delivered from their fate, so would we. All the songs at the Seder table were sung with new emphasis and new meaning and great religious fervor. When we read that "in every generation it is man's duty to regard himself as though he personally had come out of Egypt" and "it was not only our fathers whom God set free from slavery," the identification was complete.

Prinz was describing what has caused so many to cling to Judaism over generations of turmoil, trouble, and persecution. It cost much to be a Jew. In the Middle Ages, Jews insulted by Gentile children paid with loss of their dignity. Jews attacked by the Crusaders paid with their lives. Spanish Jews chased from their homes paid with their wealth. German Jews were paying with their rights as citizens; they soon would pay more. Despite all, however, they remained Jews because they understood that their religion "was not historic memory. It was not history at all. It was the reality of every day and the hope of every man. Some day, we said, we shall be free." And the Jews read at Passover: "For not one man only has risen against us to destroy us, but in every generation men rise up against us to destroy us; but the Holy One, Blessed be He, always delivers us from their hands."

If Passover offered hope, the holiday of Purim offered the opportunity for defiance. In this festival the Jews read in the scroll, the Megillah, the story of Haman's plan to murder all the Jews and of its thwarting through the efforts of the beautiful Esther. It is read in the service as the story of the Jews' survival against the despots. Every time Haman's name is read in the service, the children twirl noisemakers. The service is a festive one, a party, an annual and joyous reminder that the Jews survive. "It was again the story of our life," said Prinz. He continued:

When Haman's plot was announced, it bore a strange resemblance to Hitler's plot to wipe out the Jewish people. Many came to ask me if Hitler ever read the story of Haman . . . [When] the turning point came, Haman was demasked and exposed to disgrace and death. Never had I heard such applause in a synagogue . . . Every time we read Haman, the people heard Hitler, and the noise was deafening. The little noisemakers which had become part of the Purim festival became more than toys. They were the instruments of a demonstration in the midst of frustration.

Outside the synagogue the Jews could not speak critically or reject Hitler without fear of arrest and punishment. "But here in the synagogue," said Prinz, "there was no limit to our rejection."

Of the holidays that had the most impact on the German Jews, Prinz ranked Chanukah highest. The eight-day festival commemorates the victory of the Maccabees in the first recorded war for religious freedom. Its significance in the 1930s to the Berlin Jews apparently lay in what it had become. Chanukah is celebrated in December, near Christmas, and Jews had adopted it as a Christmaslike holiday for themselves. Gifts were exchanged, and Christmas trees were displayed in some Jewish homes. Under Hitler, however, the ersatz Christmas quality disappeared. The Christmas tree was replaced by the menorah, the candelabra, the Jewish symbol which was traditional for Chanukah. The Chanukah story, not the opportunity to imitate the gift-giving of Christmas, became the essence of the holiday. It was a story of a few victorious against the powerful many, the story of Jewish courage and stamina, "and, above all, of the Jews' ability to be victorious. . . . So a perfunctory holiday, which used to satisfy Jewish children and teach them not to be envious of their Christian neighbors, now returned to its original meaning. When we placed the menorah on the windowsills in accordance with Jewish tradition, we wanted to proclaim loudly and clearly and visibly that this house was inhabited by Jews, and we were proud of it . . ." Hitler had stripped the Jews of their citizenship, denied them the opportunity for a decent livelihood, chased many from their homeland. More important, however, as Leo Baeck said, "The Nazis could take our property but not our spirit. So far as possible we wanted the individual Jew, when exposed to persecution, to feel that he could find refuge in the protective mantle of the Jewish community."[21]

Jews turned not only to their synagogues but also to their music and theater. When the Nazis banned Jews from participating in commercial theatrical, musical, and other cultural events, some of the artists left Germany to resume their careers in other nations. Many remained, however, reluctant to make a final judgment against their homeland, refusing to give up the hope still gripping many German Jews—that someday they could resume their normal lives in Germany. These unemployed Jews formed their own theatrical, concert, and lecture groups. If they were not allowed to perform before non-Jews, they would perform before their Jewish brethren.

In April 1933 some young Jewish stage producers asked Baeck's help in developing a cultural association of German Jews. Baeck agreed, and with Martin Buber and several other prominent Jews he became a member of the cultural association's board. When theaters or large halls were unavailable for the dramatic productions, concerts, and lectures, the synagogues were used; this was in keeping with the Jewish view of the synagogues not only as houses of worship but also of education and of assembly, truly a community center. A popular presentation of the Jewish group was the play *Nathan der Weise*, a drama of a Jew at court in the Middle Ages. Baeck traveled with the drama group at first, introducing the play to audiences and lending his name and prestige to the Jewish company.

The cultural group never forgot that it was a German group. Louis P. Lochner, a newspaper reporter in Berlin during the 1930s and a non-Jew, told his children about attending a play presented by this Jewish cultural group.

I had to go alone to an exceedingly interesting evening; a premiere in German of Priestley's *Men at Sea* in—the Jewish Theater! I had to go thru considerable red tape to be permitted to attend, for gentiles are strictly forbidden ordinarily to go to this one-and-only Jewish theater. That is, it is not a Yiddish or Hebrew theater; all the acting is in German, by German Jews. But it may play no Aryan German poet's work, such as Schiller's dramas, and when they have a concert in the same hall, the artists may not "sully" the memory of Beethoven or Mozart by daring as Jews to perform the works of any Aryan composer! They may, however, play Mendelssohn, who in turn may not appear on any Aryan programs in Germany!

The Germans, with their cultural restrictions, had attempted to push the Jews into a new ghetto. The Jews had responded with a new pride in their religion, while simultaneously refusing to rebuild the ghetto walls.

"In these hard and difficult days," said Leo Baeck, "art enters the hours of men. Perhaps it may be thought, as it is sometimes, that the graceful appearance of art is an escape, a flight from reality . . . But it is entirely another thing! It is not the act of turning away but that of facing reality"—"*nicht eine Abkehr, sondern eine Einkehr.*"

This return to religion and creation of their own cultural world were acts of defiance and of courage. Eva G. Reichmann, who lived through this period in Berlin, reflected upon it many years later. "We were not always downhearted," she said. "It was a time of Jewish reawakening—adult education, theater, an intense Jewish atmosphere—not entirely an unhappy time. The synagogues were crowded, far different from the lax observances of the 1920s." She paused in her London home for a moment, remembering those years under Nazi rule, and then continued: "We thought we had conquered Hitler from within ourselves, but it was misleading—because of what happened."[22]

There was much in Germany, especially in Berlin, during the 1930s that was misleading. Berlin never had been a center of anti-Semitism, particularly in the Schoeneberg area where Leo Baeck and many of the German Jews lived their middle-class lives. "You never heard 'Heil Hitler' in Berlin," recalled Eva Reichmann. "Berlin was a haven," she said. "There was nothing to bother you there." Said a Hochschule student later, "There was too much civility around. Jews came from the middle strata, from an intellectual and professional class. Germany was a highly stratified society; the lower, rougher classes always were disregarded. We always assumed that members of society would reflect the civility they knew."

Another said, "the trap we fell into" was thinking, "Oh, it's not so bad," arguing that Hitler and Nazism would pass. There were many incidents supporting that argument in Berlin. "If taxicab drivers recognized you as a Jew," said Eva Reichmann, "they made anti-Hitler remarks." Otto Hirsch and another Reichsvertretung official went to the Foreign Office one day to meet with a German official. After closing his office door and checking that no one was listening at the windows, the official told them: "Don't panic. How long can that spook last?" And the Jews laughed with the other Germans at jokes like this one:

Q. Do you know which is the best paid choral society?
A. The Nazi Reichstag. The members sing the *Horst Wessel Song* and *Deutschland über Alles*, vote "Ja" and go home with a month's pay in their pockets.

When President Hindenburg died in 1934, Berlin Jews held a memorial service in the Prinzregentenstrasse Synagogue. Leo Baeck, appearing in the program as the president of the Reichsvertretung, said the memorial prayer. Joining with the other German Jews, including some veterans of the first World War, he sang the song that German soldiers traditionally sang of a fallen comrade: *"Ich hatt' einen Kameraden . . ."*[23]

In the 1930s the Jews in Germany did not and, of course, could not understand their real alternatives. Instead they believed their prospects to be either death if they chose armed revolution or life if they worked toward the time when the situation under the Nazis would improve. They were not alone in this opinion. A textbook produced in 1934 by the Union of American Hebrew Congregations, the Reform branch of American Jewry, for use in American temples and religious schools said:

There is doubt, however, that fear of widespread pogroms [in Germany] at the present is well grounded. It is probable that the masses of the Party, if not some of the leaders, originally envisaged a program which would wipe out the entire Jewish community. The response of the world to the atrocity reports made it clear, however, that such a policy could never be put into execution. The Jewish community will probably continue to be recognized by the authorities as a legalized corporation with power to speak for Jewry. It is also likely that the Nazis with their passion for "coordination" will mold the loosely federated National Committee of German Jewish State Associations [the original Reichsvertretung] into one centralized authoritative Jewish body. ... Such is the charter which the Third Empire will probably offer to the German Jews. The Jews in Germany, though opposed to any charter which will crystallize their disabilities, are nevertheless anxious to have their status fixed so that they may know where they stand.

Never was there a feeling within the Reichsvertretung during the 1930s that there was a choice between anything other than futile physical revolt or the course the Jewish leaders chose, that is, to save as many individuals as possible. "The Reichsvertretung members saw their duty in protecting the life and security of the Jews in Germany rather than their own . . ." said Max Gruenewald, who was on the board. "At no time was there an 'outcry,' a dramatic action, such as a wholesale resignation of the governing body. Such a demonstration to the best of my knowledge was never considered. Moreover, it is doubtful whether there existed true insight into the dynamic and demoniac character of the Nazi movement until the time when the lesser criminals gave way to the large-size criminals."

Another factor working against organized physical resistance was the disappearance of the ghetto in the nineteenth century. The Jews had become dispersed geographically. Within the country and in each city the Jews had moved out of the narrow confines of the *Judengasse*. Geographically they were not cohesive as were, for example, Jews in the Warsaw Ghetto, where physical resistance did develop. Also, as emigration of the young was encouraged, the average age of the German Jew rose; by 1938 virtually three out of four Jews remaining in Germany were over forty years of age. By the end of the 1930s physical resistance would have had to be carried out by elderly men and women, many of whom never had held a weapon in their hands.

Their also was the fear of reprisals—even before the Nazis began rounding up fifty innocent persons for every Nazi hurt, of using any act of violence as an excuse for a greater, more systematized violence. Still, the Jews never doubted that physical resistance would bring retaliation to more than the one taking the action. Schlomo Adler-Rudel, when walking home from his job with the Reichsvertretung in the mid-1930s, often passed a stand with propaganda posters for *Der Stürmer*, the Nazi anti-Semitic publication. Every night Adler-Rudel had a strong desire to pick up a brick and hurl it at the posters, to destroy the vile caricature of the Jew that the Nazis had created. He did not because he feared the Nazis would exploit the story of a Reichsvertretung official breaking the glass. "The value of the act," he said years later, "was not more important than the damage that would be done to the cause. It would not do any good."[24]

Each time a Jew walked in the streets of Berlin he or she braved ridicule, harassment, and sometimes physical abuse. Still the Jews stood erect and with pride before such onslaughts. In the 1930s they resisted Nazism forcefully by encouraging the migration of the younger people, by strengthening their own cultural institutions, and by showing pride in their heritage.

In view of the effort in the next decade to destroy all Jews, a development that could not be foreseen in the 1930s, many Jews who lived in Berlin at the time have since pondered—as well as have many others—whether there should have been a more physical resistance. Max Kreutzberger, a Reichsvertretung official in those years, responded to the question this way: "If the Jews had fought in 1934, would it have been possible for those who escaped to do so? That question must be considered in any discussion of physical resistance." Also, in declining to use physical force, the Jews were not alone among the minority groups in Germany. "The Social Democrats with three million members and the Communists with almost as many, both well organized," said Kreutzberger, "didn't resist physically."

Frank Rosenthal, a rabbi in Germany at that time, added another point. "In Poland," he said, "the Nazis eliminated the Jews in two months. In Germany nine years were required, time enough for many to escape."

In addition to the inability to visualize the horror that lay in their future, the lack of a geographic cohesiveness, and the aged quality of their population, there was yet another reason why the Jews did not resist with physical force—their religious heritage had forced them to renounce violence as a way of life. Manfred Swarsensky, a young rabbi in Berlin, summed up this attitude with three words: "Jews were Jews."[25]

10 *KRISTALLNACHT*

Little by little. That is how the survivors of the Berlin Jewish community describe the Nazi attack upon them. First, a Jewish lawyer could not practice unless he had been a lawyer prior to 1914 or had served in the First World War. Emil Fackenheim's father met both these conditions; still the Nazis disbarred him, claiming he had defended some Communists in 1918–1919. In 1933 the Nazis enacted forty-two laws restricting the Jews' rights to earn a living, to enjoy full citizenship, and to educate themselves. In 1934 there were nineteen such laws, twenty-nine in 1935, twenty-four in 1936, twenty-two in 1937, and seventy-eight in 1938. Clothed in the mantle of law, the Nazis acted arbitrarily, aggressively, immorally, and sometimes violently against the Jews. "You couldn't murder anyone in Germany," said Emil Fackenheim, "unless the law allowed you. The weakness of men is that they fall into that trap." Robert Weltsch recalled, "When the doorbells rang, we were never certain who it would be. Someone to take us away? Would we ever be seen again? Often we watched through curtained windows to see where the Nazi patrols were going, whom they were going to arrest."[1]

Between 1933 and 1938 the most significant of the laws enacted against the Jews were those referred to as the Nuremberg laws. They began, in September 1935, as laws "for the protection of German blood and honor," prohibiting marriage as well as extramarital intercourse between Jew and non-Jew. Then, at Hitler's sudden order, the laws were broadened to include a new definition of German citizenship: Jews or those with Jewish ancestry no longer were German citizens.

Hitler appeared to change his mind about the Jews on occasion. In

1936, the year following enactment of the Nuremberg laws, Germany was host to the Olympics. For Germany the event was a twofold opportunity, to show off the athletic prowess of the Nazi "superman" and to gain stature in the world by having the other nations accept Nazi Germany as the Olympics site. There was little difficulty with this second point. Most nations, arguing that sports and not politics was involved in the Olympics, accepted Germany as the site of the event. To allay some sensitivities, however, anti-Semitic posters disappeared from walls and *Der Stürmer*, the anti-Semitic newspaper, vanished during the Olympics. For a period the entire anti-Semitic campaign faded. "Nothing happened to the Jews then," recalled Werner Rosenstock, a Reichsvertretung official. "That was a boon in itself."[2]

But that was only a respite. On March 13, 1938, the Nazis took away the public status of Jewish associations. Jews no longer were members of their Jewish communities. The state no longer collected taxes for the Jewish communities for redistribution to Jewish agencies. The communities no longer enjoyed tax exemptions. The Gemeinde was dead. As president of the Reichsvertretung, Baeck called upon German Jews to continue their loyalties to the Jewish communities, to pay taxes direct to the communities, and to give the community offices full support. His message was, in effect, that nothing has changed. Privately, however, officials were more concerned. Otto Hirsch, in a discussion about the situation a few weeks later, said: "All is lost."

That year the Nazis enacted a law requiring male Jews to assume the name of Israel and all female Jews to take the name of Sarah. Leo Baeck then became Leo Israel Baeck. The following year Jews with family names such as Deutschland, Deutschländer, Deutsch, Deutscher, Deutschmann, or any other name referring to Germany had to change it in court. However, such names as Land and Länder were acceptable. The decree stipulated that Jews should not be charged for the court action.

Kosher meat became more difficult to find. When meat from Argentina marked "kosher" arrived, the Orthodox community opposed its use, saying there were no assurances that the religious ritual had been carried out properly. Baeck argued with the Orthodox on this point—and won. His position was that the elderly especially needed meat and should not be denied it because of the suspicions of the Orthodox. As Jews gradually began to accept the "neukosher"—meat that probably was not kosher—out of necessity, Baeck urged his rabbi friends not to interfere. Health was the determining factor in his long explanation to his colleagues. Then, after he had persuaded them to accept, if only grudgingly, the relaxation of tradition, he said to them: "But, of course, you and I shall not eat of this 'neukosher.' "[3]

During the 1930s, as he carried out his customary duties at the Hochschule, as an officiating rabbi, and as head of the Reichsvertretung, Baeck tried to maintain his equilibrium by seeking diversions. "From 1933 to 1938 he translated three times the whole of the Gospels from Greek into Hebrew," recalled a friend, "in order to sift the oldest parts by Hebrew-speaking Jews, including Jesus himself, from later extensions and accretions." This activity reflected that creed of Baeck's life that one continually invest something more of himself each day. He talked about this at the end of 1934 with his Christian friend Baron von Veltheim. The coming of the new year prompted von Veltheim to speak of being reborn. The only way he understood the concept was through reincarnation. Baeck's interpretation was different. "We are entering a new day," said Baeck, "and we can experience in each way this miracle of being reborn . . . It doesn't come to us, however, as a miracle; only the thinking person experiences it. To that person who does not think, the New Year is a mark on an artificial calendar. But to the one who thinks, to that person, the day says a lot. It is the knowledge, the hope, and the wish—and to that person wishes may speak."

During this period he tried to maintain his home on Am Park in Schoeneberg as an oasis, an area free from outside pressures. Schoeneberg, where Baeck and his family had moved in 1932, was one of those areas marked so much by the "civility" that lulled the Jews in the 1930s; there were few Nazi uniforms in evidence there. Leo and Natalie lived in a pleasant apartment facing the park—"We are glad about the view into the green, which is right beyond our windows." As Baeck took his regular walks through the park, his neighbors gave a friendly greeting to this tall, slightly stooped, bearded man, always dressed so fastidiously. There were a few cafes nearby where one stopped for coffee and to read the newspapers hanging on the racks. Most residents had their major meal in the early afternoon and spent their evenings at home. In this environment Leo Baeck was less the rabbi and more the German professor, the educated and cultured gentleman, like his neighbors.

Saturday afternoons, as the Sabbath neared its close, the apartment was a haven for his students and friends, a place where they had the traditional piece of cake and cup of tea and found relief from the presence of Nazism in their lives. "The peace of the Sabbath was maintained," said one of those friends, Heinz Warschauer. "You went to other people when you had a political question, but you went to Leo Baeck when you had a spiritual question." Recalling a particular Sabbath afternoon in Baeck's study, Warschauer said, "Leo Baeck had optimism; he could restore your spirit." Warschauer had returned from Palestine where he had witnessed Arab-Jewish riots. The newspapers were filled with news of the civil war in Spain, representing another triumph of fascism. Outside in the streets the spectre of Nazism hung over the city he had loved. In Baeck's study, after the sponge cake had been eaten and the tea sipped, Warschauer poured out his feelings, his concern for the future, to the sympathetic Leo Baeck. When he was done, he remembered, Leo Baeck looked carefully at him and said: "Hitler and his like cannot turn back history. We Jews will suffer. Some of us may die. But we will survive. We Jews have old eyes"—"Wir Juden haben alte Augen."[4]

During this time Leo Baeck presided over the Reichsvertretung with its sometimes conflicting concepts, tried to keep the Gestapo at arm's length, and dealt with dozens of Jewish politicians. Through it all he maintained his reputation as a conciliator. To some this was his great strength, that he was the central point into which all the conflicts funneled. If they weren't solved at that point, at least they were defused and kept from exploding. To others it continued to be his great weakness, that he did not take stronger positions. Baeck obviously had not changed his belief that he could be more helpful by not becoming identified with any particular side; he had lived that way for most of his life. Also, he genuinely preferred accommodation if possible rather than saying "No" to anyone.

Baeck generally avoided public challenges to the Nazis; he believed he served his community better by assisting its members to emigrate and by strengthening their pride in their identity. To be arrested, to lose his position, perhaps to be forced to emigrate would serve no purpose. However, his conciliatory attitude confused both his friends and his enemies. He also knew that sometimes conciliation would not work. Baeck realized that for each person a time comes to step in front of the crowd. For him it came at Yom Kippur of 1935.

"In those early years," said Leo Baeck, "the Jews suffered severely from the propaganda and calumnies by which the Nazis slyly tried to turn all of the German people against them. It depressed them so gravely that something had to be done to raise their spirits." In his rabbinical way Baeck had used the bimah to protest Nazi actions. On one occasion the Nazis ordered the Jews to refrain from saying a prayer in which God is asked to bestow His blessings upon their fatherland, a prayer integral to the Jewish services. At his next service Leo Baeck ignored the Nazi order to read the prayer as he had before, except to replace the plea for a blessing on Germany with a plea for all men of good will.

In Germany there was a tradition of the *Hirtenbrief*, the shepherd's letter, which church leaders sent to their member congregations to be read at services. Baeck occasionally followed that practice as leader of the Reichsvertretung, although it was not a religious organization. In the summer of 1935 one such *Hirtenbrief* dealt with the question of finding comfort and trust "in these days when we must endure a flood of insults." The answer, said Baeck, came from three directions—Judaism, the individual's honor, and the youth of the German Jews. First, "We place all abuses aginst the nobility of our religion; against the insults and the constant troubles, we place our effort to live the way of our Judaism, to follow its commands." Second, a person's honor is not bestowed upon him by another. "Each gives himself the true honor—through a life which is inviolable and pure, plain and upright; through a life also of reserve, which is the mark of inner strength. Our honor is our honor before God; it will endure alone." And third, he asked German Jews to respect the young people. Those were the ones denied the opportunities they had believed theirs, who were turning to new training, new professions. "Our youth," said Baeck, "does it not give us an example of modesty and of courage as it masters new ways of this difficult life? Allow us, parents and teachers, to draw near to a generation, strong and hard; its members ready to help each other, with strong bodies and fresh spirit, believing strongly in Judaism."[5]

This *Hirtenbrief* was sent out prior to the Nuremberg laws of 1935, which stripped the Jews of their German citizenship. Those laws were a blow not only to the legal standing of the Jews but also to their morale. The legal tradition they treasured, the concept of justice in which they believed, suddenly had been used to call them less than human. Even if Hitler were replaced within the next several years, a hope some Jews clung to—the Nuremberg laws still would exist.

Shortly after the laws were passed, the Jews observed their High Holy Days, the sacred period of the ten Days of Awe, in which they welcome the beginning of the religious year and then consider their lives. On the last day, Yom Kippur, they ask God to forgive their sins against Him and vow to improve their lives in the coming year. Two decades earlier Leo Baeck had stood on the battlefield with other

German Jews leading them through the Yom Kippur observance, helping them to regenerate their spirituality, to come to terms with their understanding of God, to bring their lives into conformity with their religion. Now, after the enactment of the Nuremberg laws, Leo Baeck again used the time of Yom Kippur to lead the German Jews. He wrote what he called a prayer—others sometimes refer to as a sermon—to be read in all the synagogues in Germany.

"The Reichsvertretung of the German Jews speaks to us," it began. The German Jews who heard the prayer that day or who read it later were moved emotionally by it, never forgot it, and spoke of it years later. It was a prayer, a sermon, an exhortation, a challenge to the oppressors, a statement of religious strength. It outlined the moment of decision for the individual, the point beyond which he will not bend, the pressure to which he will not succumb, the sacrifice he will not make.

In this hour all Israel stands before its God, the God of righteousness and of mercy. Before Him we want to test our way fully, to test what we have done and what we have failed to do, to test where we have gone and where we have not gone. Wherever we have failed we wish to confess openly: "We have sinned"; and wish, with a strong desire, to ask for a return to God: "Forgive us!"

While acknowledging the failings of both the individual and of the community, the essence of Baeck's prayer was that "we pronounce our abhorrence and see trampled deeply beneath our feet the lies which are turned against us, the slander turned against our religion and its character." In this Yom Kippur message Baeck then recounted the triumphs of Judaism:

Who has knowledge of the mystery of eternity, of the one God? Who has revealed to the world the sense for the purity of conduct, for the purity of family? Who has given to the world, to the attention of mankind, the image of God? Who has shown to the world the command of righteousness, of social responsibility? The spirit of the prophets of Israel, the revelation of God to the Jewish people has produced all of them.

"Against these facts," declared Baeck, "each insult rebounds."

Reiterating that the Jews "stand before God," he said, "In Him our history, our perseverance in all changes, our steadfastness in all oppression has its truth and its honor." Baeck reminded the Jews that

Our history is the history of the grandeur of the human soul and the dignity of human life. In this day of sorrow and pain, surrounded by infamy and shame, we will turn our eyes to the days of old. From generation to generation God redeemed our fathers, and He will redeem us and our children in the days to come.

Concluded Baeck: "We stand before our God . . . we bow to Him, and we stand upright and erect before man."

The prayer is both Jewish and German. Scholars have dissected it to show how Leo Baeck's German-Jewish culture influenced its shape, its organization, its wording. The prayer, however, is more than the sum of its parts. It is a human prayer, a statement by the individual of his right to hold beliefs, of his pride, and of his dignity—no man can humble him. It defines the ultimate condition of humanity: No matter how weak people are, no matter how small the minority to which they belong, no matter how oppressed they may be by their neighbors, no matter how abruptly their former friends turn from them, they cannot be defeated. They will maintain their belief, their pride, and their dignity. They will stand upright before man and bow only before God. The Hebrew Bible tells man that he was created in the image of God. That knowledge is the individual's ultimate power, the protective barrier, which no other person can destroy.[6]

The Nazis quickly learned of the prayer; apparently a rabbi who received a copy went to the Interior Ministry and asked if there was objection to it. Once the Nazis saw it, there was. Before the prayer could be read in the synagogues, a message went out to all rabbis informing them that the Gestapo would arrest anyone reading it in services; Gestapo officials showed up at some Yom Kippur services, especially in Berlin. No count ever was made of how many rabbis read the prayer at the service; many did, so many that it was almost a collective act of defiance on the part of the German rabbinate.

The only rabbi arrested, however, was Leo Baeck.

The arrest was not made by underlings. Befitting his position—the Gestapo considered these things significant—Baeck was arrested by a top official of the agency, a man named Kuchmann, who went with him to the Prinz Albrecht Strasse jail. As if sensing that the arrest of such a prominent Jew as Baeck would cause difficulties, Kuchmann grumbled: "Why did you not show us that?" Baeck was not maltreated. He was placed in a cellar cell, and a guard brought him rice mixed with cinnamon and sugar when he refused to eat the nonkosher jail food. In the evening Baeck and a number of other prisoners were taken in a police wagon to Gestapo headquarters at Alexanderplatz. The other prisoners were unloaded while Baeck was taken on to Columbia House at Templehof Air Field and placed in a cell with two beds.

At first he was alone, but later a second man arrived who said he had been arrested on charges of homosexuality. The man was friendly, insisting on making Baeck's bed in the morning and bringing him his breakfast. After breakfast the other prisoners were taken on a walk for exercise, but Baeck—the only Jewish prisoner there—was not allowed to join them.

Later that day, after approximately twenty-four hours in jail, Baeck was released. "You have had some luck," a Gestapo official told him. He was driven back to the Prinz Albrecht Strasse station and told to remain in the courtyard. Finally he was allowed to telephone Natalie and was released.

No charges had been placed against him, no warrant issued; the Nazis were acting purely as a show of strength, to stifle the kind of resistance exemplified by the Yom Kippur prayer. Baeck believed his quick release was due to the many inquiries by his Jewish friends in Berlin; the Nazis, afraid of a public protest, were reluctant to move too aggressively. Also, the Berlin correspondent of the London *Times* filed a lengthy report on the incident, which had embarrassed the Nazis.

Pressured into releasing Baeck, the Gestapo sought to continue its harassment by arresting Otto Hirsch. Baeck returned to the Prinz Albrecht Strasse station to demand the release of Hirsch, insisting that he could not operate the Reichsvertretung without Hirsch and threatening to close it down. The Nazis promised to release Hirsch the next day. But when Baeck returned to the station then, Hirsch was not released. The Gestapo played out its petty game a total of eight days from Hirsch's arrest to his release. Baeck and Hirsch's wife appeared at the station every day. The day Hirsch finally was released, they had waited two hours for him.

The arrests of Baeck and Hirsch generated publicity outside of Germany. In Washington the German embassy received a protest from a group of Christian ministers in the United States and passed it on to the foreign office in Berlin with this covering note:

In the enclosure I have the honor to send you one of the statements presented to me by the "Universal Christian Council," in which the arrest of Oberrabbiner Dr. Leo Baeck and the president of the Zentralverein deutscher Juden Dr. Otto Hirsch is protested. The "Universal Christian Council" is a branch of the "Federal Council of the Churches of Christ in America," including some of the different Protestant faiths, and is a very influential organization.

The importance of its position in regard to Germany should not be under-valued for our political connections to the United States.

The protest was signed by a dozen prominent Protestant clergymen in the United States, including Harry Emerson Fosdick and Reinhold Niebuhr. The protest came quickly to the point: The arrest of Baeck and Hirsch "without legal charges or the privilege of communicating with friends, appears to us almost unbelievable." It closed:

We would earnestly point out that any government which permits or condones such actions toward religious leaders—whether they are Jewish or Christian—cannot expect the leaders of religious life in other lands to take seriously its claims to be friendly to ethics, religion, and the standards of civilization.[7]

No German Christian leaders protested the arrests, but the action by the American church leaders in 1935 demonstrated Baeck's standing around the world, and the Nazis treated him carefully until finally they gave up any pretense at good relations with foreign countries.

Baeck exploited his international reputation in subsequent dealings with the Gestapo; in the five times he was arrested he refused to eat nonkosher food, forcing his captors either to find him food that did not violate the tradition or to buy him kosher food, rather than allow him to starve. Baeck was arrested in 1937 when the Gestapo ordered the dissolution of the B'nai B'rith and confiscated its property, valued in millions. Baeck still was the national president, and the Gestapo placed before him a statement in which he agreed to cede all the B'nai B'rith's property to the Nazi government. "I refused to sign," he recalled. "Thus their act stood as the theft which it was."[8]

Another time Baeck showed his refusal to surrender was when the dispute between the Reichsvertretung and the Berlin Gemeinde headed by Heinrich Stahl again erupted. Stahl had not been satisfied with the Reichsvertretung since its organization in September of 1933. He never had accepted the basic premise that a single prestigious agency was needed to represent the German Jews. He continued to believe that it was a needless bureaucracy that duplicated the work his own organization was capable of performing. The Reichsvertretung, an organization that Stahl's community could not dominate, had taken over much of the responsibility and authority of the Berlin Gemeinde. As the primary recipient of funds from abroad, the Reichsvertretung controlled the purse strings. And it had the stature. While there were no charges either that the money or the prestige was misused, the Reichsvertretung had powers and position that the Berlin Gemeinde missed. The dispute continued without pause, establishing a rhythm of bickering and reconciliation. At a meeting of the Reichsvertretung council on February 9, 1937, for example, Otto Hirsch announced that he had met with Stahl and both men agreed to place "the greatest value on close cooperation" between the two organizations. Hirsch asked all members of the Reichsvertretung council "to do their share in working together with the Berlin Gemeinde."[9]

That kind of effort—really only papering over the dispute without resolving it—was not adequate for Stahl. In the spring and summer of 1937 he gave his support to a move aimed at changing the leadership structure of the Reichsvertretung and ousting Baeck. The move was led by a man named Georg Kareski.

"Whatever Georg Kareski was," said one man who knew him well in those years, "he wanted to be first." The verdict, even after four decades, still is out on Kareski. To some he was the first Jewish quisling, the man who sold out to the Nazis. A kinder version is that he simply was a man on the make, looking out only for his own best interests, ready to use and be used by the Nazis in behalf of those interests. To some, however, his primary interest was in encouraging the emigration of Jews from Germany. Whatever his motivations, he had the support of the Gestapo when he sought to take over the leadership of the Reichsvertretung.

Kareski was a banker and the leader of an extreme Zionist group he had formed when the leadership of the regular Zionist movement was denied him. He believed, or at least he said frequently, that the Nazi movement "will blow over and one has to talk to them in their own language"—an attitude not too different from that adopted by many German Jews. How he transformed that attitude into policy, however, caused numerous doubts among the Berlin Jews. In 1932, for example, when the Nazis and Franz von Papen were competing for popular support, Kareski publicly proclaimed: "The Papen government has written the protection of the Jews on the flag." With anti-Semitism so pervasive in Germany at the time, the quote by one considered to be a prominent Jew did much to turn Germans away from von Papen and toward the Nazi party. In 1935 Kareski's bank provided funds for a German Jew who had been sent to England as a spy for the Gestapo. The funds had come from the Gestapo and then been "laundered" by passing through Kareski's bank. His defense was that he had been forced into the act by the Gestapo.

The following year Kareski proposed a plan for the annual emigration of 25,000 German Jews to Palestine. The proposal had some serious flaws. One was that no provision was included for persuading England to change its long-standing opposition to that kind of major migration to Palestine, over which it then exercised a League of Nations mandate. The second flaw was that the emigration was to be handled by a new organization headed by Kareski. This organization was to have absolute control over all property owned by the Jews in Germany. Kareski would control it all.

He served on the board of the Berlin Gemeinde and also on the fifty-member Reichsvertretung council, but not on the executive committee of a dozen or so members that actually ran the organization. He was a friend of Stahl's, apparently having provided financial assistance to him in earlier years. He also was, as a newspaper account of the time described him, a man "welcome in the offices of the Nazi officials."[10]

The Reichsvertretung drama involving Kareski and Baeck opened in the spring of 1937. The first acts were in the newspapers. Kareski's influence was with the *Gemeindeblatt*, the Berlin Jewish community newspaper, while Baeck's was with the *C.V. Zeitung*, the newspaper published by the Central-Verein. The newspaper stories carried charges of mismanagement by the Reichsvertretung and defenses against those charges, sometimes in heated language. The controversy finally became too serious to be left to newspaper squabbling, and the matter was scheduled for discussion at a meeting of the Reichsvertretung Council. The sides were the same as they had been in 1933: the land associations, led by the Berlin Gemeinde, versus the national associations such as the Central-Verein.

The night before the meeting of the Reichsvertretung council, Baeck invited the representatives of the land associations to a private dinner in hopes of winning them over before the regular session, to steal Stahl's and Kareski's apparent support from them. Said one participant: "The invited agreed to appear but to refuse all discussion of the subjects to be treated the next day. This agreement was adhered to. The guests could not be moved to private conversations." Unknown then was whether the silence that night at Baeck's dinner was a sign of support for Kareski or only a refusal to publicly take sides before the formal session.

With the Gestapo officials present, as usual, the regular meeting was held the next day. Julius Seligsohn opened for the Reichsvertretung, reviewing its work, praising its accomplishments, and deriding the criticism that had come from the Berlin Gemeinde. He was followed by Kareski, who sounded as if he were speaking of an entirely different organization. "No working area remained untouched," states an account of the session. "He gave a negative judgment on everything." He demanded a complete reorganization of the Reichsvertretung with power going to the land associations. From the beginning, however, Kareski was on weak ground. He received support that day from no land association except the Prussian, which was dominated by the Berlin Gemeinde. Also, four members of the board of the Berlin Gemeinde were present at the meeting but did not join Stahl, their elected leader, in endorsing Kareski's remarks. The silence the previous evening at Baeck's dinner had not been a sign of support for Kareski.

The result was the appointment of an investigatory commission to examine every charge made by Kareski; the Berlin Gemeinde would have representation on the commission. The second vote that day was one of confidence in the leadership of Baeck and Hirsch. One Reichsvertretung member was critical of Baeck for allowing the investigatory commission to be appointed, writing: "Unfortunately Baeck, who was drained of energy by all the events, did not have sufficient strength to use the good mood of the majority and agreed to a vote on the motion of the Prussian Landesverbände to put in a commission to clarify the manner of the Reichsvertretung's working." Rather than being fatigued, Baeck probably was being politically astute. Two weeks later the commission reported back and, with the concurrence of its members from the Berlin Gemeinde, said that all charges made by Kareski against the Reichsvertretung were groundless. Baeck not only had had his leadership exonerated, he had done it with the agreement of the representatives of his opponents.

That should have ended the dispute, but it did not. The Berlin Gemeinde continued to insist that Kareski be given greater authority; it wanted him placed on the executive committee. Since the Berlin Gemeinde already had two men on that committee, Stahl and another, the appointment of Kareski to the twelve-man group would have given the Gemeinde an extraordinary power.

At this point the Gestapo showed its backing for Kareski.

According to one account the Gestapo wanted "above all' to capture control of the Reichsvertretung, which had not yet come under its legal jurisdiction. Max Gruenewald, a rabbi in Mannheim and a member of the Reichsvertretung council, was called before the Gestapo and criticized for a speech he had given recently. "I could put you away for what you said," the Gestapo official told him. After that threat there was a pause and then the unexpected question: "Are you ready to form together with Kareski a new executive leadership of the Reichsvertretung with Dr. Baeck remaining as its titular head?" Gruenewald knew that the question coming after the spectre of arrest was an attempt to coerce him. He held his ground, refusing to join the move to push aside Baeck, believing that neither he nor Kareski enjoyed the confidence of the German Jews as did Leo Baeck. He also made clear he was not interested in serving under "borrowed authority."

The Gestapo then turned to Leo Baeck. Still aware of his international reputation, the Nazi officials continued to handle him deferentially. One Jew who was present at a meeting where Gestapo officials and Baeck discussed the Kareski matter, said, "Baeck was treated by [the Gestapo official] in a way that was surprising and was so respectful that it was almost embarrassing to Baeck himself. [The official] expressed several times that he understood how Baeck enjoyed the greatest authority among the German Jews." No matter how respectful the Gestapo officials were, however, there still was no hiding the pressure under which they were placing Baeck.

His opposition to Kareski was based on several points. One was Kareski's connection with the Berlin Gemeinde. Another was his generally unsavory reputation as a financial manipulator as well as an associate of the Nazis. Also, Kareski, who had been spurned by the regular Zionst organizations as a leader, had been critical of Chaim Weizmann, the Zionist representative in London working to help German Jews emigrate to Palestine. Baeck considered it politically unwise to give authority to a man whose appointment would offend Weizmann, one of their most important contacts abroad. Finally, of course, Baeck could not welcome to the Reichsvertretung leadership a man who was supported so strongly by the Gestapo. That would make the Reichsvertretung not a Jewish organization but a Nazi one.

"You can force me to appoint Kareski as a member of the executive council of the Reichsvertretung," Baeck told the Gestapo officials. "But you cannot force me to continue as president of the Reichsvertretung."

The final step remaining for the Kareski forces was to coerce an appointment on the council. The Berlin Gemeinde continued to be a powerful influence in German Jewry. If it bluntly demanded the appointment of Kareski, could it be refused? Which would be a greater loss to the Reichsvertretung, the resignation of Leo Baeck as president or the withdrawal of the Berlin Gemeinde? Ernst Herzfeld, one of the original founders of the Reichsvertretung from Essen, then stepped in. At a meeting with Stahl he said: "You have acquired in a long life a very honorable name. I can predict that you will lose the success of your life's work if you do not give up in this twelfth hour what you began so unfortunately. The deciding meeting takes place in one week. I am ready to come to Berlin a day earlier and be a mediator."

Herzfeld arrived a day earlier as promised and found two messages from Stahl. One sought an immediate appointment; the second was a copy of a message Stahl had sent to the Reichsvertretung announcing the intention of the Berlin Gemeinde to leave the Reichsvertretung. Herzfeld caught up with the beleaguered Stahl, who had allowed himself to be maneuvered into an impossible position to support his friend Kareski, and they worked out a compromise. The Berlin Gemeinde remained in the Reichsvertretung and was given a greater voice on the executive committee. Kareski was not on the committee, however, and was relegated to the budget committee, far from power.

Kareski never had the opportunity to exercise even his limited authority. He was head of the Ivriah Bank, a cooperative bank for middle-class Jews. A few days after his appointment to the budget committee of the Reichsvertretung he tried cashing a check at the Ivriah Bank for 50,000 marks from the account of the Berlin Gemeinde, an account that required two signatures. Kareski's check had only his own. When the cashier refused to accept the check, Kareski directed him to do so. The cashier complied but reported the incident immediately to Heinrich Stahl. An investigation followed—the accountant in charge, coincidentally, was Leo Baeck's son-in-law, Hermann Berlak. It showed that Kareski had authorized unsecured loans to friends and that he needed the 50,000 marks of the Gemeinde's money to save his Ivriah Bank. It was not saved. It collapsed, destroying the savings of many of its depositors and ruining what was left of Kareski's reputation in Germany. When Stahl and his friends turned against him, Kareski resigned all of his positions and emigrated to Palestine.[11]

After the Kareski incident Baeck was so drained that he took a week's vacation. The politics of that affair had not been all that had caused his emotional and physical exhaustion; a few months earlier his beloved Natalie had died.

In the mid-1930s Leo and Natalie had taken a trip to Palestine, partly as a vacation for Natalie, who had been showing signs of stress under the strain of living surrounded by Nazism. She still was not her regular self, and in August of 1936 Baeck took her to Switzerland for a *Kur*. He reported that she was "recovering slowly with good food and air." They spent four weeks in Switzerland, hiking along the trails they knew and loved so well. Natalie seemed much better when they returned to Berlin, but the pressures of living in that city again began to tell on her. "Suddenly one heard rumors that she was ill," recalled a friend, "and that she couldn't be visited." On March 5, 1937, she died of a stroke.*

The funeral was a private one for the family and a few close friends; if there had been an announcement, more people would have come than could have been accommodated. Natalie was buried in the Jewish cemetery, Weissensee, in Berlin, along the Ehrenreihe, the section where many famous German Jews were interred. "You can study history there," is how the section is described. In Proverbs there is a poem entitled "A capable wife" which near its end (31:29) has these lines: "Many a woman shows how capable she is; but you excel them all." On Natalie Baeck's gravestone her husband had those last words inscribed in Hebrew, "but you excel them all.".

Leo Baeck and Natalie had been married thirty-eight years. Their life together had started in Oppeln when he was a young rabbi fresh from the seminary. She had devoted her life to him, to his causes, to his comfort. The home she made for him had been an extension of his rabbinate, a place to bring his students and friends. And when the Nazis had come to power and new duties and responsibilities had been placed upon her husband, she had worked even harder to give their home the aura of peace that could provide shelter, even briefly, from the duties and the struggles outside. She had been *die Rabbinerfrau*.

Now the husband stood over the grave of his wife to bid her farewell. He had written the words himself:

We shall be without you. Living our lives without the blessings of you; you who were so pure, so honest, so clear; you who were so bright, so true, so pious, so devout, so good, so helpful, so warm, so open to everyone, so selfless,

---

* There have been persistent rumors through the years that Natalie Baeck committed suicide because of the pressure of living under the Nazi regime. Undoubtedly the stress of living in Berlin contributed to her death, but there is no indication that she died of other than natural causes. This author has spoken with several close friends of the Baeck family who would have known of any suicide. Her son-in-law Hermann Berlak wrote to a friend at the time that Natalie Baeck had died of a stroke. A search for her death certificate in Berlin during the summer of 1976 was fruitless; apparently it was destroyed in the World War II bombing of Berlin.

so without envy, so undemanding, so without concern, never thinking of yourself, so simple, so thankful for the smallest thing; you who were so full of hope and youth, whose house was so full of joy, so full of love, because you gave all; without you now, you who wanted to live only for us, who only enjoyed living if you could think of us, care and work for us without rest and without becoming tired, knowing each wish, guessing every thought. You have gone home and have left us without you.

He paused there and concluded: "God give us the strength to go through the days without you."

Leo Baeck was an austere person, one who rarely showed emotion publicly. But with those to whom he felt close, he relaxed and allowed his feelings to show. Months after Natalie's death he conceded to his friend Baron von Veltheim, "It is still very hard to write about personal things." Magnus Davidsohn, the cantor who had been Leo Baeck's friend from their student days, said that in the years after Natalie's death, if Leo were reminded of her, "an indescribably sad expression came over his face and tears flowed from his eyes." Cantor Davidsohn recalled that Leo Baeck, when he preached at the Fasanenstrasse Synagogue in the months after Natalie's death, would by habit, at the sermon's end, look up at the women's section seeking that customary nod of approval.[12]

Always there was the Gestapo. Two of them showed up at the Reichsvertretung meetings, dressed in their black uniforms, their boots shining, their faces without expression. One never knew whether they were listening or not—mostly they looked bored—but there were dozens of stories of Jews being arrested or harassed because they had said something when everyone was certain the Gestapo was not listening. Gestapo officials attended services on Friday nights and Saturday mornings, dressed in civilian clothes but still recognizable by their thin moustaches, their military bearing, and their looks of discomfort, searching for some sign or mark of disrespect for the Nazi government. Max Nussbaum, a rabbi in Berlin then, said that the Nazi officials usually were recognized and "for many years it did not disturb us. We dressed up what we wanted to say in old Midrashim, and instead of talking about Hitler and the Nazis, we talked about the Romans and the Babylonians. Every person in the synagogue understood that. However, the spies of the Gestapo were too dumb to understand it." But in the late 1930s, Nussbaum reported, the Gestapo caught on. "The stories with the old sources," said one Gestapo official to Nussbaum, "which you cite, we know. We are no idiots. You say Rome and Babylon, but mean Germany." From then on the rabbis became more careful, Nussbaum said, but added: "Even now I am somewhat surprised at what we risked then with our sermons."

Gestapo headquarters was at Alexanderplatz. Once a niece of Leo Baeck's was walking with him when he stopped at the S-Bahn station. He said he had to go to Alexanderplatz, and the niece understood that meant the Gestapo. She was afraid—"that was no place for a Jew," she recalled years later. But she remembered that her Uncle Leo showed no fear. "He always was poised," she said. "He never was afraid."

One who worked with Baeck at the time said, "He was the last person the Gestapo would touch because he was so much the representative of Judaism." That statement romanticizes Baeck's situation somewhat. Certainly the Nazis had learned from the time they had arrested him in 1935 because of his Yom Kippur prayer that criticism from abroad would be extensive. Also, at this point the Nazis were not ready to unleash a full-scale assault against the Jews. There was a general attitude, rather, of forcing Jews to leave Germany after first robbing them of their possessions and humiliating them. The Nazis needed someone with whom they could deal. Ideally for them it would have been someone like Georg Kareski, whom they could have controlled. Instead they had Leo Baeck, whose role was to maintain his own dignity and that of his fellow Jews while helping as many Jews as possible to emigrate. "Leo Baeck and the others were in an untenable position under the Nazis," said one who was part of that experience with them. "They represented people who could not be represented because they were prisoners." To make the situation worse, many German Jews did not understand the limits upon them or how high the prison walls were.

Baeck understood. He also understood his own role. Joachim Prinz was asked who was the most courageous man he knew when he was a rabbi in Berlin, and he answered that it was Baeck. "Leo Baeck one day simply refused to go to the Gestapo because it was the Sabbath," Prinz said. "He had been warned to appear on the Sabbath and he had refused. 'I'm not in the habit of going to an office on Saturday,' he told the Gestapo. 'It is the Sabbath. I go to services.'"

There never was any doubt about his attitude toward the Nazi officials. "On those occasions when he had to meet a German official," said Max Gruenewald, "he would speak to him with that pointed courtesy which was the nearest thing to contempt. Aristocrat that he was, given to restraint and self-discipline, he was quite capable of contempt." Eva Reichmann remembered being in a group called before the Gestapo. Jews were not allowed to sit down in the Nazi officials' presence. Baeck advanced before them, as if to place his body between the Nazis and his fellow Jews. "He stood there like a rock," said Eva Reichmann. "He was beyond death. Nothing could touch him." That perhaps was the secret of his strength. Once Natalie had died, no hurt could touch him.

And he never lost his faith in the ultimate downfall of the Nazis. Adolf Leschnitzer, who had nicknamed Baeck "the cardinal," recalled that "after some brutal and malicious steps by the Nazi regime, Leo Baeck made a comment which caused a great deal of excitement among us at a meeting of the Reichsvertretung. 'This system,' he said, 'cannot endure. It must fail and it will fail because it is built on lies.' " Leschnitzer and his friends listened to the remarks with skepticism. "Even afterwards," he said, "we laughed about it. Had the 'cardinal' still not learned how things are in this world, that coarseness and lies triumph in this world . . ." Leschnitzer later conceded that the skepticism may have been based on envy of Baeck's faith in the ultimate triumph of righteousness: "how strong he was in his understanding so that he could not be shaken."[13]

His strength before the Nazis, his leadership of the community, and his continuing role as a teacher had significance only if Leo Baeck and the organization he headed were able to persuade a large number of German Jews to leave. He had to convince them that they had no future in the land that had been so much their past, that it was worthwhile for them to surrender their economic security and brave a new world that did not show much in the way of hospitality.

Although he appreciated the need for emigration, even Baeck could not criticize his fellow Jews for refusing to realize, as he did then, that their thousand-year history in Germany had come to an end. In the spring of 1933, shortly after Hitler came to power, a friend talked to him about the necessity of emigrating and of the reluctance of the German Jews to leave. Baeck tried to make the friend understand "that the old Jewish families have grown together with the history of Germany." Many years later, when Baeck looked back upon the 1930s, he commented, "It was especially hard for German Jews to believe that *Mein Kampf* and [Hitler's] Nazi program were more than the projections of a deranged rabble rouser."

The attitudes of some German Jews were simply inexplicable. Joachim

Prinz told of a discussion he had with a prominent Jew who refused to accept Hitler as anything other than a temporary aberration. "The tower and the clock are right here in this country," said this prominent Jew. "And if I read it well, it is not midnight at all. Tomorrow will be a new day, and someday the hour will strike, and we will be free." When Rabbi Prinz visited the man in his Berlin home, he found that the Jew had sent his valuable collection of Impressionist paintings to Belgium for safekeeping. "I looked at him with great amazement," said Prinz, "and said: 'Evidently to save the paintings is important; to save Jews is not.' " Prinz did not identify the prominent Jew further, except to say that "he was a victim of his own convictions. He died in Theresienstadt."

Rudolf Callmann was a Cologne lawyer who worked with Baeck on the Reichsvertretung and then emigrated to the United States in 1935. Years later Callmann, by this time a successful lawyer, sat in his Manhattan office and said: "People told me I was smart to leave Germany. But I wasn't smart. I was lucky. I had a chance to go."

In addition to his official duties Leo Baeck also worked at a personal level to persuade people to emigrate, especially the young. In 1935 the Hebrew Union College in Cincinnati, the seminary for Reform rabbis in the United States, invited the Hochschule to send five students for training in the United States. At the time the Hochschule had difficulty finding five students willing to make the trip because the feeling of alarm still was not pervasive among the German Jews. The five who eventually did go, at the urging of Baeck and other Hochschule officials, were Alfred Wolf, Hermann Schaalman, Leo Lichtenberg, Wolli Kaelter, and W. Gunther Plaut. Kaelter remembered Baeck, who previously had visited the United States, telling him that in America one is served much chicken and at Hebrew Union College, "They have such a swimming pool!" In traveling to the United States Leo Lichtenberg had a very specific problem. He needed twenty-five marks to pay for shipping his baggage from Berlin to Paris. Baeck supplied the funds.

Jews who left Germany and then returned had a sharpened awareness of what was happening in Germany—the change could be abrupt. In 1935 Germans still told jokes on the S-Bahn and U-Bahn about Hitler; twelve months later they did not. Wolli Kaelter remembered returning to Germany after a year in Cincinnati and discussing with Baeck what the changes indicated for the future of the Jews in Germany. After listing a number of bitter prospects, Baeck said one thing that Kaelter remembered after many years: "We must make a golden book of those Germans who help us; they must not be forgotten." Leo Baeck was the one searching for and anticipating the good in his fellow man; the one who believed that, ultimately, he would not be disappointed.[14]

His acquaintances also were advised by him to leave Germany. Gertrud Gallewski had known Baeck as a young woman in Oppeln. Her husband was an accountant and, because he was Jewish, could deal with his customers only if he visited them by the back door. "I cannot do that," he said. "I am not a criminal. I have done nothing wrong." He had gone to Canada, determined he could make a living there, and returned for Gertrud. She still had three older brothers and a sister in Germany and was reluctant to place so much distance between herself and them, even when her husband begged her to leave. She heard that Baeck was vacationing nearby, and even though she hadn't seen him for thirty years, she wrote him and asked if she might come and seek his advice. When she walked into his room, he raised his hands to his forehead as a sign of the pleasure of recognizing her. She told him the situation, and he replied: "You must go with your husband. You can come back at any time, if this whole thing ends." She reflected on that meeting years later and said: "He handled me as if he were giving candy to a little girl."

Fritz Friedländer and his bride visited Baeck in 1938 before their departure. Friedländer was an old friend whom Baeck had not seen for several years. They talked in Baeck's apartment—"in his study which had a commanding view of the park; behind the desk an entire wall was covered with books. Dr. Baeck seemed to be filled with loneliness," said Friedländer, "since he had lost his wife the previous year." Baeck supported their decision to leave. "The young must go because they have no future in this land!" he insisted to them. They joked about the Friedländers' ability to speak English. Fritz Friedländer had only a rudimentary knowledge of English, but his wife was fluent in the language. "Frau Doktor," said Baeck to the wife, "if your husband continues to speak German with you, cover your ears!"

Baeck was aware of the trauma of moving to a new country, leaving behind family and friends. Letters continually went out from his home to acquaintances all over the world, introducing the German emigrants. A person coming to New York, for instance, could be "especially recommended" to an acquaintance of Baeck's there. If Baeck did not know anyone in a city, he searched out the name of a rabbinical colleague. Chief-Rabbi Landau in Johannesburg in South Africa was informed of a woman coming to his country who "has been involved for a number of years in the service of the Jewish community of Berlin and had proved herself in the best way." To those in foreign lands who were helpful there also were letters of appreciation—"I especially wish to thank you for the sincerity which you have shown to us all and especially to those who came to the New World." The letters often were handwritten by Baeck personally rather than dictated; they were his efforts to help the emigrants quickly find companionship in their new environment. They were small steps, but he believed in taking the small steps as well as the large ones.

In the late 1930s his students and associates also began to leave, and Baeck made no effort to stop the young ones. He thanked them for their help and wished them well. "You felt sort of funny," said Fritz Bamberger. "He was staying and he wanted you to leave." Baeck understood this feeling and did his best to minimize it. Once he encouraged a young teaching associate at the Hochschule to leave with his family. The young professor made all his arrangements but still felt hesitant, especially when Baeck was staying. "Don't worry," Baeck assured him, "[the Nazis] will collapse any day." Said the associate: "Perhaps I shouldn't emigrate." Baeck recovered quickly, saying: "Since you have all your papers, you might as well go. But, to be cautious, don't quit the Hochschule now. Just take a leave of absence."

The young professor left with his family; recalling the incident years later, he said: "I still have my leave of absence."

Baeck could have been helpful to his relatives; he had been one of eleven children, and his brothers and sisters had produced a large crop of nephews and nieces. However, a nephew recalled that "His own relatives were at the end of the line. The family was somewhat upset by that but never reproached him. We were told that we shouldn't speak to him about it."[15]

There were countless obstacles for those wishing to emigrate. The largest Jewish community in the world at the time was in the United States. It was generous in raising funds to help the Jews in Germany but was reluctant to encourage wholesale emigration. Robert Weltsch, editor of the *Jüdische Rundschau*, met in 1934 with a group of prominent American Jews who insisted to him that the German Jews should not renounce their German rights by wholesale emigration. "You don't understand what is happening in Germany," Weltsch shot back. The next year Max Kreutzberger and Otto Hirsch of the Reichsvertretung had a similar experience with other American Jews. If the United

States could be persuaded to accept the German Jews, the Americans said, in effect, then Poland and Rumania might decide to oust their Jews also, convinced that the United States would accept them.

Whatever the attitudes of the American Jews, there was nothing they could do to change the immigration laws, which at that time blocked entry of any substantial number of newcomers. A decade earlier the United States had closed its doors to the tired, the hungry, and the oppressed.[16]

The United States and the rest of the western world were not free of the virus that affected Germany. Anti-Semitism was prevalent. The restrictions under which German Jews had lived in the 1920s were little different from those Jews faced in the United States and England. They could not buy property in certain locations. Many hotels and resorts refused to admit them. Schools like Harvard University made no secret of their quota systems. Advancement in many careers was denied Jews. Violence often erupted. Anti-Semitism existed at all levels, in the country club and at the corner bar. Intellectuals like Toynbee in England wrote histories of civilization that dismissed the Jews as insignificant. In the United States during the early 1920s the Ku Klux Klan, which opposed blacks and Catholics as well as Jews, gained control of the Democratic Party in some states and exerted a powerful influence on the party in others.

In the 1930s Germany claimed it was doing no more than other countries did or would like to do. "... [I]t is scarcely surprising that Germany's policy towards the Jews should have had such a resounding echo throughout the world," went one propaganda diatribe against the Jews directed by Germany toward the English-speaking world. "Germany is suffering the fate of all those, who, whether nations or individuals, have sufficient courage and sense of responsibility to practise and defend a conviction fundamentally opposed to the dominating principles of the times. No great human achievement has been accomplished, save at the cost of struggle and sacrifice." This German concept of heroic service carried over to the 1940s, when the Germans believed they were solving not only their own Jewish problem with the death camps but also that of the other nations of the world.[17]

Between Hitler's coming to power at the beginning of 1933 and July 1, 1938—five and one-half years—the total number of German Jewish refugees who were admitted to the United States was 27,000, only 1,000 more than the German emigration quota for one year. Why such a small number? The bureaucracy of the American State Department was filled with men who had emerged from the country clubs and the college fraternities which did not admit Jews. Its offices abroad were staffed with men who had grown up believing that Jews were a people apart from the normal strata of society. Scholars have found comments in records of the period like "Let Hitler have his way," America should not be "flooded" with liberal professors, and on and on.

Officials with that attitude were staffing the American consulate offices in Germany. Max Nussbaum, a rabbi in Berlin at the time, charged that "the greatest misfortune for the Jews in Berlin" was an American official there "who sabotaged the entire emigration." A Jew who obtained the Nazis' permission to leave Germany then had to apply for a U.S. visa. At the consulate offices every piece of red tape and obstruction possible was placed in front of the applicant. The highest task, said Nussbaum of the Jews in the United States with influence in the government, was to have that particular official removed. But that official was not atypical. Harold L. Ickes, who served as Secretary of the Interior in President Franklin D. Roosevelt's administration during this period, accused the State Department of being "a conglomeration of ambitious men consisting mainly of careerists who, because they are career men, feel no obligation to follow Administration policy. I believe that, in substance, it is undemocratic in its outlook and shot through with fascism." Representative Emanuel Celler, whose Brooklyn district was almost entirely Jewish, had a more succinct criticism, describing the State Department as having a "heartbeat muffled in protocol."[18]

In England the situation was not significantly different. Chaim Weizmann, whose responsibility was assisting German Jews to emigrate to Palestine, frequently visited British government officials to seek help in easing the Jews' path to Palestine. No, that couldn't be done, he was told. Could the officials then assist the plight of the Jews in Germany by publicly denouncing the Nazi treatment of Jews in Germany, thus bringing international pressure on the Nazis? No, that couldn't be done either. The reasons offered were endless—one could not interfere with the internal affairs of another nation; initiatives for emigration should come from the Germans; trade relationships were important; on and on went these explanations, always adding up to one point: Almost nothing could be done.

France, Germany's neighbor, was perhaps the easiest place, in terms of emigration, for the Jews to find refuge; all they had to do was cross the border. But modern anti-Semitism, which had begun in France with the Dreyfus affair, had not ended there. In 1938 the German foreign minister, Joachim von Ribbentrop, met with his French counterpart, Georges Bonnet. The problem of the Jews emerged toward the end of their conversation. Bonnet expressed his concern—but not at the plight of the Jews. The Nazi treatment of the German Jews had caused so many to move into France that the French economy was strained. That was the problem.[19]

Palestine was one of the few countries where the Jew could feel welcome. Also, because of its historical and religious attraction for the Jew, it exerted a strong appeal for those German Jews emigrating. But emigrating to Palestine presented difficulties also. In addition to the British unwillingness to allow emigration as the decade ended, there was the problem of hostilities between Arabs and the Jews. Not only would the Jewish professors or lawyers have to give up their books and their cultured lives to become farmers and pioneers, they also would have to keep their rifles at their sides. Baeck, because of his many acquaintances in Palestine and because of his real concern for the plight of the minority, maintained an abiding interest in the welfare of the Arabs. He also held the pragmatic view that Jews and Arabs would have to live side by side if Palestine was to be a land of peace.

Leo Baeck had written in *The Essence of Judaism* that "the measure of justice is always its application to the few." When he wrote that, he was referring to how Jews were treated. He knew, however, that the same statement also applied to how Jews treat others. In a long letter to Chaim Weizmann in December of 1936 he wrote: "The essential point is that a constructive positive program of relations with the Arabs can be developed." He wanted to look the facts "in the eye." Conceding that a total answer might not be available, Baeck insisted that "a program not entirely complete is always better than evading a program or having no program at all." Baeck said the "basis and presumption of every program is the historical and legal right of the Jewish people to emigrate to Palestine." He then envisioned a program of Jew and Arab working together—"Every division into cantons must be avoided" —to turn the desert into productive land. The best way to achieve the proper cooperation, said Baeck, "is through production facilities financed by state help." A year later Baeck wrote to a Zionist friend, "Maybe now is the psychological moment for a new try at a connection with the Arabs," and sent a copy of his letter to Weizmann.[20]

The cooperation of which Baeck spoke never came about in any meaningful way, something that Baeck and others would regret for decades. The political situation of the time being what it was, there may never have been a chance for such cooperation. Baeck was talking of developing a relationship between individual Jews and Arabs, bringing them together in their workplaces and developing a joint pride in their achievements. In contrast Zionism at the time was banking its political hopes on dealing not with individuals but with factions—the British who had the Palestine mandate, the Arab leaders—because at the time that was how the game of international politics was played.

Almost any country a Jew sought to visit was inhospitable. Alexander Guttmann, a young Hochschule faculty member, was getting married in 1937 and wanted to honeymoon in a foreign country. "I visited many foreign consulates in Berlin to obtain visitors' visas," he recalled. "Invariably, the first question of the consul, or his representative, was: 'Are you Jewish?'" Since his answer was affirmative, the visas were not granted. The reason was "'Rather than return to Germany, you might remain in our country just to save your lives.'" Guttmann said those Jews who tried crossing borders illegally were chased back by the French and interned by the Swiss in camps no better than prisons.

Those German Jews who found a country willing to accept them still faced the problem that the move would bankrupt them, requiring all of their savings and whatever estate they and their families had accumulated for generations. Before the Nazis had come to power, Germany had a "flight tax" law requiring that any persons wishing to emigrate surrender 25 percent of their possessions to the government. After the Nazis came to power, the law was aimed especially at the Jews. Eventually the Jews had to surrender almost 100 percent of their possessions, meaning the emigrant arrived in the new country penniless.

The shortage of countries willing to accept Jews and the profits to be made by the unscrupulous from emigration led to the development of rackets to exploit the emigrants. Money was paid by the Jews, but then disappeared. People sold information on what visas were available; the price was high and the information generally was wrong. A Nazi official in Berlin did well for himself by confiscating the passports of wealthy Jews and then reselling them back to their owners for exorbitant prices. The policy in the 1930s, a Nazi official conceded later, had been one of robbing the Jews. "That wasn't very nice," he said, "but it wasn't criminal."

Influenced by the money to be made from the Jews, the Nazis encouraged their emigration in the 1930s. In 1938, for example, the only non-Jewish firms allowed to advertise in Jewish newspapers were transport and shipping companies selling passage to emigrants. "We have the greatest interest in encouraging the emigration of Jews . . ." explained the order.

Transportation was not cheap. Shanghai was the only city in the world not requiring a visa, but the costs of traveling there were prohibitive for many Jews. For the first six months of 1937 the Hilfsverein der Juden in Deutschland, a Reichsvertretung affiliate, provided almost 400,000 marks to help Jews emigrate. In addition the American Joint Distribution Committee provided 225,000 marks and the emigrants themselves paid 150,000 marks. Agencies then were paying about four times what the migrants were paying. The grants were limited to actual emigration expenses, namely third-class rail and steamship lines, the cost of translating and stamping documents, immigration fees, and the like.[21]

For some years there had been concern outside the borders of Germany about the plight of German Jews. James G. McDonald, in charge of refugees for the League of Nations, resigned that post dramatically in 1935 to protest the ineffective and callous attitude of the member nations to the plight of the German Jews. He said in his resignation:

When domestic policy threatens hundreds of thousands of human beings with demoralization and exile, the considerations of diplomatic correctness must take second place to the considerations of simple humanity. I would feel unworthy if I would fail to draw attention to this situation, if I would fail to advocate that world opinion, represented by the League of Nations, its member states and also other countries, must move to abate the already existing and still threatening tragedies.

The numerous newspaper stories emanating from Germany, the appeals of the Reichsvertretung leaders, and the reactions of visitors to Germany all finally forced a call for action. President Franklin D. Roosevelt of the United States asked the nations of the world to send representatives to a meeting at Evian-les-Bains in France to discuss the refugee problem and its possible solutions.

The Evian meeting had been suggested to Roosevelt by Sumner Welles, the number-two man in the State Department. This is the meeting's origins as described by Theodore C. Achilles, a State Department official who was acting as secretary of the intergovernmental committee on refugees:

The Secretary [Cordell Hull], Mr. Welles, Mr. Messersmith [the American ambassador to Germany then] and Mr. Moffet decided that it would be inadvisable for the Department merely to resist the pressure [to ease the immigration laws], and that it would be far preferable to get out in front and attempt to guide the pressure, primarily with a view toward forestalling attempts to have the immigation laws liberalized. The idea of the Evian intergovernmental meeting was suggested by Mr. Welles and approved by the President on March 22 . . .

Roosevelt's motivations can only be speculated upon. Domestically he was pushed from two sides. He had managed to wrest Jewish political support from its traditional home in the Republican party and wanted to retain it for the Democrats. At the same time, he was aware of the widespread anti-Semitism in the United States; his New Deal had been attacked as the "Jew" deal. One of the most popular politicians in the United States at the time was the Catholic priest, Charles E. Coughlin, who spewed forth weekly diatribes against the Jews over the radio. Caught between those two pressures, Roosevelt did what he often did in such cases: He attempted to placate both sides and succeeded—in this instance, at least—in helping no one. What resulted at Evian was a tawdry public relations move that created new problems rather than solving old ones.

Achilles wrote that "It is easy to dismiss the whole problem by saying 'nobody wants any more Jews.' That is unquestionably true." His own recommendation was that the United States agree to absorb the number of Jews equal to its regular German quota, between 27,000 and 30,000 annually, and encourage other nations also to take additional refugees so that the total number of German Jews absorbed by these countries each year would total 100,000. In effect his plan was for the emigration of all German Jews within five years. That could have solved the problem if any nations—including the United States—had been willing to help the Jewish refugees. But as he had reported: "Nobody wants any more Jews."[22]

Delegates from thirty-two nations attended the conference, which was held from July 6 to July 14, 1938. A few months earlier Hitler, contrary to his expressed promises, had annexed Austria. This further exacerbated the refugee problem as those trying to escape that country were added to those attempting to flee Germany. For these people Evian held much promise. However, the United States said in advance that it had no intention of changing its immigration policy and expected that no other nation would do so. England attended only on the basis that Palestine, and its availability as a refuge for Jews, not be discussed. A Jewish commentator on the Evian conference later described the meeting as the "Jewish Munich," saying that, instead of helping Jews, it broke down "all the protective barriers defending the Jews as individuals and as communities." There was no beneficence on the part of the attending nations as they stood up to announce that they had no room at the inns in their nations for the latter-day Josephs and Marys.

In Berlin the Reichsvertretung officials looked to the Evian conference as a sincere rescue effort. They sent a report to the conference of seventeen pages plus six appendices with statistics about Jewish emigration, age breakdown of the remaining Jews in Germany, occupations, education—all the information required by a conference sincerely interested in assisting refugees. The paper began with the statement that "The Jews in Germany are determined to exert all their strength, to place their organizational and financial leadership ability in the service of the progress of a major emigration plan . . ."

The Reichsvertretung asked that receiving countries ease their demand that each individual emigrant possess a certain amount of money to require only that the family unit possess such a sum—this would help to prevent the breaking up of families. It also asked that the site where the refugees were allowed to settle be capable of providing an economic base. There were other requests and provisions, based on the assumption that help would be forthcoming.

None was. The delegates to the conference made their speeches, then went home. A new committee was appointed, but it produced no results. It was not designed to. No country increased its quota. No country eased its immigration restrictions. No country protested formally to Germany over its actions. And in Berlin the Jews, who had hoped for so much, realized that once again their neighbors had turned their backs on them. "Nichts ist so schlimm," said Leo Baeck, "wie das Schweigen"— "Nothing is so sad as silence."[23]

Against all these difficulties—the reluctance of many Jews to admit their world in Germany had ended, the thievery of the Nazis, the cost of travel, the resistance on the part of the nations of the world to providing a refuge for the Jews—how well did Leo Baeck and the other leaders do in persuading the Jews to leave?

Years later Baeck himself said: "What is a number? We think too much in numbers. We forget that each is a man with his soul and his body and his fear." Still, numbers are a measurement. Against all the difficulties the German Jews faced, by the end of 1938 one-third of them had emigrated. They had left their homes, their friends, their possessions, and gone to a strange land, to take up new careers, to begin their lives again. Approximately two-fifths, 60,000, of these emigrants had left in the first two years of the Nazi regime. They were the younger ones— the writers, professors, the politically and culturally active. Through the next five years another 90,000 to 100,000 Jews also left. In addition to the 27,000 that went to the United States, approximately 50,000 went to Palestine and perhaps 40,000 emigrated to other European countries. Small numbers went to the Union of South Africa and to South American nations (only Argentina accepted any appreciable number of Jews, 13,000; Brazil took 7,500, and a few other South American nations took no more than 1,500 each). More than half of those who left Germany were under the age of forty; Leo Baeck had been successful in his efforts to persuade the young to leave. At the beginning of 1933 one-fourth of the German Jews were under the age of twenty-five. At the time of the Evian conference that had been reduced to 17 percent. In 1933 two-thirds of the German Jews were under fifty years of age; by the Evian conference slightly more than half were under fifty.

This was a modern exodus, perhaps even more daring than the Biblical one. In that ancient exodus the Jews were armed with two strengths; they left as a unit and none among them could argue that it might be more advantageous to remain in Egypt, where they had been slaves. In this modern exodus there was no large caravan of men with their families, shepherding their possessions, crossing the border like a great army with the Holy Ark before them. Instead, there was the son, traveling alone in a third-class carriage, without possessions—if all went well, to be followed by parents, brothers, and sisters; grandparents, if possible. For those who left, like the participants in the Biblical exodus, the dangers were great, but they had been urged to take the chance to preserve their heritage and to fulfill their lives. As Leo Baeck said in 1934:

For us German Jews it has become today a special, almost historical task to assure childhood and youth to the young people who have been given to us. To us has the responsibility been entrusted to protect the new generation from psychological pain, and wherever it is needed to assist them to find a place where the soul that wants to breathe in the light may develop in the clean air, protected from disagreeable and evil things. To create man's life through youth stands before us as a duty.

Baeck and his fellow Jews achieved that goal to a remarkable degree against outstanding difficulties.[24]

This emigration of one-third of the German Jews took place prior to the closing months of 1938, when it still was possible to believe that there was a future in Germany for a Jew. In the fall of 1938 events destroyed that illusion. The sequence of events began in September when Adolf Hitler, having secured Austria, sought to gain the Sudeten area of Czechoslovakia, and the nations of the world capitulated. Prime Minister Neville Chamberlain of England returned from Munich, where the deed was done, to announce the securing of peace "for our time." Hitler, astonished at his ability to subdue the nations of the world, moved freely to the next step. Truman Smith, the military attaché at the American embassy in Berlin, reported: "The national security won at Munich created those international conditions which permitted Hitler to proceed, without danger of foreign interference, to the liquidation of that non-German element within the German people, which in his eyes, stood in the way of the realization of the concept of National Socialism on a racial basis."

Munich led then to the event known as *Kristallnacht*, the night of the crystal glass, so described in history because of the shattered crystal glass from the broken windows of the synagogues strewn through the streets of Germany. On the night of November 9 the Germans, with the open support of their government, went on a rage of destruction, thievery, violence, and animalism.

"How often have the scenes of that night returned to us," said Leo Baeck some years later, "whether we wished it or not, that night . . . when the great blasphemy took place—the destruction of the synagogues. Once again we seemed to hear, even though we stopped up our ears, the voices of those who shouted to us: 'The synagogues are burning!' What is it that was then destroyed? Not only were the synagogues demolished, but with them there collapsed the pillars and supports of a human bond in which we had trusted." A human bond? "One thing," said Baeck, "we thought, would still bind us together: a reverence for that place to which men come in order that they may be made one with the Eternal, raised above the narrowness and hardship of their everyday life, where the invisible is made known to them and the infinite silence embraces them."

No Jew had any hope of a future in Germany after that evening and the following day. "Many can remember how they stood in the street that night," said Baeck. "A fearful, oppressive silence lay over the town. But then the silence began to speak and when this happened, its language was powerful and overwhelming. And those who heard it also saw something at the same time. It was a dark night and it seemed to them that they saw, on the nocturnal horizon, far above the land of Germany, an invisible handwriting, adding word to word—these words which the Prophet had seen." Baeck then quoted from Daniel 5:26–28— "*Mene mene tekel upharsin*—*Mene:* God has numbered the days of your kingdom and brought it to an end; *Tekel:* you have been weighed in the balance and found wanting; *Upharsin:* your kingdom is divided and given to the Medes and Persians."[25]

In retrospect *Kristallnacht* could have been anticipated. For years German Protestants had read the words of Martin Luther that the synagogues should be burned. For years Germans had accepted their government's anti-Semitic policies. "The German public was deeply anti-Semitic," reported a military attaché at the American embassy in a report on the events. Catholic church leaders had watched it all; not speaking, only protecting themselves and their institution. And the Germans had learned that the rest of the world did not appear to care what Germany did to its Jews. At Evian nations had made lukewarm protests but took no action. At Munich nations had demonstrated their willingness to accept unlawful behavior by Nazi Germany. Adolf Hitler had free rein.

The tragedy of *Kristallnacht* was not the destruction. No nation has been free of violence. No nation has been free of the rowdiness of the ignorant. The tragedy, rather, was that government, which should protect the individual and his property against violence, in this instance encouraged and abetted the violence against the Jews. The violence was a joint act by the government and the populace. Early the day of November 9 a message went out from Gestapo headquarters: "There will be very shortly in Germany actions against the Jews, especially against the synagogues. These actions are not to be interfered with."[26]

The excuse for the outburst was the murder of a German embassy official in Paris by a Jewish youth. There was nothing spontaneous about the events, however. An American military attaché in Berlin reported, "As early as Tuesday, November 8th [the day before the violence], rumors that reprisals would be taken in case [the embassy official] died, were heard in Berlin and the German official press commenced an inflammatory anti-Semitic propaganda." When the news of the official's death reached Berlin, late on the evening of the ninth, "preparations had been completed for a simultaneous demonstration throughout the Reich." The report, by Major Percy G. Black, continued:

Squads of men dressed in civilian clothes and armed with clubs set out under a prearranged plan to destroy Jewish property throughout the city. The operation of the squads, some of which were personally witnessed, was conducted under the direction of a leader who had been provided with a map giving the area which he was to cover and the location of Jewish property in that area. These squads proceeded from store to store, breaking windows, upsetting show cases and in some instances entering the store, scattering the goods on the floor and destroying the fixtures. As these squads, some in trucks, some on foot, proceeded with their work of destruction, the crowds looked on idly. Some instances of disapprobation occurred and occasional disorder. During the entire day, the police did not interfere. Traffic policemen remained at their posts, while squads of city police were held in readiness in case of serious rioting and to keep order and prevent the spread of fire where synagogues were burned. Late Thursday afternoon the work of destruction was officially halted by Dr. Goebbels over the radio.

While the crowds looked on in some cases, in others the populace joined enthusiastically in the attacks. Michael Bruce, a non-Jewish Englishman, provided this eyewitness account:

...hurriedly we went out into the street. It was crowded with people, all hurrying towards a nearby synagogue, shouting and gesticulating angrily.

We followed. As we reached the synagogue and halted, silent and angry, on the fringe of the mob, flames began to rise from one end of the building. It was the signal for a wild cheer. The crowd surged forward and greedy hands tore seats and woodwork from the building to feed the flames.

Behind us we heard more shouts. Turning we saw a section of the mob start off along the road towards Israel's store where during the day piles of granite cubes, ostensibly for repairing the roads, had been heaped. Youths, men and women, howling deliriously, hurled the blocks through the windows and at the closed doors. In a few minutes the doors gave way and the mob, shouting and fighting, surged inside to pillage and loot.

By now the streets were a chaos of screaming bloodthirsty people lusting for Jewish bodies. I saw Harrison of the News Chronicle, trying to protect an aged Jewess who had been dragged from her home by a gang. I pushed my way through to help him and between us we managed to heave her through the crowd to a sidestreet and safety.

We turned back towards Israel's, but now the crowd, eager for fresh conquests, was pouring down a side road towards the outskirts of the city. We hurried after them in time to see one of the foulest exhibitions of bestiality I have ever witnessed.

The object of the mob's hate was a hospital for sick Jewish children, many of them cripples or consumptives. In minutes the windows had been smashed and the doors forced. When we arrived the swine were driving the wee mites out over the broken glass, bare-footed and wearing nothing but their nightshirts. The nurses, doctors and attendants were being kicked and beaten by the mob leaders, most of whom were women.

Emil Fackenheim, a student at the Hochschule, rushed to the building the next morning. "I saw a piano in the middle of the street, and a German was playing it. He laughed. 'Ha, ha. It still works. The Jew piano can still play.'" Selma Schiratzki, a teacher in one of the Jewish schools founded by the Reichsvertretung, tried to conduct classes the next morning, but the classes were canceled because so many parents took their children out of the building. That turned out to be fortunate. Later in that day a mob of 200 German children, led by adults, broke into the building. Not finding any Jewish children to molest, they smashed windows and destroyed books and musical instruments.

Werner Rosenstock remembered hurrying that night to the Fasanenstrasse Synagogue. At its opening in 1912 it had been described as an architectural beauty. Located near the Kurfürstendamm, it symbolized the movement of the Jews into the middle-class residential areas. The Kaiser was represented at its opening, along with the army. That event had been an important one to all Germans; late on the night of November 9, 1938, Werner Rosenstock watched the Fasanenstrasse Synagogue burn while across the street fire engines stood unused.

Said Ernst Herzfeld:

I saw the ruins of burned-down synagogues and homes, empty stores with shattered glass, furniture ruined and left-over goods strewn around. I was told that especially loyal teachers were leading the classes which were entrusted to them to show "the just punishment on the Jews." These educators didn't have anything to say against the children filling their pockets with chocolate or bonbons belonging to Jews. The police standing on the street didn't notice that very close to them, in the light of day, the work of destruction continued. They concentrated exclusively on the "order" of the large crowd of people and especially on the remarks of the people passing by on the street. Whoever dared a word of criticism was immediately arrested and transported away.

Police were ordered to arrest a certain number of Jews in their homes. They obeyed those orders literally. Some Jews avoided arrest by spending the night walking through the streets of Berlin far away from their homes. Other Jews were hauled from their apartments and their beds and brought to the police station at Alexanderplatz, where officials had not "the slightest idea of what they should do with us. They were confused and telephoned in our presence for further instructions," said one who had been arrested. Another Jew complained that he had influenza, but police ignored his protests and dragged him to the police station anyway.

Attacks and arrests were widespread throughout Germany. In Oppeln, in 1897, Leo Baeck had dedicated the new synagogue there by saying that more important than its appearance was the spirit existing within it to shape great and powerful things. This was the "tranquil, dignified structure, so much in harmony with the tranquil, dignified people." That synagogue burned so brightly on *Kristallnacht* that those who saw the flames never forgot them. Thirty-six years after *Kristallnacht* a Franciscan monk who had witnessed the scene in 1938 jumped from his chair, raised his hands before his eyes, and, as he recalled the flames sweeping up through the synagogue tower, cried: *"Der Turm! Der Turm!"*

There were some minor triumphs on *Kristallnacht*. Rabbi Max Nussbaum was awakened by a telephone call from Louis Lochner, the American newspaperman. "Lochner was a Christian," said Nussbaum, "from whom we often received in the quickest way news about the plans of the Nazi government and which I, in the last years, would immediately pass on" to Baeck and other Jewish leaders. Lochner told Nussbaum of the burning of the synagogues. The rabbi dressed and rushed to the Friedenstempel Synagogue, where he usually officiated. It was burning: "the fire engines stood by, protecting, however, only the neighboring buildings from destruction." The synagogue's cantor and Nussbaum managed to enter the burning building through a rear door, hoping to save the Torah scrolls. Inside the synagogue Nussbaum and the cantor found that the Holy Ark, where the scrolls were kept, already had been pulled open and the scrolls had been torn apart. "I entered unseen behind the Torah cabinet," said Nussbaum, "and was able to save a small Torah scroll and was able to hide it under my coat. We went out and although an SS lieutenant looked at us in a threatening way, we got away without being disturbed." Rabbi Nussbaum came to the United States in 1940, bringing that Torah scroll with him to use in his new congregation. On Simchat Torah, the day when Jews carry the Torah scrolls through their congregation as a sign of their joy that God has given them the Torah, "I myself carried it always in the processions," said Rabbi Nussbaum, "through the synagogue." That Torah scroll was a symbol that Judaism had survived.[27]

Ernst G. Lowenthal, a Jewish newspaper editor, was brought to Gestapo headquarters at Alexanderplatz. He and some other editors were informed by Nazi officials that their publications would cease printing as of that moment. They were told also that they had agreed to this. After several hours the editors were released, and Lowenthal returned home, stunned. Shortly afterward he was visited by Julius Seligsohn of the Reichsvertretung "with his hat pulled low and his coat collar up." Seligsohn knew the Gestapo wanted to arrest him, and he had to get information to Leo Baeck. His informants had told him that the Nazis, not content with destroying the Jews' property, intended to make them pay a cash penalty, too. Seligsohn assumed that Baeck's apartment was being watched and asked Lowenthal to deliver the information for him.

Lowenthal agreed, and early on the morning of November 10 he went to Baeck's apartment. "When Leo Baeck opened the door," recalled Ernst Lowenthal, "he had his suit jacket off and was in his shirt-sleeves. He seemed bewildered." Never in his life to that point had Leo Baeck been seen by his associates in his shirt-sleeves. Never had he been seen bewildered, in less than perfect control of himself. "He soon recovered himself," said Lowenthal of Baeck, "and within five minutes was discussing everything clearly." But for a few minutes Leo Baeck—the man who believed in loving one's neighbor because he "is as thou"—had been undone by those who celebrated the gods of violence and of bigotry, of power and of hate.

Baeck hurried to the Reichsvertretung office where the reports of damage were coming in. Synagogues, homes, and businesses had been attacked throughout all of Germany; many Jews had been arrested and taken to the concentration camps that were then already an established part of the Nazi order. There never were exact figures, but approximately 200 synagogues were destroyed; 8,000 shops were destroyed, looted, or badly damaged. Three dozen Jews were killed. Thousands were arrested. But those figures are only minimum estimates. After a point it became impossible to count.

It now was early in the morning, and Baeck and Otto Hirsch began a futile journey, a pathetic one. Together they trooped from government office to government office, hoping to see some official, anyone, with whom they could plead for an end to the violence, an end to the arrests. By nine in the morning they had returned; no one would see them. A Jewish official named Ernst Marcus said years later: "I still see the small room of Paul Eppstein [a Reichsvertretung administrator] before me. I hear clearly the throbbing in his voice when he reported to me hastily of the situation and the unsuccessful effort which Dr. Baeck and

Otto Hirsch had made to meet with someone either in the Reichs chancellory or the Interior Ministry."[28]

Richard Fuchs, a Hochschule official, ordered the building closed and the iron gates at the main entrance shut—an order that saved the building from being looted. He then went to the Reichsvertretung offices on Kantstrasse where he met Baeck, who told him of his own failure to make contact with any government official. Fuchs knew the Prussian minister of finance and offered to approach him. Because Baeck and the others now were operating on the assumption that all their telephones were tapped, Fuchs went to a booth outside the building to telephone the minister, Dr. Johannes Popitz. Popitz agreed to see Fuchs at his home. "This was in the then circumstances rather courageous of him," said Fuchs. He hurried back to the Reichsvertretung office to inform Baeck and Hirsch. "I hardly had time . . ." he said, "when the Gestapo appeared at the Reichsvertretung and forbade us harshly to leave the house." The Jews thought they were being arrested, but as it turned out they were only searched for documents and then allowed to leave the building singly. The Nazis then locked the building.

When Fuchs met with Popitz that afternoon, the minister said there was nothing he could do to stop the persecution of the Jews—"I gathered that he was, in fact, powerless," said Fuchs. "The ultimate instigator of this persecution was beyond his reach." When they parted on the porch of Popitz's house, the minister put his hand on the shoulder of the Jew. "We have picked a bad period for our life, Fuchs," he said. Popitz was executed by the Nazis in 1944.

With the Reichsvertretung office closed, Leo Baeck's apartment became the central meeting place for leaders of the Berlin Jewish community. There they gathered the statistics on the arrests and destruction and received information from embassy officials of various nations about the possibilities for emigration. *Kristallnacht* had done something that the Jews had not been able to do themselves; it shocked some countries—especially England—into arranging for the entry of more Jews.

Another activity originating in Baeck's apartment was the dissemination of information to the members of the foreign press. The correspondents were ready. They knew that they had witnessed a story that had to be told. Louis Lochner called *Kristallnacht* "the most terrible experience in all my life . . . I never dreamed that human nature could descend to such depravity and sadism and cruelty as I was witness to . . . We have all become much older, and we sometimes wonder when we shall ever be able to really laugh again." Lochner and many other non-Germans living in Berlin turned their homes into refuges. "Haunted and hunted creatures pitifully begged for a night's lodging, and no Christian that I knew said no," he told his children. "We left it to the heathens to take upon themselves the odium of perpetrating crimes that will some day cost the country dearly." The Nazis tried to suppress the story or tone it down. "They've done everything to gag us," said Lochner, "but I am determined to tell the truth honestly, though with understatement."

Lochner and his fellow correspondents could not be suppressed; the story did get out of Germany. The world was shocked. The scab had been pulled off the festering sore. The reaction of President Roosevelt was representative. He no longer worried about anti-Semitism in the United States, about the references to his "Jew" deal. He angrily recalled the American ambassador from Berlin and condemned the Nazi atrocity. "I myself," he said, "could scarcely believe that such things could occur in a twentieth century civilization."[29]

The situation for the Nazis in world opinion was made worse by their continued attacks on the Jews. Not only had the Nazis destroyed the Jews' property and their houses of worship, they also ordered that Jews be prohibited from collecting on their insurance as well as pay a substantial cash fine. Two days after *Kristallnacht*, at a meeting in Goering's office, the decision was made: "For the aryanization of the economy, the basic thought is the following: The Jew will be cut out of the economy and will give his economic goods to the state." Almost six years earlier Leo Baeck had told a disbelieving audience that the thousand-year history of the Jews in Germany had come to an end. Finally, no one doubted him.

Church groups around the world, Protestant and Catholic, denounced *Kristallnacht*. The event did much to persuade them to sympathize with the Jews' plight, if not to support the migration of Jews. In Germany, however, with a silence that was impressive, no church groups protested. A few months later the Catholic church in Germany honored Adolf Hitler on his fiftieth birthday with special masses to implore God's blessing upon him. None realized, as Leo Baeck commented later, that during *Kristallnacht* "a hand was also laid on the Church . . . Jewish and Christian houses of worship share in the ultimate resort an indivisible fate. What is inflicted on one causes injury to the other. Many a day later this was made clear in Germany, and only the person who willfully blinded himself failed to see this, either then or later."[30]

A few weeks after *Kristallnacht* Otto Hirsch was arrested. He had been in poor health, and, said Baeck, "he suffered much hardship under the deprivations and the pressures of arrest." Again, Baeck traveled to the Gestapo headquarters seeking the release of his friend and coworker. Hirsch had been transferred to the Sachsenhausen concentration camp. The Gestapo refused Baeck's request, then directed him to reopen the Reichsvertretung to handle the large number of Jews wanting to emigrate. Baeck said he could not operate unless Hirsch were released. "Why?" demanded a Gestapo official. "Is Hirsch your right hand?" Baeck replied: "No, I am the left hand of Hirsch." The Gestapo ordered Hirsch released. When Hirsch returned from the concentration camp, although he had lost a great deal of weight and his head had been shaved, "He was still the same," recalled Baeck. "The first words which he spoke were words of jest, just as if he might have returned from a trip. Without pause he returned to his work."

Leo Baeck could speak and act as he did with the Gestapo because he did not fear arrest. A young rabbi named Alfred Jospe was picked up by the Gestapo. "I was thereby contaminated," Rabbi Jospe said. "Leo Baeck was only one of two persons brave enough to visit my wife to console her and to offer to help her. He had to walk up five flights to the apartment."[31]

Baeck's interest in persuading young rabbis to leave Germany became his passion. One of his problems was locating specific positions abroad for them so they could obtain visas outside the ordinary quota system. In a letter of January 25, 1939, to his friend Ismar Elbogen, then living in the United States, Baeck reported on his efforts. First, he said, all the rabbis, except one, and all the Hochschule students, again except one, had been released from prison, "and I hope the same will happen soon with the others." Certificates for Palestine had been obtained for several rabbis, and for "a couple of others, permits for England." The most important thing, he wrote, was that a camp for the emigrants had been opened in England. "I was there in England for that, a couple of weeks ago," said Baeck. Several of the Berlin rabbis would receive permits to officiate there, "and I will have the opportunity to place three or four of our students there as helpers." France seemed to be opening up slightly, he said, but "From America, nothing tangible has arrived." He closed the letter with "There is a lot to do here . . . but it has to be carried out."

Rabbi Jospe remembered a meeting of a group of senior rabbis shortly after *Kristallnacht*. They recognized the need for leaving and spoke about using their contacts and their influence to find positions abroad. "This is the only time I ever saw Leo Baeck angry," said Jospe. "He wasn't yelling; he never yelled. But he was really forceful, bearing down. He said to the older rabbis: 'Let the younger men go. You have lived your life. They haven't had a chance to live theirs. You have no right to take advantage of the fortuitous circumstances which can help you.'"

A young rabbi, Ignaz Maybaum, was scheduled to depart from Germany with his wife on a Tuesday. Saturday morning, the Sabbath, the couple visited Baeck. They had a problem. Allowed to take only ten marks out of Germany, should they go to the bank that morning for the funds and violate the Sabbath, or should they wait until Monday and risk the Nazis changing their mind about the money? Leo Baeck, who would not violate the Sabbath by going to the Gestapo office, advised them to go to the bank that morning.

Baeck himself had opportunities to leave—the trip to England he mentioned to Elbogen was only one of the quick trips abroad he would make in 1939—but he had determined to remain in Germany to help his fellow Jews. How long would he stay? Michael Bruce, the Englishman who had been so shocked by *Kristallnacht*, persuaded a friend, Pat Malone, to carry two passengers to safety in a private airplane. Bruce asked Wilfred Israel, a Jew who owned a large store in Berlin, and Leo Baeck if they wanted to use the opportunity to flee from Germany.

Wilfred Israel replied, "I will go when the Rabbi goes." Then he looked at Baeck.

"I will go," said Leo Baeck, "when I am the last Jew alive in Germany."[32]

11 WAR

ALTHOUGH THE REACTION abroad to *Kristallnacht* surprised the Nazis, they would not relax their drive against the Jews. Adolf Hitler would lead the Germans to even greater excesses. There continued to be a political shrewdness to his exploitation of anti-Semitism. Two decades earlier Hitler had used it to gain support among German dissidents; now he used anti-Semitism to gain support in eastern Europe, where he wished to expand his power. Truman Smith, the military attaché in the American embassy, reported shortly after *Kristallnacht* that Germany's army, "her inexhaustible market for southeastern European products," and her anti-Semitism were the devices for establishing a German "imperium" in eastern Europe. "The last of these weapons," Smith wrote, "is in many ways the most trenchant of all. In fact the advantages accruing to her from anti-Semitism in eastern Europe would seem to balance or outweigh the manifest losses this policy will bring her in Anglo-Saxon countries." Then Smith listed the eastern European areas where anti-Semitism was a powerful force—Slovakia, Hungary, Rumania, Poland, and the Carpathian Ukraine.[1]

In Germany the pressure on the Jews to emigrate increased. In the six years prior to *Kristallnacht* one-third of the German Jews had left Germany. In the next ten months, until the beginning of the Second World War in September 1939, another third emigrated. After *Kristallnacht* none had to be persuaded. Said Max Nussbaum: "The struggle for a visa to a foreign country, any country, regardless of what kind or how far away it was—'How far from what?' we used to ask as a joke—became the main preoccupation of every single Jew and of our Jewish organizations. Sometimes there were flurries of hope: Bolivia is opening up! Or: San Diego is selling visas against a guarantee of $1,000 to $2,000 a piece . . . Rumors spread like wildfire, and our people would leap on any opportunity that offered itself if it promised escape from Germany."

England, which had been as uncooperative prior to *Kristallnacht* as any country, relented after November 1938. Werner Rosenstock, in a study of the Jewish exodus from Germany, estimated that England took on "the greatest part of the rescue work . . . Despite the economic depression and the loss of jobs, England allowed approximately 40,000 of the 100,000 to 150,000 German emigrants to settle there."[2]

Among those 40,000 were Baeck's daughter Ruth, her husband Hermann, and their daughter Marianne. Marianne had attended German schools until *Kristallnacht*, when the Nazis flatly prohibited Jewish children from attending secular schools. Years later she remembered that when she left her school, clutching her records, that her teacher—a non-Jew—had defied the wrath of her Nazi superiors and written on those records of Marianne: "This child's conduct has been impeccable." The name has been forgotten, but the teacher is one of those Leo Baeck would have inscribed in the golden book he talked about so frequently in those years.

When Ruth, her husband, and daughter left for England, Baeck traveled with them as far as Hamburg, where he said goodbye. Then he hurried back to Berlin to write the first of the letters to *"Geliebte Kinder!"* As was typical for him, the letter said nothing of his loneliness or of his concerns for himself. He hoped they had found the English Channel "in a peaceful way." He was certain they would be comfortable in the home of the family friends where they were to stay. He assured them he had spoken with Hermann's father, Leo Berlak, and that all was well there. Three days later he wrote again. "New things are in front of you and uncertainty," he told them, "but I am confident that you will find your way and that you will achieve your goal."

In Hamburg, while seeing off his children, Leo Baeck had performed one other task. The Nazis had decreed that the Jews should surrender all their silver, including ceremonial pieces. In the Baeck house there were some religious objects, many of which had belonged to Natalie Baeck's family. Rather than let the Nazis find them and melt them down, Baeck rented a rowboat, went out into the harbor where the Elbe River met the channel, and dumped them. He chose that spot because it was tidal, and he could feel certain the silver mementos would never be found again.[3]

While England showed humanitarianism in allowing an unusually large number of refugees to enter, she also at this time showed that she had not given up the game of international politics. In May 1939 she issued the Palestine White Paper, a document curtailing Jewish emigration into Palestine. For centuries England had enjoyed carrying the "white man's burden." Buying raw products from colonies at cheap prices, transforming them into manufactured products, and selling them at high prices always had been good business. For young men who traveled to the colonies, perhaps to win glory, fame, and fortune, there had been an opportunity for adventure. The sons who died and the natives who were killed represented, to the English mind, an unfortunate price paid, accepted, and then forgotten. In the twentieth century, however, things had not worked that way. Given the mandate to govern Palestine by the League of Nations after the First World War, England could not take and enjoy as she once had. She wanted oil and peace in the Middle East; she had to placate the Arabs. She wanted to help the Jews in Germany and quiet those Jews in England demanding help for their brothers; she had to placate the Jews.

The Arabs believed the immigration of Jews into Palestine eventually would lead to the establishment of a Jewish homeland and the loss of Arab power in that area. The Jews believed they had a Biblical right to the land as well as a right based on their struggles to develop the land in the twentieth century. They also felt that England, in the Balfour Declaration, had promised them that homeland. After *Kristallnacht*, when emigration had become a necessity for the Jews, England responded to the political pressures by choosing to placate the Arabs and, in the White Paper, closed Palestine to Jewish emigration.

Leo Baeck always had maintained personal and warm relations with Chaim Weizmann, who led the effort in England to settle Jews in Palestine. "For me it is a necessity to tell you in these days that my thoughts are always with you and to assure you of my thanks . . ." said Baeck in a letter to Weizmann early in May 1939. When the White Paper was announced a few days later, Baeck and Hirsch wrote a formal letter to Weizmann. For them the reality was of thousands of Jews looking for somewhere to go and, with Palestine closing down, unable to find any place. They wrote:

As the representatives of the Jews in Germany, we feel the responsibility to inform you of the emotions which move our people in these days.
With deep consternation the Jews in Germany have learned of the Palestine

White Paper of the Mandate government. They feel that its realization would mean the renunciation of the Balfour Declaration and a suspension of the recognized rights to the Jewish national home. In a time in which the preservation and increase of the possibilities for emigration for the Jews of many lands is a vital necessity, the White Paper will check the emigration to the Jewish national home. The thought of a future closing of emigration must appear to all as incomprehensible and intolerable. The Jews of Germany feel that especially—both those many who in the last years have built a new home in Eretz Israel and those, of whom there are still so many, for whom the thought of Palestine as an ultimate home still remains . . .

"I have received in these recent weeks," Weizmann wrote back to them, "many letters but scarcely none has moved me as deeply as the words which you have sent me after the appearance of the White Paper. I ask you to be assured that I, again and again in these years, have thought of you, your position, your sacrificing achievements, and that before my eyes I have the picture of you, especially in these dark hours which we are going through." Weizmann had struggled for years to help his fellow Jews; it was his life's work. Now they seemed confronted with failure. He could not acknowledge that, however, to his friends in Germany who must live with the consequences of that failure. "I am in no way discouraged and hopeless," he told them. "I know that the White Paper is not the last word that is to be spoken in this situation, and that the Jewish people, if they only courageously and trustingly use their strength for the Jewish national homeland in Palestine, will reach their goal."[4]

In these months Jewish leaders exerted themselves as they never had before. They were not dealing with policy but with people. Leo Baeck wrote hundreds of testimonial letters for those Jews who managed to leave Germany. As was his habit, he wrote them by hand, wording each one differently, knowing that a personal endorsement would be more significant than a typed, routine message. With other Reichsvertretung officials Baeck sought help from Jews abroad to finance the transportation of German Jews—"Everything depends on paying for the cost of passage which can be paid only in foreign currency. We turn to you personally because we know about your willingness to help. We ask you, also, to contact your friends and acquaintances and ask them to help us."[5]

Although the Reichsvertretung had been shut down after *Kristallnacht*, the Nazis soon realized that they needed a Jewish organizational structure. Emigration still was their announced policy, and it was easier for the Jews to handle the mechanics of that than it was for them. Also, there were a number of other administrative problems that the Germans wanted to turn over to the Jews. The Nazis therefore set about resurrecting the Reichsvertretung. This time, however, it would not be an independent organization. The authority would not come from Jewish organizations but from the Nazi government. It was reconstituted in February 1939 as the Reichsvereinigung. The Reichsvertretung had been the representative of the German Jews; the Reichsvereinigung was the alliance of the German Jews. The first had been watched carefully by the Nazis. The second was bossed.

The announcement of the organization of the Reichsvereinigung was circulated on February 2 and 3, saying that it had been "created as the blanket organization of all the Jews in the German Reich . . . seeing the social concerns of the Jews as its highest task." It was signed by Conrad Israel Cohn and Hannah Sarah Karminski, two officials of the new organization.

Raul Hilberg, writing some two decades later in his monumental *The Destruction of the European Jews*, judged this change harshly. He said:

In watching this transformation, we have to keep in mind that the Reichsvereinigung and the Kultusgemeinden [the Berlin Gemeinde] were not puppets picked by the Germans to control the more unruly elements of the Jewish population. The Germans had not created the Reichsvereinigung; they had taken it over. The Germans had not deposed or installed any Jewish leaders. Rabbi Leo Baeck, Director Stahl, Dr. Hirsch, and all the others were the Jewish leaders. The Germans controlled the Jewish leadership, and that leadership, in turn, controlled the Jewish community. This system was foolproof. Truly, the Jewish communal organization had become a self-destructive machine . . .

When the bureaucracy stood at the threshold of most drastic action, the Jewish community was reduced to utter compliance with orders and directives . . .

Hilberg exaggerated the authority the Reichsvereinigung had over the German Jews. It could not dictate or "control" anyone as the German government—the agency with which he compared it—could dictate or control people. The Reichsvereinigung had no guns, no secret police, no capacity or reputation for terror. The more serious of Hilberg's criticisms—the implication of an active collaboration by the Jewish leaders —has been picked up by other writers, Hannah Arendt in particular. The charge hangs over this period.

Hans Erich-Fabian was an official of both the Reichsvertretung and the Reichsvereinigung, one of the few who survived the Nazi period. In trying to explain that the Reichsvereinigung leaders saw themselves as serving their fellow Jews and not the Gestapo, he wrote:

In order to fully appreciate the situation, one must understand the conditions in the first half of the year 1939. One cannot rely on later developments. The [Nazi] party program called for the separation of the Jews from the economic and political life in Germany and had the goal of eliminating the Jews from Germany. This goal was, however, to be achieved through the forced migration of the Jews. And such a migration was to the advantage of every individual. Because of the measures taken by the Nazis it was impossible for Jewish people to find jobs in Germany and to secure a means of livelihood. It was the task of the individuals and of the community to care for those affected so that they could be brought into an orderly situation again as quickly as possible. That was, however, only possible outside of Germany. Therefore the migration must be carried on at any price. Any resistance against the migration was impossible and illogical, and supporting the migration was in no way "collaboration and supporting" the Nazi regime.

Also it was clear that there was a part of the Jewish people for whom migration was not possible because of physical or psychological reasons, they could not tolerate resettlement and must be cared for, after the state had ceased to care for them, and that the future of these people to their deaths must be assured because their relatives could no longer care for them. That was the "solution of the Jewish question" as it was presented in the years 1939 to 1941. The concept of the "solution of the Jewish question" as it is understood today, i.e., the physical destruction of the Jewish people, was then unknown.

In July 1939 the German government issued what was known as the Tenth Ordinance, which officially established control over the Reichsvereinigung. Otto Hirsch said that the leaders of the new organization would continue their work of assisting the German Jews to emigrate and of educating and caring for those Jews who could not leave "with firm nerves, with definite objectivity and justice and yet with feeling love."[6]

Expenditures by the Reichsvereinigung in 1939 reflected this urge to carry on the work of the Reichsvertretung. Money for vocational training went up by one-third; the number of people emigrating increased by almost a third from May to June. Welfare costs went up. Costs of educating children soared as they were transported to large cities from small towns, where the organized Jewish communities were disappearing. Almost the only expense that went down was the cost of religious instructional institutions; the rabbinical seminaries in Breslau and Berlin, except for the Hochschule, were closed. The figures in the Reichsvereinigung budget for that year tell a story of the Jews begging, scrounging, demanding funds from whatever source—Jews still in Germany, Jewish organizations outside of Germany, welfare organizations, the wealthy; anyone—because a few extra marks meant that transportation could be paid for one more person, that a visa to safety could be secured for another family, that one more group of elderly people could be fed and sheltered, that another small number of children could be educated in their religion.[7]

As Leo Baeck sat with his students or friends listening to radio bulletins about the war, he recalled his own experiences at the front in the First World War, often under enemy fire or near combat. If he could survive those years, he insisted to his friends, then the Jews would survive World War Two. He considered it his responsibility to grasp at any possibility for survival and to urge any such possibility on his fellow Jews. He sent a young rabbi, Frank Rosenthal, on a special mission to the Jews in the ghetto of Lodz, Poland. The message was for the Jews there to put aside their internal differences, organize as a group to deal with the Nazis, and be willing to become members of German work groups. The rationale was that the Nazis would not kill members of a work group. Rabbi Rosenthal went to Lodz with the message from Baeck and found that the killings already had begun with the sweep of the German army through eastern Europe. "There were unburied corpses in the street," he recalled. He met with the Jewish leaders there, but they wouldn't listen to him. Much of their distrust stemmed from his being a German Jew as well as a representative of the leading Berlin Jew; the Lodz Jews could not forget the offensiveness that they and their fellow eastern European Jews had met when they had come to Berlin. Rosenthal's mission was a failure.

The massacres in eastern Europe of Jews, Armenians, members of other ethnic groups were massive, involving thousands of people at a time; often the population of an entire village was lined up and gunned down. Usually the murders were carried out by regular army troops, commanded by, in many cases, men who had professional careers in civilian life: clergymen, physicians, and lawyers. Said one account: "These men were in no sense hoodlums, delinquents, common criminals, or sex maniacs. Most were intellectuals."[8]

In Berlin, Leo Baeck preached optimism but knew perfectly well what was the fate for the Jews remaining in Germany. If he could not conceive of the death camps then germinating in the Nazi minds, he knew there was no safety for any Jew in Germany. He demonstrated this knowledge in an encounter with a Christian woman, Fräulein Lange, who was a student at the Hochschule. She asked Baeck and Alexander Guttmann, another faculty member, to convert her to Judaism. Her motive was not only her love of Judaism but also her desire to demonstrate to her fellow students and professors at the Hochschule that some German Gentiles wished to stand with them, to share their fate. Although deeply moved, Baeck and Guttmann refused to convert her, suggesting instead she become one of the Yir'e HaShem—Reverers of God. This was a reference to non-Jews in ancient times, especially in Alexandria, who attended Jewish services and observed Jewish laws and customs without formally converting to Judaism. The resistance of Baeck and Gutmann to converting her was based on their fear for her life, a fear that was well-founded. Fräulein Lange persuaded an Orthodox rabbi to convert her; the Nazis killed her in a concentration camp.[9]

Why not give up hope? Leo Baeck articulated the answer in response to a report of a conversation his friend Baron von Veltheim had with Mahatma Gandhi in India. "I am always aware of the deeply moving impression [Gandhi] made on me in our last talk about the attack on the Jews by the Nazis in November 1938," said von Veltheim. The Baron had asked Gandhi if he had any advice for Leo Baeck. Gandhi's advice to the Baron was consistent with his philosophy of Satyagraha—a form of passive resistance. All the German Jews at a given moment should commit suicide. The collective action, Gandhi insisted, would shock the conscience of the world. After the war Gandhi defended that advice, saying there had been no hope for the German Jews anyway—most had lost their lives without the positive value that the human, collective sacrifice would have had.

Leo Baeck received Gandhi's advice but did not pass it on to his fellow Jews; he could not say to them there was no hope. "Wir Juden wissen," he said, "es ist ein Gebot von Gott, zu leben"—"We Jews know that the commandment of God is to live."[10]

In the summer of 1939 Baeck and Otto Hirsch brought a transport of Jewish children to England. War was only weeks away. Eva Reichmann, who had emigrated in 1938, begged them to stay in England, but they refused. A former German rabbi, Leo Trepp, ran into Baeck in the British Museum. "Yes," said Trepp, "Baeck was going to go back. Yes, he knew what the situation was. Yes, he had the opportunity of staying or of making use of the visas offered him. But he had to go back, he felt. For two hours, however, he wished to relax. He had gone to the Babylonian department of the Museum where I found him, to relax in study."

Within Germany his friends begged him to leave. He now was close to seventy years of age. He had exhausted himself for almost a decade helping his fellow Jews resist the terrors of Nazism. Nothing more could be done, his friends insisted. Always the answer from Leo Baeck was the same: "I shall be the last to leave . . . As long as a *minyan* exists in Berlin, here is my place . . . Not until the last Jew is saved."

Some years later Leo Baeck gave a lecture about Moses Mendelssohn, saying in part: "History never provides anything ready made . . . All that history gives is the possibility which is granted to the individual man or nation. The soul and the hour can meet each other." Baeck said then—and his comments about Moses Mendelssohn at the end of the eighteenth century obviously can apply also to himself under the Nazis —"It is a crime in history and a fault in the life of the individual if man fails to understand that." Leo Baeck understood that certain opportunities had come to him. His international prestige was a buffer between the Nazis and the remaining Jews in Germany. His reputation in Germany assisted Jews there. His contacts abroad brought as much help into Germany as possible. For him to have left would have been a denial of the opportunity that had come to him, a denial of the meeting between the soul and the hour.

Wolli Kaelter, a student Baeck had encouraged to attend the Hebrew Union College in Cincinnati, said: "Leo Baeck's staying was not from any sense or desire for martyrdom but because it was his *mitzvah*," his responsibility willingly assumed.[11]

The precarious situation of a rabbi of Leo Baeck's prominence was not ignored by the Jewish communities outside Germany. His book *The Essence of Judaism* had been available for some years in English and was widely read both in England and the United States. His activities with the B'nai B'rith and the World Union for Progressive Judaism had helped make him internationally known. Finally, he was to those Jews who had contact with German Jewry the epitome of all they admired in that group: He was scholarly and obviously sincere in his religious beliefs; his refusal to involve himself in petty disputes had given him a dignity that all admired; and his courage before the Nazis was becoming legendary. This man could not be allowed to languish in Germany, perhaps—most likely—to die there. He must be brought out.

Late in 1939, after war had begun in Europe, the Central Conference of American Rabbis and the Independent Order of B'nai B'rith in the United States launched a rescue attempt. They arranged for Baeck to be appointed an associate rabbi at the Rockdale Avenue Temple in Cincinnati with a salary provided by the two organizations. The Rockdale Temple was chosen because of its proximity to the Hebrew Union College; Baeck's duties there would be minimal, whatever he wished to do. The temple's trustees approved the offer unanimously, after hearing from Alfred M. Cohen, honorary president of the B'nai B'rith, and Julian Morgenstern, president of the Hebrew Union College, whose presence at the meeting underlined the significance that Jewry attached to getting Baeck out of Germany. The general membership of the temple then also voted on the invitation. One temple official reported that while there was some minor objection, "these voices were drowned out by the strong positive vote of the congregation, which was conscious of engaging in a potentially historic mission."

Preliminary negotiations had been undertaken with Baeck's son-in-law, Hermann Berlak. The route of having a rabbinical position offered to Baeck had been chosen because that meant he could enter the United States on a nonquota visa without waiting. Now with the vote of the congregation behind it, the temple sent Baeck its formal offer. Although the United States then was not yet at war with Germany, mail delivery was uncertain, and so the offer went by diplomatic pouch. Baeck had been aware that the offer was being prepared, and in late April or early May of 1940 he received it by way of the American consulate—a formal invitation to live in the United States.

The war then was a year old. Living in Berlin was dangerous. The massacres of Jews in eastern Europe were common knowledge. Everyone was trying to get out—everyone except Leo Baeck. He had vowed to stay in Berlin until the last Jew had left, and he would maintain that vow if he could. In September of 1940 the Rockdale Temple heard from the American consulate in Berlin: "Rabbi Baeck is not contemplating any immigration at this time . . . his case is considered to be dormant."[12]

Baeck was not alone in staying. Heinrich Stahl, the leader of the Berlin Gemeinde, with whom Baeck never could agree, also refused opportunities to leave. Julius Seligsohn and Otto Hirsch remained at the Reichsvereinigung. Many of the other workers did, too. Cora Berliner, who had joined the Reichsvertretung when it first was organized, stayed. Her married friend had emigrated, and she spent much of her time trying to assuage her loneliness in work. Another woman joined the staff, Hannah Karminski. Unlike Cora Berliner, Hannah Karminski had worked all of her adult life with Jewish groups, primarily with the *Jüdische Frauenbund*, an organization of German Jewish women involved in social welfare causes. When the Nazis ordered the Frauenbund disbanded in 1938 after *Kristallnacht*, she immediately joined the Reichsvertretung staff and continued her welfare work there. She was an ebullient person. "I am always happy," she said, "when I can think about something happy and festive because spontaneously there is that feeling of joy with somebody." Often she was asked: "Why don't you emigrate yourself? How well you could continue the social tasks in the foreign countries, where so many of your friends live already." The answer she gave was the same as that given by other German Jews who stayed behind: "But here they need me the most." Hannah Karminski used the office next door to Baeck's at the Reichsvertretung, and they had become good friends. "It was always a nice and pleasant experience for me to know that she was in the room next door," said Baeck. After the death of his wife, Natalie, Baeck found Hannah Karminski the person with whom he could speak "about all those things which moved me."[13]

About this time, through his relationship with Otto Hirsch, Baeck came into contact with an underground movement of industrialists from Stuttgart, Hirsch's home city. "I was in constant touch with the men of the Resistance, my contact being a well known industrialist in Stuttgart . . ." said Baeck later, declining to name the industrialist. The man was Robert Bosch, a leading German businessman who long had opposed Nazism and the Nazi treatment of the Jews. In 1933 a Bosch associate, Hans Walz, had come from Stuttgart to Berlin to protest the treatment of the Jews to the Nazi government. In those discussions, Walz made clear, he was speaking for Bosch; the hope was that the prestige of Bosch would influence the Nazis to ameliorate their measures against the Jews. That effort failed, but still Bosch and his associates gave large sums of money to help Jews emigrate and personally assisted many Jews. Deportation to concentration camps of some of Bosch's Jewish employees was prevented when the Bosch company elevated their status and claimed they were needed if production was to continue. When the Nazis ordered the Bosch company to print an anti-Semitic diatribe in its employee newspaper, the company discontinued the newspaper rather than comply. When the Nazis criticized Bosch and his associates for being "prominent advocates of the Jews," they replied: "No, of humanity."

In visits to Berlin, Hans Walz met Leo Baeck and soon began meeting regularly with him in his apartment. "It was soon recognized that, whatever the desire, there were no more possibilities to help the Jews," recalled Walz. "The wheel which was running against the Jews already was too fast to be stopped."

Baeck did not know all the names of the people he met through his Stuttgart connections. "Names were not divulged for security reasons," said Baeck. Gradually this group of Stuttgart businessmen and civic leaders realized that Hitler must be deposed. "My industrialist contact told me people realised that the time for the assumption of power would have to be carefully prepared in the press and by writers," said Baeck. "A manifesto to the German people was to be issued. Among others I had been requested to draft such a document and my contact informed me that my version for 'The Day After' had been chosen."

More than one manifesto would be needed. For a decade the German people had been brainwashed by Nazi propaganda, and measures to counter that decade's work were needed. "It was suggested," said Baeck, "that a book on the development of the position of the Jews in Europe should be written for the information of the public after the liberation. I was given this assignment." Working with three assistants, Baeck developed a volume called *Die Entwicklung der Rechtsstellung und des Platzes der Juden in Europe, vornehmlich in Deutschland, vom Altertum bis zum Beginn der Aufklärungszeit*—The Development of the Legal Position and Place of the Jews in Europe, Especially in Germany, from Ancient Times to the Beginning of the Enlightenment. It is about 200 typewritten pages and attempts to demonstrate the intertwining of the Jews and European history. Its message is simple and obvious: The Jews belong in Europe; despite Nazi claims to the contrary, they have a right to be there.

Some of Baeck's Stuttgart connections were involved in the unsuccessful attempt to kill Hitler on July 20, 1944. By that time Leo Baeck was in Theresienstadt and no longer involved. The manuscript he had produced never was published, either in Germany or elsewhere. There is a sidelight to that story. At the same time he was writing the manuscript for the resistance movement, he also was producing that same manuscript for officials in the German government. There were two attitudes among the Nazis toward Jews. While both attitudes reflected a tendency to maltreat the Jews, one group was more lenient and encouraged either using Jews as laborers or allowing them to emigrate. Officials within this group suggested to Baeck that their case might be strengthened by a documentation of the cultural contributions of the Jews to European civilization. It was because the manuscript also had this audience that Baeck in his source notes followed the Gestapo-prescribed practice of putting a "(J)" after Jewish authors in his foot-notes.[14]

During these early days of the war, when the Jewish community in Berlin constantly diminished, the Jews continued the observance of their religion as much as possible. In April 1941 Hannah Karminski wrote to a friend of the Passover festival: "We had three wonderful days, beginning with a beautiful Seder evening at the Henschel's. On the Sabbath I was in the synagogue; Dr. Baeck preached." This was the Levetzowstrasse Synagogue, which had not been destroyed on *Kristallnacht;* the Nazis eventually used it as the staging area for the deportation of Jews. In the early 1940s there still were Friday-night services in the small room outside the synagogue chamber. However, the Torah service, which traditionally took place the next morning, no longer was allowed.

In 1941 the Jews held their last Yom Kippur service in Berlin. The Nazis decreed that the Jews no longer were allowed to own radios and must turn them into their local police stations on Yom Kippur—violating the sacredness of their holiest day. Almost three decades earlier Leo Baeck had led Yom Kippur services on the battlefield for Jews fighting for Germany. Six years earlier, on Yom Kippur, Baeck had defied the Nazis by writing a prayer that declared Jews bowed before God but never before man. This time, knowing the Nazis were looking for an excuse for arrests and physical assaults, he told his fellow Jews that they could take their radios to the police stations on Yom Kippur, the holy day. Although not wanting to place his fellow Jews in jeopardy, he himself showed his personal defiance by not turning in his own radio during the holy day. In one of his favorite stories, he told in later years of appearing at the local police station with his radio only after Yom Kippur had ended. The police sergeant there, a man who was not a Nazi and who had known Leo Baeck for years, slapped his knee and said to the other policemen: "I told you that Rabbi Baeck would not show up on his holy day."

Leo Baeck told that story years later to his grandson-in-law, Rabbi A. Stanley Dreyfus. Rabbi Dreyfus recalled that Baeck, in telling that story, was "not attempting to describe his own courage. He did not have to." Rather, Baeck's purpose was to point out that, although institutions failed to speak out against the anti-Semitism of the Nazi government, there always were some individuals who showed their sympathy for the plight of the Jews. For every group of industrialists who supported Hitler's policies, there was a Robert Bosch to speak against them. For every group of teachers who encouraged their students to attack Jewish children on the street, there was a teacher like Marianne's who defied the wrath of the Nazis by describing her conduct as "impeccable." For every mob that had run through the streets of *Kristallnacht* screaming for Jewish blood, there was the Christian who hid Jews in his or her home. And for every group of persons in uniform, there was the one who, like the sergeant in that local police station, could not stifle his admiration for the conduct of the Jews while under pressure.

Others had similar experiences. Ernst Ludwig Ehrlich, a Hochschule student, had entered the police station and thrown his radio on the floor, smashing it. There was no retaliation. "I don't understand now," he said years later, "how I had such nerve."

Chanukah also was observed that year. Friends gathered in Hannah Karminski's apartment to celebrate the Festival of Lights, to commemorate the time when the Maccabees led the Jews to victory against overwhelming odds in history's first war for religious freedom. "We set three tables in the large room . . ." said Hannah Karminski. "Then the candles were lit by Dr. Baeck. After the singing there was gift giving. The presents lay, neatly wrapped, under the menorah. . . . For some we had made calendars ourselves, and their appearance was especially admired—the making of them had been the greatest joy." Baeck spoke for a few moments, telling friends and coworkers that the occasion "is for me a twelve-times joy." Hannah Karminski wrote a friend: "If you remember still Dr. Baeck's style, then you know how the good passed from him." Those holy days and festivals were the last the friends observed together.[15]

Julius Seligsohn and Otto Hirsch were the first of this group to become Nazi targets. Seligsohn had made even more frequent trips abroad than Baeck to seek help for his fellow Jews. He had always returned; warnings could not persuade him to remain abroad. In Germany he was active as a vocal critic of the Nazis; in October 1940 he called for a fast day by the German Jews to protest Nazi deportation of Jews from the states of Baden and Pfalz. For this defiance Seligsohn was arrested and sent to the Sachsenhausen concentration camp. He died there early in 1942.

Otto Hirsch had become like a member of Baeck's own family during the eight years they had worked together. When Hirsch was arrested early in 1941 and detained in the prison at Alexanderplatz, Baeck fought for his release. This time, however, his influence was not enough. The Nazis were moving toward their "final solution" and did not respond to Baeck's pleas. Word of Hirsch's arrest was circulated abroad, and friends in the United States sought to obtain visas for him and his wife Martha. That was a lengthy process, and there were still no visas when Hirsch was taken from Alexanderplatz to the Mauthausen concentration camp. Said his brother later: "The name Mauthausen was at that time still completely unknown; one heard only that it was a camp near Linz in Austria; that it was a death camp, no one knew."

On June 23, 1941, a police officer came to Martha Hirsch's apartment late in the evening to announce that her husband Otto had died June 19. The body had been cremated. Added the officer: "The urn cannot be given over. Heil Hitler!"

A few days later the United States visas for both Otto and Martha Hirsch arrived, and the Nazis were asked to allow Martha to emigrate. The argument made in her behalf was that, since Otto's death, she was entirely alone in Germany and should be allowed to join her children and relatives out of the country. A Nazi official named Adolf Eichmann retorted: "But she still has a father-in-law and a brother-in-law in Stuttgart." Eichmann became furious when informed that they had emigrated a few days earlier without his knowledge. Relatives in Germany could be hostages; relatives outside of Germany were of no value to the Nazis. Martha Hirsch was denied her visa, then deported to the East by the Nazis.

Leo Baeck had had a friendly relationship with Otto Hirsch's son, Hans Georg Hirsch, who had left Germany in the late 1930s for the United States. "Shall I say to the son who the father has been?" Baeck wrote to Hans Georg Hirsch after his father's death in Mauthausen. "But that I may say that he has been one of the rare men who are true personalities. Each idea became for him soon a task and each task was carried in him by the idea and by the ideal . . . He was realist and idealist in one . . . the son of his people."[16]

The next year Heinrich Stahl was deported to the East. Why hadn't he left the country? "I am an old man," he once said to a young rabbi who was leaving. "I have a visa to Belgium. My family is there. But if you and I both go, who will remain here with our Jewish community?" Stahl had remained with his Jewish community, to die in the East with its members.

Cora Berliner was the next of the old Reichsvertretung officials to be deported. On June 21, 1942, she wrote a letter to her friend, the married man. She was leaving the next day, and she wanted to say farewell to the man who had been so much an important part of her life for two decades.

"Really the post should have brought a letter from you," she began, "but perhaps one will come in the morning. These days are full of memories. It has been just a year that Otto [Hirsch] has been gone from us. One is so occupied at the moment that one has not time to think of much." Then she wrote: "In the morning I go on a trip with a group of good friends, among them Franz Eugen. The decision came very suddenly so that the preparations had to be pushed through. Teka helped me a great deal, really, so that I could be ready in time. It will be of interest to you to know that I have been examined quite thoroughly again and that I am quite well. That is a big relief . . ."

A woman friend wrote that Cora and another woman sat in the sun and read Goethe, and then, "On the next day the people of the land of Goethe came and took both women to their death."[17]

Hannah Karminski was next. The Gestapo arrested her in November 1942. "The hope fills us of seeing her again in good days and in an association of new work," said Baeck. But she was not seen again.[18]

For Leo Baeck the circle of acquaintances became "narrow and more lonesome." He did not make those kinds of comments in the letters to his "Geliebte Kinder!"—he would write nothing to worry them—but to some close friends. "Around me it has become so very lonely . . ." he said, "it is often difficult to be alone." A friend, Rudolf Löb, had emigrated to Buenos Aires and sent Baeck food packages occasionally. "I do not want to seem more idealistic than I am, and I openly admit," responded Baeck, "that the coffee—an unusual pleasure—fills me with a feeling of cheerful well being." To another friend who had sent him some matzo for Passover, Baeck was pleased that "I will not have to count out my matzo at one and one-half for each day . . . and will also be able to provide friends with some."

To everyone who sent him a package Baeck wrote that he was living adequately and was pleased that he could still be of assistance to his fellow Jews. There still was much to do. A German Catholic, Gertrud Luckner—another of those persons Leo Baeck would have liked inscribed in the golden book of Germans who helped the Jews—became involved in Baeck's work. She had been a social worker who knew Hannah Karminski and through her had come to know Leo Baeck.

"He was a great comfort to everyone who saw him in those years," she said. "He was standing up, alert and ready to do whatever he could." Sometimes, however, even Leo Baeck could offer nothing. Gertrud Luckner met Leo Baeck on Yom Kippur of 1942. The Nazis no longer allowed services, and she located Baeck at the Reichsvereinigung offices. "I entered," she said, "and saw him surrounded by mothers. They were crying to him that their children—young Jews, most sixteen years of age—were being taken away." Baeck stood among these women, Gertrud Luckner remembered, unable to help.

Gertrud Luckner was a secret courier, carrying funds and messages to Jews outside of Berlin—messages about relatives, about who had or had not been able to emigrate, about how one could, perhaps, emigrate, and also about those relatives who were not seen again. Each time she visited a Jew on one of these courier missions, she risked arrest. Her stop in Berlin at Baeck's apartment was a regular one, every two or three weeks, on the Sabbath morning at about eleven o'clock. For an hour to an hour and one-half they went over names. At each visit the list was shorter.*[19]

There were no more trips outside of Germany for Baeck after 1939. In addition to the trip to England he had made that summer, shepherding refugee children, he also had gone to a Zionist conference in Geneva. The Nazis had encouraged that trip—its purpose was to stress to the Zionist groups the need for emigration from Germany—because they still were encouraging Jews to emigrate. Another trip had been scheduled, but "as you can imagine," he said after the war began, "I had to give it up." The most traveling he did in the early 1940s was to Dahlem, a small village that had been incorporated into the city of Berlin. It was approximately fifteen minutes from Schoeneberg. Leo Berlak, Hermann's

---

* Gertrud Luckner eventually was arrested by the Nazis. For nine weeks she was interrogated by Gestapo officials, who wanted to know her contacts in the German Caritas Association (the Catholic welfare organization for which she worked). Asked who her bosses were, she replied: "My Christian conscience." She then was sent to the Ravensbrück concentration camp for two years. She survived, and since the war has devoted her life to improving relations between Christians and Jews. On June 5, 1977, Gertrud Luckner, then 76, was awarded an honorary doctorate of humane letters by the Hebrew Union College—Jewish Institute of Religion in New York City. Alfred Gottschalk, president of the rabbinical seminary, said of her: "She represents the symbol of all people who have decency in them and who were willing to risk their lives for it."

father, lived there, and Baeck enjoyed visiting him and relaxing in the suburban atmosphere. "The days in Dahlem have done me much good," he conceded.

In September 1941 Leo Berlak, age seventy-seven, came to live at Baeck's apartment. A room was cleared to make him a bedroom, and after that all of Baeck's letters to Ruth and Hermann included news about Hermann's father—"my dear namesake." In one letter Leo Baeck reported that "My health is satisfactory; appetite and sleep, my old good dowry, are fine. I can communicate the same of my dear fellow lodger. He is in his consistent freshness and sprightliness, appearing well and feeling very well in the new home . . ." Leo Berlak added postscripts to many of the letters. "I am, considering my advanced age, rather well. I am spoiled by my *Pflegevater* whenever he can, and I have to be thankful to the Creator that he takes such good care of me . . ."[20]

Baeck continued to be interested in the young men he had encouraged to leave Germany, keeping in contact with them whenever possible. A letter drop was set up in Lisbon with a friend who forwarded Baeck's letters both to Ruth and Hermann and to Baeck's acquaintances. "It is certainly a difficult beginning that is asked of all of you," he wrote to a young student who had emigrated. "It is very painful for me," added Baeck, "that I cannot be helpful and useful to you from here." To another student who had escaped to London he wrote, "*Sind Sie im Guten*"—"You are in the good." He continued: "You can begin to look around you. The future lies immediately in front of you." He suggested that this person use his security and opportunity to help other German Jews. "Whatever the decision in London will be," said Baeck, "it will open up a room, a way for the people in the country and for the many who want to come there . . ."

It was almost as if he understood there would be a phenomenon known as the "guilt of the survivor"—the feeling of apology or shame on the part of the one who escaped while others were abused or killed. Leo Baeck would not contribute to any such feeling on the part of those who escaped while he stayed; that was a burden he would not place upon them. To Leo Baeck, those who left were right.

He continued a friend to the remaining Jews, the students, the elderly, the few rabbis still in Germany. In 1941 he met with the last assembly of rabbis in the Rhineland, telling them that "Next year we will sit together around the table." Neither Leo Baeck nor anyone with whom he spoke at this time believed that from the mysticism of their religion would emerge a messiah to lead them into a land of bright sunshine. He was of that group of Jews who believe that the messiah exists in men's hearts. Still, they understood as Baeck had said, *"Es ist ein Gebot von Gott, zu leben"*—One must live to survive, live as if there will be a tomorrow.[21]

There was much time now for pondering, for trying to understand what had happened to Germany. In Baeck's search for an answer he turned to the figure in United States history he most admired—Abraham Lincoln. The United States was surviving as a nation, working toward true equality, Baeck believed, because it allowed religion to permeate all aspects of its existence, and the career of Lincoln seemed to symbolize that for Baeck. "A short time ago I read again the magnificent speech by Abraham Lincoln, on November 19, 1862, in Gettysburg, in which he said: '. . . this nation, under God, shall have a new birth of freedom . . .' " In these years, early in the 1940s, Leo Baeck often reread Lincoln's Gettysburg Address, pondering its religious significance and the impact of a truly religious man on a nation's history as well as the religious orientation of a nation willing to accept such a man as its leader. "Happy is the nation to which these words could be said by this man," said Baeck.[22]

The Nazis continued to enact laws against the Jews. The laws were petty and meant a significant amount of bureaucratic red tape for the Nazis. They prohibited Jews from attending movies, denied them drivers' licenses, banned them from certain streets, required them to carry identification cards stamped *Jude.* In addition Jews could not purchase new clothes, were subject to a curfew, could not use public telephone booths, and had to turn in their typewriters and electrical appliances.

Of the various restrictions on Jews "the heaviest burden from the psychological point of view," said one who lived through this period, "was no doubt the compulsory wearing of the 'Jewish star,' " the *Magen David*—a six-pointed star. The *Magen David* had appeared in Jewish history sporadically for centuries, but was not used as a Jewish symbol until the nineteenth century, when some Jews and Gentiles began to think of it as a Jewish counterpart of the Christian cross. The Zionists incorporated the *Magen David* into their publications, and by the Nazi era it was widely accepted as a Jewish symbol. When the Nazis had first come to power in 1933, Robert Weltsch had written an editorial in the Zionist newspaper *Jüdische Rundschau* calling on Jews to wear the star with pride, as a mark of defiance. However, the Nazis saw the star as a badge of submission, meant to frighten the Jews even more.

The star was to be worn by all Jews. Yellow in color, four inches in diameter, it carried the word *Jude* in large dark letters. The stars were issued through the Reichsvereinigung. Paul Eppstein, who had replaced Otto Hirsch as executive director, was summoned before the German authorities and told that the Reichsvereinigung was to purchase the stars, which the Nazis called *Kennzeichen*—characterizing mark— for five pfennings and sell them for ten, the difference going to cover administrative costs. The order appearing over Eppstein's name stipulated that there were no exceptions to the wearing of the star and that all resistance would be useless. No one living there could doubt that last point.

As the Jews walked along the streets with the yellow star on their coats, they were to fear the abuse of their neighbors, the return of the violence that marked *Kristallnacht*. That was generally what happened, but not always. Ernst Ludwig Ehrlich, a student of Baeck's, was forced to stand on a train by a railway official. The train was half empty, but the official didn't care—Ehrlich was wearing the star. Then a German soldier beckoned to Ehrlich. The soldier asked the Jewish student to sit with him, in effect offering him his protection. "I didn't do it," said Ehrlich, "but I thanked him very much. It was a very courageous act on the part of that German soldier."

Leo Baeck made the act of wearing the yellow star one of defiance. Once, wearing his star, he was ordered to appear before the Gestapo. "Well, Dr. Baeck," said a Gestapo official to him when their meeting had ended, "even you cannot deny that the whole German nation endorses the Führer's actions including his policy towards the Jews." As the official spoke, he pointed towards the star on Baeck's coat.

"I should not like to comment on that point," answered Baeck, "but I will say this: When I now walk home, because public transport I will not use, I shall not suffer any mishap—I am quite sure of that. There will be people, here and there, trying to approach me, strangers looking around a little frightened, and then grasping my hand. Perhaps they will surreptitiously slip an apple into my pocket, a bar of chocolate or even a cigarette. Otherwise I don't think anything will happen to me." Baeck paused a moment before this parting line to the Gestapo official: "I do not know whether the Führer, were he in my place, would find the same thing happening to him."[23]

Years later Baeck often talked about the non-Jewish Germans who were kind to him in those years. "Sometimes the only way Germans could express their opposition to the Nazis was to be helpful to a Jew," he said. "In the last years a countess came to my apartment every Friday and left vegetables which were not on the Jewish ration card. Occasionally I found a bag of fruit at the apartment door left by an anonymous donor. One Sunday in the crowded S-Bahn a man stepped close to me and asked, 'Is Tiergarten the next station?' He added in a whisper, 'I am from the country. I just put a few eggs in your pocket.' Another time a man came up to me on the street and dropped an envelope. As he picked it up he handed it to me, saying, 'You dropped this.' It was a package of ration stamps." Baeck conceded knowing of instances in which Jews were harassed after they began wearing the star, "but the populations of Hamburg and Berlin treated Jews much more decently than those of many other communities."[24]

During the years following *Kristallnacht* the Nazis, curiously, did not shut the Hochschule. There's a popular story as to why. Immediately after *Kristallnacht*, classes were not held at the Hochschule; the only room open was the library. According to the story, a Gestapo official strolled into the building one day wanting to know its purpose. The only person he met there was the librarian, who made some vague answer about education. The Gestapo official then assumed it was a poor-quality school established for those Jews expelled from German schools, and the building was not closed. Given the Nazi penchant for detail, however, it is probable that the building's purpose was known and that the local story is inaccurate. In all likelihood the Nazis simply were not ready to close all Jewish institutions. Richard Fuchs, a Hochschule official, said protests from Christian religious figures outside of Germany "may perhaps have been the cause of the government's attempt to appease the disgust abroad by letting a few cultural activities of the German Jews, such as those of the Kulturbund and the Hochschule, continue." So, for almost four years after *Kristallnacht*, while those Jews who could were fleeing Germany, while the Jewish population was dwindling in Berlin, as the Nazis were preparing "the final solution," young Jews could study for the rabbinate in the building on Artilleriestrasse.

Everyone knew it was only a matter of time until the building would be shut permanently. The Hochschule report for 1938–1939 stated, "We hope that when the work of the Lehranstalt ceases in Berlin equally free research for the Wissenschaft des Judentums will be continued at another place and that men and women will be found who, faithful to the command of our Law, will work for the Wissenschaft des Judentums."

There was hope at the time of transferring the school to England. Richard Fuchs discussed it with educators there, and in 1939 Leo Baeck drafted a memorandum (which Fuchs reshaped into English) to scholars in London, asking their reaction. The proposal might have become a reality except that Baeck was not interested in leaving Germany to head the institution in England, and then in September the war broke out. Leo Baeck did not surrender the idea. At the end of 1942, when one of his students was about to begin an escape attempt out of Germany, Baeck told him, "If we survive the war, I shall see to it that the work of the Lehranstalt is continued in England."

Many of the prominent scholars at the Hochschule had accepted posts abroad. As a result the faculty now included a twenty-two-year-old rabbi for Bible studies and an elderly, retired rabbi who taught Jewish history. Despite the demands on Baeck's time and energy, he continued to teach Midrash and homiletics, as always. He became chairman of the faculty. In the past this position had been rotated among faculty members. Now he maintained the position alone because he was virtually the only faculty member remaining who had any experience at the school.

In addition to a few young men studying for the rabbinate, other persons continued to take advantage of the educational opportunities offered at the Hochschule. "They belonged to all age groups and came from every walk of life," went one description of these students. The description continued:

A rabbi emeritus sat next to a widow, a former lawyer shared his Bible with a former merchant, while a dismissed civil servant, after the lecture, discussed a point of interest with a former bank official and a physician. This participation of men and women in the academic work of the Lehranstalt had a very wholesome influence on the regular students. These men and women had a varied background of considerable standing, and they applied themselves to the work in the seminars with a sincerity and eagerness which could not fail to have an impact on the rabbinical students who would have felt embarrassed had the quality of their work been inferior to that of the older generation dedicated to the Bildungsideal.[25]

"The examinations have been held," said Baeck in the spring of 1939; "we go on lecturing at the Lehranstalt and we try to make them meet the old standards." Again, education, the preparation of people knowledgeable about the Jewish religion, people capable of instructing and inspiring others, was all-important. It was another example of God's commandment. In that same letter, however, Baeck had to concede, "Unfortunately a large number of the rabbis are discouraged, especially the 'involved' ones from the old times. Some have simply disappeared without trouble. But yet some have stayed at their place— among the younger I name, above all, Swarsensky, and among the older, I mention Dienemann, who returned after several weeks to his place and then, when his community ceased existing, he departed in an upright manner."

In his letters about the Hochschule, Baeck did not dwell on those difficulties with the teaching. Rather, he spoke most often of the students "that we enjoy." Those young pepole in the early 1940s represented another curious facet of Jewish life under the Nazis. They barely had been in their teens prior to the coming of the Nazis to power; they didn't know that the life they led was unusual. "The sense of abnormal," said one of them, "did not exist for any Jew who had been fifteen or younger in 1933." Said another: "When I began attending the Hochschule in 1940, I thought it still possible to live in Germany and practice as a rabbi." If Baeck represented the aged who were willing to sacrifice themselves for the benefit of the younger people, the students in the early 1940s represented the very young who did not realize there existed another life, one that could be sacrificed for. They soon would learn. Baeck still urged them to leave. One remembered discussing with Baeck whether he should leave Germany, and he recalled the passion Baeck gave to his answer: *"Sie müssen gehen!"*—"You must go!"[26]

But after the outbreak of the war in Europe, and especially after December 1941 when the United States entered the war, emigration became virtually impossible. For those students who could not leave, the school continued. "We have celebrated the holidays in the usual way," wrote Baeck in October 1940, "and had many services, at which some of our candidates participated." The students not only officiated at regular services but also conducted prayer services at homes for the aged and in hospitals. *Zu leben*—to live—that was the creed.

That holy day season he wrote to Ruth and Hermann in London that his work was going "in the usual way, and I also find always a few hours for scholarly activities. On occasion I am together with one or the other from our circle. Also from the family I hear good things. I am very well taken care of in my home . . ." He added a few words to his granddaughter Marianne, now in her teens. *"Geliebte* Janne," he said, "for you I add a few special lines, to congratulate you for your good report card and for going on to the next grade ... I can imagine how beautiful it is in the garden, and how you are a good helper in the house."

One of his students then recalled Baeck, although in his late sixties, still spry—"dressed well and running up steps with agility, springing over some." He still gave his Friday-morning lectures "bitter early" at eight o'clock on homiletics, and he had not changed his teaching techniques. When it came to criticizing a student sermon, if Baeck began with something like, "the sermon demonstrated honest thinking," then the student as well as his colleagues knew that a devastating summation of the mistakes quickly would follow. Baeck also continued to be interested in the students' welfare. He insisted they participate in a gymnastics course developed at the school because he believed that physical endurance was a quality they would need whether they stayed in Germany or emigrated. Each Hochschule graduate in those years received a personal letter from Baeck attesting to his completion of the required work for the rabbinate and also to being eligible for the title "rabbi." All the teachers helped, badgering Gestapo officials to release students drafted for compulsory labor, rescuing those students marked for deportation. "It was an uncanny, weird life which teachers and students led in an atmosphere appearing almost unreal," said one.

During that period Baeck consistently spoke of the "admirable" industriousness of the students—"one must slow them down sometimes," he said. Later he said that what was accomplished in this period in connection with education "will go down in history as perhaps the outstanding achievement of the doomed Jewish community."

Much of that industriousness was Baeck's own, but he did not allow the strain to show. "What really is important," he told the students, "is the task of the day. What is given to us, we have to do." Watching him, the students learned something of the meaning of words like dignity and spiritual resistance. One of his students described a lecture by Baeck in the winter of 1940 on "The Basic Thoughts of Judaism." The audience included students studying for the rabbinate as well as "Jews who had still not been called up for hard labor and others who were already too old." These people all hoped for "strength to last through the day. Here they are in another world." Baeck's bearing gave no hint that he was carrying any responsibilities or confronting any problem other than that of presenting a lecture. "He incorporated Jewish pride and Jewish spirit," said the student, "and he did not allow himself to show anything else." There was a strange quality to that lecture; Baeck seemed to be above everything, above all the turmoil and the dangers outside the Hochschule building, and yet at the same time everyone felt that he was speaking directly of that turmoil and those dangers.

"The good always is annoying to mankind," he told the students that day. "Persecution is the fate of all who come to mankind with strong, moralistic thoughts." All that is different is objectionable to the great masses of people, he said, and the Jews are different. "Israel is the servant of God, and incumbent on Israel is the responsibility for all people. Therefore, it is the suffering servant." Baeck spoke of the power-seekers. "If the tower of the powerful is erected," he said, "the prophet already is pointing out the cracks in the walls; that, which remains, is alone the spirit."

To those few people who heard him that cold morning in the building on Artilleriestrasse, Jews who had not managed to escape and—it now was obvious—would not escape, he offered a spiritual security; it was the only hope, the only chance they had. "History," he concluded, "is the history of moral and spiritual ideas. If at one time a moral genius emerges in humanity, that event can never be erased. Each idea remains. It is permanent. No catastrophe can destroy even one idea." He became like the Biblical prophets of old as he warned that man exists not by might. "Power," he said, "has as its only fate to perish." That was difficult to believe then, difficult for people—weak, hounded, with no future—surrounded by uniformed madmen who already were engaged in mass murder. The glory of Leo Baeck in those final months was that he made them believe. He made them understand that survival, the fulfillment of the commandment of God, was both possible and worthwhile.[27]

The year 1942 was even bleaker than 1941. "So many who were near are far," said Baeck. In January he sent birthday greetings through the Lisbon letter drop to his granddaughter Marianne, who was in England and whom he had not seen for almost eighteen months. Years earlier, in the First World War, when he had worn the uniform of the German army, he had sent birthday greetings to his daughter Ruth. Like any father, he had rejoiced at his daughter growing into adulthood, finding happiness in marriage, and starting her own family. With little Marianne he had been the typical grandfather, doting on her, going with her to services, watching over her education. In England she at least would have the opportunity to become an adult, to develop her own family, and to pursue the happiness to which every person is entitled. There was not much he could say to her now, not without worrying her. "My lines today are above all for your birthday, dear Fräulein Marianne," he began. "I need not say to you how sincere are my wishes for you and how everything good that I hear about you fills me with joy. How I hope all happiness comes to you."[28]

The situation worsened at the Hochschule. The Nazis forced the school to move from Artilleriestrasse, first to some vacated offices and then into empty rooms at the headquarters of a Jewish welfare agency. In the spring perhaps a dozen students attended. Then came the inevitable. On June 30, 1942, the Nazis declared that the Hochschule must cease operations.

For Baeck the announcement was devastating. He had been referred to as the one who epitomized the German Jew. The two words, *German* and *Jew*, had gone together when used in reference to him. He was the German scholar and the Jewish believer. The representative of rationalism and of faith. Through his scholarship, his preaching, and his own life, he had demonstrated that being German and being Jewish could be entwined to the advantage of each. Rationalism and faith had both been advanced because of their involvement together, as both Germany and Judaism had gained when the two were mixed. Leo Baeck was a better Jew because he was a German, more of a believer because he had subjected his beliefs to rational examination. He also was a better German because he was a Jew, more of a rationalist because he had subjected his knowledge to the test of faith. And the Hochschule had been the institution in which this intertwining had taken place. Here the study of Judaism had been approached with the same scholarship that had typified the German university. Franz Rosenzweig had once begged not to be forced to choose between being German and being Jewish. To cut one from his heart, he said, would destroy him. The closing of the Hochschule, perhaps more than anything else up to that time, symbolized the Nazi intention to rip the two apart. The symbiosis known as the German-Jew was destroyed.

"I never saw Leo Baeck appear desperate," said one of his students in his final class, "except once. That was when he learned that the Hochschule would close." The student remembered Baeck, the lines on his face tight, his voice deeper, hoarser than usual, stating to the handful of students in the room: "Whatever happens to us, we still have produced the three greatest influences on the modern world: Marx,

Freud, and Einstein." Then Baeck added: "Just as we produced Jesus two thousand years ago."

Several of those students in the final days managed to escape from Germany. Herbert Strauss was ordered to clean the streets of Berlin while wearing his star. When the Nazis finally came to arrest him, the janitor of his building—one of those German Christians to be inscribed in Baeck's golden book—delayed them for a few moments at the bottom of the stairs, allowing Strauss to escape. The last time Strauss saw Baeck during the war years was in January 1943. Strauss, who was living underground, constantly hiding from the Nazis, came to Leo Baeck's apartment. "It was courageous of Leo Baeck even to see me," recalled Strauss. They talked of the failure of the German middle class, particularly its failure in the early 1930s before Hitler came to power, to perceive where nationalism was taking Germany. Baeck urged the student to continue underground, to hold onto the opportunity to live.

Another student who escaped was Ernst Ludwig Ehrlich. He also went into hiding and eventually made his way to Switzerland. Before leaving, each student received from Leo Baeck the traditional letter describing his qualities as a rabbi and recommending him for employment.[29]

During these months there was little sympathy for the Jews and their institutions from the other religious groups in Germany. The American Office of Strategic Services, the OSS, did a study on the possibility of religious opposition to the German government in 1942. The study is perhaps the best summation of the attitudes of the time and reveals them as, basically, a continuation of past attitudes of support for the Nazi government. It read:

Neither Protestants nor Catholics as such have any great feeling of loyalty to the National Socialist regime. This has been true since 1933. There have been outspoken representations against the Nazis from both groups, notably in recent months from Catholics. Despite great pressure, the Catholics have not, officially at any rate, endorsed the Russian campaign as a "crusade." Yet neither current evidence nor the traditional role of the Church in German society justifies the inference that active political opposition against the Nazi regime is to be expected from either group. Individual German Lutherans or German Catholics function in their allotted tasks as soldiers, administrators, workmen, and so forth, *first* as Germans, *then* as Lutherans or Catholics. Despite the reality of a Church-State conflict in both cases we must not forget that the Lutheran Church recognizes the legitimacy of the prevailing government of Germany, as "die Obrigkeit" and as such to be obeyed; and the

Catholic Church, whatever it may say about Nazi policies, has not yet denounced the Nazi regime in as uncertain terms as it has used toward Soviet Russia. There is ground for believing, however, that the difference reveals not so much a distinction in Vatican point of view as an appeasement dictated by necessity.[30]

If institutions failed, individuals came forth. The names of clergymen like Niemoeller and Bonhoeffer and others could fill up a golden book themselves. During the next several years a small group of Christian clergymen was imprisoned, beaten, or killed. Its members organized against the Nazis, hid Jews in their churches, publicly prayed for them, went to the concentration camps with them, stood with them before the threatening Nazi officials. How many Jews they saved is problematical; they perhaps were too late—and certainly too few—to save many. However, they demonstrated before the other Germans that Jesus' directives to assist the weak and the humble were not mere words to be repeated by rote on Sunday mornings.

One of those who became involved was Probst Heinrich Grüber. His story is typical. Although one of the more prominent of the Protestant clergy in Berlin, at first he had ignored the Nazi threats and attacks against the Jews. However, when the Nazis began to attack members of Grüber's own faith—former Jews who had converted or Protestants who had a Jewish parent or grandparent—Grüber became the Protestant leader who worked to assist those Protestants to leave Germany. This was the same responsibility that Leo Baeck had for people who identified themselves as Jews, and the two men met because of that connection.

At first Grüber helped only the members of his own church, but through the years his work transcended parochial interest. He became a defiant figure in Germany, protesting against the maltreatment of all people. When he spoke out in the early 1940s, Heinrich Grüber did not know that the German Jews were being killed, or were about to be killed, en masse. He did know, however, that they were being arrested and imprisoned without cause and that they were being deported. Every Christian in Berlin knew that much through 1943.

Grüber publicly identified himself with Baeck. Once the two men were ordered to the Gestapo offices. A chair was brought for Grüber to sit on; none was brought for Leo Baeck, the non-Aryan. Grüber refused the chair. "If Leo Baeck cannot sit," he said, "then I will not sit." The two men became close friends. "When I was arrested," Grüber recalled, "Leo Baeck was the first person to visit my wife." In addition to being arrested, Grüber was beaten by the Gestapo and imprisoned for years in a concentration camp.[31]

One day Leo Baeck read in the newspaper that an SS officer named Adolf Eichmann had been placed in charge of a special Jewish department in the Gestapo. "I knew Eichmann," said Baeck, "since as representative of the German Jews I had had to see him occasionally. He was a bitter hater of the Jews and in the past always had been one of the worst persecutors. His department had been given special powers. It was a bad omen." Years later, when Eichmann was captured, one of his captors, a woman, thought Eichmann looked so ordinary that she found it difficult to believe he was the man who had pronounced the death sentence on millions of Jews. Eichmann could scarcely believe it himself. "I can't understand how we could have done such things," he said years after the war. He continued: "I did what everybody else was doing. I was conscripted like everyone else—I wanted to get on in life." At the time, however, he appeared more enthusiastic than those later comments indicated. A telegram to the American Joint Distribution Committee from one of its European representatives read: "Eichmann appointed head of Jewish affairs . . . evil forebodings."[32]

The appointment of Adolf Eichmann as head of the department of Jewish affairs meant that the phrase "final solution" was taking on a new meaning. Prior to the early 1940s that phrase had been a euphemism for expelling Jews from Germany and for stripping them of their property. Now it came to mean the mass murder of Jews.

Hitler's language against the Jews had escalated. In 1939 he spoke of the *Vernichtung*—destruction—of the Jewish people. He always had talked of being at war with the Jews; and in 1939, shortly after the beginning of the Second World War, he said, "Wars will always be ended only by the annihilation of the opponent." To his subordinates Hitler's intentions always were clear. "The Führer once more expressed his determination to clean up the Jews in Europe pitilessly," reported Goebbels early in 1942. "There must be no squeamish sentimentalism about it. . . . Their destruction will go hand in hand with the destruction of our enemies. We must hasten this process with cold ruthlessness . . . The Führer expressed this idea vigorously and repeated it afterward to a group of officers."

In September 1942 Hitler recalled his threat three years earlier about the destruction of the Jews and said: "At one time, the Jews of Germany laughed about my prophecies. I do not know whether they are still laughing or whether they have already lost all desire to laugh. But right now I can only repeat: They will stop laughing everywhere, and I shall be right also in that prophecy."

The Nazis began using gas chambers in the late 1930s to annihilate the very elderly or those considered incurably ill. Perhaps it was because the gas chambers were first used against the sick that the Germans began to speak of the murders as a "medical" action. The first time the chambers were used to kill for ethnic and racial reasons was in the spring of 1942. The camps multiplied, each one becoming more sophisticated than its predecessor. Before the end of the war millions of people had been killed in these camps. Most of them were Jews, but not all. Hitler's wrath was aimed primarily but not exclusively at the Jews. He also detested many members of other ethnic groups living in eastern Europe and also those who disagreed with him—all were his helpless victims.[33]

No one holding a gun on those helpless victims had a gun held at his back. No doctors who used their medical knowledge to destroy those people were forced to so distort their life's purpose. No industrialist who constructed the gas ovens was ignorant of their use. No one who robbed the dead of their clothes, their final possessions, the gold fillings in their teeth was unaware of how those people had died.

They all, in Eichmann's words, "wanted to get on in life." It was not war in any traditional sense. It was deliberate, carefully planned genocide.

Whether or not the German people knew about the death camps during the war years has been debated ever since. There is substantial evidence that they must have known of the mass killings, certainly by late 1943 and 1944. Still, the question is a false one. Even if the German people did not know that Jews and others were being murdered, they knew enough about the maltreatment of their fellow human beings to protest. They had known enough about it since boycott day in 1933. The burden the Germans have had to bear ever since is that the protests were not made by great masses of people and not by institutions, but only by scattered individuals.

For the Berlin Jews the "final solution" began to take shape on March 20, 1941, at a meeting in the propaganda ministry concerning the number of Jews still in Berlin. A few days earlier Goebbels had pointed out to Hitler that 60,000 to 70,000 Jews remained in the city. This was unacceptable. Some of these Jews maintained relationships with members of the diplomatic community. Some leased rooms to foreign students and journalists and "so had the opportunity to spread rumors that were not good for the state." Adolf Eichmann, who was present, said that Hitler had given his approval for the removal of Jews from Berlin about eight or ten weeks earlier, but the plan had not been put into effect because there was no place to receive the Jews. Arrangements had been made for the deportation of 60,000 Jews from Vienna, but only 45,000 remained there. Perhaps the difference, the 15,000, could be made up by Berlin Jews.

That last suggestion was generally acceptable to those at the meeting, particularly because it would mean ridding the city of elderly Jews who could not work. A Jewish labor pool still was needed; there was even talk at the meeting of moving young Jews into the city, to use as laborers. Another point was brought up by a representative of the army's construction office. In Berlin the Jews occupied 20,000 apartments, which might be needed if other residences were destroyed in bombing raids and fires.

Three proposals were agreed to at this meeting. Jews were forbidden to rent part of their residences to non-Jewish foreigners. Because Jews ignored shopping times prescribed for them and because they walked streets where they were not allowed, a "street hunt with police forces" would be undertaken. The third proposal was that Adolf Eichmann would develop a plan, to be submitted to Goebbels, for the evacuation of Jews from Berlin.

A small-scale deportation of Jews from Germany actually had begun before this. "The first news from the east that I saw," recalled Leo Baeck, "was postcards from Lublin and Warsaw. From them we gathered that the deportees were wretched, that hunger and disease were widespread, and that the Polish Jews were trying to help . . ." Baeck said he had his first indication of the scope of the Nazi bestiality in the summer of 1941.

A gentile woman told me that she had voluntarily gone along with her Jewish husband when he was deported. In Poland they were separated. She saw hundreds of Jews crowded into busses which were driven off and came back empty. The rumor that the busses had a gassing mechanism was confirmed by the apparatus attached to all but one of them. This one carried a group to bury those who were gassed; afterward the gravediggers were shot. Similar stories were told by soldiers who came back on furlough. Thus I learned that the lot of Jews shipped east was either slave labor or death.[34]

The Nazis made their first widescale move against the Berlin Jews just as Yom Kippur ended in 1941. A service had been held in the Levetzowstrasse Synagogue, the only synagogue not destroyed on *Kristallnacht*. When the service was over, the Gestapo appeared, located some officials of the synagogue, and demanded the keys to the building. The religious structure, they announced, would be used as a staging area for the deportation of the Berlin Jews. Adolf Eichmann's plan, promised at that meeting in March, was about to take effect.

The actual movement began October 18. The Jews were told they were going to a labor camp in Lodz, Poland. "There was a ghetto, there were official reports, packages, money; luggage was allowed. This first transport used passenger cars," recalled one Jew who witnessed it. He was an official of the Jüdische Gemeinde, which provided food, blankets, and some clothing for the deportees. The cooperation the Jewish organizations gave with this deportation has long been a matter of conflict. One Jewish official recalled:

In retrospect . . . it appears astonishing to me with what self-possession and stoical calm the highest administrative body of Jewish autonomy let themselves be forced into the deportation work by the National Socialist authorities. I recall very clearly the evening in which a hundred of the employes of the Jewish community and Jewish institutions were called together in the meeting room and given the job of bringing together an orderly list by profession and age from material the Germans gave them. I belonged to those who had to check over these lists. These were the lists for the first group of deportees. The work on these lists lasted deep into the night and another day . . .

Said one official: "You can ask, how could you do this work? We could not determine whether we had done correctly. But the thought we had was that our doing this would be milder and easier for the Jews being deported than if the Nazis did it. The gathering place was the Levetzowstrasse Synagogue. There was the food supply. The clothing source. There one received implements for eating . . . The condition of the deportees was surprisingly calm. Naturally one did not know where the transports went, what it truly was." There were 500 people on that transport. Six days later a second transport left with another 500. Before the war's end sixty-three transports had taken more than 35,000 Jews away from Berlin.

Another official also witnessed these deportations. He said:

In the official language it was called, to be sure, evacuation or emigration and the expression deportation was prohibited. To the Reichsvereinigung fell the sorrowful task of collecting the people chosen for deportation and tending them at the departure of the transports, as far as it was possible. Who had seen these people as they lay or sat together in a great room, herded together like animals for hours, as they had suffered those indignities of the gray formalities of the Gestapo, as they went through the city to the loading sites watched over along the way by SS people, with raised heads and without showing the violent emotions; those who saw this picture can never forget it—the picture of a community, which had experienced the frightful and replied to it; who, despite the ruse and the chase, walked without crying over the fate, who neither moaned nor weeped.

The Reichsvereinigung tried to make the Jews more comfortable at Levetzowstrasse and to give them the supplies that might be needed to make their new homes more comfortable. Said one involved in this work: "The Reichsvereinigung was to receive orders from the secret security police or the Main Security Office of the Reich, and transmit them to the population. But the work of those active in the Reichsvereinigung, to soften or modify the anti-Jewish activities of the Gestapo, will endure never to be forgotten." There was another persuasive point, not mentioned in these accounts: Any Jewish official who had refused Nazi demands for cooperation would have been imprisoned or executed.[35]

Although Leo Baeck still was the nominal head of the Reichsvereinigung at this time, he had receded in importance at the organization. "In accordance with my memory," said one of the officials who survived, "the name of Dr. Baeck was not mentioned in discussions very frequently when we were all in the mousetrap. . . . The Reichsvereinigung was more and more Dr. Eppstein." Paul Eppstein was then in his early forties, a teacher who had joined the Reichsvertretung in its early days, working at first with its social welfare agencies and then later replacing Otto Hirsch as executive director. By no means a collaborationist, Eppstein believed the best hope for ameliorating the conditions of the Jews was cooperation between the Reichsvereinigung and the Nazis.

For Baeck the extent of that cooperation between the Reichsvereinigung and the Nazis was too great. "I believe it probable that Dr. Baeck, more and more, suffered because the Reichsvereinigung was so deeply involved in the work of the deportation preparations," said one man associated with the organization at the time. Unlike the Reichsvertretung of the 1930s, which had been a Jewish organization, the Reichsverein igung was a Nazi-controlled one, and Baeck could not change its direction. A threat of resignation by him at this time would not have had any significance either. Neither Eppstein nor Baeck did anything dishonest or immoral, said one of their coworkers. However, there obviously was a dispute between the two men as Baeck found he could not dissuade Eppstein from his course. "Dr. Baeck was responsible for actions," said the coworker, "which oppressed him internally, but which, however, he had to allow to be pushed through by his chief executive [Eppstein]."

In later years Leo Baeck never commented publicly about the dispute with Eppstein or about the extent of the Reichsvereinigung's cooperation. He did say: "I made it a principle to accept no appointment from the Nazis and to do nothing which might help them. But later, when the question arose whether Jewish orderlies should help pick up Jews for deportation, I took the position that it would be better for them to do it, because they could at least be more gentle and helpful than the Gestapo and make the ordeal easier. It was scarcely in our power to oppose the order effectively."[36]

Nor was there any possibility of their joining any underground movement in Germany. Except for a few individuals, such as Baeck's associates in Stuttgart and, later, some military men who objected to Hitler's war leadership, there was no underground resistance to the Nazi regime within Germany. This was in contrast to almost every country that Germany had conquered, where the underground had strong support from the population. In Germany, however, the general population did not oppose Hitler; it supported him.

Also, in fairness to those Jews who cooperated with the Nazis, they were leading a group of prisoners—no other word can describe the Berlin Jews at this time—who were elderly, tired, beaten. Still, these Berlin Jews hoped to survive, and they would not believe that deportation meant death. Bolstering their hope to survive in 1942 was a faction within the German government that wanted to use Jews for slave labor. In addition, the preparation for the deportations—the luggage, the food—suggested a new residence in a labor camp. Baeck said he did not learn about Auschwitz and the systematic murder of the Jews until 1943. Norbert Wollheim, who ran a clandestine information service for the Reichsvereinigung, said he and the other Berlin Jews did not know about Auschwitz. "I was sent there in March of 1943," he said, "and I could not believe it until I was there."

Ernst Ludwig Ehrlich told of hearing from a Hochschule employee—

The Nazis did not object to the Reichsvertretung but wanted to place a man whom they could control near its top. Their candidate was Georg Kareski. "Whatever Georg Kareski was," said one who knew him, "he wanted to be first." Baeck blocked the Gestapo's move when he told the Nazis: "You can force me to appoint Kareski as a member of the executive council of the Reichsvertretung. But you cannot force me to continue as president of the Reichsvertretung." (*Photo courtesy of the Central Archives for the History of the Jewish People*)

Four persons who helped Leo
Baeck run the Reichsvertretung
(and its successor, the Reichsvereinigung) were Otto Hirsch,
Julius Seligsohn, Hannah Karminski, and Cora Berliner. All
had the opportunity to leave
Germany and oppose the Nazis
from abroad, but they chose to
remain in Germany and help
their fellow Jews there. All were
killed by the Nazis. (*Photos
courtesy of the Leo Baeck Institute, New York*)

Kristallnacht in 1938 represented a wave of terror and bestiality by the German people against the German Jews, with the wholehearted support and encouragement of the Nazi government, which still stands as a record. Of the many synagogues destroyed, the one on Fasanenstrasse represented a particularly tragic event. When it had opened in 1912, it had been described as an architectural beauty; the Kaiser and the German army had sent representatives to its opening. After Kristallnacht, as shown here, it was a shambles. (*Photos courtesy of Landesbildstelle Berlin*)

The Prinzregentenstrasse Synagogue was another landmark of the German Jews. An architectural beauty, its opening in 1930 attracted leading Berlin Jews. It was here in 1934 that Leo Baeck led the services when Hindenburg died. He had been their commander in the First World War, and the Jews wished to honor their fallen comrade. The synagogue was burned on Kristallnacht. As with the other burning synagogues, no effort was made to put out the fires until the building was virtually destroyed. (*Photos courtesy of the National Archives; Wide World Photos; Leo Baeck Institute, New York; Wide World Photos*)

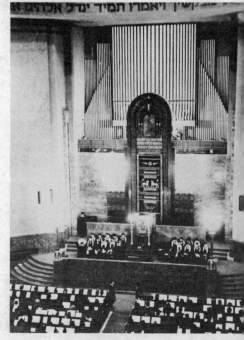

Abschied
von Hindenburg
Die Trauer=Gedenkfeier des R.j.F. in Berlin

Ein tiefer Eindruck haftenden Erlebens, eine unvergeßliche Gedenkfeier war es, die der Reichsbund jüdischer Frontsoldaten am Sonntag, dem 5. August, dem verewigten Reichspräsidenten Generalfeldmarschall von Hindenburg in der Synagoge Prinzregentenstraße widmete. Die Bundesleitung, die gemeinsam mit dem Landesverband Berlin und Mark die Veranstalterin war, hatte in das Gotteshaus zu ehrfurchtsvollem Gedenken und in dankbarer Treue zu dem großen Toten mit den Berliner Kameraden die Vertreter aller weltanschaulichen Organisationen und aller religiösen Körperschaften des deutschen Judentums geladen. Etwa zweieinhalb Tausend deutsche Juden Berlins waren im Zeichen des Frontbundes dem Rufe gefolgt und in feierlichem Gedenken an den großen Verblichenen versammelt.

Oben:
Der Präsident des Reichsvertretung der deutschen Juden, Rabbiner Dr. Baeck bei der Gedenkrede.

Unten:
Der Aufmarschmarsch bei der Trauer-Gedenkfeier des R.j.F. in der Synagoge Prinzregentenstraße.

Photos: Schwartz

The yellow star worn by Leo Baeck. In 1933 a Jewish newspaper editor in Berlin had called for the wearing of the star as a symbolic statement of pride by the Jews in their religion. But the Nazis forced the Jews to wear the star as—so the Nazis hoped—a sign of shame. Leo Baeck wore his star as a signal of defiance. He refused to fear the Nazis, saying in a famous Yom Kippur prayer that Jews bow before God but never before man. (*Photo by Leonard Baker*)

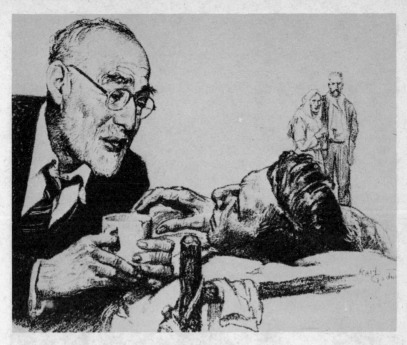

The drawing of Baeck by Karl Godwin shows Leo Baeck as the people of Theresienstadt remembered him—kind, healing, one who nursed the ill. But the photograph
of Baeck, taken at Theresienstadt in 1944, shows the reaction of the man of the
spirit and of the intellect to the inhumanity he witnessed around him. Leo Baeck
had expected more from his fellow men. (*Photos courtesy of the Leo Baeck Institute, New York, and author's collection*)

In the postwar years, Leo Baeck made frequent trips to the United States
(shown here arriving with his daughter Ruth Berlak) to teach, lecture, and
renew his friendships with the German Jews living in the United States. An
international celebrity, he symbolized both the survival of Judaism and the
gestalt of the German-Jewish society which no longer existed. He and Martin
Buber resumed their acquaintanceship. A young American rabbi sitting in a
restaurant next to the two men said, "The sight of the two beards wagging at
one another did extraordinary things to me." (*Photos courtesy of the Leo
Baeck Institute, New York*)

Leo Baeck to the artist—by Lottie Reizenstein, by Yehuda Bacon, by L. Moos, and by Eugene Spiro—in the postwar years. (*Photos courtesy of Lottie Reizenstein; Leo Baeck Institute, New York; and author's collection*)

Leo Baeck, as captured by the photographer, in the postwar years. (*Photos from author's collection, except one of Leo Baeck with his finger raised, taken by Alexander Guttman and courtesy of American Jewish Archives*)

Leo Baeck (*Photo courtesy of the Jüdische Gemeinde, Berlin*)

a woman whose non-Jewish brother-in-law often went to Poland—that there were camps in Poland that had vast "pools," but with gas instead of water. "We knew it," said Ehrlich. "I believed it." But he then conceded, "There was a problem believing it."[37]

This was the same problem the Jews had faced ever since Hitler had come to power: They could not believe it. They could not believe they would be stripped of their citizenship until it happened. They could not believe their houses of worship would be destroyed until it happened. They could not believe they would be torn from their homes and families until it happened. And now they could not believe they would be murdered systematically.

The Hochschule students sometimes were assigned to distribute deportation notices. Before Ernst Ludwig Ehrlich escaped to Switzerland, he delivered two such notices, one to a non-Jew who had a Jewish parent and the second to an elderly Jewish woman, a servant. The non-Jew refused to accept the notice, saying it must be a mistake. The elderly Jewish woman accepted hers, then later, when she was alone, committed suicide. Ehrlich was asked to deliver the notice to the non-Jew a second time, but he refused. He returned the notice and heard nothing more about it.

Gertrud Luckner, who met with Leo Baeck at the Reichsvereinigung frequently during 1942, said she never discussed the matter—the deportations and the ultimate destination—with him. "It was too great a burden," she said. "We were all asking, Is it true? We didn't know."[38]

Baeck and the other Jewish leaders now were counting out lives by the handful. He constantly urged those younger people still in Berlin to flee. He frequently met with them, although in some cases, as with Herbert Strauss, they were wanted by the Gestapo; and he risked his own safety to have contact with them. Some did manage to escape to Switzerland—several hundred did so in 1942. Others were hidden by Gentile friends—again in the hundreds. For the elderly and the sick, those who had only a present and not much of a future, there were the visits, prayers said with them in their homes, sharing of food that came in packages from abroad.

His passion to save lives caused Baeck anxiety about a small group of Jews who had organized a splinter-Communist group. The Communist underground in Germany had not been effective. Its critics believed it to be more pro-Russian than anti-Nazi; they cited the period of the German-Soviet nonaggression pact, when the Communist underground's activity virtually ceased inside Germany, reviving sporadically only after war broke out between Germany and the Soviet Union. There was distribution of some leaflets and illegal papers, but there was no physical resistance to the Nazi government or open confrontations with Nazi officials. The Communists were much less sophisticated than the Nazis, who had infiltrated their ranks thoroughly. Seeking to conceal themselves more effectively, the Communists decided to exclude Jews from membership. The argument was that Jews were more visible to the Nazis than were Gentiles. This decision so angered a small group of Jewish Communists that they determined to pull off a feat that would force the Communist underground to notice them.

In May 1942 the Germans opened an exhibit called the "Soviet Paradise." Its purpose was to create enthusiasm for the war in the east by demonstrating that life in the Soviet Union was anything but a paradise. On May 13 eleven members of the Jewish Communist group arrived at the exhibit at the Berlin Lustgarten and set it afire. All the Jews escaped. Five Nazis died in the fire.

The Gestapo quickly learned, through one of its spies, that the arsonists were Jews. All prominent Jews were arrested, including Leo Baeck and other officials of the Reichsvereinigung. "We were stood against the wall of the great hall," said one, "and forced to stand there from nine o'clock." Baeck, because of his age and position, was permitted to sit for a fifteen-minute period. At one o'clock a Gestapo official entered the hall and apologized for keeping the Jews waiting so long. He then said that he wanted the Jewish leadership of Berlin to know that 250 Jews had just been shot. He stressed the number: fifty dead Jews for each dead Nazi. Before releasing them, he announced: "*Das nächste Mal würden es für jeden zwei hundert und funfzig sein*"—"The next time it will be two hundred and fifty dead Jews for each dead Nazi."

To Baeck and the other Reichsvereinigung leaders the situation was intolerable. The dissidents had to be contacted, informed of the consequences of their actions, and told to stop. The problem was in locating them.

In the 1930s Norbert Wollheim had had casual contact with the Jewish Communists; he knew that some of them were friends or relatives of people he knew. Gradually he had grown away from those contacts, particularly after *Kristallnacht*, when at the request of Otto Hirsch he went to work for the Reichsvereinigung, handling emigration of children. This work ended for him in 1941, when the Nazis placed him in a forced-labor program. They required him to work in a factory, but he was fortunate—he could go home at night. Jews then were not allowed to have radios, but Wollheim knew people with radios who listened to the British Broadcasting Corporation from London at three o'clock in the morning. They passed on the radio news to Wollheim, who delivered it to Paul Eppstein at the Reichsvereinigung. This was how the leaders there followed the progress of the war.

Wollheim's practice was to stop by the Reichsvereinigung's offices on his way home from the factory. He happened to be there following the Communists' attack on the "Soviet Paradise" exhibit and the warning by the Nazis of large-scale reprisals. Paul Eppstein told them: "It's a terrible threat, to take two hundred and fifty of us." Eppstein wondered aloud if he could somehow meet with the Jewish Communists and tell them of the consequences of their actions. Wollheim then conceded he might still have some contacts in that group, but doubted they would agree to meet with Eppstein, who was being watched by the Nazis.

A few days later Wollheim again discussed the matter with Eppstein. Baeck was present this time. In the minds of all three men the idea had been forming that Wollheim himself try to make contact and deliver the message of the Reichsvereinigung leaders. "I have no right to ask you this," said Baeck. "It could endanger your family, if you were caught." Wollheim said he would consider the idea. Years later he said that he was certain that Baeck had not intended to apply moral pressure on him.

Wollheim decided to make the effort. Reaching back into the earlier years of his life, he contacted a school friend and then the brother of that friend, who described himself as an intermediary. They met one night near Alexanderplatz. The streets and buildings of Berlin were blacked out against bombing raids. Dark clouds covered the stars. In this darkness, enshrouded in fog, the two men moved cautiously through the streets. In the Nazi world they could be arrested for their meeting, perhaps executed. So they walked, always alert for the slightest sound, glancing over their shoulders, nervous at every strange shadow, turning corners slowly.

Wollheim told the intermediary that the Jewish leaders wanted the Communists to cease their violent actions. They were accomplishing nothing except to endanger the members of their own group and other innocent people. Wollheim recalled the man's answer, the words hissing out, this way: "What you're telling me is not of interest to us. We're just not interested. If we think we should retaliate, we will. We're not interested in what the Jewish leaders think. Our only consideration is what will serve our cause."

Wollheim remembered Leo Baeck when he reported the conversation back to him—the skin drawn tightly over the face, the hands clenched, the voice hoarse. "Frankly," said Baeck, "I didn't think that in these circumstances reason would prevail. What they did was folly in the first place. Now, at least they are aware of it." Then he added: "There is nothing more we can do."[39]

Baeck knew that soon his turn for deportation would come. He had survived these years because of his international reputation and because the organization he headed was valuable to the Nazis. He had used those two factors to aid his fellow Jews, but he knew he was losing his bargaining power. There were two reasons for this: First, the Nazis, at war with most of the world, had little regard for their reputation outside their own borders. Second, the Reichsvereinigung was becoming less important as the number of Jews dwindled. Since early 1941 Baeck had been working on a new book, *Dieses Volk*—This People, in which he was attempting to summarize his understanding of Judaism as a constant revelation through its history. He knew the manuscript would not be safe with him, particularly as his position in Berlin became more precarious. Someday the "knock on the door" would be at his apartment. He sent the pages of the manuscript as he finished them, therefore, to his Christian friend Baron von Veltheim. ". . . I am sending you further pages of the manuscript, p. 47 to 100," he wrote in May 1942. "The section has gotten a little long, the chapter about the revelation. The further ones, desert and land, will follow. If you could confirm the arrival of the manuscript, I would be very thankful."

Von Veltheim was risking his own security by befriending Baeck, but that was not discussed—he was that kind of friend. "For a long time—so long that I am concerned about you—I have heard nothing of you," von Veltheim wrote two months later. "Also I have not received any further pages of your manuscript . . . Today I have the occasion to send these lines into the city. Please give me a life-sign and write me an address where I can write to receive news of you and of what is happening to you . . ." Baeck answered that his address hadn't changed. "If there should be a change," he said, "you shall be notified."

In June 1942 the Gestapo began arresting Reichsvereinigung officials for deportation. "On this day," said one of the survivors, "at eight o'clock in the morning, the Gestapo occupied the building of the Reichs-vereinigung. Each person who came after eight o'clock—even if it were only one minute later—was chosen for transport. In addition, some fifty members of the office staff were chosen . . ."[40]

Leo Baeck was not in that group. He realized that if he were not in the next, he would likely be in the one after that, or perhaps the next one. In September 1942 his house guest, Leo Berlak—his daughter's father-in-law—was deported to Theresienstadt, a town near Prague in Czechoslovakia. All the residents there had been evicted, and the town had been transformed by the Nazis into a ghetto for elderly and promi-nent Jews. It was not considered a concentration camp. Still, it was deportation and it was a camp. Baeck wrote his daughter and son-in-law and explained the move. He began by telling them how pleased he was that their new home in London "is a center for many of your friends and acquaintances which to a large extent are mine." He used the German phrase *die Meinen* which has an intimate quality. Then he wrote about how well he and Leo Berlak were getting along. Then, "Now these days unfortunately come to an end. My housemate"—*Hausgenosse*—"is moving to Theresienstadt." He used the phrase *verlegt seinen wohnsitz*, which means, literally, "is putting his living place." The Germans use this phrase casually, when they are in control of their actions. "We hope dearly to see each other again in quiet and peaceful days," closed Baeck, "and to be reunited with all our loved ones."

Berlak wrote at the bottom of the letter about how much he would miss his *Pflegevater* and that the farewell was not easy.

Baeck wrote frequently to his daughter and son-in-law, through the Lisbon letter drop, about Leo Berlak. "Maybe he has sent to you already news from there [Theresienstadt]," Baeck wrote in November. "The reports which I receive from there say that he is well, even if new cir-cumstances requiring an adjustment surround him there."[41]

At this time Berlin was being bombed frequently. The Allied bombs did not differentiate between Jew and non-Jew, and everyone spent a great deal of time in the shelters. The Nazis had decreed that Jews and Aryans would have separate shelters. "We were in the basement room with the hot water pipes," recalled one Jew, "so if there had been a direct hit, we would have been killed first. If the bombs didn't get us, the hot water would." That particular shelter happened to be in a building with a number of Nazis, and the Jew remembered that he and his fellows, huddled together in the shelter near the hot water pipes, sometimes hoped for a direct hit so that the Nazis in the building would be killed. He explained the emotion with Samson's line from Judges 16:30, "Let me die with the Philistines."

"Leo Baeck played the old soldier in the air raid shelters," said one witness. He reminded the other Jews of his World War One experiences and claimed to be an authority on bombs, informing everyone that a bomb had hit much farther away than its sound had indicated. "He explained to everyone that there was nothing to worry about," said one who sat through many bombing attacks in one of those shelters, "that they should be calm."[42]

The increasing frequency of the air raid attacks emphasized for the Germans in Berlin that they were beginning to lose the war. In North Africa the brilliant German thrust at the Suez Canal by Field Marshal Erwin Rommel had been blunted. The entry of the United States in the war was strengthening the Allies, and in Russia the Germans were being challenged and defeated by the enemy that always had conquered the invader of Russia, the bitter winter. General Friedrich Paulus had promised Hitler that Stalingrad would be captured by November 10, 1942. It was not. On November 19 the Russians began a major offensive. Hitler, who always had been visible to the German people, became more and more withdrawn. The air raid attacks, the bad news from the fronts, and the pessimism of Hitler and the other leading Nazis cast a pall over the city.

The fall had passed, and no leaves remained on the trees for the wind to tear off and hurl down the long gray streets. Winter had come, gloomy and cold. Men and women plodded through the snow, their heads down against the cold, their collars up. The days were short, and in the wartime blackout there were no lights at night to pierce the city's gloom. Perhaps because of that pervasive feeling of despair Baeck finally wrote to Ruth and Hermann in London a little of how he felt. "Every day brings its work," he said. "I am thankful when I can fulfill tasks and can be something to people and can give something to them. In my house I am well cared for, and I have there quiet hours. The circle has narrowed. However, I experience many loyalties from old friends."

The apartment on Am Park was empty now, without young nephews and nieces to ride the ladder around the wall in the library. There were few students left to come for Sabbath cake and tea. And, of course, nothing could fill the void left by the passing of *die Rabbinerfrau*. But there were within those walls many memories and many reminders of the life and the society now coming to such a brutal end. There was a

silver cigarette case that had belonged to Natalie's grandfather, Rabbi
Adolf Wiener, and that Leo Baeck had hidden from the Nazis. Decades
earlier, when Rabbi Wiener had been granted the freedom of the city in
Oppeln, truly a new era for the Jews began in Germany—or so it
seemed. There were the leather bound books, many not connected with
Judaism—*Art of the Early Renaissance* and *The Netherlands Artists of
the 17th Century*, for example—which symbolized that this had been the
home of sophisticated, cultured, and educated people; people who had
wrapped around themselves the mantle of German middle-class society.
There were the personal things, too—silver napkin rings, some jewelry
of Natalie's, a lace bed cover—all reminding Leo Baeck of the years
when this apartment had been filled with a happy home life. There was
his unfinished manuscript of *Dieses Volk*, some religious artifacts—
Sabbath candlesticks, a large brass star etched with Hebrew letters—
reminders that his obligations and his work still continued.[43]

An old friend, Herman O. Pineas, saw Baeck early in 1943 before he,
Pineas, went underground with his wife. Much later he recalled those
weeks: "The agony you don't remember any more. You know about it,
but you don't feel it any more."

Through 1942 the German army commanders had insisted that Jews
working in factories were of value to the war effort and should not be
deported. At the beginning of 1943, however, the army influence was
replaced by the Gestapo decision to make Europe *Judenrein*. It was as
if the Gestapo, after the Nazi retreats in North Africa and Russia,
realized that the war against the Allies was doomed and decided to
secure victory in the war against the Jews. Hildegard Henschel, the wife
of Heinrich Stahl's successor as president of the Berlin Jüdische Gemeinde, reported:

The year 1943 set in and the morale of the Jews of Berlin was sinking
lower and lower. Almost everybody had lost one of his dear ones in the deportations. Besides, it was well-known that the Army authorities were ready
to compromise with the Gestapo and refrain from protesting against the
seizure of Jewish labourers. The meaning of all this was that the end was
near; there was no doubt about that. When, on January 26–27, 1943, the
three popular functionaries of the Jewish community, Dr. Paul Eppstein,
Dr. Leo Baeck and Mr. Phillip Kusover, the last with his three children, one
of whom was ten weeks old, were all deported to Theresienstadt, the faith in
the continuation of any kind of Jewish activity or Jewish institutions, was
shattered forever.

If Baeck had expected arrest and deportation that month, he gave no sign of it, either to his acquaintances in Berlin or to his children in London. In a letter he wrote to Ruth and Hermann on January 22 he did little else except comment about how pleased he was that things were going well with them in London. He congratulated Hermann on the growth of his practice, Ruth on her new social duties—"how much that all gives you"—and Marianne on her school work—"of course, chemistry takes the first place, before zoology and botany." He assured them that the snow was disappearing; in Berlin there was almost spring weather.

Five days after he wrote that letter, on January 27, he rose earlier than usual. At a quarter of six he was fully dressed. The doorbell rang. "Only the Gestapo would come at that hour," he recalled. His housekeeper opened the door and ushered in two men wearing civilian clothes.

"We have orders to take you to Theresienstadt," one said.

"Please wait a little while. I must get ready."

"You must come with us at once."

"You are two and can use force to take me. But if you will wait an hour I will go with you as you wish."

One left to make a telephone call. When he returned, he said: "We will wait."

Leo Baeck sat down at his desk and wrote a farewell letter to his children via the Lisbon letter drop. Then he wrote postal orders for his gas and electric bills. "My housekeeper had packed my bag," he said. "I was ready to go."

He was taken to the collection center at the Grosse Hamburgerstrasse, where he was locked alone in a room. Later he was given a meal, which he ate alone. At night he was transferred to another building, still alone.

The next morning, he said, "I was taken to the Anhalter station where hundreds of unfortunate Jews were boarding a train. I was put into a compartment by myself. Before long the train moved out and I was occupied with my thoughts. Only once was I disturbed. In Dresden an SS man looked in and asked if I wanted water."

Leo Baeck continued: "Theresienstadt meant much to me even before I saw it. Three sisters of mine had died there, and a fourth died shortly after my arrival."[44]

12 THERESIENSTADT

LATE IN JANUARY 1943 Gertrud Luckner telephoned Leo Baeck's home. *"Der Herr Doktor ist nicht hier,"* she was told. "I realized," she recalled, "that he had been arrested." A friend of Baeck's wrote Baron von Veltheim that "Herr Dr. B. is no more in his home. . . . Today on my own I have taken up the task, difficult for a lady, to write to you and this is my third effort . . . You must forgive me this great sadness." Another friend sent von Veltheim the remainder of the *Dieses Volk* manuscript, which she had found among Baeck's possessions. "Hopefully," the friend added, "the time is not too far away when the other part can reach you."

When Baron von Veltheim received the manuscript, he wrote on it: "This is that last work, the last manuscript, which Dr. Leo Baeck wrote from 1941 until January 1943. Because I have known the author for more than twenty years, I have willingly undertaken the task of keeping the manuscript and of sending it to his daughter as soon as conditions will allow." Von Veltheim not only was concerned about Baeck's survival, he also believed he himself might be in danger because of his friendship with "enemies of the state" and his own opposition to the Nazis.[1]

Theresienstadt where Baeck was headed—Terezin, as the Czechs called it—had been built in 1789 by the Austrian Emperor, Joseph II, as a military installation, and named after his mother, the Empress Maria Theresa. There were two fortresses—a large garrison and a small military prison—one on each side of the Ohre River. When Theresienstadt became part of the Czechoslovakian Republic, the small fortress still was used as a prison for dangerous criminals, but the large fortress fell into disuse. By the end of the nineteenth century it had become a small provincial town of a few thousand occupants. There were no water mains until the 1930s, and they were connected only to a few buildings. Despite an attractive square in the town's center, Theresienstadt epitomized drabness. The buildings were gray stone, architecturally pedestrian, and the streets were narrow. There was no industry. It was the kind of small European town that people generally were happy to leave. In 1941 the Nazis evicted the approximately 3,500 people still living in the town from their 219 houses and announced that Theresienstadt would become a ghetto for "privileged" Jews.

One of the Jews interned there remembered Theresienstadt as being crossed by three roads. One led to Bohusovice, a town approximately a mile away. Here the transports arrived—Theresienstadt had no rail lines of its own—and Jews unloaded and began walking, clutching their possessions, to what was for them a prison. The second road led from the town itself across a narrow bridge to the small prison fortress where a Jew, for almost any infraction, was sent and crowded into a filthy cell. The third road led from Theresienstadt to Prague. "With its signpost, 'Prague 63 kilometers,' [it] was the highway of memories and dreams. This highway was the prisoners' only link with friends, homes, life, and future."

The Ghetto Theresienstadt resulted from the Nazis' queasiness at their treatment of Jews. Eichmann and many others wanted to destroy the Jews, to carry out Hitler's vow to make Europe *Judenrein*. At the same time they feared that if their brutality became known, they would be in trouble with some elements within Germany and they might engender unnecessary hostility abroad. Their solution was to develop one site as a "showplace," one area they could show to visiting Red Cross dignitaries and other skeptics as proof that the Jews were not being maltreated.[2]

Some Jews bought their way into Theresienstadt, considering it the least of the evils facing them. "Contracts" were entered into by individual Jews and the Reichsvereinigung in which the Jew agreed to turn over his resources in return for "the acquisition of residence" at Theresienstadt. The usual contract stipulated that the Jew must pay not only for himself but also for other less-affluent Jews.* Five categories

* Hannah Arendt in *Eichmann in Jerusalem*, 1965 ed., p. 158, reported that after the Reichsvereinigung officials had been sent to Theresienstadt, the "Reich simply confiscated the considerable amount of money then in the Association's treasury" which had been gained from such contracts. The Reichsvereinigung records were

of German Jews were eligible for Theresienstadt: those over sixty-five and their spouses (even if the spouse was under sixty-five), invalids from the First World War and recipients of significant German medals in that war, Jewish partners in mixed marriages (if the marriages had produced non-Jewish children), Jews of mixed religious parentage, and high officials of the Reichsvereinigung. Within these five groups were many prominent Jews about whom the Germans feared international inquiries and many, such as World War One veterans, who still had some friends and supporters within Germany. Whatever its original purpose, the Ghetto Theresienstadt eventually became a way station for Jews being sent to Auschwitz. Although Theresienstadt was not a death camp as were the other concentration camps in the sense that mass murders took place there, it became a death camp of its own kind. So many died there of illness, starvation, and despair that Theresienstadt became another example of Nazi bestiality.[3]

The first transport of Jews arrived at Theresienstadt at four-thirty on the morning of November 24, 1941. It included 342 young men from Prague. They had feared they would be sent to the camps farther east, about which they already heard rumors, so for them Theresienstadt was a welcome relief—at least they had a chance for survival. They were told they could write to their families, that they would have decent living conditions, and that they would be paid for their work. Ten days later the second transport from Prague arrived.

By the fall of 1942 Theresienstadt, built to hold perhaps 10,000 people at most, housed more than 60,000 Jews. The few decent buildings in the town, the Hotel Victoria in the square and a few other modern structures, had been taken over by the SS for its own members. Barbed wire bordered the streets leading to these buildings. On the other side of the barbed wire lived the Jews. Rooms that once had housed a family of three or four now housed sixty persons. Men and women, husbands and wives were separated. Children over twelve did not live with their parents. Eventually the Jews began to take over the Ghetto administration; the Nazis had no objection because it saved them the trouble. The Jews organized a laundry, operated the bakery and the food depot, and built a sewer system. They examined the wells and shut down those found contaminated. Water was always in short supply—

---

destroyed in the war, and the size of its treasury is unknown. Whether there was a "considerable amount of money" is doubtful, however. Few Jews in Germany by this time had much money, and most people who went to Theresienstadt were sent there as prisoners and did not purchase their way in.

four gallons a day to each person when twenty gallons were considered necessary, but the four gallons were more than the Jews could have had otherwise. Latrines were built and connected with the sewer system, but because of the large numbers of people and the cramped quarters, toilet facilities always were inadequate. For Jews, administering the Ghetto themselves meant that whatever facilities available were being administered as efficiently as possible, whatever food available was being distributed as fairly as possible, whatever living space existed was being allocated as honestly as possible.

Problems multiplied because the age of the Jewish inhabitants became increasingly higher. In January 1942 people over sixty-five represented 6 percent of the total population. By May of that year the figure was 27 percent. These elderly were less able to work in the Ghetto, needed more food and care, and had more difficulty coping with the living conditions. This was evident in the increasing number of persons becoming ill—ten times as many in the second half of 1942 as in the first half.

Although the Nazis called Theresienstadt a Ghetto, and many Jews referred to it by that name, it had no resemblance to the ghettos of the Middle Ages. They had been communities of people bound by their religious beliefs. The members of those communities had been born into them, usually were comfortable within them, and believed they could fulfill their religious lives within them. The ghetto of the Middle Ages was an environment restricted by hostile civil laws. Yet the Jews still could walk outside the ghetto walls in the Middle Ages, converse with their Gentile neighbors, trade with them, learn from them, and—if the Gentiles would allow it—assist them. The Theresienstadt Ghetto was made up of people who had been uprooted from their homes, transported against their wills, ordered by guards to stay within the confines of the Ghetto walls, and forced to live in conditions alien to them.[4]

At the time of Leo Baeck's arrival there were 46,735 Jews in Theresienstadt. Slightly more than half—25,730—were under sixty years of age, and the remainder—21,005—were over sixty. The work details broke down this way: 6,000 Jews did construction work, repairing streets and building a railway line from Bohusovice to Theresienstadt; 2,300 did maintenance work in the Ghetto; 4,800 Jews were needed simply to care for the elderly and the sick. A report from a Nazi official at Theresienstadt to his superiors in Berlin at this time said that "because of the difficult hygienic conditions and the insufficient sanitary facilities, it is calculated that the daily number of persons ill from typhus in the early part of 1943 will reach a very high level; currently it is 406." The report requested permission to deport 5,000 Jews over the age of sixty to Auschwitz, to eliminate contact between those capable of working and the infected. The promise in the report was to deport only Jews "who do not have special relationships and connections, and who do not have any special war honors."

The request was denied in a February 16, 1943, telegram to Theresienstadt. The Nazi officials in Berlin did not want to upset the belief of the elderly Jews that they could live in Theresienstadt without fear of execution. One Jewish inmate recalled that period and said Jews believed they could remain in Theresienstadt, "where they would enjoy a modicum of peace though life would be hard."[5]

Leo Baeck arrived on January 28, aboard transport 1/87 from Berlin. He then became the number 187984. It was of this last that he said he had resolved "not to become a mere number and always to keep my self-respect." People arriving at Bohusovice were marched by police and orderlies to the entrance gates at Theresienstadt, where they were told not to speak to anyone while personal information was indexed and they were searched by the Germans for valuables—cigarettes, cosmetics, soap, and the like. "For many people," said one who experienced it, "arrival at Theresienstadt was the first and one of the worst experiences, a major traumatic one. After the arrival you went through this business of being undressed." A woman who went through the experience as a child, on the verge of entering her teens, recalled: "You were told to strip to your birthday suit, and the women stood in front of some men who were chatting and laughing and questioning them. Nothing in particular was done, but it was just the experience of having this kind of thing happening." The woman recalled that after going through the receiving center, "You began meeting your old friends who told you that the big concern which was even more important than how much food there is that day or how much space you have to sleep in, was that you never know whether you are really going to be staying."[6]

The day before Baeck's arrival the camp commandant, Siegfried Seidl, received a special report from Berlin, sent at the direction of Adolf Eichmann. "Important functionaries from Berlin, Vienna and Prague start this morning to Theresienstadt," it said. One of those listed was Baeck. The report requested special treatment for several of the prominent Jews, including Paul Eppstein, who was to have two rooms—but no mention is made of any special treatment for Baeck.

As a prominent person, Baeck probably did not have to go through as arduous an ordeal on arriving as did others. But he did not receive any favored treatment at the beginning of his stay. Every inmate of the Ghetto, male and female, who arrived at Theresienstadt had to belong to a labor battalion for a fixed period before being assigned to a regular job. During Baeck's first few weeks at Theresienstadt he was assigned to a labor battalion and actually pulled a garbage wagon through the Ghetto's streets.

"I had heard of the crowded conditions," Baeck later said of Theresienstadt, "but not until I saw with my own eyes did I fully understand what it meant. Bunks often were constructed in four and five decks, with so little space between them that one had to lean far forward when sitting on the edge. Often people did not have enough room to stretch out. It was a luxury to have an opportunity to sit on a chair." One of the worst problems, he said, was the shortage of latrines. "Many had dysentery," he said of his fellow elderly Jews, "and it was humiliating for these good people to defile themselves when they had to wait. When I too was affected, I fasted for three days and was blessed with recovery."

What was the impact on a person entering Theresienstadt for the first time? Leo Baeck described the experience this way:

When he had entered the fortress gates between the walls and bastions, a gate of destiny was closed behind him, perhaps forever. He was locked in. And inside he was yet again segregated; one part of the fortress-town, the better and healthier part, was separated as the precincts of the S.S. guards. In a space that before, even in the narrowness of military quarters, had been meant to harbour scarcely more than 3,000 people, now there were often almost 45,000 penned together in barracks and other buildings, pressed against each other, packed above each other. Covering the streets there was, when the sun shone, the thick dust that the high ramparts did not keep out and when rain or snow had fallen, there was the deep sticky mud that seemed to grow daily. And from everywhere and into everything there came the vermin, a great host—crawling, jumping, flying—in their onslaught against the hungry human beings, waging a war hour by hour, day and night. For months and months, maybe for years and years this was now to be the world.

But Baeck realized that the great danger was not the hunger, the crowded conditions, the filth, or the vermin. Rather, he said:

Here the mass submerged the individual. He was enclosed in the mass, just as he was encircled by the crowded narrowness, by the dust and the dirt, by the teeming myriads of the insects and encircled, as it were, also by the need and distress, always together, as it were, the hunger that seemed never to end—enclosed in the camp of the concentrated, never alone by himself. It was like a symbol that each had received his transport number. That was now his characteristic feature, was the first and most important sign of his existence. It officially ousted his name and it threatened inwardly to oust his self. That was the mental fight everyone had to keep up, to see in himself and in his fellow man not only a transport number. It was the fight for the name, one's own and the other's, the fight for individuality, the secret being, one's own and the other's. Much, perhaps everything, depended on whether one stood this test, that the individual in one remained alive as an individual and continued to recognize the individual in the other.[7]

On May 23 of the year of his arrival at Theresienstadt, Leo Baeck became seventy years of age, and with the other elderly he was excused from physical labor. Eventually he became one of the "prominents," people whom the Germans considered either of international repute or having a special value. Their living conditions were better than average. Baeck acquired a two-room apartment; the back room was his bedroom and the front room had a table, chairs, and some books. It eventually became a center for many of his old friends from Berlin. They came by for tea, conversation, and some reminder of the life they once had led. The apartment obviously had belonged to a very poor man by the standards of the Berlin Jews, but in the realm of Theresienstadt it was elegance. "To be served with a real tea cup," marveled one of his guests, still charmed even thirty years later by that touch of civilization. Baeck was not involved with the Jewish Council of Elders, which ran the Ghetto—it had been organized before his arrival—but he did take on the responsibility for administering the welfare program at the camp, first for the elderly and then for the entire camp. This kept him moving throughout Theresienstadt, visiting the sick and talking to the elderly. He had been allowed to bring clothes with him, and his appearance continued to be that of the German burgher—suit jacket always on, vest, and tie. He managed to maintain the dignity of his position, to remind those whose lives he touched at Theresienstadt of the life they all had known in Germany.

"Leo Baeck was untouched by Theresienstadt," said one of his fellow inmates. "He never really was there."

That Leo Baeck was untouched by Theresienstadt is not true. He was deeply moved by the experience, but he was disciplined. As in Berlin, he tried to be the ultimate resource person, the one to whom both sides in a dispute could come, the one who—by not showing distress—could offer solace to others.[8]

One woman who had been at Theresienstadt for a year before Baeck's arrival recalled that within hours after he came to Theresienstadt, "He was at my side. Nothing great was said. No wordy comfort was given. But he was there." He always looked through the list of new arrivals to see if there was anyone he knew from Berlin, members of any family he had known in the old days in Duesseldorf and Oppeln. If he recognized a name, he quickly made a visit.[9]

Baeck had said that God's commandment was to live, and the immediate problem was physical survival. Living at Theresienstadt, he believed, involved "the fight . . . for the individual day." The first problem was housing. If the Jewish Council of Elders complained to the Nazi authorities about inadequate space, the probability was that the Nazis would respond by ordering Jews deported. So the Council crowded more and more people into the small houses and the barracks. Living space averaged out to two square yards for each person, counting storage, lavatory, and cooking space. Those who were fortunate had a bunk with some bedding; others slept on the floor. The bunks began as two tiers, then became three tiers. "Living conditions in the large barracks," said a former prisoner there, "tended to be better than in the small ones because these small houses tended to be tremendously crowded, more so than the barracks. I suppose because the barracks were built to accommodate many people and you had these dormitory-like rooms. I suppose the ceilings were higher so that maybe the air was better."

The rooms were unheated, and those who survived Theresienstadt often were unable, in the years following their liberation, to work in anything but a cold room. In the postwar years a friend of Baeck's visited him at the Hebrew Union College in Cincinnati and was astonished at how cold Baeck's room was. "I was cold," said the friend, "but he was very comfortable."[10]

Food was another problem. A woman who went to Theresienstadt as a young child recalled that in Berlin, "My father very deliberately, for a long period, encouraged us not even to attempt to obtain more food than was available. My parents absolutely refused food that was ordinarily not available. My father felt we would probably go to Theresienstadt sooner or later, and wanted us to learn abstinence." She added: "I think that was one of the very smart things he did for us." Those who were disciplined in their eating habits survived Theresienstadt better than those who were not. But even the survival was grim. Wrote one of the inmates:

Only he who himself had to queue in front of the communal kitchens for a plate of soup or a few potatoes, who himself has been in the terrible scramble for the little bit of daily food when rain was pelting down, only he who has seen old ladies—ladies still in distress—beg for a few spoonfuls of a thin soup, who has seen old men rummaging in the dustbins for potato scraps, only he who has noticed what a bag of stale bread crusts means to a hungry person or witnessed the happiness given by a sandwich or two, only he can fully realize what hunger meant in Theresienstadt. Only he who has seen the old ladies walking along with legs like thin sticks, or has seen the emaciated bodies of the men in the bath—mere bones and skin—knows how malnutrition has left its mark on the people . . .

The main diet was a small portion of margarine, sugar occasionally, and potatoes. The potatoes were prepared this way: "Four of us carried heavy sacks of potatoes to a small room in the barracks . . . where about a hundred women, mostly elderly, peeled potatoes from early morning till late evening. At noon and night we carried the peelings to a cellar where hungry people were waiting to search for anything edible among them. The atmosphere in the crowded rooms was stifling. The women sat on hard boards till they could scarcely sit any more and peeled till their hands were sore. Many of the women who had come from comfortable circumstances adjusted better to deprivations than those who had always been poor." Most of the women who worked peeling the potatoes tried to save a few scraps to augment their rations for themselves or their families. "The women showed astonishing imagination and skill at finding hiding places in their clothes or on their bodies," said this account.

Packages were received from the outside, but not always their contents. "A package came for me not long after I arrived in Theresienstadt," said Baeck. "Its contents had been removed and it was really only an empty cardboard box." That particular package had been sent by an individual. Food packages from the International Red Cross and the American Joint Distribution Committee had better success getting by the Nazis. The Council of Elders tried to parcel out this food in proportion to needs. "A shipment of dried prunes and condensed milk has arrived," said one announcement of the Elders, ". . . dried prunes will be distributed among the Ghetto inmates over 70 years of age; the condensed milk to the public health agency and to the youth welfare, and, as far as it is possible, to manual and administrative coworkers."

Baeck hoped to persuade individuals who received food packages to give up part of them for general use; he did this on a voluntary basis along with some others. "The respect enjoyed by Dr. Baeck in the entire free world," said one of his fellow Jews at Theresienstadt, "made him a favored receiver of packages . . . which made him the benefactor for the oppressed of the Ghetto." Many people survived almost solely because of the food packages from outside. These packages were remembered primarily for figs, considered a delicacy in the camp, and also for the tinned sardines. A joke at Theresienstadt through the years was "Are we having sardines again?"[11]

Given the food and housing conditions, widespread disease was to be expected. There were outbreaks of typhus, encephalitis, and scarlet fever as well as the effects of malnutrition. Many women, in their first few months in the Ghetto, stopped menstruating. Often one-third of the Jews in the camp were ill. Many of the Jews were medical doctors and nurses, and the rudimentary health facilities were better staffed than many hospitals outside the Ghetto, but they lacked proper supplies. The Nazi officials had mixed reactions to the health facilities—they feared that an epidemic would not respect uniforms, but they still could not bring themselves to provide Jewish medical personnel with all the supplies they needed. At times the Gestapo restrictions were without purpose except harassment. For example, lights were not allowed in the lavatories; because of the large number of people and the shortage of lavatories, those rooms had to be used twenty-four hours a day; without lights it was impossible to keep them clean.

Even against these odds Jewish medical personnel managed to establish a preventive health program. People between the ages of three and sixty-five were vaccinated for typhus; between the ages of one and one-half to forty, for scarlet fever; from one and one-half to eighteen, for diphtheria. The vaccination schedule was listed on a mimeographed announcement distributed by the Jewish Council of Elders. On the announcement, which went on the barracks' walls, was a drawing of a man in a white coat, holding a huge hypodermic needle and chasing a small boy.[12]

Still, they died. There was not enough food, not enough blankets, not enough medicine. There were too many people in too small a space; many were old, without coats to keep them warm in the winter and without the strength to survive the stifling summer heat. Carrying the dead away, said Leo Baeck, who officiated at many of the funerals, was a "long procession out to the great army of those who had gone before."

The mortuary was "a deep, dark passage in a fortress wall, itself almost like a mass grave . . . There stood, often in a long, long row— the plain coffins of the dead, always two or three on top of each other, and the names were read and the old, thousands of years old prayer for the dead was said." This prayer was the Mourner's Kaddish.

Although the Mourner's Kaddish is a prayer for the dead, it is not about death or about those who have died. Rather, it is an affirmation of the Jews' faith in God; they say that prayer when they lose a loved one to show that, even in the most dire circumstances, they cannot renounce their faith.

After the recitation of this prayer, "The coffins were taken up and carried forth, while the psalm was sung that for generations has accompanied the dead on their last journey, the psalm that begins: 'He that dwelleth in the shelter of the Most High!' and ends: 'With length of days will I satisfy Him, and will let Him see my salvation.'" This is the Ninety-first Psalm. It includes these lines:

> you shall not fear the hunters' trap by night
> or the arrow that flies by day,
> or pestilence that stalks in darkness
> or the plague raging at noonday.
> A thousand may fall at your side,
> > ten thousand close at hand,
> > but you it shall not touch.

"It was like a demonstration when that psalm was intoned, a demonstration of freedom in serfdom," said Baeck.

"Outside there stood big, heavy lorries and the coffins were placed on them. For about fifty paces the people were allowed to follow them; then the enclosure of the camp was reached. Only the dead went forth . . ."

The dead were taken to a mass grave in a large field outside the Ghetto. Every morning men came and dug into the wildflowers until a shallow pit was ready for the bodies, which arrived about noon. The bodies were removed from the wooden coffins—which were reused for other bodies the next day—placed in the pit and covered with dirt. "My fellow workers' disgust and horror of the corpses seemed strange to me," said one who buried the bodies. "To me they were only outer shells from which the soul had gone and become free. But the thin bodies were not a pretty sight. Sometimes the cloth with which they were covered showed traces of dysentery, and occasionally a dried-up limb would hang out of the covering."[13]

In the early history of Theresienstadt Ghetto many people tried to escape, but only thirty-three succeeded. Those caught were imprisoned in the Little Fortress across the river, tortured, or deported. Anyone who still considered the possibility of escape was warned that he or she "must reckon with the strongest measures of the state police. Also, relatives in and outside of Theresienstadt [would] have to expect severe disadvantages."

There was no need to speculate on "severe disadvantages." Punishments in Theresienstadt were harsh for the smallest infraction. One person was sent to the Little Fortress for four weeks for stealing potatoes; another, ten days for stealing a piece of satin; a third, twenty days for smuggling a piece of salami into Theresienstadt. One man accused of having written a clandestine letter was kicked and beaten while lying ill on a stretcher. Another man accused of having cigarettes and money was beaten and then ordered to stand naked next to a red-hot stove. The Nazis pushed him against the stove and seared his eyes and his hands with a red-hot poker. In March of 1943 sixteen persons were hanged with the full knowledge of Ghetto inmates. The Germans claimed the sixteen had been guilty of bribery, but a Red Cross report after the war charged they had been executed for minor causes. "One of them was found guilty for having sent a completely harmless note to his wife," said the Red Cross report of the executed men. It continued: "Another was sentenced to death because he had received, without permission, a suitcase of supplies from the outside." Seven of the prisoners were hung on March 9, and the remaining nine were hanged on March 16. In the process of hanging one of the sixteen, the rope broke; the man had to be hung a second time.[14]

The Nazis decreed that childbirth in the Ghetto must end—"You are reminded, with all forcefulness, that women who find themselves pregnant or believe themselves, due to existing conditions, to be pregnant, are obliged to report immediately to a gynecologist at the proper health center." An American government report about Theresienstadt after the war said that a "tragic fact" was that no children were born at Theresienstadt. That was inaccurate; a small number of babies were born in the Ghetto, at least in its early years—according to one history, 207 children were born there. It is true, however, that the Nazis demanded that pregnant women have abortions; giving birth in the later years of the Ghetto, if the Nazis found out about it, could be cause for deportation to the east.

Leo Baeck had some young friends, Willi Groag and his wife, who was pregnant and hoped to have her child. Frau Groag worked in a section dealing with agricultural products and turned for help to her supervisor there, a non-Jew, who had been friendly toward her and Willi. He refused to intercede with the German authorities, explaining that his position was not high enough for him to be influential, and suggested she go to a member of the Jewish Council of Elders.

"What can I do?" said this Jewish official. "I'm under pressure from the Germans."

When Frau Groag was seven months pregnant, she was called before a health division official. Her pregnancy was evident, and she was informed that she must have an abortion. She refused and heard nothing about it for another month. Suddenly she was directed to the health clinic, and her husband Willi was called before the same Jewish official of the Council of Elders who earlier had refused to help his wife.

"You should know," said the official, "at this moment your wife is in the clinic, and they will perform an abortion on her."

"I understand that you want to shock me, but I believe that I can call on your humanity to prevent this abortion in the eighth or ninth month. It would kill my wife."

"I cannot go with that to the Germans. It is an unfortunate thing. Briefly, you must give your consent to it."

Rather than give his consent to the killing of his wife, Willi Groag went to the clinic and brought her back to the barracks. They would face the consequences together of wanting their child and defying the Nazi restrictions.

Leo Baeck always had been fond of the young couple. He had assured Frau Groag that her child would be born on the Sabbath. "You will have a *Sabbath-kind*," he told her. When he heard of their plight, he was not a member of the Council of Elders. He was a "prominent," however, and not afraid of placing his prestige and position on the line in a confrontation with the Nazis. Groag never learned the details except that Leo Baeck interceded with the Nazis so that the child could be born without fear of retaliation.

The child was born at approximately four o'clock on a Friday afternoon, shortly before the Sabbath was to begin at sundown. A few days later, when Frau Groag could walk, Willi took her to see Leo Baeck. "I checked when the Sabbath actually had arrived, and it was at five o'clock," said Groag. "So I said to Dr. Baeck: 'Everything is fine except that you have not proved yourself as a prophet.' " Leo Baeck turned to Frau Groag and replied: "I am truly sorry for that. I have underestimated your ability."[15]

Sometimes Baeck helped simply by listening and understanding. A woman in her early twenties, daughter of a wealthy family Baeck had known well in Berlin, had arrived at Theresienstadt some months before him. This lovely young woman had known all the comforts that money can bring, and she missed them in Theresienstadt. The crowded conditions, the shortage of food, and the dirt eroded her sense of pride and decency. In hopes of an extra scrap of food, a feeling of warmth, space to breathe in, she became a prostitute. Years later she said: "I don't know why I did what I did. You can't explain those things." Judaism has no dark and private confessional booth. It does, however, have love and sympathy for the troubled individual. "I needed someone to understand my action," she said, "and I used Baeck. His compassion for human errors would not allow him to hold my acts against me. He was my conscience, like my father."[16]

All Jews at Theresienstadt were required to wear a yellow star on their clothes. "The orders regarding the wearing of the Jewish star are called again to your attention," read one notice. "The Jewish star is to be worn also within the buildings, on the walks and in the courtyards. The superior authorities will put suitable controls in effect..." This symbolism was important to the Nazis. A notice in the summer, for example, ordered those Jews working without shirts to attach the star "on their pants with a pin and [to] wear it there until they put on a jacket with the Jewish star." People caught without the star were struck by the guards.[17]

The Nazis were brutal and sadistic, and enjoyed the power they held over their victims. One SS chauffeur toured the Ghetto streets in his car, deliberately running down Jews. Another official inspected the Ghetto's hospital late one night, waking up the tubercular patients and forcing them to stand naked in the open doorways. This sadism was not limited to Nazi underlings. The first camp commander was Siegfried Seidl, an SS leader who had a doctor of philosophy degree. He collected handsome commissions on supplies ordered for Theresienstadt and enjoyed arriving unexpectedly in the shower rooms when the Jewish women were taking their baths.[18]

Despite the Nazi harassment, the illnesses, the poor food, the shortage of proper clothing, and the crowded living conditions, the Jews used the physical facilities of the Ghetto as best they could, dispensed food as fairly as possible, looked after their health as well as they could. That they did live—many of them, at least—is a triumph of the Jews at Theresienstadt.

In addition to physical survival something more was needed. "Whether one survived in a concentration camp," Leo Baeck said when the experience was over, "outwardly depended on circumstances; disease, torture, annihilation could destroy one's life." But whether one could survive inwardly depended upon two other qualities—"patience and imagination." Baeck defined patience as "this power of resilience that did not let the will to live give way" and imagination as "the vision that ever again and in spite of everything makes him see a future." The Jews, with their tremendous optimism, their desire to fulfill God's commandment to live, lost neither their patience nor their imagination. Against all the pressures a sense of community developed at Theresienstadt. "People who had not known each other endeavoured to help each other, physically and spiritually," reported Baeck. "They gave each other of whatever they had, of their belongings and of their spirit. Human beings found each other, and where the individual held on to himself, there also arose community."

Despite harsh living conditions, brutality, and doubts about their future the Jews at Theresienstadt determined not only to survive, to live, but to live as human beings. They developed a community that included their own theater, musical productions, lectures, and religious services. The Nazis could rob them, beat them, attempt to humiliate them, and, ultimately, kill them. The only thing the Nazis could not do was defeat them.

Many of the Jews at Theresienstadt had been famous composers, artists, and actors. The actors began by giving poetry readings in the barracks and then progressed to stage productions. The musicians began playing together and gradually combined to produce symphonic music. Actors and musicians joined together. Smetana's *The Bartered Bride* was one of the most memorable productions. The scenery was non-existent, the costumes greatly resembled the everyday clothes of the participants, and the theater was the corner of a barracks or a courtyard. The young children were introduced to Verdi, Mozart, and Bizet, to *Cyrano de Bergerac* and *Liliom*. Artists painted—desolate scenes of the elderly, hugging their emaciated bodies for warmth, standing in long lines for food; of children huddled in purposeless groups. Poets and musicians tried to capture the hunger, cold, and sadness in words and music.

Much of the creative work produced at Theresienstadt has been lost; some was destroyed by Nazis, some misplaced by families deported to Auschwitz, some buried in the debris of a crowded barracks. Some of this work has survived, however. There is a famous poem by a child lamenting at never having seen a butterfly. There are the sad drawings of cold, hungry, lonely people. There are plays and operas that say much of how the people felt. One opera, *The Emperor of Atlantis*, which surfaced years after the Second World War, is an example of how the artists of Theresienstadt used their creative abilities to protest. In the opera, the ruler of Atlantis loses his power because death has taken a holiday, and in the absence of death people lose their fear of him. To make certain that no one missed their point, the Czech composer Viktor Ullmann and the librettist Peter Kien made references to the Nazi goose-step and to the song *Deutschland Über Alles*. The Nazis at Theresienstadt prohibited performances of the opera. Even they realized the work's bitter commentary.*[19]

The artistic quality of the work produced at Theresienstadt was not the important point about it. Rather, its real purpose was to nourish the "patience" and the "imagination" of the Ghetto inmates. That was part of the learning experience the Jews underwent in Theresienstadt; learning to live so as to be ready for tomorrow was a process that gave meaning to each day.

The Jews never were certain why the Nazis allowed these activities. Speculation centered on several reasons. Certainly the Nazis did not appreciate how far the cultural program would develop and the significance it would have for those in the Ghetto. Probably the guards believed these activities made their own lives easier because they kept the inmates involved. And there was an effort, especially in 1943 and 1944, to stabilize the conditions in Theresienstadt. It was supposed to be a "model" ghetto, and in the Nazi minds cultural activities contributed toward that image. For whatever reason, the Nazis generally did not interfere, and the Jews made the most of that neglect.

The care of the children was an important activity in Theresienstadt, one that eventually came under the welfare program, which Leo Baeck headed. Many children were separated from their parents, who had to

* The opera was performed in the mid-1970s. Although successful because of its political background, it was found to be lacking as a musical accomplishment. The critical feeling was that Ullmann and Kien had lacked the time needed to develop their style. They died at Auschwitz.

work long hours. Special homes were set up for these children, and activities were devised for them—athletics, crafts, as many diversions as possible. A program of formal education was established. The Nazis had a strict rule against any such educational program, and so the teaching was done in secret, with people watching at barracks windows to warn when a guard approached; then the lesson was disguised as a game. "Some of the physical punishment that did occur," recalled a woman who had been a student there, "occurred when people had been caught teaching. There was a lot of teaching going on, but it was very definitely a dangerous business. My mother had a small group which she taught. I remember one day we had very little notice that someone was coming through. It was the kind of thing where somebody came dashing by and said, 'They're down the corridor!' and so everybody started singing. And when the guards came in and asked what are you doing, my mother replied: 'Oh, keeping them out of trouble by singing some songs,' and that was all right." Against such difficulties the Jews managed to develop a system of elementary and secondary schools, along with vocational training for the older children. They enlisted whomever they could find with almost any kind of teaching background. The children sometimes wrote their lessons on toilet paper.

Much of this education was in the hands of the Zionists. They seemed to have a greater sense of organization and perhaps a greater sense of purpose than did the other Jews. The Zionists looked beyond Theresienstadt, to the time when Jews would be free to go to Palestine, and they acted on the assumption that this would happen. One student had a schoolbook at Theresienstadt with the name *Natiw* on it—Hebrew for "path." The cover indicated that the path led toward Palestine. This cover had a crude drawing on it of a ship, with the word *Aliyah* written on it. The word is Hebrew for "ascent," and it has several uses. When a person is called to the *bimah* during a service to read the Torah or the Torah blessings, for example, his ascent to the *bimah* is called an *aliyah*. The Zionists used the word to mean a return to Palestine; when the Jews return to Jerusalem, they not only ascend physically, by climbing a mountain to the city, but also spiritually. This textbook at Theresienstadt reflected the belief not only that the children would survive but that they would return to Jerusalem, making both the physical and the spiritual journey. In the *Natiw* book the history was Jewish history; the characters were Palestinian. Many of the lessons were taken up with map reading and knot tying, an orientation toward living elsewhere than in Germany or in eastern Europe; toward living in a young Jewish land where farmers and foresters would be needed more than lawyers and doctors.[20]

Of the many activities at Theresienstadt that turned the people there from a mass to a community, probably the one best remembered, praised, and considered the most valuable in a spiritual and intellectual way was the series of lectures given by Leo Baeck and some of the other scholars in the camp. There are several stories about their origin— probably all of them are true. A young Zionist at the Ghetto, Zeev Shek, talked to Baeck about the spiritual hunger of the people there. "My thesis was that the Germans could break us physically but needed our help to break us morally. When I said that to Leo Baeck, he rose from his chair and said: 'I'm with you in everything you say about that.' " The next step was to develop a program appealing to the Jews. Almost all of them had come from middle-class backgrounds in Germany and were highly educated. Given the number of scholars at Theresienstadt, a lecture program seemed appropriate.

Leo Baeck once told a rabbi friend this story about how the lecture series began: "I stood there when the Jews from Holland came on a lorry. A Gestapo agent read off their names for them to come down. When I heard the names, I literally heard the history of the Jewish Netherlands which dated back to the seventeenth century. I heard a list of the Dutch aristocracy." This was an intellectual aristocracy. "It was then," Baeck continued, "I decided to institute the lecture series. I taught Plato. We didn't have any books. I remembered Plato in Greek, and I taught all of Plato in Greek."

Another time Baeck wrote:

There existed an unbelievable pressure toward spiritual nourishment. So Professor Maximilian Adler, a fervent Zionist from Prague, who had distinguished himself in the scholarly world, Professor Utitz from the University of Halle, and I decided to begin a series of lectures, "From Plato to Kant." I undertook the first lecture about Plato myself. We invited the audience using the "snowball" approach. At first three people knew it; a few minutes later twenty-five, and after an hour, five thousand. Half secretly, in the protecting darkness of the night, we went to the so-called Dresden barracks where more than seven hundred people would stand closely packed in the drafty attic in the winter cold to listen for one hour and fifteen minutes with great excitement to a lecture on an academic subject which was not easy to follow.

At this first lecture both Baeck and his audience wore coats, scarves, and hats because of the cold. "And," he said, "while over the auditorium hung the dreaded danger of deportation to the death camps, at the same time the eternal world of Platonic ideas arose brightly over the auditorium. Later I spoke to the same circle about Maimonides and finally about Kant. The audience did not decrease but, as far as the room permitted, it increased. I asked myself: Is there another people on earth which has such a deep and true connection to the spirit, as ours—that although it is facing such humiliation and danger, it asks for the word of the philosopher."[21]

Because the Ghetto inmates had to be inside their own barracks by eight o'clock in the evening, the lectures began at six. The program offered over the years was comprehensive. In the month of July 1943, for example, there were sixteen lectures, including "Rabbiner Dr. Leo Baeck: 'Spinoza.' " Recalled one person:

I was in Theresienstadt from June 1943 to September 1944. There I, along with many other interested fellow prisoners, heard the series of lectures which Dr. Baeck organized about the philosophy of Kant. So far as I remember, there were five lectures of between ninety and 120 minutes. They took place in a loft attic of one of the notorious barracks and hundreds of persons attended. Dr. Baeck spoke extemporaneously, without a manuscript. Whether he had been able to prepare it in advance by writing it out and whether he generally had otherwise required literature available, I strongly doubt.

Said a woman listener:

The lectures of Dr. Baeck offered always the same picture. In a cold, dark loft, a collection of people sit or stand on beams; before them, on a wooden stand, the speaker appears as a prophetlike figure from an older time. Whether he speaks about Plato, Kant, Maimonides, whether he handles themes like "The Time of the Enlightenment," or "The Thoughts of the Nineteenth Century," or is speaking about "Return and Reconciliation," "Soul and Body," his audience is seen listening, absorbed, in breathless silence, forgetting hunger and cold, going away with new strength—to suffer the torments of the camp after some hours in the building.

To these people the lectures were a part of their past recalled for them, a way of life they had known, a homage to the intellectual world that once had been theirs. As another person said of Baeck's lectures: "For a moment it was like it used to be."

The lectures were not secret. The Germans knew about them and allowed them, probably for the same reason they allowed the other cultural developments—they didn't understand their significance. That the lectures might appear—by their titles, at least—to be insignificant seemed calculated. The Jewish speakers chose titles and subjects— Plato, Kant, Spinoza, Maimonides—totally divorced from current events, often from Judaism, from anything suggesting protest or rebellion. But in the context of the lectures there was the cry of protest, the shout of defiance.

An example is a lecture Leo Baeck gave to a Czechoslovakian group one evening, "Great and Small Nations." One member of the audience, a doctor, recalled that "To be sure this lecture was not announced. It took place in the Hamburger barracks in a great subterranean store- house, announced surreptitiously from mouth to mouth. Despite that, the room was completely filled." Leo Baeck began by recalling the troubles of the early Greeks as they were conquered by their neighbors with more powerful weapons, but he then reminded his audience that despite those defeats the Greek culture survived thousands of years. Then he told of Jan Hus, the fourteenth-century religious reformer who was martyred in Czechoslovakia because of his beliefs. Baeck stressed that the important fact about Hus was not his death but that an entire people rose up in protest. "Farm workers left their fields; craftsmen, their work benches; the entire people struggled for truth." Baeck went through other examples of the history of the people in his audience, always stressing that in the end might failed before truth. In Judaism to hope is a duty, and Baeck's lectures gave those people reason to fulfill that duty. Said the Czechoslovakian doctor: "His lecture in Theresienstadt was an evidence of high courage, since a traitor in the audience might have delivered him to the torture chamber in the Theres- ienstadt fortress. To us Czechoslovakians the name Leo Baeck remains unforgettable."[22]

Baeck's lectures were not written down, but one has survived as reconstructed by Baeck after his liberation. Given in June 1944, its title is "The Writing of History." Its content shows how Baeck managed to take an historical theme and transform it into a contemporary cry of defiance. He began with a definition of history, one that very much shows the influence of his old teacher, Wilhelm Dilthey. Baeck said history was neither a listing of events nor a collection of themes. It was not a story of economics or of wars. Rather, it was a record of the "continuity of life," with equal emphasis upon life and community. Life was not "an aimless vegetating, a state of random movement swinging vaguely to and fro at the will of external impulses." Instead, life was "an existence that has become aware of itself, conscious of its yesterdays and tomorrows, of the paths leading up and those leading away from it, conscious of its course and destiny." He defined continuity, too, first negatively. "This is no mere medley, no accidental sequence of juxtaposition, but a structure with its own definite lines, with its own architectural framework, its own divisions and extensions, its own connections, affinities, and contrasts . . . a totality and unity that is clearly aware of itself, that can become a subject of meditation, a task for self-realization."

Baeck went on to say: "The basic premise of all writing of history . . . is that there is sense and meaning behind all manifestations and that these are subject to laws." To understand this meaning, a dual ability is needed—"scientific competence with which to grasp and examine all the details, and an artistic vision . . . science and art . . . a sense of the rational and of the irrational . . . of critical assessment and imagination, of research and intuition."

"Understandably enough," Baeck continued, "historical awareness and the writing of history developed first and only among peoples of marked self-assurance, who were certain of their own specific character and of being favoured. In antiquity this feeling of nobility and singularity existed among two peoples, the Greeks and the Israelites. Both groups undertook the writing of history, first the Israelite people and a few centuries later the Greeks . . ." Then he began tracing the historians, beginning with the Greeks. Herodotus, he said, "searched for laws. The first law, to his mind, was the action of the gods." Next was Thucydides, who "saw men determining and deciding, men as the measure of things."

Baeck then turned to the Israelite writers of history. This people, he said, experienced an historical awareness at an early age. "This is understandable," he continued, "since their life as a people began, according to their own recollection, with an historical event, the Exodus from Egypt." The purpose of Baeck's lecture, its message to its listeners, was the concept that there is a progression in life that—despite all appearances to the contrary, despite the swastikas worn on the arms of the guards—is not arbitrary, but is bounded by law.

Baeck added that the Hebrew prophets had sought "an understanding of the realities of history and the laws contained within them." These prophets had seen the empires of Egypt, Assyria, and Babylon proceed in triumph. "They had seen the edifices of power being erected and crumbling once again." More than the rise and fall of empires, the prophets had seen another struggle, "a wrestling of the spirit, of faith and ideas, a conflict between spirit and power, between faith and egotism, between ideas and interests. And history, to them, was present only when spiritual values existed and ideas ruled." To the study of history and to the experience of life, the Jewish contribution was one of spiritual values, faith, and ideas. The prophets, said Baeck, "turned against every misdeed of history that seeks its vindication in success or expediency. They turned against the sort of politics that creates its own moral code; they objected to any justification of right by victory."

For the Hebrews law was "derived from a single Being, from an eternal, everlasting moral justice." The law also went with God's commandment to live. "For living means living for justice," said Leo Baeck to the imprisoned people of Theresienstadt, "for goodness and truth; the ultimate continuity of life is the continuity of this permanent verity ... True history is the history of the spirit, the human spirit, which may at times seem powerless, but ultimately is yet superior and survives because, even if it does not possess the might, it still possesses the power, the power that can never cease."

Baeck did not speak of the Third Reich that day, but everyone in his audience knew what he was saying. The Hebrew people had survived a long time. Their traditional Biblical history was more than 5,000 years old—and they had seen many despotic powers collapse. They would see the Nazis collapse, too. This particular lecture was given on June 15, 1944; nine days earlier the Allied forces had landed on the Normandy beaches in France to pierce Hitler's hold on the European continent. *"Wir Juden haben alte Augen"*—"We Jews have old eyes" —Baeck once had told a friend.[23]

There were religious observances at Theresienstadt. Many attended services conducted by their own rabbis—the Berlin Jews usually attending Baeck's. Since many of the people at Theresienstadt were Protestants or Catholics, services were held for them, too, in the barracks. Indicating the relentlessness with which the Nazis pursued anyone with a Jewish parent or grandparent, the percentage in the Ghetto of those people with some Jewish ancestry who were Protestants or Catholics increased significantly. In May 1944 that group represented 15 percent of the total population at Theresienstadt. A year later, at liberation, the figure had risen to 36 percent. Many of these Christians knew and liked Leo Baeck. Said a Catholic of Baeck: "He derived no benefits from his position as did some of the other leaders." The Catholic said also that Baeck was "a link between those of different religions and ideas. We Catholics honored him especially, and he was a frequent guest at our meetings. When he lectured on philosophic subjects or commented on current problems, his appearance, his personality, the depth of his thought, and the clarity of his expression made an extraordinary impression." The Catholic concluded: "Respect and tolerance for his fellow man formed the basis of his ethics."

Community seders were held to celebrate the festival of Passover, commemorating the Jews' exodus from slavery in Egypt. Matzo was usually available from the Red Cross and other organizations outside of Europe. For Purim the Jews at Theresienstadt had an Esther Megillah, a scroll telling the story of how Esther and Mordecai saved the Jews from destruction by Haman, which they read during the service.

Some weeks after Theresienstadt had been liberated and Baeck had left, the Esther Megillah was found there and given to a young American chaplain, Eugene J. Lipman. He promised to give it to Baeck, and when he was in London, he met Baeck and offered it to him. Baeck picked up the Megillah for a moment—"I remember his hands; they were huge hands and he used them well," said Lipman. "This is not for me," Baeck had said. "If I have it, it is a museum piece. The Megillah we used at Theresienstadt was not a museum piece. We read it. We used it. Take it. Use it in your congregation. Tell them all about Theresienstadt. Don't let them forget Theresienstadt." Rabbi Lipman took back the Megillah and has used it in every Purim service since.

Of the many services conducted at Theresienstadt perhaps the Bar Mitzvahs were the most impressive. In them the Jews reaffirmed a resolve to pass on their religion and their life to their children. One Bar Mitzvah boy at Theresienstadt was Ralph Blume, who became thirteen in August of 1944. Years later Blume recalled his Bar Mitzvah ceremony:

Leo Baeck's appearance is very vivid in my mind as one of a beautiful and handsome man. His posture is one of erectness, if I may use the term. Tall and handsome with a shock of white hair . . . The Bar Mitzvah took place in one of the barracks in which one of the smaller rooms had been converted into a synagogue. We had a Torah . . . Eight people were called up and Leo Baeck called me for my Torah portion. He had no singing voice although a beautiful speaking voice, deep and impressive . . .

In his address to me on this day, Leo Baeck mentioned how sad this occasion was and also how far away we were from our "Heimatland." Yet, Baeck continued, we should rejoice for after all it is a happy occasion and how fortunate I am to celebrate this together with my mother. The white shirt which I wore then was made from a set of shrouds normally used for the dead.

Rabbi Baeck said further that despite the terrible circumstances, I was still brought up as a Jew . . . I think the point Leo Baeck made which, in my opinion, was the most important, was that, despite all I had gone through so far, I should never change my religious beliefs.

By the way, we "celebrated" the occasion by having a special treat; we had dry bread and mustard . . .[24]

The Jews at Theresienstadt had managed to maintain and enrich their culture—music, theatre, literature, and their religion. They had come to the Ghetto as people of taste, sentiment, and with a love of God. That they would leave the same way was another triumph of the Jews at Theresienstadt.

It was at Theresienstadt that Leo Baeck became an ardent Zionist. Actually, he had been moving toward that position most of his adult life. At the beginning of his career he had supported the right of Zionists to speak, although he disagreed with their position. Later he had accepted that some Jews, if not the German Jews, might need Palestine as a homeland, and that the development of Palestine created renewed interest in Judaism even for non-Zionists. As the Nazis had become more powerful and more threatening, he had realized that even the German Jews might find Palestine a necessity. By 1943, at Theresienstadt, Baeck was acknowledging that the Jews needed the security of a homeland, the assurance that comes from knowing that there is a refuge when one's neighbors turn their backs.

After he left Theresienstadt, Baeck said that the Jews there had been nurtured by the religious experience, the services that took place in small rooms—"Jews, who knew nothing of the matter and who had lived their entire life far from Jewish tradition, took part in these *minyans*"—but, he said, "Above all, however, the thought of Palestine clearly was the vital spark for us all." At Theresienstadt, Baeck officiated at the burial of a woman who had a very strong connection with Zionism, and at that ceremony he confessed his error in not having been a Zionist earlier. The woman was Trude Herzl, daughter of Theodor Herzl, the early leader of the Zionist movement. "If we had listened to the words of the father of this unfortunate woman," said Baeck at the service, "we would not all be here today."[25]

Mail was limited at Theresienstadt. Prisoners were allowed to send one postal card a month, with a maximum of thirty words printed in block letters, to anyplace in Germany. German was the only language allowed. The cards could not have political content or disparaging references to the German Reich; they were not allowed to "include untrue reports or distorted pictures about the conditions in the Ghetto." The cards as they left Theresienstadt carried the stamped message: *"Ruckanwort nur an Postkarten in deutscher Sprache"*—meaning that responses from outside Theresienstadt could be only in German on postcards.

Baeck occasionally received mail and packages from old friends in Germany. What few messages he sent out did not dwell on his own discomfort. "Let me thank you again from my heart and let me say again how much your kindness has touched me. The excellent things that your packages gave me are good for my physical well being. Just as much and also more, your kindness and loyalty gives to me in a spiritual way. Many thanks to you." Writing shortly after the High Holy Days, Baeck reported: "The holidays passed here well, with their services and community activities. I hope that you also spent them well and enjoyed them. I would certainly enjoy hearing from you again and hearing how you are."

His reluctance to complain to his acquaintances was another aspect of his self-discipline. At this point in his life, the keeping up of defenses and dignity was a habit that could not be broken except under extreme provocation. Then, however, those defenses would be broken in different ways. Once at Theresienstadt, in July 1944, he scrawled out these words:

> Tage gehen,
> Erinnerungen bleiben
> > Theresienstadt, 16. Juli 1944
> > L. Baeck

The meaning was: Days go, memories remain.[26]

Although Baeck rarely showed his anger, it was effective when it did erupt. One such occasion involved a demand by Baeck to one of the Jewish elders of the camp for relief of the crowded conditions in a building that was one of the worst at Theresienstadt. Some juggling could relieve the worst parts of the problem. The elder had not seen the building himself, made no offer to go, but assured Baeck that changes would be made by the next day. The next day, however, there had been no improvement; the elder had ignored the problem. "Leo Baeck became angry," said a witness, "and took the official by the scruff of the neck and forced him up the stairs to see the crowded conditions for himself. Conditions were then corrected."[27]

Whatever resourcefulness the Jews developed at Theresienstadt, they could not avoid the harshness and stupidity of the Nazis. An example was the census taken in fall 1943. "One November day all of us had to walk out of the camp and stand in a field until evening," said Leo Baeck. "We did not know what was to happen to us. I was afraid that they would use gas bombs to kill us on the spot. It turned out that they were checking up on account of irregularities in the list of inmates."

The Nazis simply had no idea how many inmates Theresienstadt held. So many people had come in, so many had died; records had been kept, but the inconsistencies and errors had overwhelmed the Nazis, who decided the simplest way to discover how many people were in the Ghetto was to count them. On the morning of November 11 some 40,000 people were ordered to line up in front of their barracks and march in columns of five to an old drill ground outside the fortress. From four o'clock in the morning until noon, the Jews—some very old, some young children—marched to the parade ground. An hour later some SS officers arrived by car from Prague. They established a system by which all the Jews walked past two groups of Nazis to be counted in rows of five. When the two groups of Nazis compared their figures, the totals never agreed, of course, so the marching and counting began a second time. Whatever the original purpose, for the Jews watching the Nazis it was apparent that the Nazis considered ridiculing the inmates more significant than counting them. The weather was cold; the Jews were hungry, forbidden to use a latrine, and frightened. Late in the afternoon the SS officers gave up the idea of counting the Jews and left. No one in charge had any idea of what to do with the 40,000 Jews: Should they be kept in the field all night or returned to Theresienstadt? The people panicked. According to one eyewitness account several people died on the drill ground, and many of the elderly became ill and eventually died. "Altogether between two hundred to three hundred prisoners paid with their lives for the census," according to this account. The Nazis tried the census count a few days later; this time they ordered prisoners to turn in their identification cards, which were counted and then returned.[28]

Several hundred Danish Jews had been sent to Theresienstadt; Danish officials insisted on knowing their status, sent food packages and demanded that the Red Cross be allowed to visit Theresienstadt and examine living conditions there. The possibility of a Red Cross visit in the summer of 1944 frightened the Nazis who, facing the possibility of losing the war, knew they would be in trouble if actual living conditions were discovered by the Red Cross. They decided to create a false front.

Days before the Red Cross appeared the Jews were ordered to clean the streets. The healthiest children exchanged their dirty rags for new clothing. Buildings were painted and street signs erected. Children were rehearsed to play games on the streets; they were told to call the Nazi commandant "Uncle Rahm."

Karl Rahm, the camp commandant from early 1944 until liberation, was a mechanic with no organizational ability. He possessed a temper which he frequently exhibited against the Jews. Without Nazism he would have been nothing, since he lacked the intelligence or the ability to perform anything but the simplest task. As a Nazi, however, he had power over other people and importance. The night before the Red Cross visit Rahm directed Paul Eppstein, the former Reichsvereinigung official, to inform the Jews of the Red Cross' arrival and to instruct them not to speak of the true conditions at the camp. A squat, ugly man, Rahm stood by Eppstein's elbow, obviously enjoying the plight of the helpless Jew telling his fellow prisoners to lie. The Jews listened to Eppstein, but they watched Karl Rahm. They would remember that scene.

Some by-products of the Red Cross visits were advantageous to the prisoners. Living conditions did improve somewhat in preparation for the visits, and the interest of the Red Cross guaranteed delivery of its food packages. Still, to the majority of Jews the "show" aspect of the visits brought only anguish and disappointment. The International Red Cross, said Baeck, "appeared to be completely taken in by the false front put up for their benefit. Many of the houses were so overcrowded that a tour through one of them quickly could have revealed the real state of things. But since only the ground floor could be seen from the street, the SS shrewdly ordered two-thirds of the people living there to move to the upper floors. Flowers were put in the windows. The commission never bothered to climb one flight of stairs. Perhaps they knew the real conditions—but it looked as if they did not want to know the truth. The effect on our morale was devastating. We felt forgotten and forsaken."

A camp orchestra had been organized to entertain the Red Cross officials, and it occasionally gave an afternoon concert in the weeks after they had left. Baeck was so angry at the false front put up for the Red Cross visit that he refused to attend any of these concerts. He expected others to boycott them, too, "without considering," said one of his friends from Berlin, "that they were for many of the elderly people an interruption in their drab existence."[29]

The Nazis decided to make a film about Theresienstadt. An inmate overheard Rahm and another SS official saying: "We should film Theresienstadt so that the Jews will not say later that they were badly treated by us." A reasonable surmise is that in the summer of 1944, with the Allies storming across the French beaches and the Russians pushing in from the east, some Nazis decided the time was appropriate for fashioning alibis. Cameramen from Prague were imported to do the filming. Jewish actors and other theatrical personalities were forced to direct and act in the film. Some of the scenes were ludicrous—tragically so—to the Jews. The only time they were allowed to swim in the river during the entire period of Theresienstadt Ghetto was the one day when the cameras filmed the scene. Cafes suddenly sprouted on the sidewalks. Food was put on the tables. In one scene a group of Jews was shown sitting in the town square describing their happiness at living in Theresienstadt.

The film never was shown publicly. The few people who saw it considered it such a blatant and false propaganda effort that it became a joke. Also, by the time the film was ready for showing, in the spring of 1945, no one would have believed it. By that time the world had an accurate idea of what was happening to the Jews in Germany. So did the Jews in Theresienstadt.[30]

There had been occasional deportations "to the East" from Theresienstadt, but they had not been numerous or organized and did not involve large numbers. Generally the Jews in the Ghetto believed that if they could exist under the harsh living conditions there, they would survive until the war ended. During the spring and summer of 1944 living conditions improved because deaths and a small number of deportations had decreased the Ghetto's population. In May this decrease had brought the population down to approximately 36,000. By the end of September the number had dropped still further, to 28,000. In that month a systematic program of deportations to the east had begun. On September 23 the Nazis issued the following order:

It is imperative that Theresienstadt should provide more manpower than hitherto for the war effort. Careful investigation has brought us to the conclusion that Theresienstadt lacks the space required for the transfer of essential war industries to the Ghetto. Hence it has been decided that 2,500 able-bodied men will leave Theresienstadt for this purpose on the morning of Tuesday, the 26th of September, to be followed by the same number of able-bodied men on Wednesday, the 27th of September. They will set up a new labour camp under the direction of Otto Zucker.

Those proceeding to the new destination will take only light luggage, one change of linen, etc., and food for twenty-four hours. The destination of the transports is in the direction of Dresden. The nature of the work to be carried out will be similar to that which is being performed in the camp of Zossen. The wives and children of workers will remain in Theresienstadt, where H.Q. guarantees their good treatment. Excess luggage of single men, which cannot be taken on the journey, will be safely stored, while the luggage of married men may be left with their families.

Although that kind of order obviously was designed to disarm the deportees, it was questionable whether the language fooled anyone. Certainly it did not dispel all the shadows that hung over deportation. "Transports to other camps in the East went out, in some months day by day," recalled Leo Baeck, "no one knew quite where to; one only knew: eastward into new uncertainty. A cloud of questions, of anxiety and of terror ever anew descended on the camp. It seemed to be the secret watchword of the overlords: Never let the Jews come to rest!"

The destination for many of those deported was Auschwitz, farther east. In the history of mankind Auschwitz holds a unique position. The number of people murdered there totals one million. They were brought in crowded railroad cars, on trucks, by foot—led into small, sealed chambers, gassed, and then carted away to crematoriums. These were noncombatants—in addition to the healthy there were the elderly, the sick, the children. Almost all of them were Jewish. But the total number killed is not the only reason for Auschwitz's claim to infamy; more have been killed in other places. Rather, Auschwitz represents the horror of technology as the servant of power. The technological achievement of the Germans enabled Hitler and the Nazis to kill Jews in an organized, untroubled way. The crematoriums were surrounded by newly planted trees. Special elevators made the moving of the dead bodies easy. Powerful gasses made the actual killing simple; the murderer did not have to be in the same room with the victim and did not have to witness the act. Technology had made the mass murders a statistical event, numbers to be collected each day and added to previous totals. Technology took killing out of the realm of humanity; it preserved the psyches of the killers.

Arrival at Auschwitz happened this way, as told by one survivor:

Transports arrived when it was dark. One did not know where one was. One knew nothing of gas chambers. The Nazis went to infinite trouble to keep them a secret. Presently loudspeakers announced that a long march into the camp lay ahead and that transport was being provided for the sick and the weak. After months or years of captivity in one camp or another, everyone was weak and there was a rush to the lorries conspicuously bearing Red Cross signs. Needless to say, they went straight into the gas chambers.

This division no doubt facilitated the task of the SS doctor in front of whom the rest paraded in a single file, being waved either to the left or to the right. A temporary separation, one assumed. One waved "see you soon" to one's relatives. Members admonished their children to button up their coats lest they should catch cold. Those "new" arrivals, waved to the side of death, who did not know—and who could have imagined it, even after two years of ghetto life, that gas instead of water would pour out of the shower—were the only people physically, mentally and morally fit to revolt.

Baeck described the deportation from Theresienstadt to Auschwitz this way: "Those for whom by inexorable chance the lot had been cast were rounded up in one of the barracks, and they were given a new transport number; they had become other beings, an existence had ended for them; what would be the other existence? In front of the barracks there stood, between two files of the SS, the train of cattle trucks. Human beings were penned up in them and the train drove out of the camp, away from those who yet remained."

No longer in control of their lives, watched over by armed military robotlike men, the people began this trip quietly. "Transports were dreaded," said Baeck, "but when they did leave people were careful not to give the SS satisfaction by creating scenes. I had already learned in Berlin to admire the self-restraint and inner strength of our people—even when families were torn apart."[31]

The deportees were quiet and orderly, not for the benefit of their Nazi guards but to ease the pain of their relatives and loved ones remaining behind. "Don't cry," they were saying, in effect. "We are going not to one of those dreaded places you have heard about but to a work camp, and we will be together again." Nothing could be gained by causing a relative standing in a barracks door to make a fruitless gesture against an SS guard carrying a machine gun. Nothing could be gained by telling a young child that he or she never would see parents again. Better to ease the pain.

One inmate who witnessed the deportations from Theresienstadt said:

Anyone who has seen the hurrying, bewildered masses of humanity, anyone who has witnessed those days of horror and despair will understand that the small pleasures of life were essential to counterbalance this misery. Just because the danger of deportation was menacing everyone at every moment, the people in the Ghetto had to live as if this danger did not really exist, as if a life of freedom and human dignity was waiting round the corner for those now banished behind the walls of the Ghetto.[32]

After the war Baeck reported that he had first learned of the death camps in August 1943. According to his account a half-Jew escaped from Auschwitz and sent a message to Theresienstadt to warn Baeck, whom he knew, before he fled again. "So it was not just a rumor, as I had hoped, or the illusion of a diseased imagination," said Baeck when he received the eyewitness account. Despite this knowledge Baeck continued to walk through the streets of Theresienstadt, stopped to chat with old friends, went to the hospitals, watched out for children, lectured the people about the ultimate triumph of law, spirit, and decency—choosing not to say that many of them soon would be sent to their deaths.

"No one should know," he had decided. "If the Council of Elders were informed, the whole camp would know within a few hours. Living in the expectation of death by gassing would only be the harder. And this death was not certain for all—there was selection for slave labor; perhaps not all transports went to Auschwitz. So came the grave decision to tell no one. Rumors of all sorts were constantly spreading through the ghetto, and before long the rumors of Auschwitz spread too. But at least no one knew for certain."

After the war Paul Tillich, the German-born theologian, criticized Baeck for his refusal to confirm the rumors. "No one can fully judge the events within the concentration camp," said Tillich. "But, in a way, I would criticize Baeck for not giving the last iota of information which he possessed. If he did know that Auschwitz meant certain death, he should have spoken out. The full existential truth should always be made available, just as the uncurable patient should always be told the full truth." Tillich was quoted by Albert H. Friedlander, whose study of Baeck is subtitled "Teacher of Theresienstadt." Friedlander suggests that in addition to Baeck's announced reason he might also have doubted the accuracy of the report and been reluctant to spread a false story.

There were many rumors. A report to the American OSS in November 1943 commented on postcards smuggled from Theresienstadt, written by Danish Jews, saying that "These said that before the Dutch and Danish Jews were sent to this place, which was overcrowded, the Germans, after blowing up the dam in the Ruhr, killed 50,000 Jews in this camp with gas to make room for the new ones." There also were accounts the other way. "Extermination and its gruesome connections were not known to us until after the liberation," said one of the inmates.

The conflict between the accounts indicates a people in limbo, not knowing their future, dreading the worst and hoping for a miracle, trying to survive until liberation. H. G. Adler was at Theresienstadt, knew Baeck well there, and survived to write a definitive account of life in the Ghetto. He has considered Leo Baeck's explanation for not informing about Auschwitz and found it lacking. "It is certain," wrote Adler, "that the general lack of information about the true fate of all those who went from Theresienstadt to the death camps of the east led to a thoughtlessness and self-deception which was barely limited by a darkening of consciousness."

An account in a Red Cross report written after liberation is not as negative toward the concept of deception as Adler. "The fact that they [those remaining behind] knew nothing of the fate that awaited those who were deported to the east," it said, "allowed the population to keep up their morale during this time and to be disciplined."

Many at Theresienstadt knew, as did Baeck, or could surmise the fate of those being deported. Like him they felt that nothing would be gained by eliminating the possibility of hope. "Transports?" said one woman who had been at Theresienstadt. "We didn't talk about them. Leo Baeck would not have answered. He wouldn't have said anything. A lot of people committed suicide and more would have, if they had known."

A woman who was at Theresienstadt while in her teens reflected years later on the question of whether the people knew and whether anything could have been gained by discussing the death camps. "I think you knew pretty well," she said. "Even if you weren't certain or didn't know exactly how, you knew the transports weren't good. It really was a very dreaded thing. Some people had some words, they had some ideas; but even if you didn't know exactly what was going on, it was quite dreadful. I cannot recall any of my friends or relatives leaving without our saying goodby in such a way as if we really did not expect to see each other again."[33]

Transports to the east rolled out of Theresienstadt with regularity after September 1944. There had been almost 30,000 prisoners at Theresienstadt at the beginning of that month. In the next four months 4,500 died there of illness and malnutrition and about 15,000 were deported, leaving about 11,000 in the camp.

Karl Rahm, the camp commandant, did not miss the departure of any train. As he stood uniformed, his black boots shiny despite the dust, his garrison cap squashed down on his glistening forehead, he could have been counting cattle, watching the Jews drag themselves by him, tags around their necks, their possessions tied in bundles on their arms.[34]

Leo Baeck was not a member of the Council of Elders through the end of 1944. The Council was headed by the Chief Elder, who had a deputy and used the Council as an advisory group. The position of these people was of course quite tenuous. They were supposed to represent and look after the best interests of the Jews at Theresienstadt. At the same time, however, they were constantly under the Nazi guns. Their discretion and ability to maneuver was limited by that German authority, and any judgment of those people must include that factor. Baeck's judgment of those serving on the Council was that most of its members used their position to help as many of their fellow Jews as possible and not themselves. One exception was a certain rabbi. After the war, when this rabbi applied for a position, the community asked Baeck for a reference. Baeck declined, explaining to a friend that the rabbi "has still to prove himself a good man." Another exception was an associate of Baeck's from Berlin who had other problems. He used his position on the Council to take advantage of the women at Theresienstadt. Even though the Nazis eventually executed him for other reasons, the man's name could not be mentioned in Baeck's presence in the years following the war without the disciplined, self-controlled Leo Baeck exploding with anger.

As a "prominent," Baeck could have benefited from his position but did not. "Dr. Baeck practiced the hardest ethic," said one with him at the time. "In the knowledge that for every scheduled deportee saved, another must be sacrificed, he allowed to go on the transports his nephew and his niece, both doctors."[35]

In the late fall of 1944 the Council of Elders was so depleted that Leo Baeck was obliged to become a member and finally, the Chief Elder, the administrative head. In the next few months he tried to hold the organizational structure of the Ghetto together, although little could be done at this time by anyone.

As always he had little regard for his own safety. One of his friends in the Ghetto, for example, was H. G. Adler, whose interest and background were in music but who was assigned at Theresienstadt to be a mason. He was not a very good one. "Whenever Leo Baeck needed a laugh," said Adler, "he would come by and watch me do my masonry work." Adler had resolved that the record of Theresienstadt must be reported after the war. For months he collected documents and made notes about the conditions there. In the closing months of the Theresienstadt Ghetto, Adler's mother-in-law was sent to Auschwitz, and Adler and his wife insisted on going with her. He asked Baeck to hold onto his documentary material, and Baeck agreed without a moment's hesitation. They all lived so close to death and danger that Adler didn't consider the extra hazard under which he placed Baeck. Baeck kept the materials safely, and they became the nucleus of Adler's damning study of the Nazis and the Ghetto Theresienstadt.[36]

What became important to Baeck in these last few months before the war ended was preventing the moral and physical collapse of the few remaining Jews. He had contacts with the outside world through an old family friend who worked frequently outside the Ghetto walls and who provided Baeck with Czechoslovakian and German newspapers. "The death penalty was exacted for possession of newspapers," said this acquaintance. "Dr. Baeck knew that as well as I knew it, but he took the risk." With his personal knowledge of eastern Europe from his First World War experiences, Baeck was able to track the Russian advance and estimate the time of Theresienstadt's liberation. He began sending messages to the other inmates to hold on, to survive just a little longer. Help no longer was a remote possibility. Underground acquaintances were willing to cooperate with Baeck. They would not work with some Jewish leaders because, as one said: "A great number of the leading German Jews always wanted to prove that they were loyal to the SS camp leaders and followed their orders exactly, and because of that, often did more than they would have had to do. Dr. Baeck was one of the few who did not have that inclination to demonstrate loyalty to the SS leaders."

Baeck's arrival in Theresienstadt in 1943 had been reported within Jewish circles around the world, and as early as September 1943 his family knew he was there. But his family and friends lost track of him as information from inside the German Reich became increasingly difficult to obtain. Finally, in February 1945, his daughter received a letter from Switzerland, written by a Dutch Jew who had left Theresienstadt the previous week with a transport of 1,200 Jews whom the Nazis had released in a reconciliation effort. Baeck was given the opportunity to join the group but had refused, again preferring to remain with his fellow Jews rather than seek safety. Baeck asked the Dutch Jew to write to Ruth, and his letter reported that Baeck's "health is well and mentally he is unbroken, and that last strength has made him a great support for others." The letter described Baeck as a member "of the so-called prominent group, which is treated better in many respects." Baeck by this time was the leader of the Council of Elders, the letter reported, continuing: "Everybody who gets to know him, either in a private capacity or through his duties, loves him. I myself think that one of the few good things in Theresienstadt was that I got to know him and that he has taken care of me and my family." The letter continued with a few more personal items. The Dutchman and his family had been in Theresienstadt for sixteen months; it was their third camp. "We are overwhelmed to have survived the pressures under which we have lived for so long a time," he concluded, "and that we don't have to work ourselves to death anymore and that we are rid of the fears that have haunted our recent life."[37]

In those closing weeks Baeck did not speak to anyone about the possibility of his own rescue, of his own return to his family. There still was too much work, too much danger, too much potential for vengeance by the Nazis to make plans. He almost did not survive that last violence. Toward the end of March several people expressed astonishment at finding him alive. "I just heard that you were dying," said one. He learned later that a Moravian rabbi in the camp named Beck had died. Baeck did not appreciate the significance of that death until a few weeks later, when he was in one of the offices of the Ghetto. "The door opened and an SS officer entered. It was Eichmann," Baeck recalled. "He was visibly taken aback at seeing me. 'Herr Baeck, are you still alive?' He looked me over carefully, as if he did not trust his eyes, and added coldly, 'I thought you were dead.'" Eichmann obviously had confused the dead Beck from Moravia with Leo Baeck from Berlin. Baeck replied: "Herr Eichmann, you are apparently announcing a future occurrence." Eichmann quickly recovered himself. "I understand now," he said. "A man who is claimed dead lives longer."

"Feeling certain that I had little time left to live," Baeck later said, "I wasted none with him. I walked to the door, he stepped aside, and I went to my quarters. I gave my wife's and my wedding rings to a friend and asked him to hand them onto my daughter in England. Then I wrote farewell letters and was ready for what might come."[38]

Eichmann never carried through on his implied threat, probably be-

cause there was an event on the last day of that month that put an end
to the organized violence of the Third Reich. On April 30, 1945, Adolf
Hitler killed himself in a Berlin bunker.

April had been a chaotic month at Theresienstadt. The Nazis burned
as many documents as possible. Some of the officials advocated the
building of gas ovens to destroy the remaining Jews there; others tried
to placate the Jews, hoping for help from them after the war. One night
rumors circulated that the war was over. The Jews actually packed their
belongings, but the SS guards, headed by the commandant, Rahm,
crossed the barbed wire and ordered them to return to their barracks.
A representative of the International Red Cross, Paul Dunant, appeared
at the camp early in April, then disappeared. He was negotiating to take
the camp over from the Germans even before liberation by the Russians.
But the inmates didn't know that; they only knew he had come and
gone. Then the transport trains carrying the sick and the dying from the
death camps, bringing even more disease and despair, began arriving at
Theresienstadt.

Early in May an American Flying Fortress flew over and dropped
leaflets announcing that help was near. Then there was a different sound
in the sky. A small blue-and-yellow airplane arrived with the returning
Red Cross official, Dunant. "Something had disappeared," noticed a
woman inmate; "the swastika, the sign of our terrible humiliation was
not hanging any more on the Rathaus tower. And soon it was spoken
everywhere. The whisper was a certain truth, that instead of the
swastika, the flag of the Red Cross had been raised. Mr. Dunant, the
representative of the great organization, had succeeded in getting the
leadership of the prison camp into his hands. The danger of gassing
was ended."

Another woman inmate recalled looking up and down the streets of
Theresienstadt: "One thinks that nothing has happened. That all is as it
has been. One ventures forward. Looking toward all sides one goes a
few steps. And looks and is astonished and understands it not: Nowhere
can a German uniform be seen. No guards; no watchers. In the jumble
of the bombing uproar and fear the Germans have fled. Unobserved.
The Germans are gone! They have fled!"

But the Germans were not yet finished. A regiment intent on defending Prague against the uprising of the Czechoslovakian partisans and
the advancing Russian army was forced to turn back. As they retreated
past Theresienstadt, they began firing off their excess ammunition
toward the town. They had become animals, killing for vengeance,

killing for sport, just killing. "Everybody was looking for protection," said one inmate. The few Red Cross officials present were no defense.

"A hand grenade fell into a small house and hurt an old man badly. With the children we lay under the windows on the floor while the bullets flew through the room over our heads," said one inmate. Then there was silence. The women and the men gripped tightly the young children, whom they had protected with their own bodies. They waited for the howling soldiers to explode into the rooms, determined to find victims.

Like that, they waited.

There was a scream, but not the scream of death. It was a jubilant shout. The Germans had fled, really fled! The Russians had arrived! They were liberated! They were saved! Now it was truly over. "We opened all the windows, looked outside," said one woman. "The Russians were there. They entered, the liberators. No one who has not himself experienced it can understand the joy of that hour of freedom. A band marched through the city, everybody came out and joined the procession. One played the *Internationale*." The experience of Theresienstadt was beginning the process of becoming a memory.

Dunant of the Red Cross took over the camp's administration on May 3. "Dr. Leo Baeck awaited us at a corner," he said. "Between the words of greeting, I said to him that in a short time all would be free and there was no reason to worry in the last hours. I pleaded with him to convey that to the prisoners."

The Council of Elders was abolished, and Dunant asked several of the more prominent Jews, including Leo Baeck, to head the camp. Dunant was particularly concerned about the sick in the Ghetto and in the Little Fortress. On May 6 Leo Baeck and three other prominent Jews issued the following directive to the Ghetto inmates:

Men and Women of Theresienstadt!

The international committee of the Red Cross has undertaken the protection of Theresienstadt. The representative of this committee, Herr Dunant, has been appointed leader of Theresienstadt. He has entrusted the undersigned members of the existing council of elders with the leadership of the self-government.

In Theresienstadt you are safe. The war is still not ended! Those of you who might leave Theresienstadt expose yourselves to many dangers.

Theresienstadt has undertaken the caring of the martyred of the small fortress. This means increased work, which also is necessary for the preparation of the transportation back.

The mail now is permitted in any language, without censorship and without any other restriction. For the introduction of this postal service every resident of Theresienstadt, who wishes, will receive a franked postcard, to the extent that a sufficient number is available.

Newspapers will be received and will be posted so all can read. Seriously ill persons still are present here, meaning that a strong observation of the quarantine rules is necessary. For that reason, observe them carefully.

When the war ends, the transports back will begin promptly and then authorities will begin putting out instructions for the handling of the return.

Obey rules and laws! Help us with our work, the return home shall be made possible. Go each of you to your designated work place.[39]

There was one other incident that happended at Theresienstadt in those closing days. When the main body of the Germans had fled and the Russians had not yet arrived, one German officer remained. This was Obersturmführer Karl Rahm, the mechanic turned despot, the man who enjoyed power at the expense of the Jews, the man who watched with pleasure as wives and husbands and children and friends had been loaded on transports to the east.

Karl Rahm—on a bicycle and without a weapon—went from gate to gate at Theresienstadt, closing each one and collecting the keys. The Jews watched him from the sidewalks and from the windows of the crowded barracks. There was no one else present at this time except the Jews and the German soldier they believed responsible for so much of their persecution.

Silently the Jews watched. Not one of them moved. Willi Groag stood with Leo Baeck as Rahm pedaled by. Groag remembered Baeck taking his arm and saying: "Look at it. This can only happen with Jews. Of all these Jewish people here, not one person lifted a stone to throw at him. They could have strangled him if they wanted."

Jews believe that vengeance is taken away from man by God, that man has no right to vengeance. After the Nazi barbarity, they still believed that—that was the ultimate triumph of the Jews at Theresienstadt.[40]

13 FINAL YEARS

EARLY IN MAY an American jeep drove into Theresienstadt carrying a United States Army major. He introduced himself as Patrick Dolan and said his orders were to take Leo Baeck home. Baeck refused to go immediately because there still were Jews in the Ghetto who needed his help. Two months later, when Baeck was certain the ill had been cared for and the others were assured of transportation, he left Theresienstadt.

"July 1, 1945," Baeck wrote, "I left the concentration camp Terezin; an American bomber brought me to Paris. Having obtained there some necessary papers, I was flown on July 5 by a British military plane to London where after six years I saw again my daughter, son-in-law, and granddaughter."

He still was the disciplined man, revealing very little of his emotions, becoming again the one who calmed. Some friends from his Berlin days saw him three days after his arrival in London. "We three were very upset because we did not know how we would find him. We made the greatest effort not to allow our excitement to intrude on the meeting," said one. "Then Leo Baeck came towards us, unchanged and unbroken, and it was his appearance that immediately pulled us out of our anxiety. He calmed us only by the fact of talking to us." Ruth and Hermann Berlak had a small house in a London suburb, which became Leo Baeck's home. "I arrived here twelve days ago," he told a friend, "and I am so grateful that I can stay here in my children's house."[1]

Baeck was an international personality by this time. His reputation as the leader of German Jewry had spread throughout the Jewish world. Already his symbolism as the survivor of the Holocaust was understood. Even before he left Prague, Chaim Weizmann wrote asking him to participate in a Zionist conference. Baeck did not receive the letter until after he arrived in London, and then he quickly agreed. He was ready to move again, to be active once more. When he had gone to Theresienstadt, he had been in good health, and he had managed to emerge well, although with a substantial weight loss. He regained his appetite, something not all the Ghetto inmates were able to do. "All the old likings have come back," he told a friend, "but that is human nature and can't be changed." His old friends soon found him little changed in appearance; at least they noticed little change. "I don't remember him as showing signs of weight loss or concentration camp scars," said one of his former students. "But the impact of Leo Baeck would be the same even if his body had been made of sticks. You must understand that with Leo Baeck the physical body was not the essential point."[2]

His first task when he arrived in London was a painful one. Many old friends who had survived the Holocaust wrote him, hoping he might have some positive news about their relatives. Each one received a handwritten note from him. "I suspect that she was on one of the numerous transports that were sent to the East," was a line which appeared frequently in his letters, or, "Our dear friend . . . was sent to the East in the fall of 1942, to my great pain." In some instances the friendships went back almost half a century. Fritz Muhr, a student when Leo Baeck was rabbi in Oppeln, now lived in Santiago, Chile. The resumption of the friendship with him was, like the others, tinged with sadness. "I was with your sister Elly a couple of times before she was sent to the East . . ." Baeck wrote. "Since then I have heard nothing of her but hope should not be given up. Since the end of May people and signs of life have shown up again and again from the East. May it be the same way with your dear sister. . . . I hope that the band of loyalty which connected me for forty-eight years with the Muhr family will be kept up by my family."

In the years following the war Baeck could speak more personally of his own experiences. "It almost appears to me like a miracle how I have gone through everything," he said, "when I think how I have passed on a close fringe in the hard years, always, as if in the last minute, protected and guarded." He remembered that "for twenty-eight long months, my longing dream was to see once again a meadow, a field, or even a wood; to go once again one day to bed without being hungry; it was a great dream to be once again among the living and not among the dying—sometimes, day after day, a hundred of the men would die in the camp. I cannot speak about the even greater misery there and about the greater longing."

It could not always be relegated to the past—"Before me so often appears the shadows, the shadows of those who died and the shadows of those who led them to their deaths." Scarcely a day would go by without a picture appearing before him of someone rushing to his door, seeking his help. "It is difficult to become totally re-established after a difficult time, and perhaps the healing process sometimes lasts as long as the illness," he said.[3]

The survivors of the German Jewish community of which he had been so much a leader now were scattered. Some lived in England, and through the years many of them came to visit their *seelsorger*. As Baeck traveled in later years, he made a point of seeking out old friends, as if he was trying to maintain the surviving German Jews as a family unit with himself as father. He again met Jeannette Wolff. When he had officiated at the Bat Mitzvah ceremonies of her daughters years earlier, he had advised those young ladies to study the troubles of others so their own would not appear so bad. All of Jeannette Wolff's family, including those daughters, had been killed in the Holocaust. She remembered that meeting with Leo Baeck after the war, Baeck taking her hands in his. "You won't give up," he said to her, and she remembered it more as a command than as a question. She did not give up, resuming her activities to further social causes, adopting a child whose parents had been killed by the Nazis, being elected to the Bundestag, and—still not giving up—becoming a leading advocate of equalizing women's role in Judaism.

Many of the survivors of the German Jewish community lived in the United States, and Baeck enjoyed seeing them when he visited there after the war to make a series of speeches on behalf of various organizations in the American Reform Jewish movement. When his hosts scheduled his trips too tightly, he grumbled that "I didn't come here to make speeches, but because I wanted to see my German Jews again." Once, visiting the United States, Baeck met Wolli Kaelter, whom Baeck had befriended when Kaelter's father had died and whom Baeck had persuaded to attend the Hebrew Union College in Cincinnati in 1935. He had invited Kaelter, now an American rabbi, to meet him at a hotel where he was conducting a meeting. Kaelter remembered: "When I entered the room, Leo Baeck was in the middle of a sentence. He stopped abruptly, walked over to me and said, 'Now that you're so much older, you look more like your father.'" Baeck then launched into a total recall of the Kaelter family. "It was as if it had been only a few months since we had seen each other," said Kaelter, "rather than ten years."

For many he did more than visit with them. For some he wrote letters of introduction to his friends. To others he gave money. One former student who suddenly lost his job in Chicago received 300 dollars from Baeck. Baeck made a regular practice of turning over payments for articles he wrote to needy acquaintances. Since the payments he received often were in German marks, he had to convert the marks to English money. "He would be exact," said one who frequently benefitted from Baeck's kindness, "and I often received a check for so many pounds and pence, rather than for a rounded figure."[4]

After the war Baeck also did not forget his non-Jewish German friends who had been so kind to him and still lived in Germany. During the war their opposition to the Nazis had been known, and they had been stripped of their possessions. In the bleak postwar years in Germany they were in great need, and Baeck tried to help them. "Today I have sent a package to you with a couple of things," goes a typical letter by him. "I hope they arrive all right. My daughter wants to know what you and your wife especially need so that we can send it to you ..." His old friend Baron von Veltheim survived and managed to return Baeck's manuscript to him. The Baron's situation gave some indication of the living conditions in Germany in the mid-1940s. "I have gone through a lot and it is a miracle that I did not drown in the Nazi terror as did many of my relatives and friends," the Baron wrote. "My cousin ... was beheaded one year ago. Another cousin was murdered in February 1945 in a concentration camp." In those years immediately after the war the full horror of the Nazi experience was unfolded in gruesome detail. "Even if I personally don't need to feel guilty about the suffering and tragedy and death brought on the world by the Nazis," said von Veltheim, "and which have been brought on me and my family also, I still do find it somehow right and fair to undergo the suffering from the revenge which is being inflicted upon this people into which I was born."[5]

Leo Baeck became a British citizen on December 18, 1950, and never returned to Germany to live. The Jewish community that developed there after the war was built around Jews from eastern Europe who had migrated west, and never totaled more than 10,000 people. The German Judaism of which Leo Baeck had been so much a part and so much a representative no longer existed. Gershom Scholem commented on this when he wrote about the translation of the Hebrew Bible into German which Franz Rosenzweig and Martin Buber had begun in the 1920s but which was not finished until after the Second World War. The translation was intended, Scholem recalled, as "a kind of *Gastgeschenk* which German Jewry gave to the German people, a symbolic act of gratitude . . ." but instead it became "the tombstone of a relationship that was extinguished in unspeakable horror. The Jews for whom you translated are no more."

Baeck hoped that the German Judaism he had known would live on, at least in the legacy of its achievements, in the scholarship of its survivors, and in the memories of those whom it had touched. His friends and followers did much to see that this hope was fulfilled. Leo Baeck Institutes exist in New York, London, and Jerusalem as repositories of material relating to German Judaism and as centers for research. The Leo Baeck College in London trains people for the rabbinate and for lives as modern Jews, influenced by Baeck's liberal Jewish philosophy.

"German Jewry," Baeck said, "during its history of more than a thousand years has achieved very much. It has taken a leading part in the intellectual development of the last century. The three decisive spiritual revolutions, the new orientations that humanity has won during the last one hundred and fifty years, all three of them were initiated by German Jews: Marx, Freud, and Einstein."

Baeck believed that although German Judaism "lives no more on that soil . . . it has not come to an end. To those who lived there, who have remained alive, dispersed throughout many countries, there has been entrusted something that must not be lost: A yearning for the things of the mind, of the spirit, for the humane, the messianic, for everything that is great and beautiful and harmonious. To cherish this has become the task of all Jews everywhere."

Baeck realized that Germany would not again be home to a large Jewish community. Not only did the physical destruction of the Jews by the Germans negate that possibility but also "what has been endured and experienced during the past twelve years. There has been too much inner destruction to permit the restoration of any true spiritual relationship to the German nation, to the German people." Although acknowledging there could not be a resumption of the spiritual relationship that had existed for so long a time between the Jews and the Germans, Baeck still believed he had a responsibility for nurturing some kind of a relationship. In the fall of 1948 he became one of the first of the prominent German Jews to make a return trip to Germany. It was a well-publicized tour of the country, and Baeck was feted by both Jewish and non-Jewish groups. He spent most of the time studying the living conditions of Jews remaining in Germany and investigating how Jewish organizations outside of Germany could help them. He traveled through the western zones of Germany, attending services at the synagogue in Luebeck, one of the few remaining in Germany. While there he gave a talk on establishing peace in Europe, and a number of non-Jews attended, including a Protestant bishop. He also participated in a study conference in Darmstadt with a group of Protestant clergymen. A commentary at the time said that his short trip "made a deep impression on the remnants of a once large and distinguished Jewish community and was also of great importance to the non-Jewish world, in particular to leaders of the Churches."

Baeck's purpose was obvious, both in his visit and in his attitude toward the Germans he met. A person who traveled with him then said, "Leo Baeck always behaved well toward Germans and never said a word to non-Jews in Germany about his own experience." Again, he was the conciliator, the one reaching out the hand of friendship. "He could do it," said one of his acquaintances, "because he was so well respected."[6]

Nonetheless, his attitude toward the German people after the Second World War was especially hard, but in a particularly Jewish way. Rabbi Nelson Glueck, president of the Hebrew Union College in Cincinnati, once asked Baeck if he ever could forgive the Germans. Baeck answered: "I, forgive the Germans? It is for the Germans to forgive themselves." The Germans must struggle not to correct the harm they had done—that never could be corrected—but to overcome the attitudes within themselves that allowed the flourishing of Nazism and the acceptance of the Holocaust, to overcome the drive for self-gratification that allowed them to ignore their neighbor's plight, to overcome the love of power that caused the destruction of the meek and innocent. They themselves would have to look deep into their psyches, into their history, their symbols, their aspirations, and their religion. They themselves would have to rip out those elements that had led to war and genocide. In the Hebrew Bible, God says in Deuteronomy 30:15 to each individual: "Today I offer you the choice of life and good, or death and evil." Leo Baeck understood that the choice was not his or that of any other Jew; it was the choice of the German people.[7]

Baeck also was a realist. His trips to Germany, Israel, and to the United States in the postwar years gave him an understanding of the economic plight of those former German Jews who had survived with their careers, homes, and savings destroyed; he devoted a good deal of his remaining years to helping them. "Whenever a moral weight was needed for a cause," said one who knew him well in those years, "Leo Baeck was enlisted." It was not only his reputation that was used but also his personal friendship with Theodor Heuss, president of West Germany, and a German non-Jew whom Baeck had met years before at the home of Otto Hirsch in Stuttgart.

Various Jewish organizations scattered around the world organized the Council for the Protection of the Rights and Interests of the Jews from Germany with its main offices in London. That city was chosen because reparations were being handled from London and because Leo Baeck was living there, and the assumption was that Baeck would head any such organization. He did so and continued as its head when it became the Council of Jews from Germany in 1950. A journalist friend said that Baeck "could appeal urgently, even violently, to the public conscience and to a common responsibility of the German people; for him restitution was not an affair of money but of right." The journalist quoted Baeck as saying: "If I give up the right, I give up myself also." Baeck outlined his position in a 1946 letter reacting to a proposal for reparations that he considered inadequate because "a considerable part of the victims of Nazi persecution are Jews, yet in the recommendations neither the unique position of the Jewish victims nor the safeguarding of Jewish interests had been taken into account at all." In 1951, when the German Bundestag approved a reparations resolution acceptable to Baeck and the Jewish organizations, he described it as an answer by the Germans to the confidence shown in them by the other nations of the world. The Council of Jews from Germany continued active, and Baeck attended its meetings and took a prominent role in its work for many years.[8]

In the United States, Reform Jewish groups often used the presence of Leo Baeck on a platform or as a speaker to attract attention for themselves and, sometimes, as a fund-raising device. Baeck usually entered into the fund-raising wholeheartedly as, decades earlier, in the First World War, he had assisted his colleagues at the Hochschule. As he had said then, "First you have to live, then you can be a philosopher."

In 1947 the Union of American Hebrew Congregations, the Reform branch of Judaism, was sponsoring an "American Jewish Cavalcade," and decided the event could be publicized with a visit by Baeck to President Harry S Truman in the White House. The Union then approached Edward Jacobson, Truman's former haberdashery partner in Kansas

City and his close friend. Jacobson often was the Jews' link to the White House, and he managed to arrange the meeting for January 8, 1947 (after the White House had the State Department check its Palestine desk to determine whether Baeck had any "political" connections that might embarrass Truman—the Palestine desk never had heard of Baeck). The brief meeting did take place, and the Cavalcade was properly publicized.

More significant for Baeck probably was another event in Washington the next month. He was invited to give the opening prayer in the House of Representatives. Before the war Baeck had criticized the silence of the United States and other nations in the face of the Nazi abuse of Jews. Since that time he had witnessed the massive American effort to defeat Germany and to assist refugees. When he stood before the House of Representatives in 1947, it was as an appreciative man. The date was fortuitous—February 12, the birthday of Abraham Lincoln, the American most admired by Baeck.

"Our Father, our God," he began, "we pray unto Thee on this day on which six score and nineteen years ago was born that man who came to be Thy servant." He described Lincoln as the man who, for "the sake of this land became a witness and testimony of humanity, herald of Thy command and Thy promise, to the everlasting blessing of this country and of mankind." He recalled that Lincoln had once told Congress, "We cannot escape history." Then Baeck said: "So help us, O God, that we may not evade history, but we may be granted history." And then the man who represented the people who owed so much to the American efforts in the Second World War closed with: "Reverently I pray Thee to bless Congress, its men, and its days. From the bottom of my heart I pray: God Bless America."[9]

In the fall of 1948 he accepted a position as visiting professor at the Hebrew Union College in Cincinnati. "The atmosphere in the college in which I live is nice and I am surrounded by kindness," he told a friend. He found at the school "the peace and quiet for the work which I have been involved in for years." This was a reference to completing *Dieses Volk*, the book he had worked on before being sent to Theresienstadt and which his friend Baron von Veltheim had hidden for him. "I give lectures for two hours a week for students in their senior year," he said, "and the other time I have essentially for myself." He stayed at the rabbinical seminary from November through April each year. "I live very comfortably in a separate apartment—living room, bedroom, bathroom, and hall. The college lies with its four big buildings on a hill surrounded by meadows with its own swimming pool, heated in the winter," he said, describing it as "a little world in itself." The food there was so good, he continued, that he was forced to diet.

He was remembered at the school as "a big, tall, hulk of a man . . . no sense of being an emaciated concentration camp victim . . . walking with his hands behind his back, bent forward, and fast." He always walked fast. One student recalled meeting Leo Baeck one evening on his way to mail a letter. The mailbox was at the bottom of a steep flight of stairs, and the student offered to mail the letter for Baeck. "No," replied Baeck quickly, "I want to take my evening walk." The student recalled: "Whereupon Leo Baeck proceeded to walk away from me at a rate of speed I could not match," down the steps, which "I had to negotiate carefully. Baeck skittered down those steps, had his letter in the box and was off on his promenade before I ever got halfway down."[10]

Nelson Glueck, then president of the college, hoped Baeck's presence at the school would develop a link between the *Gestalt* of German Judaism and the future rabbis. Establishing the linkage, however, was dependent upon what the students brought to the relationship. "The students did not accord Leo Baeck any great awe; it must have been a difficult time for him. In class he seemed an authoritarian personality who had mellowed. There was no barking, no humiliation in class," said one student. Another described his encounter with Baeck's lectures this way: "Because I had read and admired *The Essence of Judaism*, I tried to attend his lectures but I found it difficult to stay in his class. Dr. Baeck was healing, in his marvelously personal style, with Midrash but in a fashion which I found largely incomprehensible. I then tried attending every other session, since each lecture began with a long summary of the previous session. Even that stratagem did not work for me." The Korean War had begun then, and this student decided to give up Baeck's lectures entirely, using the time to finish up his doctoral dissertation before entering the Navy chaplaincy.

Nahum N. Glatzer, a German Jew who had known Baeck for many years but who had spent more time in the United States then had Baeck, thought the problem with Baeck's lectures at Hebrew Union was that he spoke a different language than did the students. Not only was it a difficulty with English—"it was," said Glatzer, "a different style and frame of reference. In his talks with the students, he had to assume they had the same foundation he did. He couldn't go back and explain the original Greek and German references. But American students were not in that league." In the 1920s American students coming to Germany had been unable to respond to him for those same reasons. In the late 1940s and early 1950s American students, listening to Baeck in Cincinnati, still could not respond to him.[11]

Some students found him stimulating. If they could not follow his Greek and German references, if they were lost in his lectures on the Midrash, they did enjoy his presence, his appearance and manner. "Dr. Baeck was important to me not so much for the material which he taught," recalled one student, "but because he was able to serve as a model of what a rabbi should be. It a man can present an image that will serve as a model for the young, a model that helps to form identity, this man then has a great gift."

Another student inspired by Baeck was Albert H. Friedlander, a German refugee whose rabbinical training was in the United States. Friedlander later wrote *Leo Baeck—Teacher of Theresienstadt*, a study of Baeck's theology, and also translated *Dieses Volk* into English as *This People Israel*. In his introduction to *This People Israel* Friedlander recalled a morning walk with Baeck "through the snow-covered woods surrounding the Hebrew Union College." Baeck spoke that morning with "fervor and intensity on many topics," turning at one point to the German Jews who had found refuge in America. "There is a special obligation for that generation to transmit the greatness of European Jewry's culture to America," Baeck said. Baeck believed that the European heritage and the dynamism of the American community "might well recreate what the forces of darkness had destroyed." Friedlander felt from that relationship with Baeck a particular obligation on him. In completing the translation of *Dieses Volk*, "this labor of love," wrote Friedlander, "I do not discharge the obligation placed upon me, but I begin to fulfill it."[12]

The visits to the Hebrew Union College resulted in another event. Baeck's granddaughter Marianne—"Janne," with whom he had walked to services in Berlin years earlier—had accompanied him to Cincinnati from London on some of these trips. She made certain that he had his rest, ate well, and dressed warmly. During one of these trips she met a young rabbi named A. Stanley Dreyfus. They were married in London on July 25, 1950. At the ceremony Leo Baeck offered a sermon, and other distinguished British rabbis participated. Stanley Dreyfus recalled that day and the sermon given by his famous grandfather-in-law, "the powerful voice rising and falling in ill-suppressed emotion." Rabbi Dreyfus continued: "During the drive to the synagogue, during the reception, well into the family dinner, Leo Baeck was strangely withdrawn, almost impervious to the gay chatter round about, as if he were reliving another wedding, in 1897; as if his gaze were fixed upon a dearly beloved face. Perhaps he was recalling an August day in 1923 when his daughter Ruth married Hermann Berlak." Then, quite suddenly, Baeck awoke from his reverie and began speaking "rather formally." Rabbi Dreyfus' family had been unable to attend the wedding because of illness; his family and Marianne's parents never had met. Baeck, fearing "that I might regard myself still a stranger" among his family and its many friends, began to tell them about Stanley Dreyfus' family, "their way of life in Ohio, and before, the way of the Jews of Alsace," from which the Dreyfus family had come. It was Baeck's way of introducing Stanley Dreyfus and his family to the people in London, to make him feel at home. "How sensitive, how gracious in all things he was," said Stanley Dreyfus of Leo Baeck.

With Marianne and Stanley Dreyfus, Leo Baeck was the typical grandfather. Happy in their happiness, rejoicing when their children were born, as generous with them as possible. "Thinking it allowable to send a birthday present ten weeks before the birthday," he said in a letter similar to that written by grandparents the world over, "I enclose a cheque which is intended for the best specimen of a vacuum cleaner available, with all its accessories . . ."[13]

Baeck continued his affiliation with the World Union for Progressive Judaism in the postwar years, urging it to move its headquarters from London—home city for its original English founders—to New York. Baeck predicted, correctly, that Judaism would find New York an area of strength immediately following the war. Ultimately, Baeck said, the World Union should establish a permanent headquarters in Israel, which would become the new center of the Jewish religion. The Union made these moves. Baeck was president of the Union, said a man active at the time with him, "in the English tradition of a crown and a prime minister. Leo Baeck was the crown . . . but Baeck made a contribution. He always sat at the end of the table by the presiding officer; and when he wished to speak, he would touch the officer's arm. His comments usually were in summary and to give the discussions direction."[14]

Baeck also was active within the community of German Jews who had settled in England. He became president of the Society for Jewish Study, a group of Jews who met together, and delivered a series of lectures at the Monday meetings. He spoke about European religious movements of the nineteenth century. Ignaz Maybaum, who had known him in Germany, described those lectures. "Friends of Baeck's," he said, "had revived the lecture series for which the Berlin Hochschule für die Wissenschaft des Judentums once was famous. The old sage had his regular audience of German Jewish intellectuals; German rabbis, the few who were left and resided in London, also came. People listened to the man who impressed everyone."

He also lectured frequently, returning to Germany on many occasions as part of his efforts to rebuild bridges there. His carefully prepared lectures are models of the kind of literary construction for which he was famous, each word built on the other as an architect builds brick upon brick. He also was adept as an extemporaneous speaker. As a young rabbi in 1953, Eugene B. Borowitz attended a London Conference of the World Union for Progressive Judaism, at which Baeck and Martin Buber were speaking. The two men in their talks insisted upon religion being the basis of civilization, and Borowitz, in his own words, "had the temerity to put a question to them." Borowitz's question, as he recalled it, ran this way: "Don't you understand? What has happened is that our civilization has become secular; people operate without religion. How are we going to come to terms with that?" When the answer period arrived, said Borowitz, "Dr. Baeck responded to various questions, including mine. And with that, this mild, quiet, frail man tore me limb from limb; he was ferocious. He gave me a lesson in American history, citing the compact made by the Pilgrims when they arrived in the new world, and then went on to show that the essence of American civilization had been religious, and unless it was going to be religious it would not be possible to have an American civilization."[15]

Leo Baeck retained his interest in Palestine and in Israel after it became an independent state. In 1947 he returned to Palestine for a seven-week visit, a visit of new experiences and old memories. "The weeks in Palestine were rich in valuable impressions," he said. "I was there in 1935 with my wife, and now it always seemed to me as if she accompanied me again and were talking with me." He admired the progress that had been made there in turning the desert into farmland and said of one community: "From mud and sand, as I knew the area, they transformed it as if by magic. The settlement is a place of blossoming agriculture and cattle development."

He also was pleased at the pleasant reception he had from the Arabs. "Jews and Arabs," he said, "live as good neighbors and often also in friendship." His perception was that what conflicts there were originated "from the outside, from the neighboring states, and from a few small feudalistic groups inside." He continued to be concerned about the future of Arab-Jewish relations, however. Ever since his first visit in the 1930s he had advocated that Jews do more to develop a viable relationship with the Arabs. Baeck believed the Zionists had underrated both the Arab physical presence and needs. "If later history writers were to get a picture of Palestine only on the basis of [Theodor] Herzl's diaries," Baeck said, "they would have to assume that there were no Arabs at all in Palestine." Baeck once asked Weizmann if he visited any Arab leaders on his first trip to Palestine as a Zionist leader. Baeck knew the answer was No, but was hoping the question itself would serve as a reprimand to Weizmann. Baeck had been shocked at a story told by Weizmann, of his going after a seder in Jerusalem to the Wailing Wall, the Jews' holy place in the middle of the Arab old city, to sing *Hatikvah*, the Jewish national anthem, at two o'clock in the morning. "Bad manners" was Baeck's verdict.

Baeck opposed partitioning the land between Arabs and Jews, which was recommended after the war. Instead he advocated a program of economic unity so that "Balkanization will be lessened and finally eliminated."

He had no doubt that a Jewish homeland should be established on Palestinian soil. When the United Nations was considering the proposal, he argued that a Jewish homeland in Palestine already existed in fact. The only question, he said, was "the form which shall be given to the reality." Any proposal adopted, he insisted, should allow freedom of emigration. "*Aliyah*," he said, "must be our warcry. All others shall and must retreat before this vital effort." However, he would not surrender his right to criticize his fellow Jews. His visit in 1947 to Palestine had persuaded him that the Jews there were developing in ways which "engender nationalism and chauvinism, and chauvinism, in turn, engenders violence and terrorism, and false ideals." His hope was that religious education would overcome those characteristics and "establish a standard of right."

With most Jews he was thrilled when the state of Israel was created by a vote of the United Nations, and when the Israelis turned that resolution into a reality by defeating the invading Arab armies. "The state of Israel has been founded," he said, "and it has rendered the proof of its will, of its strength, of its devotion and claim to the future . . ." He hoped that the new state would be more than just a secular state. "A state of Israel," he insisted, "can, must indeed always, also signify a moral appeal, a religious claim."

One of the aftereffects of the Israeli war for independence was the problem of the Arab refugees. The causes of this problem were many, and there was a question within Jewish groups over whether Israel and Jews everywhere should make an effort to solve their problem and to help them. Leo Baeck was one of those who believed Jews had the responsibility to assist those refugees. "We cannot stand by the Kingdom of God without standing for human need. Helping distressed people, we help our soul as well as all mankind . . ."[16]

During those postwar years, as Leo Baeck approached and then passed his eightieth birthday, he continued physically active. "He walked briskly," said a friend, "giving the appearance of always being on the alert." Herman Schaalman, one of five students influenced by Baeck to leave Germany in 1935 for Cincinnati, told of meeting Baeck in New York to escort him to a Jewish gathering. Schaalman knew that Leo Baeck enjoyed walking and anticipated having to shepherd the older man through the traffic-jammed Manhattan streets. But Baeck outran him, dodging among the cars. "It was all that I could do to keep up with him," said Schaalman; "he was like a goat." Added Schaalman: "Leo Baeck was a man almost totally alive, not just intellectually but physically also."

Baeck continued punctual, perhaps to a fault. The artist Eugene Spiro was doing a portrait of him, and a sitting was scheduled for four o'clock in the afternoon. At three-fifty Spiro looked out the window and saw Baeck striding back and forth in front of his building, refusing to enter before the appointed time. And his courtesy—always jumping from his chair to greet visitors, holding their coats for them, accompanying visitors from his daughter's house to the bus stop—became the source of many stories about him. "You'd have to dance to get to the door first," said one friend. Another gave this account:

Many will remember the last speech which Leo Baeck gave in Israel, about Judaism and Humanism. It was a hot, windy day and certainly the speech had exhausted him. But afterwards when the people pressed around him at the speaker's table, those who knew him from earlier times, from Germany or from Theresienstadt, he had time for each, without once showing his exhaustion. He greeted them all, asking after their relatives and friends. If a woman—and even if it was a very young one—spoke to him, the old gentleman stood (he was then near 80) in order to speak with her. Then the nobility of his thinking, the graciousness of his heart showed in an outer courtesy which in our land, sad to say, is in short supply.[17]

The friendship between Baeck and Martin Buber resumed. Once in London a young American rabbi said a highlight of his visit was sitting in a restaurant at a table next to one where Baeck and Buber were having lunch. "I could not make out what they were muttering to one another," said the young rabbi, "nor do I know whether they were able at that point to bridge the gaps of communication which they had had over the years. But the sight of the two beards wagging at one another did extraordinary things to me."[18]

Baeck considered that speaking out about the Holocaust was a proper role. In Germany he had been critical of German institutions and German citizens who had allowed Nazism to develop, to take power, and to run unchecked. After he left Germany, he was critical of those institutions and those people outside of Germany who had allowed the Holocaust to happen. He said in 1946 in London:

This ordeal has been so terrible, it has grown to such a torment and such a misery, because men who were responsible for parts of the world, for the leadership of the great communities remained silent when they should have stepped forth to act and to help . . . The sin of silence and of looking on lay on the world. This disaster has come over mankind because the moral enthusiasm, the moral passion was lacking power—this power that grows up out of the depth of religion; and true peace will exist only when that sacred flame will make alight the souls of men so that in the fight between ideas and interests, between commandment and advantage, the divine commandment will be victorious.

For him there was no question but that the religions of the world had responded to what he called "national" needs rather than fulfilling their religious obligations as spokesmen for a morality that transcended national borders. "Only when resort is made constantly to that which belongs to the command of God, be it to side with or to oppose and resist hereby the state, only then a religion is and remains a universal, a genuinely human religion." The distinction, insisted Baeck, is between "the universal and the political."[19]

Baeck's attitude toward Christianity in the postwar years was similar to his attitude in the years before the war—he considered Judaism superior. In an introduction to a collection of Baeck's essays Walter Kaufmann made that point and added, "It is one of the oddities of our times that this view is scarcely ever discussed in public. Yet it would be very strange if it were not shared by most Jews." He added that, while the view rarely is discussed, it is not surprising for, on the other side, "Most Christians are convinced of the immeasurable superiority of Christianity over all other religions, and quite especially over Judaism." Krister Stendahl, a Lutheran minister and dean of the divinity

school at Harvard University, did not disagree with Kaufmann's interpretation but went an additional step to place it in another perspective.
Stendahl wrote that Baeck, in viewing Judaism as superior to Christianity, "does so as a wise father who sees how his own children have
wandered astray. For to him there is always enough of Judaism in
Christianity so that he can recognize the church as the child of Judaism.
To me this is not arrogance, but love." Years earlier, when Leo Baeck
first read Adolf von Harnack's *The Essence of Christianity*, he had resolved to respond with his scholarship, his literary style, and his love
of Judaism. His opponents were blind prejudice, faulty learning, and
suspicion. His goal had been the understanding of Judaism by the
Christian world. Krister Stendahl's homage to him indicates that no
knowledgeable Christian in the modern world can ignore Baeck, his
writings and his life. The question is not which religion is superior or
inferior. Both exist and must exist together. Leo Baeck made that point
in 1953 in a paper he wrote in connection with an ecumenical celebration of his eightieth birthday. These comments by Baeck are in answer
to those made by the Very Reverend Doctor W. R. Matthews, the Dean
of St. Paul's Cathedral in London. Said Baeck:

Judaism means a question, a permanent one, posed to Christianity, and
Christianity a permanent question propounded to Judaism. The two are their
mutual problem. Neither is really enabled to vindicate itself without giving
full attention to the other. For a very long time, however, the history of
Christian-Jewish and Jewish-Christian relations was only a painful drama.
When one spoke to the other it was across a deep gulf.

Now new days are dawning, and a new idea will appear here. On our days,
it seems, is laid the solemn obligation that Jewish and Christian faiths frankly
meet—faiths indeed, and not only tendencies and policies. They are called to
face one another on the strength of being alive to a common ground and a
common outlook also, and, so to speak, to a common teacher too.

This is the import of the true teacher, that he becomes the connecting link
between the different pupils and their different ways. It may be difficult to
define here this common teacher, but one should be sensitive to him wherever
is manifested "the spirit of knowledge and of the fear of the Lord." This
spirit, this common teacher, is the uniting power in history.[20]

For Baeck the Holocaust could not be an excuse for the Jew to retreat
from the obligation to be a moral advocate. In words that are similar
to those he expressed to Martin Buber after the First World War, Baeck
wrote after the Second, "Judaism must not stand aside, when the great
problems of humanity which are reborn in every new epoch, struggle

in the minds of men to find their way." Jews could not "deny" themselves those problems or "hide" from them. He insisted: "We are Jews also for the sake of humanity; we should be there, quite especially in the world after the war; we have our questions to raise and have to give our answer. To rouse the conscience of humanity could here be our best title-deed." He appreciated that the Jewish people, fewer by one-third after the Holocaust and struggling in Israel for the existence of a homeland, were tired. He understood the emotions that had led the Yiddish poet Kadia Molodowsky to implore: "O God of Mercy, for the time being choose another people. We are tired of death, tired of corpses, we have no more prayers. For the time being, choose another people." Although understanding that feeling, Baeck argued: "We should not be satisfied, or deceive ourselves, or grow weary . . . everywhere we can be a 'creative minority.' We believe in God, and not in progress as an end in itself. We, therefore, believe in the constant task and not in the achievement."[21]

In the modern world, where more and more power is grasped by fewer and fewer people, Judaism continued necessary because its view, said Baeck, "was always that of the little, the weak, the needy. They are first to be shielded and helped; in other places laws have mostly been written from the standpoint and on behalf of the great, the mighty, the property owners." Judaism's role in history, he continued, was not only to fight against a polytheism of gods but also, "this polytheism of morals and justice, that established a different morality, a different justice, one for the great and one for the little." In the modern world, where societies nurture the impersonal and the faceless, Judaism is necessary, wrote Leo Baeck, because it insists on the recognition of the individual. "Every man is a world in himself," said Leo Baeck.

He has something which is altogether his own, belonging only to him—*his* thoughts, *his* wishes, *his* fortune and *his* burden, that of which no one else knows, only he and God know of it. Every one is, as the medieval phrase has it, "Individuum ineffabile," "an inexpressible, undefinable, individual," with an individuality which cannot be comprehended in words or ideas. Every man has similarly also his own eyes by which he takes the world into himself, his own ears through which the world impresses itself on him. No one else sees exactly what he sees, and no one else hears exactly what he hears, even when others see or hear the same thing. Just as every one has a world of his own in himself, so everyone has as his own the world which comes to him.

In 1948 Baeck was asked how to practice Judaism, how he would lead a religious revival. "I always advise," he answered, "begin not with two things or ten things; begin with only one. For instance, 'I will go every Friday night to the synagogue; I will light the candles every Friday night.' Begin only with one thing and don't plan great enterprises." Also, "I would say don't begin with theories. Begin with practice. Do something. Perhaps give a tenth part of your income to the poor; that is the first step to Judaism. Before anything and after anything, say a blessing. Learn Hebrew; that is also the first step to Judaism. This language will have a spiritual force. Begin not with theories, with philosophy, but with practice—with deeds." There he was back again where he had started, explaining Judaism as the religion of deed, of the ethical imperative.[22]

The summing up of his theology, his understanding of Judaism, his attitude toward history, and his vision of Judaism's historical role was in his book *Dieses Volk*. He had worked on the book before going to Theresienstadt, and continued his work after coming to London. He finished the second volume only a few days before he died in 1956. The two volumes were published in German in 1955 and 1957; a single American edition, *This People Israel*, was published in 1965.

The book weaves together the history and theology of Judaism to demonstrate Judaism as a constant revelation, a constant command. It brings together more than half a century of Baeck's teaching. Words like monotheism soar from the confines of a single word to the heights of the concept of a universal morality. The directive to love one's neighbor becomes a command to practice brotherhood. Religion is not a Sabbath habit but a way of life. Rationally and emotionally it is a means of infusing one's life with the techniques that allow society to continue, to prosper, and, ultimately, to survive. Because of the time when Baeck finished preparing the book, after the Second World War and the Holocaust, several sections of the book have a particular interest.

He describes the state presented by the Hebrew prophets as an institution to serve people with justice. Then the political state arose in opposition. "The state, as it presented itself in the new [political] concept," wrote Baeck, "was completely different. It was to exist for its own sake. Its task and its function were not the good of the people whom it incorporated. The people existed for it ... The head of the state was given what should be God's place on earth; his word was to be the authority and security for the Law of God ... [But] political authority dispenses no revelation. It was always fatal to nations when they thought to use it in this way."

Years earlier Baeck had said much the same thing when he had argued for the individual both to adhere to the moral law and to challenge political authority when the individual believes that authority is acting immorally. Sometimes law does not correspond with morality, and the role of the religious man is to attempt to bring them into congruence. Baeck had witnessed in Germany the tragedy that follows when the men of religion refuse to perform that role.

Baeck argued in *Dieses Volk* that this moral role is man's true genius. "Now there is something creative within him; he can form his self, he can give shape to his life. He, the created man, can become a creator. He can be free inwardly, free by reason of the commandment. He is allowed to be more than the earth upon which he was born and upon which he dies. The great commandment, which never ceases and never changes, this miracle—it renders it thus for him. This miracle of morality makes him truly man."

Baeck believed the line from Deuteronomy 16:20—"Justice, and justice alone, you shall pursue, so that you may live and occupy the land which the Lord your God is giving you"—to be a foundation for the Jewish people. "The best among this people recognized this when they fought for the rights of their people and for the rights of all human beings."

With all the tribulations, dangers, and responsibilities of being Jewish, Leo Baeck pointed out that there also was a sheer pleasure. "It is strange to say—but true—that this people, more than all other peoples," he wrote, "always carried within itself a feeling of joy and of happiness. This people never ceased writing poetry, not only for others, but also for itself."

Leo Baeck died November 2, 1956, in London, at the age of eighty-three. His gravestone carries the line in Hebrew by which he wished to be remembered—"a descendant of rabbis." He had lived the life of basic Judaism. He had learned. He had believed. He had taught. More than that, he had understood the essential point of religion, that God's commandment to live requires more than survival. The significance of Leo Baeck's life is his demonstration that it is possible to suffer any tragedy man with all his technical expertise can produce, yet still survive as a moral person. His life demonstrates that man truly was created in the image of God and that he can retain humanity; he can nurture it under any circumstances and defend it against any assault.

In his life and in his writings Baeck pointed to the cardinal rule for society, the rule he once described this way: "The right to be the avenger where justice fails, where it cannot be found, or where it is too weak (let alone to succumb to the passion of the moment) is denied to man. . . . Revenge is reserved for God . . . Vengeance is prohibited to man."[23]

If the Jew can emerge from the Holocaust and still believe that, then no person can sanctify the role of avenger or justify the path of revenge until it escalates into untold misery. No person can deny for himself or herself the path that Leo Baeck outlined the day he flew back to civilization from Theresienstadt, the day he reached out and touched the arm of Major Patrick Dolan to say: "Patrick, do not have revenge in your heart. Only love and justice."

SOURCES

1: INTERVIEWS

Leo Adam; London: May 26, 1974
H. G. Adler; London: May 25 and May 27, 1974
S. Adler-Rudel; Jerusalem: June 3, 1975
Alexander Altmann; Newton Center, Massachusetts: October 14, 1975
Siegbert Altmann; Los Angeles: February 14, 1977
Josef Amir; Hazorea, Israel: June 16, 1975
Yehoshua Amir; Jerusalem: June 12, 1975
Hans I. Bach; London: July 20, 1976
Sophie Baehr-Pineas; Tel Aviv: June 18, 1975
K. J. Ball-Kaduri; Tel Aviv: June 18, 1975
Bernard J. Bamberger; New York: January 22, 1974
Fritz Bamberger; New York: October 18, 1974
Gregory Baum; Washington, D.C.: September 27, 1974
Hildegard Biermann; New York: March 25, 1974
Sheldon H. Blank; Cincinnati, Ohio: April 20, 1977
Ilse Blumenthal-Weiss; New York: October 15, 1974
Henry Walter Brann; Takoma Park, Maryland: March 21, 1974 (telephone
    interview)
Friedrich Brodnitz; New York: February 14, 1974
Werner J. Cahnman; New York: February 24, 1975
Rudolf Callmann; New York: May 1, 1974
Klara Caro; Palisades, New York: February 14, 1974
Betty Cohen; Degania, Israel: June 14, 1975
Patrick Dolan; Eze-le-Haut, France: June 1, 1974
A. Stanley Dreyfus; Brooklyn: February 12 and March 26, 1974
Marianne Dreyfus; Brooklyn: February 12 and March 26, 1974
Ernst Ludwig Ehrlich; Basel, Switzerland: June 4, 1974
Emil L. Fackenheim; Toronto, Canada: October 10, 1973
Kurt Fischer; Haifa: June 13, 1975
Albert H. Friedlander; London: August 2, 1973
Gertrud Gallewski; New York: October 30, 1975
Helmuth H. Galliner; New York: December 9, 1974
Charlotte Gichermann; Tel Aviv: June 6, 1975
Mordechai Gichon; Tel Aviv: June 19, 1975
Nahum N. Glatzer; Watertown, Massachusetts: August 21, 1974
Perle Gold; Tel Aviv: July 1, 1975
Willi Groag; Kibbutz Maanit, Israel: July 6, 1975
Fred Grubel; New York: October 16, 1974
Heinrich Grüber; Berlin: June 18, 1974
Frau Heinrich Grüber; Berlin: June 18, 1974
Max Gruenewald; New York: May 1, 1974

Alexander Guttmann; Cincinnati, Ohio: April 19, 1977
Eleonore Heldt; Washington, D.C.: May 16, 1975
Gustav Horn; Hazorea, Israel: June 16, 1975
Etta Japha; New York: November 12, 1973
Benjamin Jeremias; Nahariya, Israel: June 13, 1975
Alfred Jospe; Washington, D.C.: February 19, 1974
Wolli Kaelter; Los Angeles: April 22, 1976
Samuel E. Karff; New York: November 12, 1973
A. E. Kaufmann; London: May 29, 1974
Henry J. Kellermann; Washington, D.C.: March 26, 1976
Max Kreutzberger; Locarno, Switzerland: June 3, 1974
Adolf Leschnitzer; New York: October 28, 1975
Leo Lichtenberg; Cincinnati, Ohio: April 19, 1977
Eugene J. Lipman; Washington, D.C.: October 20, 1975
Ellen Littmann; London: May 29, 1974
Marianne Loew; Haifa: June 16, 1975
Ernst G. Lowenthal; Berlin: June 18, 1974
Gertrud Luckner; Frieburg, Federal Republic of Germany: July 1, 1974
Sara Mandelbaum; Jerusalem: June 23, 1975
B. Manuel; Zurich, Switzerland: June 5, 1974
Jacob R. Marcus; Cincinnati, Ohio: April 18, 1977
Ignaz Maybaum; London: May 29, 1974
Uta C. Merzbach; Washington, D.C.: May 8 and October 11, 1974
Margaret Muehsam; New York: October 17, 1974
Israel Neumark; Hazorea, Israel: June 16, 1975
Arnold Paucker; London: May 30, 1974
Frederick J. Perlstein; Bridgeton, New Jersey: October 18, 1976
Herman O. Pineas; New York: September 4, 1975
W. Gunther Plaut; Toronto, Canada: May 13, 1975
Joachim Prinz; Orange, New Jersey: May 1, 1974
Eva G. Reichmann; London: May 27, 1974
Eli Rock; Philadelphia, Pennsylvania: April 8, 1975
Shoshana Ronen; Tel Aviv: June 18, 1975
Werner Rosenstock; London: May 30, 1974
Frank F. Rosenthal; Olympia Fields, Illinois: January 21, 1974
Schlomo Rülf; Nahariya, Israel: June 15, 1975
Georg Salzberger; London: August 6, 1973
Herman Schaalman; New York: November 10, 1973
Gershom Scholem; Boston, Massachusetts: October 14, 1975
Zeev Shek; Jerusalem: June 25, 1975
Ernst Simon; Jerusalem: May 30, 1975
Krister Stendahl; Washington, D.C.: November 4, 1973
Herbert A. Strauss; New York: November 11, 1973
Manfred E. Swarsenksy; Chicago, Illinois: November 15, 1974
Sefton D. Temkin; Cincinnati, Ohio: April 20, 1977
Ilse Turnheim; New York: October 18, 1974
Max Vogelstein; Rochester, New York: December 3, 1974

Eric M. Warburg; Hamburg, Federal Republic of Germany: June 24, 1974
Heinz Warschauer; Toronto, Canada: October 12, 1973
Robert Weltsch; London: May 31, 1974
David H. Wice; Philadelphia, Pennsylvania: March 12, 1975
Theodore Wiener; Arlington, Virginia: October 18, 1973
Alfred Wolf; Los Angeles: April 23, 1976
Robert Wolfe; Washington, D.C.: May 20, 1974
Jeannette Wolff; Berlin: June 25, 1974
Norbert Wollheim; New York: October 29, 1975
Walter Zander; Princeton, New Jersey: December 27, 1974

2: MANUSCRIPT COLLECTIONS

Auswärtiges Amt; Bonn, Federal Republic of Germany
American Jewish Archives; Cincinnati, Ohio
Beit Theresienstadt; Kibbutz Givat Chaim, Israel
Berlin Document Center; Berlin
Brandeis University: Special Collections Department; Waltham, Massachusetts
Central Intelligence Agency; McLean, Virginia
Central Zionist Archives; Jerusalem
Ghetto Fighters Museum; Haifa
Harry S Truman Library; Independence, Missouri
Hazorea Kibbutz Archives; Hazorea, Israel
Hebrew University of Jerusalem:
    Central Archives for the History of the Jewish People
    Institute of Contemporary Jewry, Oral History Division
    Jewish National and University Library
Institut für Zeitgeschichte; Munich, Federal Republic of Germany
Judah L. Magnes Memorial Museum; Berkeley, California
Jüdische Gemeinde; Berlin
Landesbildstelle Berlin; Berlin
Landeszentrale für Politische Bildungsarbeit; Berlin
Leo Baeck Institute; Jerusalem
Leo Baeck Institute; London
Leo Baeck Institute; New York
Library of Congress; Washington, D.C.
National Archives; Washington, D.C.
Weizmann Archives; Rehovot, Israel
Wiener Library; London
Yad Vashem Archives; Jerusalem

3: MEMORABILIA

(In some cases the following persons provided me with a large collection
of letters, newspaper articles, and other material relating to Leo Baeck; in
others, they wrote me lengthy letters of their recollections; and in a few, they
provided me a single item of information.)

Hans I. Bach; London
Peter Bedrick; New York
Ralph Blume; Kibbutz Schluchot, Israel
Kurt Boehm; Lima, Peru
Betty Cohen; Degania, Israel
A. Stanley and Marianne Dreyfus; Brooklyn
Ernst Ludwig Ehrlich; Basel, Switzerland
Emil L. Fackenheim; Toronto, Canada
Fritz Friedländer; Caulfield, Victoria, Australia
Charlotte Gichermann; Tel Aviv
Perle Gold; Tel Aviv
Willi Groag; Kibbutz Maanit, Israel
Max Gruenewald; New York
Isser Harel; Zahala, Israel
R. E. Helberg; Tel Aviv
Joseph Henninger; St. Augustin, Federal Republic of Germany
Hans Georg Hirsch; Bethesda, Maryland
Norman D. Hirsch; Seattle, Washington
N. Peter Levinson; Heidelberg, Federal Republic of Germany
Ludwig Loeffler; Hamburg, Federal Republic of Germany
Ernst G. Lowenthal; Berlin
Sara Mandelbaum; Jerusalem
Rosa Ostro; Tel Aviv
Eva G. Reichmann; London
Werner Rosenstock; London
Kurt Schwerin; Chicago, Illinois
Max A. Shapiro; Minneapolis, Minnesota
Fritz Silten; Zurich, Switzerland
Eric M. Warburg; Hamburg, Federal Republic of Germany
Norbert Wollheim; New York

4: LEO BAECK WRITINGS

(The most comprehensive listing of Baeck's writings is Theodore Wiener's *The Writings of Leo Baeck, a Bibliography*, Cincinnati, 1954. The following selections are those from which I quoted in this book or which I found of particular interest in the writing of it.)

Abschieds-Predigt, 1907
Address at the founding of the committee for erection of the Otto Hirsch and Julius Seligsohn Memorial School in Hazorea, Israel, April 8, 1949 (typescript; also printed in *AJR Information*, May 1953, p. 6)
Address on the occasion of Leo Baeck's grandson-in-law taking his first pulpit, 1951 (handwritten mss.)
Addresses before the World Union for Progressive Judaism, various years
"Conditions of Tolerance," *The Listener*, Aug. 17, 1953, p. 339

"Die Deutschen Juden," in *Ten Years—American Federation of Jews from Central Europe, 1941–1951*, New York, 1952

Dieses Volk, Frankfurt am Main, 1955, 1957 (2 vols.)

Aus Drei Jahrtausenden, Tübingen, 1958

"Dreizehnter Bericht über die Lehranstalt für die Wissenschaft des Judentums in Berlin," *Jüdische Chronik*, 1896–97, pp. 90–1 (reprinted in *Leo Baeck —Beispiel und Botschaft*, Zurich, 1959)

"Einleitung," *Zum 50 Jährigen Bestehen des Ordens Bne Briss in Deutschland*, Frankfurt am Main, 1933

Die Entwicklung der Rechtsstellung der Juden in Europa, vornehmlich in Deutschland (unpublished mss.)

Epochen der jüdischen Geschichte, Stuttgart, 1974

The Essence of Judaism, New York, 1960 ed.

"Eugen Taeubler, Creative Scholar and Thinker," undated

"Fluchtling oder Kolonist," August 1945 (handwritten mss.)

"Gedanken zur Abrüstung," *Völkerbund die Abrüstungskonferenz*, Berlin, April 22, 1932, pp. 3–4

"Gedenkrede zur Erinnerung an die Kuratoren Albert Mosse, Paul Meyer und Max Weiss und der Dozenten Martin Schreiner," October 21, 1926, in *Bericht über die Lehranstalt für die Wissenschaft des Judentums in Berlin*, 1926, pp. 17–32

"Gedenken an Zwei Tote," undated reprint from *LBI Yearbook*

"Gedenkrede, zur Erinnerung an die Während des Krieges verstorbenen Kuratoren und die im Felde gefallenen Hörer," 1919

"Haggadah and Christian Doctrine," reprint from *The Hebrew Union College Annual*, Cincinnati, Ohio; v. 23, part 1, 1950–51

"Individuum und Gemeinschaft," *Der Weg*, Berlin, March 1, 1946, p. 1

"Geleitwort," Ferdinand Gregorovius, *Das Ghetto und die Juden in Rom*, Berlin, 1935

"Israel und das deutsche Völk," *Merkur*, Munich, Oct. 1952, pp. 901–11

"Jewish Mysticism," undated reprint from *The Journal of Jewish Studies*, London, v. 2, no. 1, pp. 3–16

"The Jewish Spirit Among the Nations," *Commentary*, New York, Feb. 1949, pp. 132–9

Judaism and Christianity, Philadelphia, 1958 (translated by Walter Kaufmann)

"Judaism on Old and New Paths," *The International Review of Missions*, London, April 1950, pp. 190–200

"Judaism: Revolution and Rebirth," *The Synagogue Review*, London, Nov. 1964, pp. 52–4

"Judentum, Christentum und Islam," a lecture given in Brussels, Belgium, on April 22, 1956

"Das Judentum in der Gegenwart," *Der Morgen*, Oct. 1933, unpaged reprint

"Das Judentum under den Religionen," *Korrespondenz-Blatt*, May 1912, pp. 9–15

"Die Jüdische Religion in der Gegenwart," *Süddeutsche Monatshefte*, Munich, Sept. 1930, pp. 828–32 (reprinted in Leo Baeck, *Wege im Judentum*, pp. 260–9)

"Leo Baeck Zum Boykott-Tag," *AJR Information*, April 1973, p. 3

"Life in a Concentration Camp," *The Jewish Forum*, London, March 1946, pp. 29–32

"Martin Buber," *The Jewish Chronicle*, Feb. 1953, unpaged clipping

Memorial sermon for Paul von Hindenburg, 1934

"Neuem Tag Entgegen," *Mitteilungsblatt*, Tel Aviv, Sept. 7, 1945, p. 1

"Orthodox oder ceremoniös?" *Jüdische Chronik*, 1896–97, pp. 237–243 (reprinted in *Leo Baeck—Beispiel und Botschaft*, Zurich, 1959)

"Peace," *The World Union for Progressive Judaism: Bulletin No. 19*, London, Jan. 1948, pp. 9–10

The Pharisees and Other Essays, New York, 1966

"Plan Eines Jüdischen Konkordats," *Bulletin für die Mitglieder der Gesellschaft der Freunde des Leo Baeck Institute*, Tel Aviv, Number 1, 1957

"Geleitwort," H. G. Adler, *Theresienstadt 1941–1945*, Tübingen, 1960 ed.

The Psychological Root of the Law, London, 1952

"Recht und Pflicht!", *C.V. Zeitung*, Berlin, clipping dated 1933

"Eine religionsoziologische Linie," *Der Jude*, Berlin, March 1938, pp. 147–52

"Religion und Erziegung," *Der Jude*, 1926, undated and unpaged clipping (actually a lecture delivered in 1923, reprinted in Leo Baeck, *Wege im Judentum*, Berlin, 1938, pp. 159–73)

"Religious Education of Children in Palestine," *The World Union for Progressive Judaism: Bulletin No. 20*, London, Sept. 1048, pp. 40–2

"Rosch Haschanah 5694," *Jüdische Rundschau*, Sept. 20, 1933, p. 547

Sabbathgedenken für jüdische Soldaten, undated

"Schöpfungsordnungen," *Jüdische Allgemeine Zeitung*, Berlin, clipping dated 1936

"The Scope and Limitations of Co-operation Between Jews and Christians," *The Liberal Jewish Monthly*, London, Dec. 1954, pp. 133–5

"The Shema," 1946 (typed mss.)

"Das Soziale der Jödischen Religion," *Gleichheit*, Bonn, Aug. 1954, pp. 278–80

"Der soziale Gehalt der jüdischen Wohlfartspflege," *Zedakah*, Berlin, Aug. 1926, pp. 5–8

Speech before the convention of the Vereinigung der liberalen Rabbiner Deutschlands in Berlin, published in *Liberales Judentum*, Frankfurt am Main, Heft 1–3, 1922

Spinozas erste Einwirkungen auf Deutschland, Berlin, 1895

"Die Staatslehre Spinozas von Dr. Josef Hoff," *Jüdische Chronik*, 1895–96, pp. 188–9 (reprinted in *Leo Baeck—Beispiel und Botschaft*, Zurich, 1959)

"Staat, Familie und Individualität," *Jüdische Wohlfahrtspflege und Sozialpolitick*, 1932, pp. 193–4

"Tag des Mutes," *C.V. Zeitung*, Berlin, Sept. 20, 1933, p. 3

The Task of Progressive Judaism in the Post-War World, London, 1946

"Trauerfeier für Ludwig Tietz in Weissensee," *C.V. Zeitung*, 1933, Berlin, No. 43, p. 2

This People Israel: The Meaning of Jewish Existence, New York, 1964

Untitled and undated mss. about youth

Untitled mss. describing Baeck's activities since his release from Theresienstadt, sent to Max A. Shapiro, 1950

Untitled mss. about Orthodox restrictions on Liberal rabbis in Israel, post World War Two

Von Moses Mendelssohn zu Franz Rosenzweig, Stuttgart, 1958 (reprinted, in English, in *Judaism*, winter and spring issues, 1960)

"Wedding Sermon," delivered at the wedding of his granddaughter Marianne to A. Stanley Dreyfus, July 25, 1950

Wege im Judentum, Berlin, 1933

Das Wesen des Judentums, Berlin, 1905 ed.

Das Wesen des Judentums, Frankfurt am Main, 1926 ed.

"The Writing of History," *Synagogue Review*, London, Nov. 1962, pp. 51–9

5: PUBLISHED MATERIAL, REPORTS, AND DOCTORAL DISSERTATIONS

H. G. Adler, *The Jews in Germany*, London, 1969

H. G. Adler, *Theresienstadt 1941–1945*, Tübingen, 1960 ed.

H. G. Adler, *Die Verheimlichte Wahrheit*, Tübingen, 1958

S. Adler-Rudel, *Jüdische Selbsthilfe unter dem Naziregime 1933–1939*, Tübingen, 1974

Alexander Altmann, *Leo Baeck and the Jewish Mystical Tradition*, The Leo Baeck Memorial Lecture No. 17, New York, 1973

American Federation of Jews from Central Europe, *Leo Baeck Memorial Conference on Jewish Social Thought—1973–1974*, New York, 1974 (also referred to as "Lerntag")

American Joint Distribution Committee, European Executive Office, Paris; "Activities of the Zentralausschuss of the Reichsvertretung der Juden in Deutschland—January 1st–June 30th, 1937," Oct. 1937

Hannah Arendt, *Eichmann in Jerusalem*, New York, 1965 ed.

Hannah Arendt, *The Origins of Totalitarianism*, New York, 1968 ed.

Samuel Bäck, *Die Religionssatze der heiligen Schrift*, Lissa, 1875

Leonard Baker, *Brahmin in Revolt*, New York, 1972

Leonard Baker, *Roosevelt and Pearl Harbor*, New York, 1970

Michael Balfour and Julian Frisby, *Helmuth von Moltke—A Leader Against Hitler*, London, 1972

K. J. Ball-Kaduri, *Das Leben der Juden in Deutschland im Jahre 1933*, Frankfurt am Main, 1963

K. J. Ball-Kaduri, *Vor der Katastrophe—Juden in Deutschland 1934–1939*, Tel Aviv, 1967

Norman Bentwich, *My 77 Years*, Philadelphia, 1961

Norman Bentwich, *The Refugees from Germany*, London, 1936

Norman Bentwich, *They Found Refuge*, London, 1956

Kurt Blumenfeld, *Erlebte Judenfrage*, Stuttgart, 1962

Eric H. Boehm, *We Survived*, Santa Barbara, Calif., 1966 ed.

Fred Gladstone Bratton, *The Crime of Christendom*, Boston, 1969

Sir Michael Bruce, *Tramp Royal*, London, 1954

Martin Buber, *Briefwechsel aus sieben Jahrzehnten*, 3 vols., Heidelberg, 1972

G. K. Chesterton, *The New Jerusalem*, London 1920

Arthur A. Cohen, *The Myth of the Judeo-Christian Tradition*, New York, 1971 ed.

Emil Cohn, *Die Geschichte meiner Suspension*, Berlin, 1907

Emil Cohn, *Mein Kampf ums Recht*, Berlin, 1907

The Condition of Jewish Belief, New York, 1966

Harvey G. Cox, *On Not Leaving It to the Snake*, New York, 1967

Milton Dank, *The French Against the French*, New York, 1974

Lucy S. Dawidowicz, *The War Against the Jews 1933–1945*, New York, 1975

Max I. Dimont, *The Indestructible Jews*, New York, 1971 ed.

Max I. Dimont, *Jews, God and History*, 1962 ed.

Frances Donaldson, *Edward VIII*, New York, 1974

Frederic A. Doppelt, *Unconquerable Soul*, New York, undated

Simon Dubnov, *History of the Jews*, New York, 1971 ed.

Amos Elon, *Herzl*, New York, 1975

Amos Elon, *The Israelis—Founders and Sons*, New York, 1972 ed.

Encyclopedia Judaica, Jerusalem, 1971

The Encyclopedia of Education, New York, 1971

Max Eschelbacher, *Die Synagogengemeinde Duesseldorf 1904–1929*, Duesseldorf, 1929

Carlo Falconi, *The Silence of Pius XII*, Boston, 1965

David Farrar, *The Warburgs*, New York, 1975

Henry L. Feingold, *The Politics of Rescue*, New Brunswick, New Jersey, 1970

Joachim C. Fest, *Hitler*, New York, 1974

Festschrift zum 80. Geburtstag von Leo Baeck Am 23. Mai 1953, London, 1953

Edward H. Flannery, *The Anguish of the Jews*, New York, 1965

Franz Rosenzweig: Eine Gedenkschrift, Frankfurt am Main, 1930

Herbert Freeden, *Jüdisches Theater in Nazideutschland*, Tübingen, 1964

Albert H. Friedlander, *Leo Baeck—Teacher of Theresienstadt*, New York, 1968

Albert H. Friedlander, *Leo Baeck—Leben und Lehre*, Stuttgart, 1973

Henry Friedlander, *On the Holocaust*, New York, 1972

Otto Friedrich, *Before the Deluge*, New York, 1973 ed.

Peter Gay, *Weimar Culture*, New York, 1968

Nahum N. Glatzer, *Baeck-Buber-Rosenzweig—Reading the Book of Job*, The Leo Baeck Memorial Lecture No. 10, New York, 1966

Paul Goodman, *History of the Jews*, New York, 1959 ed.

Robert Gordis, *The Book of God and Man—A Study of Job*, Chicago, 1965

Heinrich H. Graetz, *Popular History of the Jews*, New York, 1919 ed.

Kurt R. Grossmann, "Flight or Emigration, 1933 through 1938," text of a lecture given at the Leo Baeck Institute, New York, Jan. 19, 1972

Kurt R. Grossmann, "What Happened to the German Jews? A Balance Sheet," in *Ten Years—American Federation of Jews from Central Europe, Inc., 1941–1951*, New York, 1952

Richard Grunberger, *The 12-Year Reich*, New York, 1972 ed.

Hermann Gunkel, *The Legends of Genesis*, New York, 1964 ed.

Wolfgang Hamburger, "Leo Baeck—The Last Teacher of the Lehranstalt," in *Paul Lazarus-Gedenkbuch*, pp. 120–30

Isser Harel, *The House on Garibaldi Street*, New York, 1976 ed.

Adolf von Harnack, *Christianity and History*, London, 1900

Adolf von Harnack, *Mission and Expansion of Christianity*, New York, 1904

Adolf von Harnack, *What Is Christianity?* New York, 1903 and 1957 eds.

Malcolm Hay, *Europe and the Jews*, Boston, 1960 ed.

Ernst Helmreich, *Religious Education in German Schools*, Cambridge, Massachusetts, 1959

Emil Herz, *Before the Fury*, New York, 1966

Moses Hess, *Rome and Jerusalem*, New York, 1918 ed.

Raul Hilberg, *The Destruction of the European Jews*, Chicago, 1967 ed.

Adolf Hitler, *Mein Kampf*, Boston, 1971 ed.

Aubrey Hodes, *Martin Buber—An Intimate Portrait*, New York, 1971

Peter Hoffmann, *The History of the German Resistance 1933–1945*, Cambridge, Mass., 1977

Halo Holborn (ed.), *Republic to Reich*, New York, 1973 ed.

David Irving, *Hitler's War*, New York, 1977

"In Memoriam Leo Baeck," London, undated

Jacob Jacobson, "Terezin: The Daily Life 1943–1945," in *Jewish Survivors Report—Documents of Nazi Guilt*, London, 1946

The Jewish Encyclopedia, New York, 1905 and 1925 eds.

Josef Kastein, *Jews in Germany*, London, 1934

Jacob Katz, *Exclusiveness and Tolerance*, New York, 1969 ed.

Walter Kempowski, *Did You Ever See Hitler?* New York, 1975 ed.

Hermann Keyserling (ed.), *The Book of Marriage*, New York, 1926

Max Kreutzberger (ed.), *Studies of the Leo Baeck Institute*, New York, 1967

Kriegsbriefe gefallener Deutscher Juden, Berlin, 1935

Walter Laqueur, *A History of Zionism*, New York, 1972

Walter Laqueur, *Weimar—A Cultural History 1918–1933*, New York, 1974

Zdenek Lederer, *Ghetto Theresienstadt*, London, 1953

Leo Baeck—Beispeil und Botschaft, Zurich, 1959

Leo Baeck Centenary 1973, London, 1973

Leo Baeck/H. G. van Dam, Duesseldorf, 1973

Leo Baeck Remembered, London, 1973

"Lerntag," a series of talks about Leo Baeck given by Ernst Simon, Eugene B. Borowitz, and Herbert A. Strauss on Oct. 21, 1973; for the printed text see, in this bibliography, American Federation of Jews from Central Europe

Adolf Leschnitzer, "Die Geburt des 'Modernen' Antisemitismus aus dem Geist der Neuzeit," in *Ten Years—American Federation of Jews from Central Europe, Inc., 1941–1951*, New York, 1952

Nora Levin, *The Holocaust*, New York, 1968

Shmarya Levin, *Youth in Revolt*, New York, 1930

Louis P. Lochner (ed.), *The Goebbels Diaries*, New York, 1971 ed.

Stefan Lorant, *Seig Heil!* New York, 1974

Marvin Lowenthal, *The Jews of Germany*, London, 1939

Erich von Ludendorff, *Ludendorff's Own Story*, New York, 1920

Arnost Lustig, *Night and Hope*, Iowa City, Iowa, 1973 ed.

Jacob R. Marcus, *The Jew in the Medieval World*, New York, 1960

Jacob R. Marcus, *The Rise and Destiny of the German Jew*, Cincinnati, Ohio, 1934

Werner Maser, *Hitler—Legend, Myth, Reality*, New York, 1973

Werner Maser, *Hitler's Letters and Notes*, New York, 1974

Ignaz Maybaum, *The Face of God After Auschwitz*, Amsterdam, 1965

David McLellan, *Karl Marx—His Life and Thought*, New York, 1973

Michael A. Meyer, *The Origins of the Modern Jew*, Detroit, 1967

Frederic Morton, *The Rothschilds*, New York, 1962

George L. Mosse, *Germans & Jews*, New York, 1970 ed.

Abraham Myerson and Isaac Goldberg, *The German Jew*, New York, 1933

Simon Noveck (ed.), *Great Jewish Thinkers of the Twentieth Century*, New York, 1963

John F. Oppenheimer (ed.), *Lexikon des Judentums*, Berlin, 1971

Harry M. Orlinsky, *Ancient Israel*, Ithaca, New York, 1960

Sidney Osborne, *Germany and Her Jews*, London, 1939

Otto Hirsch—Ein Lebensweg, Berlin, 1957

Lilli Palmer, *Change Lobsters and Dance*, New York, 1976 ed.

Franz von Papen, *Memoirs*, New York, 1953

Ruth L. Pierson, "German Jewish Identity in the Weimar Republic," Yale University, 1970 (a doctoral dissertation)

W. Gunther Plaut, *The Growth of Reform Judaism*, New York, 1965

Terrence Des Pres, *The Survivor*, New York, 1976

Walther Rathenau, *Die Neue Gesellschaft*, Berlin, 1919

Walter Rathenau, *The New Society*, London, 1921

Eva G. Reichmann, *Grösse und Verhängnis deutsch-jüdischer Existenz*, Heidelberg, 1974

Eva G. Reichmann, *Hostages of Civilisation*, Westport, Connecticut, 1970 ed.

Eva G. Reichmann (ed.), *Worte des Gedenkens für Leo Baeck*, Heidelberg, 1959

Erich Maria Remarque, *All Quiet on the Western Front*, Boston, 1929

Erich Maria Remarque, *Im Westen Nichts Neues*, Berlin, 1964 ed.

Karl Heinrich Rengstorff, *Leo Baeck—Eine geistige Gestalt underer Zeit*, Duesseldorf, 1958

Gerhard Ritter, *The German Resistance*, Freeport, N.Y., 1970 ed.

Ger van Roon, *German Resistance to Hitler*, London, 1971

Martin Rosenbluth, *Go Forth and Serve*, New York, 1961

Rosemary R. Ruether, *Faith and Fratricide—The Theological Roots of Anti-Semitism*, New York, 1974

Samuel Sandmel, *Leo Baeck on Christianity*, The Leo Baeck Memorial Lecture No. 19, New York, 1975

Jean-Paul Sartre, *Anti-Semite and Jew*, New York, 1972 ed.

Jean-Paul Sartre, *Existentialism*, New York, 1947

Fritz Scherbel, *Die Juden in Lissa*, Berlin, 1932

Gershom Scholem, *The Messianic Idea in Judaism*, New York, 1971

Ismar Schorsch, *Jewish Reactions to German Anti-Semitism, 1870–1914*, New York, 1972

Hermann Schwab, *The History of Orthodox Jewry in Germany*, London, 1950

Ernst Simon, *Brücken*, Heidelberg, 1965

Some Religious Aspects of Zionism, London, undated

Harold Stahmer, *Speak That I May See Thee!*, New York, 1968

Herbert A. Strauss and Kurt R. Grossmann (eds.), *Gegenwart im Rückblick*, Heidelberg, 1970

John Toland, *Adolf Hitler*, New York, 1976

Hans-Hasso von Veltheim-Ostrau, *Der Atem Indiens*, Hamburg, 1965

Eckhard Wandel, *Hans Schäffer*, Stuttgart, 1974

Friedrich K. Wiebe, *Germany and the Jewish Problem*, Berlin, 1939

The World Union for Progressive Judaism: The First Twenty-Five Years, 1926–1951, London, 1951

Michael M. Zarchin, *From Constantine to Hitler*, San Francisco, 1936

Zum 50 Jährigen Bestehen Des Ordens Bne Briss in Deutschland, Frankfurt am Main, 1933

6: PERIODICALS

AJR Information, London

Allgemeine Wochenzeitung der Juden in Deutschland, Berlin

Allgemeine Zeitung des Judentums, Berlin

The American Jewish Year Book, Philadelphia

The Atlantic Monthly, Boston

Der Aufbau, New York

Berliner Rundschau, Berlin

Blätter des Verbandes Jüdischer Heimatvereine, Berlin

Blätter Juden Wissens Bne Brith, La Paz, Bolivia

CCAR Journal, Miami

Central European History, Atlanta, Georgia

Common Ground, London

C.V. Zeitung, Berlin

Daily News Bulletin, London (published by the Jewish Telegraphic Agency in 1945)

Deutsche Bauzeitung, Berlin

EMUNA, Frankfurt am Main

Filantropia, Buenos Aires (published by the Association Filantropica Israelita)

Gemeindeblatt der jüdischen Gemeinde zu Berlin, Berlin

Gleichheit, Bonn

Herausgegriffen, Berne, Switzerland

Israelitisches Gemeindeblatt, Karlsruhe

Israelitisches Familienblatt, Berlin

Israelitisches Wockenblatt für die Schweiz, Zurich, Switzerland

Jedioth Chadaschrot, Haifa

Jewish Social Studies, New York

The Journal of Jewish Studies, London

Judaism: A Quarterly Journal of Jewish Life and Thought, New York
Jüdische Wohlfahrtspflege und Sozialpolitik, Berlin
Jüdisches Gemeindeblatt für die Britische Zone
Korrespondent-Blatt, Berlin
LBI News, New York (published by the Leo Baeck Institute)
Leo Baeck Institute Yearbook, London
Liberal Jewish Monthly, London
Liberales Judentum, Frankfurt am Main
MB (Mitteilungsblatt), Tel Aviv
Merkur, Munich
Midstream, New York
The National Jewish Monthly, Washington, D.C.
Neue Züricher Zeitung, Zurich, Switzerland
The New York Times, New York
The New Yorker, New York
Our Congregation, London (published by the New Liberal Jewish Congregation)
Revue Européenne, Zurich, Switzerland
Saturday Review, New York
Soziale Ethik im Judentum, Frankfurt am Main
The Synagogue Review, London
Time Magazine, New York
Tradition und Erneuerung, Berne, Switzerland
The Voice of Emanuel, Chicago, Illinois (published by the Emanuel Congregation)
Der Weg, Berlin
Wisconsin Magazine of History, Madison, Wisconsin
Yad Vashem Bulletin, Jerusalem (also known as *Yad Washem Bulletin*)
Yad Vashem Studies, Jerusalem
Zeitschrift für die Geschichte der Juden, Tel Aviv

NOTES

Abbreviations
CIA   Central Intelligence Agency
JNL   Jewish National and University Library, Hebrew University of Jerusalem
LBI/J   Leo Baeck Institute, Jerusalem
LBI/L   Leo Baeck Institute, London
LBI/NY   Leo Baeck Institute, New York
LBIY   *Leo Baeck Institute Yearbook*
NA   National Archives
OSS   Office of Strategic Services

1: RETURN

1. Patrick Dolan interview, June 1, 1974.
2. NA: OSS Record Group 226, L57022.
3. Eli Rock interview, April 8, 1975.
4. David H. Wice interview, March 12, 1975; R. Weltsch, "End of an Epoch," *Jewish Observer and Middle East Review*, Nov. 9, 1956, p. 27; Robert Weltsch interview, May 31, 1974.
5. Sara Mandelbaum interview, June 23, 1975; *MB* (*Mitteilungsblatt*), Aug. 22, 1947, p. 3.
6. "Red Cross Report on Theresienstadt," pp. 2, 32 (located in Ghetto Fighters Museum); Z. Lederer, *Ghetto Theresienstadt*, pp. 142–4.
7. L. Baeck, "A People Stands Before Its God," in E. H. Boehm, *We Survived*, p. 294; Betty Cohen interview, June 14, 1975; Uta C. Merzbach interview, May 8, 1974.
8. Hugo Heumann, "Theresienstadt," mss., pp. 40–1, in LBI/NY; "Typhus at Terezin," pp. 1–9, in CIA, office of the director.
9. Betty Cohen interview, June 14, 1975.
10. *Aufbau*, Dec. 21, 1945, p. 1; Eli Rock interview, April 8, 1975; Betty Cohen interview, June 14, 1975; Leo Adam interview, May 26, 1974.
11. Patrick Dolan interview, June 1, 1974; Eva G. Reichmann interview, May 27, 1974; L. Baeck, "A People Stands Before Its God," in E. H. Boehm, *We Survived*, pp. 294–8; L. Baeck letter to unknown, April 18, 1946, in LBI/NY: 16-AR363; J. L. Liebman, "A Living Saint: Rabbi Baeck," in *Atlantic*, June 1948, p. 42; Z. Lederer, *Ghetto Theresienstadt*, pp. 191–6; H. E. Fabian, "Die Letzte Etappe," in *Festschrift zum 80. Geburtstag von Leo Baeck Am 23. Mai 1953*, pp. 96–7.
12. L. Baeck letters: June 19, 1945, courtesy of Ralph Blume; June 30, 1945, courtesy of Rosa Ostro; June 30, 1945, courtesy of Willi Groag.
13. L. Baeck letter, June 4, 1945, courtesy of A. S. and M. Dreyfus.
14. Telegram, July 1, 1945, courtesy of A. S. and M. Dreyfus; Charlotte Gichermann, "Rabbiner Dr. Leo Baeck," undated newspaper clipping, courtesy of C. Gichermann.
15. Account of the destruction of the European Jews drawn from *Daily News Bulletin*, May 14, 1945, p. 4; N. Levin, *The Holocaust*; L. Dawidowicz, *The War Against the Jews*; R. Hilberg, *The Destruction of the European Jews*; M. Dank, *The French Against the French*. Lodz account: Frank F. Rosenthal interview,

Jan. 21, 1974; author's visit to Lodz, June 14, 1974. "To be German ..." quote, Gregory Baum interview, Sept. 27, 1974.

16. Patrick Dolan interview, June 1, 1974; P. Dolan letter to Lt. Cmdr. Frank Wisner, July 7, 1945, in CIA, office of the director; Friedrich Brodnitz interview, Feb. 14, 1974; Werner Rosenstock/P. Dolan interview, April 24, 1972, in LBI/NY: Leo Baeck, Allgemeine III-187 (365).

2: BEGINNINGS

1. L. Baeck, *Die entwicklung ...*", part 1, pp. 1, 14, 19–20, 27.
2. Hildegard Biermann interview, March 25, 1974; B. Manuel interview, June 5, 1974; "Notes on the origins of the Baeck family," by Hildegard Biermann, courtesy of A. S. and M. Dreyfus; H. Biermann, "Vorfahren und Familienange-hörige von Rabbiner Dr. Leo Baeck," in *Zeitschrift für die Geschichte der Juden,* 1967, no. 4, p. 257; K. Wilhelm, "Der vertraute Knecht im weiten Hause des Judentums," in *MB (Mitteilungsblatt)*, May 18, 1953, p. 3; S. Stern, "Rabbiner Dr. Samuel Bäck 1834–1912, in *Allgemeine Zeitung des Judentums*, June 21, 1912, pp. 295–6.
3. M. S. Ruest, untitled reminiscence about S. Bäck, in *Blätter des Verbandes Jüdischer Heimatvereine*, June 1937, unpaged clipping; F. Scherbel, *Die Juden in Lissa*, p. 12; S. Stern, "Rabbiner Dr. Samuel Bäck 1834–1912," in *Allgemeine Zeitung des Judentums*, June 21, 1912, p. 295; Mordechai Gichon interview, June 19, 1975; Norbert Wollheim interview, Oct. 29, 1975.
4. H. I. Bach, "Leo Baeck," in *Synagogue Review*, Jan. 1957, pp. 137–8; H. G. Adler interview, May 25, 1974.
5. S. Stern, "Rabbiner Dr. Samuel Bäck 1834–1912," in *Allgemeine Zeitung des Judentums*, June 21, 1912, pp. 295–6.
6. L. Baeck, *Die Entwicklung ...*, part 2, p. 178; H. Schreiber, "The Birthplace of Dr. Leo Baeck," in *Synagogue Review*, May 1953, p. 268.
7. H. Schreiber, "The Birthplace of Dr. Leo Baeck," in *Synagogue Review*, May 1953, pp. 265–6; interviews with Theodore Wiener, Oct. 18, 1973, and Frank F. Rosenthal, Jan. 21, 1974.
8. M. Turnowksy-Pinner, "A Student's Friendship with Ernst Toller," in *LBIY*, 1970, pp. 211–2; B. Manuel interview, June 5, 1974; H. I. Bach, untitled lecture, courtesy of H. I. Bach.
9. H. Strauss, "Pre-Emancipation Prussian Policies Towards the Jews 1815–1847," in *LBIY*, 1966, p. 117; K. Wilhelm, "The Jewish Community in the Post-Emancipation Period," in *LBIY*, 1957, pp. 54–6; W. Breslauer, "Jews of the City of Posen One Hundred Years Ago," in *LBIY*, 1963, p. 233. "Where the Poles ..." quote, S. Stern-Taeubler, "Eugen Taeubler and the 'Wissenschaft des Judentums,' " in *LBIY*, 1958, pp. 39–40.
10. H. I. Bach, "Leo Baeck," in *Synagogue Review*, Jan. 1957, p. 137.
11. Ilse Turnheim interview, Oct. 18, 1974; Theodore Wiener interview, Oct. 18, 1973; *Encyclopedia of Education*, v. 2, pp. 301–7; Georg Wiener, untitled mss. on occasion of L. Baeck's 70th birthday, in LBI/NY: ME 251.
12. C. Wilk, "Zum Gedeken an Leo Baeck," in *Filantropia*, May 1963, p. 133.
13. I. Schorsch, "Moritz Güdemann," in *LBIY*, 1966, pp. 43–4; J. Fraenkel, "Moritz Güdemann and Theodor Herzl," in *LBIY*, 1966, p. 68; A. Kober, "Die Hoch-schulen für die Rabbinerausbildung in Deutschland," in *Festschrift zum 80. Geburtstag von Leo Baeck Am 23. Mai 1953*, pp. 24–5; H. W. Brann, "Leo Baeck: Teacher of Theresienstadt," in *Judaism*, Spring 1969, pp. 251–2; M.

Gruenewald, "The Modern Rabbi," in *LBIY*, 1957, pp. 85–7. "It is inconceivable . . ." quote, in W. G. Plaut, *Growth of Reform Judaism*, p. 46.

14. Breslau records in LBI/NY: A3, A4, A5 (3982); Frank F. Rosenthal interview, Jan. 21, 1974; Max Vogelstein interview, Dec. 3, 1974; H. Liebeschütz, "Between Past and Future—Leo Baeck's Historical Position," in *LBIY*, 1966, p. 7 (for account of alleged rift between father and son); E. G. Lowenthal interview, June 18, 1974; Alfred Wolf interview, April 23, 1976.

15. R. Fuchs, "The 'Hochschule für die Wissenschaft des Judentums' in the Period of Nazi Rule," in *LBIY*, 1967, pp. 4–7; H. I. Bach, "Leo Baeck," in *Synagogue Review*, Jan. 1957, p. 138; W. G. Plaut, *Growth of Reform Judaism*, p. 47; J. R. Marcus, *Rise . . . German Jew*, p. 232. "A disgrace to . . ." quote, in S. Levin, *Youth in Revolt*, pp. 229–30.

16. H. I. Bach, untitled lecture, courtesy of H. I. Bach; Max Vogelstein interview, Dec. 3, 1974; H. H. Hirschberg, "Leo Baeck and His Teacher," in *CCAR Journal*, Winter 1973, pp. 84–9; H. Liebeschütz, "Between Past and Future—Leo Baeck's Historical Position," in *LBIY*, 1966, p. 11. Buber quote, in E. Simon, "Martin Buber and German Jewry," *LBIY*, 1958, p. 6.

17. A. Altmann, "Theology in Twentieth-Century German Jewry," in *LBIY*, 1956, pp. 198–202; W. Van der Zyl, "Memorial Tribute," in *In Memoriam Leo Baeck*, pp. 21–2; transcript of radio interview with Joachim Prinz, May 23, 1973, in LBI/NY; Leo Baeck, Allgemeine III–174 (365); E. Fischoff, "Hermann Cohen," in S. Noveck (ed.), *Great Jewish Thinkers . . .* , pp. 108, 112–3; 121, 125, 128, 130; G. L. Mosse, *Germans & Jews*, pp. 175–6; H. Liebeschütz, "Die Aufgabe einer Biographie für Leo Baeck," in *EMUNA*, March/April 1975, pp. 43–4. Cohen Sabbath dinner story, Bernard J. Bamberger interview, Jan. 22, 1974. "Be of good cheer . . ." quote, in A. Altmann, *Leo Baeck and the Jewish Mystical Tradition*, p. 5.

18. Dilthey letter, Jan. 5, 1894, in LBI/NY: A1 (3982); F. Friedländer, "Hours I Spent with Rabbi Baeck," *AJR Information*, Nov. 1970, p. 6; Leo Adam interview, May 26, 1974.

19. M. Davidsohn letter, Aug. 12, 1957, in LBI/NY.

20. L. Baeck, *Spinozas erste Einwirkungen . . .* , pp. 4, 8, 71. See also A. Altmann, *Leo Baeck and the Jewish Mystical Tradition*, pp. 6–7.

21. L. Baeck's Hochschule records in LBI/NY: A6 (3982); also report by Antoni Sylwester, Stadtarchivar von Oppeln, Feb. 6, 1960, courtesy of A. S. and M. Dreyfus.

3: RABBI

1. LBI/NY: A7, A8 (3982).

2. Oppeln history taken from L. Baeck's accounts in *Jewish Encylopedia*, 1905 ed., v. 9, p. 409, and 1925 ed., v. 9, pp. 408–9.

3. E. G. Reichmann, *Grösse und Verhängnis*, p. 257; Max Vogelstein interview, Dec. 3, 1974; G. Wiener, "Geschichte der Juden Gemeinde Oppeln O/S," unpublished mss., pp. 9–10, in LBI/NY.

4. Synagogue dedication program in G. Wiener, LBI/NY: M. E. 19; *Allgemeine Zeitung des Judentums*, July 9, 1897, unpaged clipping, courtesy A. S. and M. Dreyfus.

5. Natalie Baeck's family records, courtesy of Betty Cohen; Hildegard Biermann interview, March 25, 1974.

6. A. Stanley Dreyfus interview, Feb. 12, 1974.

7. Undated memorandum by L. Baeck, courtesy of A. S. and M. Dreyfus; "young

married happiness" quote in M. Davidsohn letter, Aug. 12, 1957, in LBI/NY; Marianne Dreyfus interview, March 26, 1974.

8. Interviews with Joachim Prinz, May 1, 1974, and Gertrud Gallerski, Oct. 30, 1975; H. W. Brann, "Leo Baeck," in S. Noveck, ed., *Great Jewish Thinkers* ..., pp. 136–7.

9. E. G. Reichmann, *Grösse und Verhängnis*, pp. 258–9; Eva G. Reichmann interview, May 27, 1974.

10. "Therefore, each will ..." quote, K. Boehm letter to author, Dec. 2, 1974; L. Baeck letter to F. Muhr, July 29, 1904, in LBI/NY; drinking story, Fred Grubel interview, Oct. 16, 1974.

11. H. L. Goldschmidt, "Der Junge Leo Baeck," in *AJR Information*, May 1963, p. 3.

12. W. Laqueur, *History of Zionism*, p. 103; H. L. Goldschmidt, "Der Junge Leo Baeck," in *AJR Information*, May 1963, p. 2; E. G. Reichmann, "Address Given at the Celebration of Rabbi Dr. Leo Baeck's 100th Birthday," text courtesy of E. G. Reichmann; Eva G. Reichmann interview, May 27, 1974; Gershom Scholem interview, Oct. 14, 1975.

13. W. Hamburger, "The Reaction of Reform Jews to the Nazi Rule," in H. A. Strauss and K. R. Grossmann (ed.), *Gegenwart im Rückblick*, p. 158.

14. E. Cohn, *Mein Kampf ums Recht*, pp. 5, 7; L. Baeck letter to E. Cohn, April 30, 1907, courtesy of A. S. and M. Dreyfus.

15. "I always admonish ..." quote, in F. Friedländer, "Hours I Spent with Rabbi Baeck," in *AJR Information*, Nov. 1970, p. 6; Herman O. Pineas, "Meine Erinnerungen am Dr. Leo Baeck," mss., in LBI/NY; Herman O. Pineas interview, Sept. 4, 1975.

16. "... Literal interpretation of God's ...", cited by F. G. Bratton, *Crime of Christendom*, p. 52; subsequent quotations from A. von Harnack, *What Is Christianity?* pp. 16, 186, 141, 174, 8, 121, 109.

17. R. Ruether, *Faith and Fratricide*, pp. 218–9.

18. L. Baeck, "Dreizehnter Bericht über ...", pp. 9–10; L. Baeck, "Orthodox oder ceremoniös?" pp. 13, 15.

19. *Monatsschrift für Geschichte und Wissenschaft des Judentums*, 1901, pp. 107–20.

20. I. Schorsch, *Jewish Reactions to German Anti-Semitism*, pp. 172–3; letter from Peter Bedrick, executive vice president, Schocken Books, to author, Dec. 20, 1976.

21. "is not really ..." quote, attributed to Max Wiener, in H. Liebeschütz, "Max Wiener's Reinterpretation of Liberal Judaism," in *LBIY*, 1960, p. 45n; "enlightenment not Judaism" quote, Ignaz Maybaum interview, May 29, 1974.

22. L. Baeck, *Das Wesen des Judentums* (1905 ed.), pp. 1–7, 21–2, 23, 28–9, 30. See also, A. Altmann, *Leo Baeck and the Jewish Mystical Tradition*, and E. Simon, *Brücken*, pp. 385–91.

23. M. Eschelbacher, *Die Synagogengemeinde Duesseldorf*, p. 23; Hildegard Biermann interview, March 25, 1974; Gertrud Gallerski interview, Oct. 30, 1975; report by Antoni Sylwester, Stadtarchivar von Oppeln, Feb. 8, 1960, courtesy of A. S. and M. Dreyfus.

24. Printed text of L. Baeck's sermon, courtesy of A. S. and M. Dreyfus.

25. M. Eschelbacher, *Die Synagogengemeinde Duesseldorf*, pp. 2, 3; Frau Heinrich Grüber interview, June 18, 1974.

26. M. Eschelbacher, *Die Synagogengemeinde Duesseldorf*, pp. 18, 24.

27. Yehoshua Amir interview, June 12, 1975; H. W. Brann, "Leo Baeck," in S. Noveck (ed.), *Great Jewish Thinkers* ..., pp. 137–8.

28. Herman O. Pineas, "Meine Erinnerungen am Dr. Leo Baeck," mss., pp. 1–3, in LBI/NY; Herman O. Pineas interview, Sept. 4, 1975; Sophie Baehr-Pineas interview, June 18, 1975.

29. L. Baeck, "Das Judentum unter den Religionen," published in *Korrespondenz-Blatt*, May 1912, pp. 9–15.

30. Undated memorandum by L. Baeck, courtesy of A. S. and M. Dreyfus; interviews with Charlotte Gichermann, June 6, 1975, and Marianne Loew, June 16, 1975; Charlotte Gichermann, "Rabbiner Dr. Leo Baeck," undated newspaper clipping, courtesy of C. Gichermann. Voice lessons reported in interviews with Herman O. Pineas, Sept. 4, 1975, and Sophie Baehr-Pineas, June 18, 1975.

31. N. Glueck, "Memorial Tribute," in *In Memoriam Leo Baeck*, pp. 12–3; Max Vogelstein interview, Dec. 3, 1974.

32. W. Hamburger, "The Reactions of Reform Jews to the Nazi Rule," in H. A. Strauss and K. R. Grossmann (eds.), *Gegenwart im Rückblick*, p. 150; M. Gruenewald, "The Modern Rabbi," in *LBIY*, 1957, pp. 89–90; Frank F. Rosenthal interview, Jan. 21, 1974.

33. M. Nussbaum, "Ministry Under Stress," in H. A. Strauss and K. R. Grossmann (eds.), *Gegenwart im Rückblick*, p. 241.

34. A. Altmann, "The German Rabbi: 1910–1939," in *LBIY*, 1974, p. 31.

35. H. W. Brann, "Leo Baeck, in S. Noveck (ed.), *Great Jewish Thinkers*, pp. 138–9; E. G. Lowenthal, "Berlin, Fasanenstrasse 79/80," unpaged clipping from *Allgemeine Zeitung des Judentums*, Nov. 1, 1957; M. Davidsohn letter, Aug. 12, 1957, in LBI/NY.

36. *Bericht über die Lehranstalt für die Wissenschaft des Judentums in Berlin*, 1904 ed., p. 19; 1911 ed., p. 18, in LBI/NY. F. Bamberger, "Leo Baeck: The Man and the Idea," in M. Kreutzberger, *Studies of the Leo Baeck Institute*, p. 5. Gymnasium story, Heinz Warschauer interview, Oct. 12, 1973.

37. R. Fuchs, "The 'Hochschule für die Wissenschaft des Judentums' in the Period of Nazi Rule," in *LBIY*, 1967, p. 7; author's visit to building, June 11, 1976; Hans Liebeschütz, "Judaism and History of Religion in Leo Baeck's Work," in *LBIY*, 1957, pp. 12–3; *Bericht über die Lehranstalt für die Wissenschaft des Judentums in Berlin*, 1912 ed., p. 8, in LBI/NY. "Greek and Jewish Preaching," reprinted in L. Baeck, *The Pharisees*, pp. 109–22; quoted lines: pp. 111, 112, 113, 119, 120, 122.

4: FELDRABBINER

1. For the history of the Jews in Berlin, I have used H. Seeliger, "Origins and Growth of the Berlin Jewish Community," in *LBIY*, 1958; M. Lowenthal, *Jews of Germany*; H. G. Adler, *Jews in Germany*; J. R. Marcus, *Jews in the Medieval World*; W. Laqueur, *History of Zionism*; P. Gay, "Encounter with Modernism: German Jews in German Culture, 1888–1914," in *Midstream*, Feb. 1975; E. Herz, *Before the Fury*; E. Hamburger, "Jüdische Parlamentarier in Berlin 1848–1933," in H. A. Strauss and K. R. Grossmann (eds.), *Gegenwart im Rückblick*. "It seems that where you live..." quote, in M. A. Meyer, *Origins of the Modern Jew*, p. 40; "Our Israelite religion..." quote, in I. Schorsch, *Jewish Reactions to German Anti-Semitism*, p. 57 (see also P. Gay/*Midstream* article cited above, p. 34); "blessing and success..." quote, in W. Hamburger, "The Reactions of Reform Jews to the Nazi Rule," in H. A. Strauss and K. R. Grossmann (eds.), *Gegenwart im Rückblick*, p. 151; "Put us to the acid test..." quote, in H. G. Adler, *Jews in Germany*, p. 56; "What are we then?" quote, in

I. Schorsch, *Jewish Reactions to German Anti-Semitism*, p. 61; "more western-ized..." quote, in M. A. Meyer, *Origins of the Modern Jew*, p. 138; "I have lived..." quote, in M. Lowenthal, *Jews of Germany*, p. 266; "rekindle the consciousness..." quote, in H. G. Adler, *Jews in Germany*, p. 99; "...a religious community..." quote, in I. Schorsch, *Jewish Reactions to German Anti-Semitism*, p. 66; "The case of the unfortunate Captain Dreyfus..." quote, in H. Arendt, *Origins of Totalitarianism*, p. 117; "Pogroms could be..." quote, Jeannette Wolff interview, June 25, 1974.

2. H. G. Adler, *Jews in Germany*, pp. 7, 100, 101, 106.

3. P. Gay, "Encounter with Modernism: German Jews in German Culture, 1888–1914," in *Midstream*, Feb. 1975, p. 51; for background on Ballin and Rathenau I used, in addition to general studies, J. R. Marcus, *Rise and Destiny of the German Jew*, p. 115; the P. Gay/*Midstream* article cited above, p. 59; W. G. Plaut, *Growth of Reform Judaism*, pp. 128–9; E. Herz, *Before the Fury*, pp. 216, 241–5; M. Lowenthal, *Jews of Germany*, pp. 321–2.

4. K. R. Grossmann, "Einfuhrung," in H. A. Strauss and K. R. Grossmann (eds.), *Gegenwart im Rückblick*, p. 18; H. G. Adler, *Jews in Germany*, pp. 114–5; E. Herz, *Before the Fury*, pp. 226–8.

5. S. Osborne, *Germany and Her Jews*, pp. 71–2; M. Lowenthal, *Jews of Germany*, p. 285.

6. Cohen quote, in W. G. Plaut, *Growth of Reform Judaism*, p. 78; see also E. Fischoff, "Herman Cohen," in S. Noveck (ed.), *Great Jewish Thinkers...*, pp. 114–5; H. G. Adler, *Jews in Germany*, p. 117.

7. I. Schorsch, *Jewish Reactions to German Anti-Semitism*, p. 27; H. W. Brann, "Leo Baeck," in S. Noveck (ed.), *Great Jewish Thinkers...*, p. 140; Georg Salzberger interview, Aug. 6, 1973; E. Simon quote, "Lerntag," Oct. 21, 1973.

8. L. Baeck, Reports 1 and 2 from the front, courtesy of A. S. and M. Dreyfus.

9. Mordechai Gichon interview, June 19, 1975.

10. Walter H. Herrnstadt letter, Dec. 1914, in *Kriegsbriefe Gefallener deutscher Juden*, pp. 28–9.

11. "Errinerungen an Rabb. Dr. Leo Baeck S.A.," by F. S. N., unidentified clipping, in Hazorea Kibbutz Archives; E. Simon, "Lerntag," Oct. 21, 1973; Israel Neumark interview, June 16, 1975; Walter H. Herrnstadt letter, Dec. 1914, in *Kriegsbriefe gefallener deutscher Juden*, p. 28; Bernardo Kusnitzki, July 1918, in LBI/NY: AR 365, No. 29; Edwin Halle, "Kriegserinnerungen mit Auszuegen aus meinen Tagebuch, 1914–1916," in LBI/NY: M.E. 527, p. 118; L. Baeck, Report 2 from the front, courtesy of A. S. and M. Dreyfus.

12. Sermon text, author's possession.

13. Leo Adam interview, May 26, 1974; Friedrich Brodnitz interview, Feb. 14, 1974.

14. H. G. Adler, *Jews in Germany*, p. 118; interviews with Yehoshua Amir, June 12, 1975, and Frank F. Rosenthal, Jan. 21, 1974.

15. Kurt Fischer interview, June 13, 1975; Kurt Boehm letter to author, Dec. 2, 1974.

16. L. Baeck letter to I. Elbogen, Sept. 21, 1917, LBI/NY: AR-C.254/696.

17. *Gemeindeblatt der Jüdischen Gemeinde zu Berlin*, v. 5 (1915), pp. 5, 6, 16; Herman O. Pineas, "Meine Erinnerungen am Dr. Leo Baeck," unpublished mss., pp. 3–4, in LBI/NY; Herman O. Pineas interview, Sept. 4, 1975; Charlotte Gichermann, "Rabbiner Dr. Leo Baeck," undated newspaper clipping, courtesy of C. Gichermann.

18. Ellen Littmann interview, May 29, 1974; L. Baeck letter to Ruth Baeck, Aug. 18, 1915, courtesy of A. S. and M. Dreyfus.

19. Herman O. Pineas interview, Sept. 4, 1975; Georg Salzberger interview, Aug.

8, 1973; Wolf Schoen reminiscences, in Yad Vashem Archives: 01/229; "With all our ability..." quote, in W. G. Plaut, *Growth of Reform Judaism*, p. 79.

20. R. R. Ruether, *Faith and Fratricide*, pp. 88–9.
21. F. G. Bratton, *Crime of Christendom*, p. 31; E. H. Flannery, *Anguish of the Jews*, pp. 36, 43.
22. R. R. Ruether, *Faith and Fratricide*, pp. 206–7.
23. J. Toland, *Adolf Hitler*, p. 703.
24. I. Maybaum, *Face of God*, p. 25.
25. Painting of Wilhelm I's coronation, by Anton von Werner, and photograph of son being inducted into the army, both reproduced in S. Lorant, *Sieg Heil!* pp. 18–9, 42.
26. E. Herz, *Before the Fury*, p. 215.
27. Hitler photograph reproduced in S. Lorant, *Sieg Heil!* pp. 50–1; A. Hitler, *Mein Kampf*, pp. 161, 164.
28. E. Hamburger, "One Hundred Years of Emancipation," in *LBIY*, 1969, pp. 25–8; S. Adler-Rudel, "East European Jewish Workers in Germany," in *LBIY*, 1957, p. 148. J. Toland, *Adolf Hitler*, pp. 66, 70; A. Hitler, *Mein Kampf*, p. 193.
29. L. Baeck, "Gedenkrede, zur Erinnerung an die Während des Krieges verstorbenen Kuratoren und die im Feld gefallenen Hörer," pp. 12–4.
30. *Gemeindeblatt der Jüdischen Gemeinde zu Berlin*, Aug. 9, 1918, p. 79.
31. L. Baeck, "Gedenkrede, zur Erinnerung an die Während des Krieges verstorbenen Kuratoren und die im Feld gefallenen Hörer," pp. 3, 4.
32. L. Baeck letter to M. Buber, Sept. 24, 1918 (with attachment), in LBI/NY: AR 2269 "B" Buber, Martin No. 1.

5: COMMUNITY

1. W. Maser, *Hitler's Letters and Notes*, pp. 213–6.
2. I. Schorsch, *Jewish Reactions to German Anti-Semitism*, p. 166; E. Helmreich, *Religious Education in German Schools*, pp. 147–9; J. R. Marcus, *Rise and Destiny of the German Jew*, p. 2; R. L. Pierson, "German Jewish Identity...", pp. 4, 5, 6, 13.
3. "Unbelievable cultural glamour" quote, Henry J. Kellermann interview, March 26, 1976; M. Lowenthal, *Jews of Germany*, pp. 333, 335; "Indeed there were far more..." quote, in W. Laqueur, *Weimar–A Cultural History*, pp. 72–3; "Yes, there was always..." quote, in O. Friedrich, *Before the Deluge*, p. 98.
4. M. Lowenthal, *Jews of Germany*, pp. 190–1; "The Jewish Community in the Post-Emancipation Period," in *LBIY*, 1957, pp. 47n, 59; A. Altmann, "The German Rabbi: 1910–1939," in *LBIY*, 1974, p. 40; Alexander Altmann interview, Oct. 14, 1975.
5. L. Baeck, "In Memory of Two of Our Dead," in *LBIY*, 1956, p. 51; Eva G. Reichmann interview, May 27, 1974; J. R. Marcus, *Rise and Destiny of the German Jew*, p. 94.
6. I. Schorsch, *Jewish Reactions to German Anti-Semitism*, pp. 15–6, 18; J. R. Marcus, *Rise and Destiny of the German Jew*, p. 227.
7. E. Herz, *Before the Fury*, p. 240.
8. D. McLellan, *Karl Marx*, p. 1; I. Schorsch, *Jewish Reactions to German Anti-Semitism*, pp. 5–8, 137–9; H. G. Adler, *Jews in Germany*, pp. 4–5, 107; J. R. Marcus, *Rise and Destiny of the German Jew*, p. 246; H. Arendt, *Origins of Totalitarianism*, p. 73; M. Eschelbacher, *Die synagogengemeinde Duesseldorf*, p. 6; J. Katz, *Exclusiveness and Tolerance*, p. 195.

9. P. Gay, "Encounter with Modernism: German Jews in German Culture, 1888–1914," in *Midstream*, Feb. 1975, pp. 24–5, 60.

10. "I felt I was a good German..." quote, Mordechai Gichon interview, June 19, 1975; F. Rosenzweig quote, in I. Maybaum, *Face of God*, pp. 51–2 (see also F. Rosenzweig letters printed in W. G. Plaut, *Growth of Reform Judaism*, pp. 129–30); M. Buber quote, in H. G. Adler, *Jews in Germany*, p. 139.

11. Shoshana Ronen interview, June 18, 1975; Leo Adam interview, May 26, 1974; Joachim Prinz interview, May 1, 1974; W. Gunther Plaut interview, May 13, 1975.

12. "private conversations with God" quote, F. Bamberger, "Leo Baeck: The Man and the Idea," in M. Kreutzberger, *Studies of the Leo Baeck Institute*, p. 4; "der Fahrstuhl," Heinz Warschauer interview, Oct. 12, 1973; Joachim Prinz interview, May 1, 1974; "His rabbinical bag..." quote, F. Bamberger citation above, pp. 3–4; "very husky, a..." quote, Herman Schaalman interview, Nov. 10, 1973; "it was something different..." quote, in untitled mss., Rudolf Simons Coll., LBI/NY; "The high point..." quote, in Conrad Rosenstein, "Der Brunnen-Eine Familienchronick," LBI/NY: M.E. 295; also Henry J. Kellermann interview, March 26, 1976; Helmuth H. Galliner interview, Dec. 9, 1974.

13. M. Buber quote, in A. Hodes, *Martin Buber*, p. 119; L. Baeck quote, "Religion und Erziehung," reprinted in L. Baeck, *Wege im Judentum*, pp. 1–3. *Bericht über die Lehranstalt für die Wissenschaft des Judentums in Berlin*, 1913 ed., p. 53, in LBI/NY.

14. Fritz Bamberger interview, Oct. 18, 1974; "America still was..." quote, Jacob R. Marcus interview, Apr. 18, 1977; "bitter early" quote, W. Gunther Plaut interview, May 13, 1975; "That was his kindness" quote, Ignaz Maybaum interview, May 29, 1974; "You may speak..." quote, Wolli Kaelter interview, Apr. 22, 1976; "Only God could possibly..." quote, in M. E. Swarsenky, "Out of the Root of Rabbis," in H. A. Strauss and K. R. Grossmann (eds.), *Gegenwart im Rückblick*, pp. 220–2; "Much of what you said..." quote, Heinz Warschauer interview, Oct. 12, 1973; "Your sermon is very good..." quote, in N. Glueck, "Memorial Tribute," in *In Memoriam Leo Baeck*, p. 19; also interviews with Israel Neumark, June 16, 1975, and Gustav Horn, June 16, 1975.

15. Fritz Bamberger interview, Oct. 18, 1974; Fritz Friedländer, "Grösse, Güte, Unerbittlichkeit—Enige Erinnerungen an Leo Baeck," unpublished ms., courtesy, H. I. Bach, pp. 1–2; Wolli Kaelter interview, Apr. 22, 1976; Manfred E. Swarsensky interview, Nov. 15, 1974; Leo Lichtenberg interview, Apr. 19, 1977; Emil Fackenheim interview, Oct. 10, 1973; Joachim Prinz interview, May 1, 1974.

16. Ellen Littmann interview, May 29, 1974; Perle Gold (nee Haskel) letter to author, July 10, 1974.

17. E. Littmann, "Der Lehrer," in *MB* (*Mitteilungsblatt*), May 18, 1953, p. 4; Ellen Littmann interview, May 29, 1974; Yehoshua Amir interview, June 12, 1975; Max Vogelstein interview, Dec. 3, 1974; Fritz Bamberger interview, Oct. 18, 1974; F. Bamberger, "Leo Baeck: The Man and the Idea," in M. Kreutzberger, *Studies of the Leo Baeck Institute*, pp. 5–7; F. Friedländer, "Hours I Spent with Rabbi Baeck," in *AJR Information*, Nov. 1970, p. 6; M. E. Swarsensky, "Out of the Root of Rabbis," in H. A. Strauss and K. R. Grossmann (eds.), *Gegenwart im Rückblick*, p. 220.

18. "It's a good thing..." quote, Ignaz Maybaum interview, May 29, 1974; "a great 'Jeinsager'" quote, Wolli Kaelter interview, Apr. 22, 1976; "You are absolutely right" story, Henry J. Kellermann interview, March 26, 1976; M. Gruenewald, "Leo Baeck: Witness and Judge," in *Judaism*, 1957, p. 196; Max

Gruenewald interview, May 1, 1974; "I told him..." quote, in M. Gerson, "Verstehen im Humanismus," in *AJR Information*, undated supplement entitled "In Memory of Leo Baeck," p. 11.

19. Theodore Wiener interview, Oct. 18, 1973; K. Wilhelm, "The Jewish Community in the Post-Emancipation Period," in *LBIY*, 1957; pp. 67–8; L. Baeck letter to I. Elbogen, Dec. 14, 1922, in LBI/NY: AR-C.254/696: G. Lotan, "The Zentralwohlfahrtsstelle," in *LBIY*, 1959, pp. 193–4; "His strong and influential position..." quote, in S. Moses, "The Impact of Leo Baeck's Personality on His Contemporaries, *LBIY*, 1957, pp. 4–6.

20. "Money alone..." quote, Frank F. Rosenthal interview, Jan. 21, 1974; 1928 B'nai B'rith meeting report, *Zum Jährigen Bestehen des Ordens Bne Briss in Deutschland*, pp. 53–4. Same citation, pp. 32–8; F. Goldschmidt, "Der Auteil der deutschen Juden an der Gründung und Entwicklung des ordens B'nai B'rith," in *Festschrift zum 80. Geburtstag von Leo Baeck Am 23. Mai 1953*, pp. 58–9; L. Baeck letter to M. Dienemann, May 19, 1928, in LB Briefe, Max Dienemann folder, LBI/NY; L. Baeck to M. Buber, Aug. 29, 1930, in JNL: Buber Coll. 75; Werner J. Cahnman interview, Feb. 24, 1975; A. Loewenstamm, "The Grand President of the B'nai B'rith in Germany," in E. G. Reichmann, *Wortes des Gedenkens*, pp. 195–6.

21. Manfred E. Swarsensky interview, Nov. 15, 1974; Hans I. Bach, unpublished lecture, courtesy of H. I. Bach; Fritz Bamberger, "Julius Guttmann—Philosopher of Judaism," in *LBIY*, 1960, pp. 11–2; K. Stendahl, from the introduction to L. Baeck, *Pharisees*, p. xvi.

22. *Franz Rosenzweig: Eine Gedenkschrift*, p. 5; Ernst Simon, "Lerntag"; Nahum N. Glatzer interview, Aug. 21, 1974; Ignaz Maybaum interview, May 29, 1974.

23. Heinz Warschauer interview, Oct. 12, 1973; Fritz Friedländer, "Grösse, Güte, Unerbittlichkeit—Einige Erinnerungen an Leo Baeck," unpublished mss., courtesy of H. I. Bach, pp. 3–4.

24. Fritz Friedländer, "Hours I Spent with Rabbi Baeck," in *AJR Information*, Nov. 1970, p. 6; H. G. Adler interview, May 25, 1974; David H. Wice interview, March 12, 1975; L. Baeck, "Judaism: Revolution and Rebirth," in *Synagogue Review*, Nov. 1964, pp. 52–3; "read the reviews" story, in F. Friedländer, "Hours I Spent with Rabbi Baeck," *AJR Information*, Nov. 1970, p. 6; "He is a well-tailored man" quote, Georg Salzberger interview, Aug. 6, 1973; "You might have done..." quote, in Fritz Friedländer, "Grösse, Güte, Unerbittlichkeit—Einige Erinnergungen an Leo Baeck," unpublished mss., courtesy of H. I. Bach, p. 6; Friedrich Brodnitz interview, Feb. 14, 1974. Also interviews with Max Gruenewald, May 1, 1974; Leo Adam, May 26, 1974; Joachim Prinz, May 1, 1974; Henry J. Kellermann, March 26, 1976.

25. W. Gunther Plaut interview, May 13, 1975; B. Manuel interview, June 5, 1974; United States trips: Leo Adam interview, May 26, 1974, and L. Baeck's notes on his trips, courtesy of A. S. and M. Dreyfus; Herbert A. Strauss interview, Nov. 11, 1973; Ernst Simon interview, May 30, 1975; Else Mediner, "Ein Wort des Dankes," in *In Memory of Leo Baeck*, p. 11; Frank F. Rosenthal interview, Jan. 21, 1974.

26. Joachim Prinz interview, May 1, 1974; Eva G. Reichmann, "Address Given at the Celebration of Rabbi Dr. Leo Baeck's 100th Birthday," p. 2, text courtesy of E. G. Reichmann; "He would sit..." quote, Ernst G. Lowenthal interview, June 18, 1974.

27. Fritz Bamberger interview, Oct. 18, 1974; H. Keyserling (ed.), *Book of Marriage*, pp. iii, ix–x; L. Baeck, "Marriage as Mystery and Command," in H. Keyserling

citation above, pp. 464, 468, 470; "gave him the possibility..." quote, Benjamin Jeremias interview, June 13, 1975. Also interviews with Shoshana Ronen, June 18, 1975; Henry J. Kellermann, March 26, 1976; Leo Adam, May 26, 1974; Betty Cohen interview, June 14, 1975.

28. Leo Adam interview, May 26, 1974; Frederick J. Perlstein interview, Oct. 18, 1976; Natalie Baeck letter, Aug. 24, 1921, courtesy of A. S. and M. Dreyfus; Henry J. Kellermann interview, March 26, 1976.

29. Baeck family letters to H. Berlak, March 3, 1921, courtesy of A. S. and M. Dreyfus; Benjamin Jeremias interview, June 13, 1975; L. Baeck letter to H. and R. Berlak, Aug. 26, 1923, courtesy of A. S. and M. Dreyfus.

30. Natalie Baeck to H. and R. Berlak, Aug. 12, 1926; L. Baeck to H. and R. Berlak, Aug. 2, 1928, courtesy of A. S. and M. Dreyfus; M. Dreyfus, "Leo Baeck," mss. courtesy of M. Dreyfus, p. 1; Betty Cohen interview, June 14, 1975; Leo Adam interview, May 26, 1974; Mordechai Gichon interview, June 19, 1975.

31. *Gemeindeblatt der Jüdischen Gemeinde zu Berlin*, Aug. 9, 1918, p. 84; apartment description: interviews with Theodore Wiener, Oct. 18, 1973, and Fritz Bamberger, Oct. 18, 1974; Paul Rosenstein, "Leo Baeck as Patient," undated newspaper clipping, in LBI/NY: AR 365, No. 15.

32. L. Baeck's *tefillin*, his black-and-white head coverings, and his white *tallith* are in LBI/NY: L. Baeck folder no. 2; Mordechai Gichon interview, Feb. 14, 1974; Leo Adam interview, May 26, 1974; Ilse Blumenthal-Weiss interview, Oct. 15, 1974; "Always wear a robe..." quote, Wolli Kaelter interview, Apr. 22, 1976; Joachim Prinz interview, May 1, 1974; "The rituals have a..." quote, Alexander Altmann interview, Oct. 15, 1975.

33. Ernst Ludwig Ehrlich interview, June 4, 1974; Jeannette Wolff, June 25, 1974; W. G. Plaut, *Growth of Reform Judaism*, pp. 67–8, 68–73, 74; Friedrich Brodnitz interview, Feb. 14, 1974; L. H. Montagu, "Rabbi Dr. Leo Baeck—A Memorial Tribute," in *Liberal Jewish Monthly*, Dec. 1956, p. 183.

34. History of World Union and L. Baeck's involvement, in W. G. Plaut, *Growth of Reform Judaism*, pp. 89–91; L. H. Montagu, "Memorial Tribute," in E. G. Reichmann, *Wortes des Gedenkens*, pp. 199–200. Also L. Baeck letter to L. H. Montagu, July 20, 1926, courtesy of Wiener Library; Henry J. Kellermann interview, March 26, 1976; Friedrich Brodnitz interview, Feb. 14, 1974.

35. "Judaism is a unique happening..." quote, Hans I. Bach unpublished lecture, courtesy of H. I. Bach; *Israelitisches Familienblatt* photograph, courtesy of Charlotte Gichermann; S. Moses, "The Impact of Leo Baeck's Personality on His Contemporaries," *LBIY*, 1957, p. 6; M. Rosenbluth, *Go Forth and Serve*, pp. 234–5; Gershom Scholem interview, Oct. 14, 1975; "Who of us is not sure..." speech text, reprinted in *Allgemeine*, Nov. 2, 1956, pp. 1–2; "startled and incredulous" quote, in L. Baeck, "In Memory of Two of Our Dead," *LBIY*, 1956, p. 53. Also, H. Liebeschütz, "Between Past and Future—Leo Baeck's Historical Position," *LBIY*, 1966, p. 14.

36. Perle Gold interview, July 1, 1975; A. Leschnitzer, "Die Geburt des 'Modernen' Antisemitismus aus dem Geist der Neuzeit," in *Ten Years—American Federation of Jews from Central Europe, Inc., 1941–1951*, p. 70; J. R. Marcus, *Rise and Destiny of the German Jew*, pp. 80–1; "That hatred for Jews..." quote, in H. G. Adler, *Jews in Germany*, p. 142; "The Church must have eyes..." quote, in R. Grunberger, *12-Year Reich*, pp. 482–3; W. Laqueur, *Weimar—A Cultural History*, pp. 17, 183–4, 193; H. G. Adler, *Jews in Germany*, pp. 125–6, 127; R. Grunberger, *12-Year Reich*, pp. 15, 335–7, 339; E. G. Reichmann, *Hostages*

of Civilization, pp. 154–5; P. Gay, *Weimar Culture,* pp. 3, 20; R. L. Pierson, "German Jewish Identity . . .", p. 24.

37. L. Baeck, "Gedenkrede, zur Erinnerung an die Während des Krieges verstorbenen Kuratoren und die im Felde gefallenen Hörer," pp. 4–7.

38. W. Laqueur, *Weimar—A Cultural History,* pp. 25–6.

39. "the religious sentimentality . . ." quote, Max Gruenewald interview, May 1, 1974.

40. H. J. Morgenthau, "The Tragedy of German-Jewish Liberalism," in M. Kreutzberger, *Studies of the Leo Baeck Institute,* pp. 50–1; E. Herz, *Before the Fury,* pp. 262–3; Georg Salzberger interview, Aug. 6, 1973; K. R. Grossmann, "Einfuhrung," in H. A. Strauss and K. R. Grossmann (eds.), *Gegenwart im Rückblick,* p. 17.

41. C. Seligmann, "Mein Leben," in LBI/NY: M.E. 369, pp. 128–9.

6: FIGHTER

1. L. Baeck, "Judaism in the Church," in L. Baeck, *Pharisees,* p. 77.

2. L. Baeck, "The Gospel as a Document of History," in L. Baeck, *Judaism and Christianity,* p. 101.

3. L. Baeck, "Essay on Neutrality," quoted in A. J. Friedlander, *Leo Baeck—Teacher of Theresienstadt,* p. 105.

4. L. Baeck, "The 'Son of Man,'" in L. Baeck, *Judaism and Christianity,* p. 29; L. Baeck, "The Gospel as a Document of History," in L. Baeck, *Judaism and Christianity,* pp. 65–6.

5. L. Baeck, "Jewish Mysticism," in *Journal of Jewish Studies,* v. 2, no. 1, undated, p. 4; L. Baeck, "Romantic Religion," in L. Baeck, *Judaism and Christianity,* pp. 204, 211, 259.

6. A. Altmann, *Leo Baeck and the Jewish Mystical Tradition,* p. 6.

7. K. Wilhelm, "Leo Baeck and Jewish Mysticism," in *Judaism,* Spring 1962, pp. 123–30.

8. L. Baeck, *Essence of Judaism,* 1961 ed., pp. 95, 191.

9. L. Baeck, speech before Vereinigung der liberalen Rabbiner Deutschlands in Berlin, in *Liberales Judentum,* 1922, p. 19.

10. "Es ist ein altes . . ." quote, L. Baeck, *Wesen des Judentum,* 1922 ed., p. ix; "Whenever the hidden . . ." quote, in *Essence of Judaism,* 1961 ed., pp. 92, 104; "und Israel war . . ." quote, *Wesen des Judentums,* 1905 ed., p. 41, and 1922 ed., p. 59.

11. L. Baeck, *Essence of Judaism,* 1961 ed., pp. 273, 274, 275.

For other discussions of Leo Baeck and his changing attitude toward mysticism see E. Simon, *Brücken,* pp. 385–91, and A. Altmann, *Leo Baeck and the Jewish Mystical Tradition.*

7: ENEMY

1. J. Fest, *Hitler,* p. 211; I. Maybaum, *Face of God,* p. 17; J. Flanner, "Führer," *New Yorker,* March 14, 1936, p. 26; J. Toland, *Adolf Hitler,* p. 49; A. Hitler, *Mein Kampf,* pp. 180, 184.

2. H. G. Adler, *Jews in Germany,* pp. 81–4; E. Herz, *Before the Fury,* pp. 110, 156–7; M. Lowenthal, *Jews of Germany,* pp. 355–6; "Pre-Fascist Groups in Germany, 1918–1933," in NA: OSS Record Group 59, R&A 1789.

3. A. Hitler, *Mein Kampf,* pp. 56, 61, 63, 338, 403, 427, 338–9, 306, 148, 430.

4. David Greenberg, in *Condition of Jewish Belief*, p. 86.
5. H. G. Adler, *Jews in Germany*, p. 129.
6. J. Toland, *Adolf Hitler*, pp. 216, 359; W. Kempowski, *Did You Ever See Hitler?*, p. 14; J. Fest, *Hitler*, pp. 522, 155; Hitler quotes: J. Toland, *Adolf Hitler*, p. 222, and J. Fest, *Hitler*, pp. 240–1; J. Fest, *Hitler*, pp. 444–5.
7. NA: RG 165:2657-B-754.
8. J. Fest, *Hitler*, pp. 323–4; L. Baeck, "Staat, Familie und Individualität," in *Jüdische Wohlfahrtspflege und Sozialpolitik*, 1932, pp. 192–4.
9. L. Baeck, "Die Schöpfung des Mitmenschen," in *Soziale Ethik im Judentum*, 1914, p. 11; A. Hitler, *Mein Kampf*, pp. 44, 4; L. Baeck, "Gedanken zur Abrüstung," in *Völkerbund die Abrüstungskonferenz*, pp. 3–4.
10. L. Baeck letter to von Veltheim, June 19, 1932, courtesy of A. S. and M. Dreyfus; W. Laqueur, *Weimar–A Cultural History*, p. 255; M. Hay, *Europe and the Jews*, p. 301.

8: STRUGGLE

1. "Das Ende des..." quote, in K. J. Ball-Kaduri, *Vor der Katastrophe*, p. 12, and R. Weltsch, "Twenty-Five Years After," in *AJR Information*, Nov. 1963, p. 1, among others; Robert Weltsch interview, May 31, 1974. L. Baeck, "Gedenken an Zwei Tote," undated reprint from *LBIY*, pp. 309–10.
2. L. Palmer, *Change Lobsters and Dance*, pp. 55, 59; D. Farrer, *Warburgs*, pp. 112–3; R. L. Pierson, "German Jewish Identity...", p. 286; W. G. Plaut, *Growth of Reform Judaism*, p. 133; W. Rosenstock, "Exodus 1933–1939," undated reprint from *LBIY*, p. 387n; M. Rosenbluth, *Go Forth and Serve*, pp. 243–4.
3. L. Baeck, "Plan Eines Judischen Konkordats," in *Bulletin für die Mitglieder der Gesellschaft der Freunde des Leo Baeck Institute*, 1957, p. 14.
4. S. Adler-Rudel, *Jüdische Selbsthilfe*, pp. 4, 5, 7; K. R. Grossmann, "What Happened to the German Jews? A Balance Sheet," in *Ten Years—American Federation of Jews From Central Europe, Inc.*, *1941–1951*, p. 44; A. Myerson and I. Goldberg, *German Jew*, p. xi; S. Osborne, *Germany and Her Jews*, p. 20; R. Grunberger, *12-Year Reich*, p. 505; Herbert Kahn, "Umfang und Bedeutung der judischen Einzelhandelsbetriebe," mss., in LBI/NY, dated Feb. 1, 1934, pp. 4–8; H. G. Adler, *Jews in Germany*, p. 132.
5. M. Kreutzberger interview, June 3, 1974; H. Gaertner, "Problems of Jewish Schools in Germany During the Hitler Regime," in *LBIY*, 1956, pp. 124–5; L. Palmer, *Change Lobsters and Dance*, pp. 43–4.
6. L. Baeck, "Gedenken an Zwei Tote," undated reprint from *LBIY*, p. 309; R. Grunberger, *12-Year Reich*, pp. 17–8; E. G. Reichmann, *Hostages of Civilisation*, pp. 221–2; T. Ferrer, "Rosemary Park," in *Saturday Review*, Apr. 20, 1963; p. 67; W. von Braun quote, in O. Friedrich, *Before the Deluge*, p. 275 (also see *N.Y. Times* obituary of von Braun, June 18, 1977, p. 1); R. Strauss quote, in R. Weltsch, "Introduction," *LBIY*, 1958, pp. xvi–xvii; F. von Papen, *Memoirs*, p. 285, 260; L. Palmer, *Change Lobsters and Dance*, p. 60; J. Toland, *Adolf Hitler*, p. 315; W. Maser, *Hitler*, p. 268; R. Weltsch, "Introduction," to S. Adler-Rudel, *Jüdische Selbsthilfe*, p. ix.
7. Von Veltheim letters to L. Baeck, July 5, 1932, and March 3, 1933, courtesy of A. S. and M. Dreyfus; L. Palmer, *Change Lobsters and Dance*, p. 301; L. Baeck letter to von Veltheim, Feb. 28, 1933, courtesy of A. S. and M. Dreyfus; N. Bentwich, *My 77 Years*, p. 126.
8. L. Baeck, "Recht und Pflicht!" in *C.V. Zeitung*, March 2, 1933, p. 1; L. Baeck letter to von Veltheim, March 2, 1933, courtesy of A. S. and M. Dreyfus; Robert

Weltsch interview, May 31, 1974; L. S. Dawidowicz, *War Against the Jews,* p. 177.

9. L. Baeck, "A People Stands Before Its God," in E. H. Boehm, *We Survived,* pp. 284–5; L. Baeck, "Gedenken an Zwei Tote," undated reprint from *LBIY,* pp. 310–11; Georg Salzberger interview, Aug. 6, 1973; L. S. Dawidowicz, *War Against the Jews,* p. 170.

10. Frederick J. Perlstein interview, Oct. 18, 1976.

11. NA: RG 165:2657-B-801/B; E. Herzfeld, "Meine Letzten Jahre in Deutschland," in LBI/NY: M.E. 163, p. 4; M. Rosenbluth, *Go Forth and Serve,* pp. 251–4.

12. J. R. Marcus, *Rise and Destiny of the German Jew,* pp. 8–11; L. S. Dawidowicz, *War Against the Jews,* pp. 177–8.

13. Berlin community letter, printed in S. Adler-Rudel, *Jüdische Selbsthilfe,* p. 84; J. Prinz, "A Rabbi Under the Hitler Regime," in H. A. Strauss and K. R. Grossmann (eds.), *Gegenwart im Rückblick,* pp. 232–3; R. Weltsch editorial, printed in W. G. Plaut, *Growth of Reform Judaism,* pp. 131–3; L. Baeck, "Leo Baeck zum Boykott-Tag," in *AJR Information,* April 1973, p. 3.

14. L. Baeck, "Leo Baeck zum Boykott-Tag," in *AJR Information,* April 1973, p. 3.

15. A. Elon, *The Israelis,* pp. 68–9.

16. L. S. Dawidowicz, *War Against the Jews,* pp. 171–2; L. Baeck, "In Memory of Two of Our Dead," in *LBIY,* 1956, pp. 51–2; also, H. G. Reissner, "The Histories of 'Kaufhaus N. Israel' and of Wilfred Israel," in *LBIY,* 1958, pp. 249–50; M. Gruenewald, "The Beginning of the 'Reichsvertretung'," in *LBIY,* 1956, pp. 59–60.

17. L. Baeck, "Gedenken an Zwei Tote," undated reprint from *LBIY,* p. 311; "The German-Jewish Question," in Institut für Zeitgeschichte: MA 108 (a copy also is at LBI/J); Franz Meyer, OHP, 00264, in Hebrew University, Institute of Contemporary Jewry; Hans-Erich Fabian, "Zur Enstehung der 'Reichsveinigung der Juden in Deutschland'," in H. A. Strauss and K. R. Grossmann (eds.), *Gegenwart im Rückblick,* p. 168; Reichsvertretung meeting minutes, June 16, 1933, in LBI/J: Folder A, Item A48; Reichsvertretung meeting minutes, June 25, 1933, in Central Archives for the History of the Jewish People: Hamburg Community Archives, AHW/871.

18. For Reichsvertretung organization I have used K. J. Ball-Kaduri, "The National Representation of Jews in Germany—Obstacles and Accomplishments at Its Establishment," p. 159 et. seq., which includes mss. by Ernst Herzfeld and Franz Meyer, in *Yad Vashem Studies,* 1958; also Hans-Erich Fabian, "Zur Enstehung der 'Reichsvereinigung der Juden in Deutschland'," in H. A. Strauss and K. R. Grossmann (eds.), *Gegenwart im Rückblick,* p. 168; L. Baeck, "Gedenken an Zwei Tote," undated reprint from *LBIY,* p. 311; also in LBI/NY: AR.C.A. 103 221 for correspondence relating to events of the summer and early fall of 1933, as well as the meeting minutes.

For the choosing of Baeck as leader I have used the above material plus the following interviews: Joachim Prinz, May 1, 1974; Max Kreutzberger, June 3, 1974; Ernst G. Lowenthal, June 18, 1974; and Friedrich Brodnitz, Feb. 14, 1974; also, *Jüdische Rundschau,* Sept. 20, 1933.

Material on Otto Hirsch included, in addition to the above material, *Otto Hirsch—Ein Lebensweg,* unpaged; *Jüdische Rundschau,* Sept. 20, 1933; Ernst Simon interview, May 30, 1975; Hirsch friend quoted is Leopold Marx, "Zur Grundsteiglegung für Jad Otto Hirsch," text of speech presented April 9, 1958, courtesy of Charlotte Gichermann; Theodor Heuss letter to R. Berlak, Nov. 2, 1956, courtesy of A. S. and M. Dreyfus.

19. L. Baeck, *Essence of Judaism*, 1961 ed., pp. 180, 248–9; L. Baeck, *This People Israel*, pp. 169–70, 196.

9: RESISTANCE

1. "all the great organizations..." quote, in LBI/NY: AR.C.A. 103 211; I. Elbogen quote, in I. Elbogen, *Century of Jewish Life*, p. 651. Also Hans-Erich Fabian, "Zur Enstehung der 'Reichsvereinigung der Juden in Deutschland,'" in H. A. Strauss and K. R. Grossmann (eds.), *Gegenwart im Rückblick*, pp. 173–4; Max Gruenewald, "The Beginning of the 'Reichsvertretung,'" in *LBIY*, 1956, pp. 60–7.

2. L. Baeck letter to C. Weizmann, Sept. 29, 1933, in LBI/NY: LB Briefe, Chaim Weizmann folder; Friedrich Brodnitz interview, Feb. 14, 1974; Joachim Prinz interview, June 3, 1975; also interviews with Werner Rosenstock, May 30, 1974, and Rudolf Callmann, May 1, 1974; untitled article by Julius Brodnitz, in *C.V. Zeitung*, Sept. 20, 1933, p. 1, and untitled clipping from *Jüdische Rundschau*, Feb. 27, 1934; Hans-Erich Fabian, "Zur Enstehung der 'Reichsvereinigung der Juden in Deutschland'," in H. A. Strauss and K. R. Grossmann (eds.), *Gegenwart im Rückblick*, p. 174; various Reichsvertretung correspondence, in LBI/NY: AR.C.A. 103 221.

3. A. Leschnitzer, "Der unbekannte Leo Baeck," in *Aufbau*, Nov. 30, 1956, p. 15; also interviews with Adolf Leschnitzer, Oct. 28, 1975; Friedrich Brodnitz, Feb. 14, 1974; Eva G. Reichmann, May 27, 1974; Ernst G. Lowenthal, June 18, 1974; Rudolf Callmann, May 1, 1974; Max Kreutzberger, June 3, 1974; Fritz Bamberger, Oct. 18, 1974.

4. L. Baeck, "Gedenken an Zwei Tote," undated reprint from *LBIY*, pp. 311–2; L. Baeck, "In Memory of Two of Our Dead," *LBIY*, 1956, p. 54; E. Simon, "Jewish Adult Education in Nazi Germany as Spiritual Resistance," in *LBIY*, 1956, pp. 72–3; *Otto Hirsch—Ein Lebensweg*, unpaged. Also, S. Moses, "The Impact of Leo Baeck's Personality on His Contemporaries," *LBIY*, 1957, pp. 6–7.

5. "Allow us to present you..." document, in LBI/NY: 5(221); other papers related to this document are in Institut für Zeitgeschichte: MA 108; Auswärtiges Amt: Dienstgebaude, Bestand Inland, II A/B Nr. 39/1; also see L. S. Dawidowicz, *War Against the Jews*, pp. 184–6.

6. Auswärtiges Amt: Dienstgebaude, Bestand Inland, II A/B Nr. 39/1; *Jüdische Rundschau*, May 18, 1934, p. 3.

7. H. L. Feingold, *Politics of Rescue*, pp. 11, 5.

8. L. Baeck, "In Memory of Two of Our Dead," *LBIY*, 1956, p. 54; "What was at stake..." quote, in E. Simon, "Jewish Adult Education in Nazi Germany as Spiritual Resistance," in *LBIY*, 1956, p. 98; "I was brought up..." quote, in A. Hodes, *Martin Buber*, p. 105; Central Archives for the History of the Jewish People: Hamburg Community Archives, AHW/871; E. Helmrich, *Religious Education in German Schools*, p. 202.

9. Max Vogelstein interview, Dec. 3, 1974; "Buber became very..." quote, Ignaz Maybaum interview, May 29, 1974; L. Baeck letter to M. Buber, June 14, 1932, in JNL: Buber Coll. 75; E. Simon quote, "Lerntag."

10. Buber quotes in F. Friedländer, "Trials and Tribulations of Jewish Education in Nazi Germany," *LBIY*, 1958, pp. 187–8; E. Simon, "Jewish Adult Education in Nazi Germany as Spiritual Resistance," in *LBIY*, 1956, pp. 68–9.

11. M. Buber, *Briefwechsel aus sieben Jahrzehnten*, v. 2; "He spoke very clearly..." quote in H. Gerson letter to M. Buber, June 13, 1933, p. 486; L. Baeck letter to M. Buber, June 21, 1933, p. 491. Buber responses in JNL: Buber Coll. 75/1,

both dated June 22, 1933; "has obviously handled..." quote in M. Buber letter to H. Gerson, June 23, 1933; M. Buber, *Briefwechsel aus sieben Jahrzehnten*, v. 2, p. 494; L. Baeck letter to M. Buber, Dec. 14, 1933, and M. Buber letter to L. Baeck, Feb. 23, 1934, both in JNL: Buber Coll. 75/1. Also see I. Elbogen, *Century of Jewish Life*, p. 650.

12. H. Gaertner, "Problems of Jewish Schools in Germany During the Hitler Regime," in *LBIY*, 1956, pp. 125–8; E. Simon, "Jewish Adult Education in Nazi Germany as Spiritual Resistance," in *LBIY*, 1956, pp. 81–4; American Joint Distribution Committee, "Activities... 1937," p. 50.

13. F. Friedländer, "Trials and Tribulations of Jewish Education in Nazi Germany," in *LBIY*, 1958, p. 199; L. S. Dawidowicz, *War Against the Jews*, p. 190.

14. G. Lotan, "The Zentralwohlfahrtsstelle," *LBIY*, 1958, pp. 203–4; American Joint Distribution Committee, "Activities... 1937," p. 65; Frederick J. Perlstein interview, Oct. 18, 1976.

15. American Joint Distribution Committee, "Activities... 1937," p. 38; also E. Helmreich, *Religious Education in German Schools*, pp. 201–2; W. Hamburger, "The Reactions of Reform Jews to the Nazi Rule," in H. A. Strauss and K. R. Grossmann (eds.), *Gegenwart im Rückblick*, pp. 158–60; S. Schiratzki, "The Rykestrasse School in Berlin—A Jewish Elementary School During the Hitler Period," *LBIY*, 1960, pp. 300–3.

16. "We had a university..." quote, in A. Guttmann, "Hochschule Retrospective," *CCAR Journal*, Autumn 1972, p. 77; "The number of inefficient..." and "We were a small community..." quotes and external student figures, in R. Fuchs, "The 'Hochschule für die Wissenschaft des Judentums' in the Period of Nazi Rule," *LBIY*, 1967, p. 20; student ratings, American Joint Distribution Committee, "Activities... 1937," p. 60; "Our Talmud discussions..." quote, in A. Guttmann, "Hochschule Retrospective," *CCAR Journal*, Autumn 1972, p. 75; Alexander Guttmann interview, April 19, 1977; W. Hamburger, "Leo Baeck—The Last Teacher of the Lehranstalt," in *Paul Lazarus-Gedenkbuch*, p. 125; Emil Fackenheim interview, Oct. 10, 1973. Also Frau Ismar Elbogen, "Die Hochschule für die Wissenschaft des Judentums in Berlin in den Jahren 1933–38," an unpublished mss., Yad Vashem: 01/140.

17. R. Fuchs, "The 'Hochschule für die Wissenschaft des Judentums' in the Period of Nazi Rule," in *LBIY*, 1967, pp. 8–9; "Formerly we were a Hochschule..." quote, O. Lehmann letter, *AJR Information*, Feb. 1964, p. 12, and Leo Lichtenberg interview, April 19, 1977.

18. "Our students live..." quote, L. Baeck letter to Dr. Kaufmann, Feb. 25, 1936, courtesy of A. S. and M. Dreyfus; Hochschule budget, American Joint Distribution Committee, "Activities... 1937," p. 53; R. Fuchs, "The 'Hochschule für die Wissenschaft des Judentums' in the Period of Nazi Rule," *LBIY*, 1967, pp. 13–4, 23; E. Simon quote and Hochschule report, in E. Simon, "Jewish Adult Education in Nazi Germany as Spiritual Resistance," *LBIY*, 1956, pp. 84–5. Also Etta Japha interview, Nov. 12, 1973.

19. G. Lotan, "The Zentralwohlfahrtsstelle," in *LBIY*, 1959, pp. 195–7, 201–3, 205–6; American Joint Distribution Committee, "Activities... 1937," pp. 29–31, 33.

20. American Joint Distribution Committee, "Activities... 1937," pp. 1–2, 8, 55, 58, 83; Cora Berliner report, LBI/NY: 24 (1578); Friedrich Brodnitz interview, Feb. 14, 1974; Hans-Erich Fabian, "Zur Enstehung der 'Reichsvertretung der Juden in Deutschland'," in H. A. Strauss and K. R. Grossmann (eds.), *Gegenwart im Rückblick*, p. 169.

21. Frank F. Rosenthal interview, Jan. 21, 1974; J. Prinz, "A Rabbi Under the

Hitler Regime," in H. A. Strauss and K. R. Grossmann (eds.), *Gegenwart im Rückblick*, pp. 234–7; L. Baeck, "A People Stands Before Its God," in E. H. Boehm, *We Survived*, p. 287.

22. L. P. Lochner, "Round Robins from Berlin," *Wisconsin Magazine of History*, Summer 1967, p. 325; "In these hard..." quote, in H. Freedom, *Jüdisches Theater in Nazideutschland*, p. 166; Eva G. Reichmann interview, May 27, 1974. Also Freeden citation above, pp. 18–20, 53, 159.

23. Interviews with Eva G. Reichmann, May 27, 1974; Herman Schaalman, Nov. 10, 1973; Emil Fackenheim, Oct. 10, 1973; Friedrich Brodnitz, Feb. 14, 1974. Also, L. P. Lochner, "Round Robins from Berlin," *Wisconsin Magazine of History*, Summer 1967, p. 323n; LBI/NY: 34 AR (363).

24. J. R. Marcus, *Rise and Destiny of the German Jew*, pp. 6, 271–2; Max Gruenewald, "About the Reichsvertretung der deutschen Juden," a paper presented at a Yivo Colloquium, Dec. 2–5, 1967, p. 4; H. L. Feingold, *Politics of Rescue*, p. 6; S. Adler-Rudel interview, June 3, 1975. Also E. H. Flannery, *Anguish of the Jews*, pp. 228–9; E. Simon, "Jewish Adult Education in Nazi Germany as Spiritual Resistance," *LBIY*, 1956, pp. 90–1; H. Arendt, *Eichmann in Jerusalem*, 1965 ed., pp. 11–2; A. Kazin, "Can Today's Movies Tell the Truth About Fascism?" *N.Y. Times*, Jan. 12, 1975, Sec. 2, p. 1.

25. Interviews with Max Kreutzberger, June 3, 1974; Frank F. Rosenthal, Jan. 21, 1974; Walter Zander, Dec. 27, 1974; Wolli Kaelter, Apr. 22, 1976. Manfred E. Swarsensky, "Out of the Root of Rabbis," in H. A. Strauss and K. R. Grossmann (eds.), *Gegenwart im Rückblick*, p. 226.

10: *KRISTALLNACHT*

1. K. R. Grossmann, "Flight or Emigration," p. 8. Interviews with Emil Fackenheim, Oct. 10, 1973; Robert Weltsch, May 31, 1974; and Hildegard Biermann, March 26, 1974.

2. J. Toland, *Adolf Hitler*, p. 379, 392; L. S. Dawidowicz, *War Against the Jews*, pp. 192–3; F. Friedländer, "Trials and Tribulations of Jewish Education in Nazi Germany," *LBIY*, 1958, pp. 198–9; I. Elbogen, *Century of Jewish Life*, p. 640; J. Fest, *Hitler*, p. 516; Werner Rosenstock interview, May 30, 1974.

3. *American Jewish Year Book*, v. 40, pp. 196–7; "All is lost" quote, in Max Gruenewald, "About the Reichsvertretung der Deutschen Juden," p. 7; L. S. Dawidowicz, *War Against the Jews*, pp. 97–8; Yad Vashem: Fa506/14, Blatt 18–19. Kosher incident: interviews with Alfred Jospe, Feb. 19, 1974; Yehoshua Amir, June 15, 1974; Israel Neumark, June 16, 1975.

4. H. I. Bach, "Leo Baeck," in *Synagogue Review*, Jan. 1957, p. 140; L. Baeck letters to von Veltheim, Dec. 29, 1933, and April 26, 1932, courtesy of A. S. and M. Dreyfus. Description of Baeck neighborhood and Sabbath: interviews with Leo Adam, May 26, 1974; Friedrich Brodnitz, Feb. 14, 1974; Ellen Littmann, May 29, 1974; Uta C. Merzbach, May 8, 1974. Interview with Heinz Warschauer, Oct. 12, 1973.

5. "In those early years..." quote, in L. Baeck, "A People Stands Before Its God," in E. H. Boehm, *We Survived*, pp. 285–6; "In these days" message, in Wiener Library.

6. There are several English versions of this Yom Kippur prayer. I have translated a copy of the original German found in the Wiener Library. Also see F. Bamberger, "Leo Baeck: The Man and the Idea," in M. Kreutzberger, *Studies of the Leo Baeck Institute*, pp. 8–9.

7. Interviews with Georg Salzberger, Aug. 6, 1973; Frank F. Rosenthal, Jan. 21,

1974; Ignaz Maybaum, May 29, 1974; Fritz Bamberger, Oct. 18, 1974. Also, see undated telegram signed "Neumeyer" to Rabbi R. Weinberg in Regensburg, in Wiener Library. Baeck's account of his and Hirsch's arrest, in memorandum by Hans G. Reichmann, Wiener Library. London *Times* account, Oct. 9, 1935, unpaged clipping, Wiener Library. Documents regarding American Christian protest, in Auswärtiges Amt: Dienstgebäude, Bestand Inland II A/B Nr. 39/1.

8. F. Goldschmidt, "Der Anteil der deutschen Juden an der Gründung und Entwicklung des Ordens B'nai B'rith," in *Festschrift zum 80. Geburtstag von Leo Baeck Am 23. Mai 1953*, p. 61; F. A. Doppelt, *Unconquerable Soul*, pp. 8–9; L. Baeck, "A People Stands Before Its God," in E. H. Boehm, *We Survived*, pp. 286–7.

9. Stahl biographical material, in E. G. Lowenthal, "Berlin, Fasanenstrasse 79/80," *Allgemeine*, Nov. 1, 1957, unpaged clipping; W. Breslauer, "Glückwunsch aus dem Kreis der 'Alten' Jüdischen Gemeinde," in H. A. Strauss and K. R. Grossmann (eds.), *Gegenwart im Rückblick*, p. 13. Stahl/Reichsvertretung dispute, in Central Zionist Archives; H. Stahl letter, Aug. 30, 1934 (A 142/123); Feb. 19, 1937 meeting minutes (A142/86).

10. Kareski background, H. S. Levine, "A Jewish Collaborator in Nazi Germany: The Strange Career of Georg Kareski, 1933–37," in *Central European History*, Sept. 1975, pp. 251–81; "Whatever Georg Kareski was..." quote, Adolf Leschnitzer interview, Oct. 28, 1975; "The Papen government..." quote, Central Archives for the History of the Jewish People: P 82/16 (also P 82/29). Also Yad Vashem: 01/156, 01/127; L. S. Dawidowicz, *War Against the Jews*, pp. 194–5; J. K. Ball-Kaduri interview, June 18, 1975.

11. The account of the Kareski/Baeck struggle is derived from the following: Interviews with Max Gruenewald, May 1, 1974, and Israel Neumark, June 16, 1975; K. J. Ball-Kaduri, "Leo Baeck and Contemporary History," in *Yad Vashem Studies*, 1967, p. 128; Max Gruenewald, "About the Reichsvertretung der deutschen Juden," pp. 2–4; K. Boehm, untitled account, in *Blätter juden Wissens Bne Brith*, 1947, pp. 16–7; *American Jewish Year Book*, v. 40, p. 203; Yad Vashem: 01/93, 01/112a; LBI/NY: Hans G. Reichmann letter, Jan. 3, 1965, to Max Gruenewald (AR C.A. 103/221–30), and Ernst Herzfeld, "Meine letzten Jahren in Deutschland," mss., pp. 35–9; "Bericht über Schwierigkeiten der Reichsvertretung," July 6, 1937, unsigned and unpaged mss., in LBI/J: Folder G II, Item G 18.

12. Interviews with Ellen Littmann, May 29, 1974; B. Manuel, June 5, 1974; Betty Cohen, June 14, 1975; Herman O. Pineas, Sept. 4, 1975; Eva G. Reichmann, May 27, 1974; Fritz Bamberger, Oct. 18, 1974; Manfred E. Swarsensky, Nov. 15, 1974; Ernst G. Lowenthal, June 18, 1974; Alfred Jospe, Feb. 19, 1974; Wolli Kaelter, April 22, 1976; Margaret Muehsam, Oct. 17, 1974. Magnus Davidsohn letter, May 23, 1957, in LBI/NY; H. Berlak to von Veltheim, March 9, 1937; L. Baeck letters to von Veltheim, Aug. 7, 1936, and Nov. 17, 1937; and L. Baeck's farewell to Natalie, all courtesy of A. S. and M. Dreyfus.

13. Max Nussbaum comments, in Yad Vashem: 01/222, pp. 3–4; H. Biermann interview, March 25, 1974; Heinz Warschauer interview, Oct. 12, 1973; "Leo Baeck and the others..." quote, W. Gunther Plaut interview, May 13, 1975; Hebrew University, Institute of Contemporary Jewry, OHP: Joachim Prinz, 00322, also Joachim Prinz interview, May 1, 1974; M. Gruenewald, "Leo Baeck: Witness and Judge," *Judaism*, 1957, p. 195, also Ignaz Maybaum interview, May 29, 1974; Eva G. Reichmann interview, May 27, 1974; A. Leschnitzer, "Der unbekannte Leo Baeck," in *Aufbau*, Nov. 30, 1956, pp. 15–6.

14. For general discussion about emigration attitudes: Central Zionist Archives,

A 142–86; Friedrich Brodnitz interview, Feb. 14, 1974; W. Hamburger, "The Reactions of Reform Jews to the Nazi Rule," in H. A. Strauss and K. R. Grossmann (eds.), *Gegenwart im Rückblick*, p. 155; W. T. Angress, "Auswanderlehrgut Gross-Breeson," in *LBIY*, 1965, pp. 168–9. L. Baeck quotes, in H. Bruening, *Briefe und Gespräche 1934–1940*, pp. 162–3; and L. Baeck, "A People Stands Before Its God," in E. H. Boehm, *We Survived*, p. 184; J. Prinz, "A Rabbi Under the Hitler Regime," in H. A. Strauss and K. R. Grossmann (eds.), *Gegenwart im Rückblick*, p. 238; Rudolf Callmann interview, May 1, 1974. Interviews with Leo Lichtenberg, April 19, 1977; Alfred Wolf, April 23, 1976; Wolli Kaelter, April 22, 1976; W. Gunther Plaut, May 13, 1975; Herman Schaalman, Nov. 10, 1973 (L. Baeck made the "golden book" comment to H. G. Adler, as well as to Wolli Kaelter: H. G. Adler interview, May 25, 1974).

15. Gertrud Gallerski interview, Oct. 30, 1975; Fritz Friedländer, "Grösse, Güte, Unerbittlichkeit—Einige Erinnerungen an Leo Baeck," unpublished mss., courtesy of H. I. Bach, p. 8. Samples of Baeck letters: LBI/NY: LB Briefe, to Mrs. Razowsky, Sept. 4, 1938, Mrs. Razowsky folder; and to Walter Heinemann, Dec. 5, 1937, Walter Heinemann folder; to Chief-Rabbi Landau, April 22, 1936, in JNL: Folder 56-B; to Rabbi J. H. Hertz, undated, courtesy of A. S. and M. Dreyfus. Fritz Bamberger interview, Oct. 18, 1974; Alexander Guttmann interview, April 19, 1977; Leo Adam interview, May 26, 1974. Also interviews with Ellen Littmann, May 29, 1974; and Werner Rosenstock, May 30, 1974.

16. Interviews with Robert Weltsch, May 31, 1974; and Max Kreutzberger, June 3, 1974. H. L. Feingold, *Politics of Rescue*, pp. 14–5.

17. "It is scarcely surprising..." quote, in F. K. Wiebe, *Germany and the Jewish Problem*, p. 15.

18. American emigration figures, in Werner Rosenstock, "Exodus 1933–1939—Ein Uberblick über die Jüdische Auswanderung aus Deutschland," undated report, courtesy of W. Rosenstock, p. 401; S. Safir, "American Diplomats in Berlin (1933–1939)," in *Yad Vashem Studies*, 1973, pp. 79–82; M. Nussbaum quote, in Yad Vashem: 01/222; Ickes quote, in L. Baker, *Brahmin in Revolt*, p. 298; Celler quote, in H. L. Feingold, *Politics of Rescue*, p. 19.

19. Weizmann Archives: Weizmann to Stephen Wise, March 27, 1933 (6); notes of conversations June 13 and 14, 1933 (53); notes of conversations March 1, 1933 (203–4). Bonnet/Ribbentrop meeting, in H. L. Feingold, *Politics of Rescue*, p. 47, and R. Hilberg, *Destruction of the European Jews*, p. 259.

20. Central Zionist Archives: L. Baeck to C. Weizmann, Dec. 3, 1936 (S 25/4580); L. Baeck to "Lieber Herr Dr. Senator," Nov. 9, 1937 (S 25/3246).

21. A. Guttmann, "Hochschule Retrospective," in *CCAR Journal*, Autumn 1972, p. 75; and Alexander Guttmann interview, April 19, 1977. E. H. Flannery, *Anguish of the Jews*, pp. 214–5; R. Grunberger, *12-Year Reich*, p. 112; "That wasn't very nice..." quote, in R. Hilberg, *Destruction of the European Jews*, p. 661. Yad Vashem: FA 506/14, Blatt 10; Werner Rosenstock, "Exodus 1933–1939—Ein Uberblick über die Jüdische Auswanderung aus Deutschland," undated report, courtesy of W. Rosenstock, p. 399; American Joint Distribution Committee, "Activities...1937," pp. 10, 22. Also, A. Prinz, "The Role of the Gestapo in Obstructing and Promoting Jewish Emigration," in *Yad Vashem Studies*, 1958, pp. 209–10.

22. McDonald statement, in K. R. Grossmann, "Flight or Emigration, 1933 through 1938," p. 22; Achilles memorandum, reproduced in *Encyclopedia Judaica*, v. 6, p. 990.

23. For general background on the Evian conference, S. Z. Katz, "Public Opinion

in Western Europe and the Evian Conference of July 1938," in *Yad Vashem Studies*, 1973, pp. 108–13; E. Marcus, "The German Foreign Office and the Palestine Question in the Period 1933–1939," in *Yad Vashem Studies*, 1958, p. 194; K. R. Grossmann, "Flight or Emigration, 1933 through 1938," pp. 29–30; H. L. Feingold, *Politics of Rescue*, pp. 26–38; W. Laqueur, *History of Zionism*, pp. 507–8. "Jewish Munich" quote, S. Z. Katz article cited above, p. 105; Reichsvertretung report to Evian conference, in LBI/NY; "Nichts ist so schlimm" quote, in Max Elk, "Leo Baeck—80 Jahre," undated clipping, courtesy of A. S. and M. Dreyfus.

24. Emigration figures from H. Eschwege, "Resistance of German Jews Against the Nazi Regime," *LBIY*, 1970, pp. 145–6; Werner Rosenstock, "Exodus 1933–1939 —Ein Überblick über die Jüdische Auswanderung aus Deutschland," undated report, courtesy of W. Rosenstock, pp. 380–400; Reichsvertretung report to the Evian conference, Anlagen 1, 3, in LBI/NY. Baeck quotes in *Time*, June 1, 1953, p. 54; and 1934 Reichsvertretung proclamation, courtesy of A. S. and M. Dreyfus. Also Eva Michaelis-Stern letter to Hans I. Bach, Sept. 4, 1973, courtesy of H. I. Bach; and L. Baeck, "A People Stands Before Its God," in E. H. Boehm, *We Survived*, p. 286.

25. Smith quote, in NA: RG 165, 2657-B-801/5; Baeck quotes, in *LBIY*, 1957, pp. 36–7.

26. NA: RG 165, 2657-B-801/5; LBI/NY: 5 (170).

27. NA: RG 165, 2657-B-801; M. Bruce, *Tramp Royal*, pp. 240–1; Emil Fackenheim interview, Oct. 10, 1973; S. Schiratzki, "The Rykestrasse School in Berlin—A Jewish Elementary School During the Hitler Period," *LBIY*, 1960, pp. 305–6; Werner Rosenstock interview, May 30, 1974; Ernst Herzfeld, "Meine letzten Jahren in Deutschland," mss., pp. 45–7, in LBI/NY (ME 163); Alexander Guttmann interview, April 19, 1977; A. Prinz, "The Role of the Gestapo in Obstructing and Promoting Jewish Emigration," *Yad Vashem Studies*, 1958, p. 213; author's visit to Oppeln, June 18, 1974; Nussbaum story, in Yad Vashem: 01/222, pp. 1–2.

28. Ernst G. Lowenthal interview, June 18, 1974 (the story of the newspaper editors' arrest also was told by Hans Klee, in Yad Vashem: 01/217); destruction statistics from Nazi records, in LBI/NY: 5 (170), pp. 582, 587; Marcus quote, in K. J. Ball-Kaduri, *Vor der Katastrophe*, p. 166.

29. R. Fuchs, "The 'Hochschule fur die Wissenschaft des Judentums' in the Period of Nazi Rule," in *LBIY*, 1967, pp. 24–5; K. J. Ball-Kaduri, *Vor der Katastrophe*, p. 195; K. J. Ball-Kaduri (compiler), "The Central Jewish Organizations in Berlin During the Pogrom of November 1938," in *Yad Vashem Studies*, 1959, pp. 261–81; L. P. Lochner, "Round Robins from Berlin," in *Wisconsin Magazine of History*, Summer 1967, p. 324; FDR quote, in L. Baker, *Roosevelt and Pearl Harbor*, p. 120.

30. "For the aryanization . . ." quote, in LBI/NY: 5 (170), p. 585; J. Toland, *Adolf Hitler*, p. 528; Baeck quotes, in *LBIY*, 1957, p. 36.

31. Baeck quotes, in L. Baeck, "Gedenken an Zwei Tote," undated reprint, pp. 312–3; and K. J. Ball-Kaduri, *Vor der Katastrophe*, p. 192. Also, *Otto Hirsch— Ein Lebensweg*, unpaged. Alfred Jospe interview, Feb. 19, 1974.

32. L. Baeck letter to I. Elbogen, Jan. 25, 1939, in LBI/NY: 6 (696); Alfred Jospe interview, Feb. 19, 1974 (similar stories told in interviews with Max Gruenewald, May 1, 1974; Yehoshua Amir, June 12, 1975; and Gustav Horn, June 16, 1975); Ignaz Maybaum interview, May 29, 1974; M. Bruce, *Tramp Royal*, p. 242.

11: WAR

1. NA: RG 165, 2657-B-801/2. Also H. L. Feingold, *Politics of Rescue*, pp. 41–4; S. Shafir, "American Diplomats in Berlin (1933–1939)," in *Yad Vashem Studies*, 1973, pp. 95–6.

2. M. Nussbaum, "Ministry Under Stress," in H. A. Strauss and K. R. Grossmann (eds.), *Gegenwart im Rückblick*, p. 240. Werner Rosenstock, "Exodus 1933–1939 —Ein Uberblick über die Jüdische Auswanderung aus Deutschland," undated report, courtesy of W. Rosenstock, p. 399.

3. Marianne Dreyfus interview, Feb. 12, 1974; L. Baeck to Berlaks, March 30, 1939, and April 2, 1939, courtesy of A. S. and M. Dreyfus; H. G. Adler interview, May 25, 1974.

4. L. Baeck to C. Weizmann, May 21, 1939, in LBI/NY: LB Briefe, Chaim Weizmann folder; "As the representatives..." in Weizmann Archives: L 13/A45; C. Weizmann to L. Baeck, June 15, 1939, Central Zionist Archives: L 13/145.

5. Ernst G. Lowenthal interview, June 18, 1974. "Everything depends on..." quote, in L. Baeck letter to Dr. J. Picard, May 28, 1940, in LBI/NY: 57 (221). Other letters in LBI/NY: LB Briefe, Karl Guggenheim, Walter Heinemann, Fritz V. Gutfeld folders.

6. For general background on transformation of Reichsvertretung to Reichsvereinigung: L. S. Dawidowicz, *War Against the Jews*, p. 105; K. J. Ball-Kaduri, "Berlin Is 'Purged' of Jews," in *Yad Vashem Studies*, 1963, p. 292; Institut für Zeitgeschichte: Eich/1444; Hans-Erich Fabian, "Zur Enstehung der 'Reichsvereinigung der Juden in Deutschland'," in H. A. Strauss and K. R. Grossmann (eds.), *Gegenwart im Rückblick*, pp. 170–6. R. Hilberg, *Destruction of the European Jews*, pp. 124–5; Hans-Erich Fabian article, cited above, p. 166; *Otto Hirsch— Ein Lebensweg*, unpaged.

7. Reichsvereinigung budget, in LBI/J: Folder G, Item G-02; financial report from Reichsvereinigung to American Joint Distribution Committee, Dec. 28, 1939, author's possession.

8. Herbert A. Strauss interview, Nov. 11, 1973; Frank F. Rosenthal interview, Jan. 21, 1974; R. Hilberg, *Destruction of the European Jews*, pp. 188–9, 661.

9. A. Guttmann, "Hochschule Retrospective," in *CCAR Journal*, Autumn 1972, p. 74; Alexander Guttmann interview, April 19, 1977.

10. H. H. von Veltheim-Ostrau, *Der Atem Indiens*, pp. 15–6; F. Bamberger, "Leo Baeck: The Man and the Idea," in M. Kreutzberger, *Studies of the Leo Baeck Institute*, p. 9; A. S. Dreyfus, "Leo Baeck: As We Remember Him," in *Leo Baeck Remembered*, pp. 5–6; A. S. Dreyfus, "Of Rabbinical Lineage," in E. G. Reichmann, *Worte des Gedenkens*, p. 156. Also, L. Baeck, "Die Schöpfung des Mitmenschen," reprint from *Soziale Ethik im Judentum*, p. 9.

11. Eva G. Reichmann interview, May 17, 1974; Trepp story, in F. A. Doppelt, *Unconquerable Soul*, p. 11. Baeck's comments about staying in Germany: E. Simon, "Lerntag"; Georg Salzberger interview, Aug. 6, 1973; undated letter, courtesy of A. S. and M. Dreyfus, L. Baeck, *Von Moses Mendelssohn zu Franz Rosenzweig*, p. 18. Wolli Kaelter interview, April 22, 1976.

12. Unsigned letter to I. I. Mattuck, Dec. 1939, courtesy of A. S. and M. Dreyfus; L. A. Katz, "Why Dr. Leo Baeck Refused US offer to Rescue Him from the Nazis in 1939," in *National Jewish Monthly*, Oct. 1964, pp. 7–8, 19.

13. LBI/NY: Hannah Karminski File.

14. H. G. Reichmann, untitled article, in *LBIY*, 1958, pp. 361–3; H. Walz letter to Leo Baeck Institute, June 16, 1967, in LBI/NY; G. Ritter, *German Resistance*,

pp. 80–1; K. J. Ball-Kaduri, *Vor der Katastrophe*, p. 42. K. J. Ball-Kaduri, "Did the Jews of Germany Resist?" in *Yad Vashem Bulletin*, March 1961, p. 31; NA: RG 59, OSS-R&A 609; M. Balfour and J. Frisby, *Helmuth von Moltke*, pp. 78–9; Alexander Altmann interview, Oct. 14, 1975; L. Baeck, "A People Stands Before Its God," in E. H. Boehm, *We Survived*, p. 289. A copy of *Die Entwicklung der Rechtsstellung und des Platzes der Juden in Europe, vornehmlich in Deutschland, vom Altertum bis zum Beginn der Aufklarungszeit* is in LBI/NY.

15. H. Karminski letter, April 11, 1941, in LBI/NY: Hannah Karminski Folder, AR-C.A. 154/330; Yom Kippur radio story: Marianne Dreyfus, "Leo Baeck," p. 4, courtesy of M. Dreyfus; and A. S. Dreyfus, "Of Rabbinical Lineage," in E. G. Reichmann, *Worte des Gedenkens*, p. 157; and A. Stanley Dreyfus interview, Feb. 12, 1974. Ernst Ludwig Ehrlich interview, June 4, 1974. H. Karminski letter, Nov. 26, 1941, in LBI/NY: Hannah Karminski Folder, AR-C.A. 154/330. Also, Herman O. Pineas interview, Sept. 4, 1975.

16. Seligsohn death details in J. F. Oppenheimer (ed.), *Lexikon des Judentums*, p. 745. Hirsch death details: Theodore Hirsch memorandum, May 12, 1960, in Yad Vashem: 01/285; *Daily News Bulletin*, July 10, 1945, p. 4; L. Baeck to Louis Hirsch (Otto's father), June 6, 1941, in LBI/NY: LB Briefe, Louis Hirsch folder; L. Baeck to Hans Georg Hirsch, Oct. 15, 1940, courtesy of H. G. Hirsch; *Otto Hirsch—Ein Lebensweg*, unpaged; L. Baeck to S. Guggenheim, Sept. 24, 1941, in LBI/NY: LB Briefe, Siegfried Guggenheim folder.

17. Stahl death details, in Yad Vashem: 01/222. Cora Berliner letter, June 21, 1942, in LBI/NY: Hans Schaeffer Coll., Cora Berliner file; Bertha Badt-Strauss, "Drei Unvergessene," in *AJR Information*, April 1958, p. 8.

18. L. Baeck letter to H. Schaeffer, Nov. 27, 1942, in LBI/NY: Hans Schaeffer Coll., Hannah Karminski file.

19. L. Baeck to Rudolf Löb, Nov. 18, 1942, and April 2, 1941, in LBI/NY: LB Briefe, Rudolf Löb folder; L. Baeck to Immanuel Loew, April 21, 1940, in *Zeitschrift für die Geschichte der Juden*, 1972, p. 4; Alfred Neumeyer mss., in LBI/NY: (M.E. 192) pp. 258–9. Gertrud Luckner interview, July 1, 1974; *N.Y. Times*, June 6, 1977, p. 35.

20. Robert Weltsch interview, May 31, 1974; two L. Baeck letters to Berlaks, undated, and letters of Dec. 8, 1941, and Feb. 27, 1942, courtesy of A. S. and M. Dreyfus.

21. Letters dated Jan. 31, 1940, and March 2, 1939, in LBI/NY: LB Briefe, Robert R. Geis folder; Klara Caro interview, Feb. 14, 1974.

22. L. Baeck letters to von Veltheim, April 30, 1941, and Dec. 31, 1941, courtesy of A. S. and M. Dreyfus.

23. Laws against Jews and "the heaviest burden..." quote, in K. J. Ball-Kaduri, "Berlin Is 'Purged' of Jews," in *Yad Vashem Studies*, 1963, pp. 271–2. Magen David history, in G. Scholem, *Messianic Idea in Judaism*, pp. 257–81. Reichsvereinigung involvement: Institut für Zeitgeschichte: Eich/1150. Ernst Ludwig Ehrlich interview, June 4, 1974. Baeck story, in E. G. Reichmann, "Symbol of German Jewry," *LBIY*, 1957, p. 25; and Werner Rosenstock interview, May 30, 1974.

24. L. Baeck, "A People Stands Before Its God," in E. H. Boehm, *We Survived*, p. 288.

25. Hochschule opening story: W. Hamburger, "Leo Baeck—The Last Teacher of the Lehranstalt," in *Paul Lazarus-Gedenkbuch*, p. 122; and R. Fuchs, "The 'Hochschule für die Wissenschaft des Judentums' in the Period of Nazi Rule," *LBIY*, 1967, p. 26. "We hope that..." quote, in W. Hamburger, citation above, pp.

120–1; *LBIY*, 1967, citation above, p. 27. Transferring Hochschule to England story: *LBIY*, 1967, citation above, pp. 26–8; and W. Hamburger, citation above, p. 130. Faculty changes: *LBIY*, 1967, citation above, p. 29; and W. Hamburger, citation above, pp. 123–4. Description of students: W. Hamburger, citation above, pp. 30–1.

26. "The examinations have..." quote, in L. Baeck letter to I. Elbogen, April 25, 1939, LBI/NY: 7 (696); "that we enjoy..." quote, in L. Baeck letter to I. Elbogen, Jan. 23, 1940, in LBI/NY: AR-C. 254/696; "The sense of abnormal..." quote, Herbert A. Strauss interview, Nov. 11, 1973; "When I began..." quote, Ernst Ludwig Ehrlich interview, June 4, 1974; "Sie *müssen* gehen!" quote, in N. Peter Levinson, "Der Lehrer von Theresienstadt," courtesy of N. P. Levinson.

27. L. Baeck letter to I. Elbogen, Oct. 26, 1940, in LBI/NY: AR-C.254/696; R. Fuchs, "The 'Hochschule für die Wissenschaft des Judentums' in the Period of Nazi Rule," in *LBIY*, 1967, pp. 29–31; L. Baeck letter to Berlaks, Oct. 16, 1940, courtesy of A. S. and M. Dreyfus; "dressed well..." quote, in Ernst Ludwig Ehrlich, "Leo Baeck in Berlin 1940–1942," in LBI/NY; Leo Baeck Allgemeine II-122 (365); W. Hamburger, "Leo Baeck—The Last Teacher of the Lehranstalt," in *Paul Lazarus-Gedenkbuch*, p. 126; L. Baeck letter to I. Elbogen, Feb. 19, 1941, in LBI/NY: AR-C.254/696; Ernst Ludwig Ehrlich interview, June 4, 1974; N. Peter Levinson, untitled article, in *Leo Baeck/H. G. van Dam*, pp. 27–8.

28. L. Baeck letters to Berlaks, July 31, 1942, and Jan. 25, 1942, courtesy of A. S. and M. Dreyfus.

29. Interviews with Herbert A. Strauss, Nov. 11, 1973; and Ernst Ludwig Ehrlich, June 4, 1974.

30. NA: RG 59, OSS-R&A 609.

31. Heinrich Grüber interview, June 18, 1974; H. Arendt, *Eichmann in Jerusalem*, p. 131.

32. L. Baeck, "A People Stands Before Its God," in E. H. Boehm, *We Survived*, p. 289; I. Harel, *House on Garibaldi Street*, pp. 204, 232; LBI/NY: Folder 3417/9.

33. Hitler quotes, in R. Hilberg, *Destruction of the European Jews*, pp. 257, 266; J. Fest, *Hitler*, p. 612. "The Führer once more..." quote, L. B. Lochner (ed.), *Goebbels Diaries*, pp. 101–2; H. Arendt, *Eichmann in Jerusalem*, p. 108.

34. Minutes of March 20, 1941 meeting, in NA: T-81, Roll 676, frames 548560-5; also Institut für Zeitgeschichte: MA 423. Baeck quotes, in L. Baeck, "A People Stands Before Its God," in E. H. Boehm, *We Survived*, pp. 289–90.

35. "There was a Ghetto..." quote, in M. Henschel, "Die letzten Jahre der Jüdischen Gemeinde Berlin," pp. 1–4, in Yad Vashem: 01/51; "In retrospect..." quote, in J. Jacobson, "Bruchstücke 1939–1945," p. 5, mss. in LBI/NY: M.E. 560; "You can ask..." quote, in M. Henschel, cited above; "In the official language..." quote, in Hans-Erich Fabian, "Die Letzte Etappe," in *Festschrift zum 80. Geburtstag von Leo Baeck Am 23. Mai. 1953*, pp. 89–90; "The Reichsvereinigung was..." quote, in K. J. Ball-Kaduri, "Berlin Is 'Purged' of Jews," in *Yad Vashem Studies*, 1963, p. 293.

36. J. Jacobson, "Bruchstücke 1939–1945," pp. 6–7; L. Baeck, "A People Stands Before Its God," in E. H. Boehm, *We Survived*, p. 288.

37. Interviews with Norbert Wollheim, Oct. 29, 1975, and Ernst Ludwig Ehrlich, June 4, 1974.

38. Interviews with Ernst Ludwig Ehrlich, June 4, 1974, and Gertrud Luckner, July 1, 1974.

39. Background on German Communist Party, in NA: RG 59, OSS-R&A 1550,

"The German Communist Party," pp. 35–6. Jewish officials arrested, in Yad Vashem: 01/297; M. Henschel, "Die Letzten Jahren der Jüdischen Gemeinde Berlin," p. 4, in Yad Vashem: 01/51; K. J. Ball-Kaduri, "Did the Jews of Germany Resist?" in *Yad Vashem Bulletin*, March 1961, p. 32. Norbert Wollheim interview, Oct. 29, 1975.

40. L. Baeck letter to von Veltheim, May 25, 1942; von Veltheim letter to L. Baeck, Aug. 31, 1942; L. Baeck to von Veltheim, Sept. 1, 1942—all courtesy of A. S. and M. Dreyfus. Yad Vashem: 01/50.

41. L. Baeck letters to Berlaks, Sept. 29, Nov. 27, 1942, and Jan. 4, 1943, courtesy of A. S. and M. Dreyfus.

42. Interviews with Alexander Guttmann, April 19, 1977, and Norbert Wollheim, Oct. 29, 1975.

43. Undated inventory, apparently made at the time of Baeck's arrest, courtesy of A. S. and M. Dreyfus.

44. Herman O. Pineas interview, Sept. 4, 1975; H. Henschel account, in K. J. Ball-Kaduri, "Berlin Is 'Purged' of Jews," *Yad Vashem Studies*, 1963, p. 273; L. Baeck, "A People Stands Before Its God," in E. H. Boehm, *We Survived*, pp. 290–1.

12: THERESIENSTADT

1. Gertrud Luckner interview, July 1, 1974; Baroness Maria von Hollitscher-Bojicevic letter to von Veltheim, Jan. 30, 1943, and Paula Glück letter to von Veltheim, Jan. 31, 1943, courtesy of A. S. and M. Dreyfus.

2. Z. Lederer, *Ghetto Theresienstadt*, pp. 2, 4.

3. K. J. Ball-Kaduri, "Berlin Is 'Purged' of Jews," in *Yad Vashem Studies*, 1963, p. 273; Z. Lederer, *Ghetto Theresienstadt*, p. 90; L. S. Dawidowicz, *War Against the Jews*, p. 137; H. Arendt, *Eichmann in Jerusalem*, pp. 79–81, 133.

4. Z. Lederer, *Ghetto Theresienstadt*, pp. 2–3, 10–1, 13–4, 16–20, 30–3, 41, 49–52, 55; H. Liebrecht, "Therefore Will I Deliver Him," in E. H. Boehm, *We Survived*, pp. 222–3; "Terezin," undated report, courtesy CIA, office of the director.

5. NA: T-175, Roll 22, Frames 2527354-6; Uta C. Merzbach interview, Oct. 11, 1974; "where they would enjoy . . ." quote, in Z. Lederer, *Ghetto Theresienstadt*, p. 88.

6. L. Baeck's arrival card is at Beit Theresienstadt; other records of train's arrival in Brandeis University: Emma Fuchs/Theresienstadt documents. Z. Lederer, *Ghetto Theresienstadt*, pp. 1–2, 37–8. Uta C. Merzbach interview, Oct. 11, 1974. J. Jacobson, "Terezin: The Daily Life," pp. 2–3.

7. Institut für Zeitgeschichte: Eich/1239; L. Baeck, "A People Stands Before Its God," in E. H. Boehm, *We Survived*, p. 291; L. Baeck, "Life in a Concentration Camp," in *Jewish Forum*, March 1946, pp. 30–1.

8. Hebrew University: Institute of Contemporary Jewry, Oral History Division, Willi Groag, p. 98; Hildegard Biermann interview, March 25, 1974; "To be served . . ." quote, Ilse Blumenthal-Weiss interview, Oct. 15, 1974; "Leo Baeck was untouched . . ." quote, Etta Japha interview, Nov. 10, 1973.

9. "He was at my . . ." quote, in E. Japha, "Dr. Leo Baeck, *Voice of Emanuel*, Nov. 1, 1962, unpaged; L. Baeck letter to H. O. Pineas, Oct. 17, 1945, in LBI/NY: LB Briefe, Herman O. Pineas folder.

10. L. Baeck, "Life in a Concentration Camp," in *Jewish Forum*, March 1946, p. 31; Z. Lederer, *Ghetto Theresienstadt*, pp. 44–7; "Living conditions . . ." quote, Uta C. Merzbach interview, Oct. 11, 1974; H. G. Adler interview, May 27, 1974; "I was cold . . ." quote, Herman Schaalman interview, Nov. 11, 1973.

11. "My father very deliberately..." quote, Uta C. Merzbach interview, Oct. 11, 1974; "Only he who himself..." quote, in J. Jacobson, "Terezin: The Daily Life," pp. 8–9; daily menus in Brandeis University: Emma Fuchs/Theresienstadt Documents; "Four of us..." quote, in H. Liebrecht, "Therefore Will I Deliver Him," in E. H. Boehm, *We Survived*, pp. 226–7. Packages: L. Baeck, "A People Stands Before Its God," in E. H. Boehm, *We Survived*, p. 291; "A shipment of dried prunes..." quote, in Brandeis University: Emma Fuchs/Theresienstadt Documents, Tagesbefehl Nr. 394, Dec. 24, 1943; "The respect enjoyed..." J. Jacobson, "Bruchstücke 1939–1945," mss. in LBI/NY: M.E. 560; H. G. Adler, *Theresienstadt 1941–1945*, p. 367; "Are we having sardines again?" quote, Hebrew University: Institute of Contemporary Jewry, Oral History Project, Willi Groag, p. 100.

12. H. Liebrecht, "Therefore Will I Deliver Him," in E. H. Boehm, *We Survived*, p. 288; Z. Lederer, *Ghetto Theresienstadt*, pp. 137–42; Klara Caro, "Stärker als das Schwert!: mss. in LBI/NY, p. 3; Brandeis University: Emma Fuchs/Theresienstadt Documents, "Mitteilungen der Jüdischen Selbstverwaltung Theresienstadt," Nr. 17, June 3, 1944.

13. L. Baeck, "Life in a Concentration Camp," in *Jewish Forum*, March 1946, pp. 30–1; H. Liebrecht, "Therefore Will I Deliver Him," in E. H. Boehm, *We Survived*, p. 224.

14. Z. Lederer, *Ghetto Theresienstadt*, pp. 61–2; "Must reckon with..." quote and examples of punishment in Brandeis University: Emma Fuchs/Theresienstadt Documents, Tagesbefehl Nr. 411, Feb. 15, 1944; Tagesbefehl, Nr. 373, Oct. 27, 1943; Tagesbefehl Nr. 367, Oct. 7, 1943; Tagesbefehl Nr. 387, Dec. 6, 1943; and in Z. Lederer, *Ghetto Theresienstadt*, pp. 78–80. Hangings, in Siegfried Seidl statements, Oct. 16, 1945, in Yad Vashem: 109/29, pp. 2–3; and June 4, 1946, in Yad Vashem: 109/51, p. 24; and Ghetto Fighters Museum, "Red Cross Report on Theresienstadt," p. 13.

15. Brandeis University: Emma Fuchs/Theresienstadt, Tagesbefehl, Nr. 384, Nov. 29, 1943; "Terezin," undated report, courtesy CIA, office of the director; births recorded in Brandeis citation above, Tagesbefehl Nr. 95, April 8, 1942; and Z. Lederer, *Ghetto Theresienstadt*, pp. 98–9. Groag birth story in Hebrew University, Institute of Contemporary Jewry, Oral History Project, Willi Groag, pp. 93–5; Willi Groag interview, July 6, 1975; L. Baeck letter to Frau Groag, Feb. 11, 1945, courtesy of Willi Groag.

16. Confidential source.

17. Yellow star records in Brandeis University: Emma Fuchs/Theresienstadt documents.

18. Z. Lederer, *Ghetto Theresienstadt*, pp. 75–7, 90–1; Siegfried Seidl statement, June 4, 1946, in Yad Vashem: 109/51, p. 1; H. Liebrecht, "Therefore Will I Deliver Him," in E. H. Boehm, *We Survived*, p. 234; *AJR Information*, Nov. 1948, p. 2; J. Jacobson, "Terezin: The Daily Life," p. 5.

19. L. Baeck, "Life in a Concentration Camp," in *Jewish Forum*, March 1946, pp. 29–32; J. Jacobson, "Terezin: The Daily Life," pp. 12–4; Z. Lederer, *Ghetto Theresienstadt*, pp. 125–31; H. Liebrecht, "Therefore Will I Deliver Him," in E. H. Boehm, *We Survived*, pp. 228–30. *Emperor of Atlantis*: *N.Y. Times*, April 26, 1977, p. 46; *LBI News*, Winter 1976/77, p. 8.

20. Uta C. Merzbach interview, Oct. 11, 1974; "Natiw" textbook, courtesy of Ralph Blume; Klara Caro, "Stärker als das Schwert!" mss. in LBI/NY, p. 15.

21. Zeev Shek interview, June 25, 1975; Joachim Prinz interview, May 1, 1974;

Schalom Ben-Chorin, "Interview mit Dr. Leo Baeck," unidentified newspaper clipping, author's possession.

22. H. G. Adler, *Theresienstadt 1941–1945*, p. 602; "I was in Theresienstadt..." quote, Ludwig Loeffler letter to author, April 28, 1976; H. G. Adler interview, May 27, 1974; "The lectures of Dr. Baeck..." quote, Else Dormitzer, in *AJR Information*, undated supplemental issue on Baeck's 75th birthday, p. 4; "For a moment..." quote, Etta Japha interview, Nov. 12, 1973; Czechoslovakian lecture, unpaged mss. by Max Poper, in LBI/NY: Ismar Elbogen Collection. Also, J. Jacobson, "Terezin: The Daily Life," p. 13; J. Jacobson, "The Gateway to Hell," in *AJR Information*, April 1956, p. 7; E. Japha, in *Voice of Emanuel*, Nov. 1, 1962, unpaged.

23. L. Baeck's Theresienstadt lecture, in L. Baeck, "The Writing of History," *Synagogue Review*, Nov. 1962, pp. 51–9. For the impact of Baeck's lectures, also Uta C. Merzbach interview, Oct. 11, 1974; Klara Caro, "Stärker als das Schwert!" mss. in LBI/NY, p. 7; Wiener Library: P. IIIh (Theresienstadt) No. 516, p. IV; unsigned Preface to L. Baeck, *Pharisees*, p. xxiv; I. Maybaum, *Face of God*, pp. 124–6.

24. J. Jacobson, "Terezin: The Daily Life," pp. 14–5; Catholics' comments, in H. Liebrecht, "Therefore Will I Deliver Him," in E. H. Boehm, *We Survived*, pp. 233–4; Esther Megillah story: Eugene J. Lipman interview, Oct. 20, 1975; Bar Mitzvah story: Ralph Blume letters to author, Jan. 22 and March 11, 1976.

25. Schalom Ben-Chorin, "Interview mit Dr. Leo Baeck," unidentified newspaper clipping, author's possession; undated letter by Lotte Liebstein, in LBI/NY: Leo Baeck, Allgemeine I, 12-365.

26. "include untrue reports..." quote, Brandeis University: Emma Fuchs/Theresienstadt Documents: Tagesbefehl Nr. 213, Sept. 16, 1942; L. Baeck letter to "Herr Dr. Plaut," Oct. 24, 1943, in LBI/NY: LB Briefe, Plaut folder; "Tage gehen..." note, courtesy of A. S. and M. Dreyfus.

27. H. G. Adler interview, May 25, 1974.

28. L. Baeck, "A People Stands Before Its God," in E. H. Boehm, *We Survived*, p. 293; Z. Lederer, *Ghetto Theresienstadt*, pp. 103–5; Brandeis University: Emma Fuchs/Theresienstadt Documents, Tagesbefehl Nr. 379, Nov. 18, 1943, and Tagesbefehl Nr. 382, Nov. 23, 1943.

29. "Terezin," undated report, courtesy of CIA, office of the director; Hebrew University: Institute of Contemporary Jewry, Oral History Project, Trudi Groag, pp. 2–3; Klara Caro interview, Feb. 14, 1974; B. Murmelstein, "Das Ende von Theresienstadt," in *Neue Züricher Zeitung*, Dec. 14, 1963, p. 14; H. G. Adler, *Theresienstadt 1941–1945*, p. 165; H. G. Adler, *Die Verheimlichte Wahrheit*, p. 310; L. Baeck, "A People Stands Before Its God," in E. H. Boehm, *We Survived*, pp. 293–4; J. Jacobson, "Bruchstücke," pp. 30–1, mss. in LBI/NY: M.E. 560.

30. "We should film..." quote, in Ghetto Fighters Museum: "Red Cross Report on Theresienstadt," p. 52; J. Jacobson, "Terezin: The Daily Life," p. 16; H. Liebrecht, "Therefore Will I Deliver Him," in E. H. Boehm, *We Survived*, p. 228; Z. Lederer, *Ghetto Theresienstadt*, pp. 53–4, 119–21.

31. "It is imperative..." quote, in Z. Lederer, *Ghetto Theresienstadt*, pp. 146–7; L. Baeck, "Life in a Concentration Camp," in *Jewish Forum*, March 1946, p. 31; "Transports arrived at..." quote, N. Wilson letter, in *New Statesman*, March 23, 1962; L. Baeck, "A People Stands Before Its God," in E. H. Boehm, *We Survived*, p. 294.

32. J. Jacobson, "Terezin: The Daily Life," p. 12.
33. L. Baeck, "A People Stands Before Its God," in E. H. Boehm, *We Survived*, pp. 292–3; A. J. Friedlander, *Leo Baeck—Teacher of Theresienstadt*, p. 47; NA: RG 226, 55106; Klara Caro, "Stärker als das Schwert!" mss. in LBI/NY, pp. 22–3; H. G. Adler, *Theresienstadt 1941–1945*, p. 156; and H. G. Adler interview, May 27, 1974; Ghetto Fighters Museum: "Red Cross Report on Theresienstadt," p. 55; interviews with Ilse Blumenthal-Weiss, Oct. 15, 1974; and Uta C. Merzbach, Oct. 11, 1974.
34. A drawing made by a Ghetto inmate of Rahm supervising the deportations is in H. G. Adler, *Die Verheimlichte Wahrheit*, p. 282; also H. G. Adler, *Theresienstadt 1941–1945*, p. 193; Z. Lederer, *Ghetto Theresienstadt*, pp. 156–7.
35. Ernst Ludwig Ehrlich interview, June 4, 1974; Yad Vashem: 02/244, p. 2; "Dr. Baeck practiced ..." quote, J. Jacobson, "Bruckstücke," p. 40.
36. H. G. Adler, *Theresienstadt 1941–1945*, p. 703; H. G. Adler interview, May 25, 1974.
37. K. J. Ball-Kaduri, "Did the Jews of Germany Resist?" in Yad Vashem Bulletin, March 1961, p. 32; unsigned memorandum of Theresienstadt experiences (apparently by Werner Neufliess, referred to in *Yad Vashem Bulletin*, cited above), in LBI/NY: AR 365, No. 18; Dr. H. Cats-Hilleson to R. Berlak, Feb. 15, 1945, courtesy of A. S. and M. Dreyfus.
38. L. Baeck, "A People Stands Before Its God," in E. H. Boehm, *We Survived*, pp. 295–6.
39. Z. Lederer, *Ghetto Theresienstadt*, p. 191; H. G. Adler, *Theresienstadt 1941–1945*, pp. 205, 216, 826; J. Jacobson, "Terezin: The Daily Life," pp. 18–21 (also the appendix to this document by David Cohen); Ilse Blumenthal-Weiss, "Im Auftrag des Reichskommissars," mss. in LBI/NY, pp. 78–9; Hebrew University, Institute of Contemporary Jewry, Oral History Project, Trudi Groag, pp. 10–2.
40. Willi Groag interview, July 6, 1975.

13: FINAL YEARS

1. L. Baeck to Max A. Shapiro, courtesy of M. A. Shapiro; Kurt Alexander, untitled mss., courtesy of A. S. and M. Dreyfus; L. Baeck to Robert R. Geis, July 17, 1945, in LBI/NY: AR 2269, Geis, Robert, No. 3.
2. C. Weizmann to L. Baeck, June 29, 1945, and L. Baeck, to C. Weizmann, July 11, 1945, in Weizmann Archives: 12120/3924 and 135; H. G. Adler interview, May 25, 1974; "I don't remember ..." quote, Alfred Wolf interview, April 23, 1976.
3. Sample Baeck letters are July 30, 1945, to Frau Hepner, LBI/NY; undated to Gertrud Heindenfeld, LBI/NY: Leo Baeck Briefe, Gertrud Heindenfeld folder; and to Heinrich Guttmann, Sept. 2, 1945, LBI/NY: Leo Baeck Briefe, Heinrich Guttman folder; L. Baeck to Fritz Muhr, Aug. 7, 1945, LBI/NY (Ar 2269); L. Baeck letters of May 23, 1947, June 23, 1947, and Feb. 18, 1947, all in LBI/NY: No. 16 (AR 363).
4. Jeannette Wolff interview, June 25, 1974; Friedrich Brodnitz interview, Feb. 14, 1974; Wolli Kaelter interview, April 22, 1976; Wolfgang Hamburger letter to R. Berlak, May 23, 1957, courtesy of A. S. and M. Dreyfus; H. G. Adler interview, May 25, 1974; also interviews with Ilse Blumenthal-Weiss, Oct. 15, 1974; Margaret Muehsam, Oct. 17, 1974; Alfred Jospe, Feb. 19, 1974; Henry J. Kellermann, March 26, 1976; and Alexander Altmann, Oct. 14, 1975.

5. L. Baeck to R. Jaser, June 9, 1947, in LBI/NY; LB Briefe, Rudolf Jaser folder; von Veltheim to L. Baeck, Sept. 12, 1945, courtesy of A. S. and M. Dreyfus.

6. G. Scholem, *Messianic Idea in Judaism*, pp. 318–9; "A Message from Rabbi Leo Baeck," in *National Jewish Monthly*, Jan. 1946, p. 158; *Aufbau*, Dec. 21, 1945, pp. 1–2; Schalom Ben-Chorin, "Interview mit Dr. Leo Baeck," undated clipping; interviews with David H. Wice, March 12, 1975; Ernst G. Lowenthal, June 18, 1974; and Werner Rosenstock, May 30, 1974. Baeck's trip to Germany reported in *AJR Information*, Nov. 1948, p. 2.

7. N. Glueck, "Memorial Tribute," in E. G. Reichmann, *Worte des Gedenkens*, p. 161.

8. "Whenever a moral weight..." quote, Arthur E. Kaufmann interview, May 29, 1974; E. G. Lowenthal, "Im Dienst an der Menscheit," in *Leo Baeck/H. G. van Dam*, p. 18; Central Zionist Archives: Zu/10.095; Robert Weltsch interview, May 31, 1974.

9. L. Baeck's visit to White House, correspondence courtesy of Harry S Truman Library; opening prayer in House of Representatives, in *Congressional Record*, 1948, p. 1275.

10. L. Baeck to Fritz Kaufmann, Nov. 29, 1948, courtesy of A. S. and M. Dreyfus; L. Baeck to Rudolf Jaser, Feb. 7, 1949, in LBI/NY: LB Briefe, Rudolf Jaser folder; "a big, tall..." quote, Samuel Karff interview, Nov. 10, 1973; Eugene B. Borowitz, in *American Federation . . . 1973–1974*, pp. 16–7.

11. Samuel Karff interview, Nov. 10, 1973; Eugene B. Borowitz, in *American Federation . . . 1973–1974*, pp. 16–7; Nahum N. Glatzer interview, Aug. 21, 1974.

12. Letter from Rabbi Norman D. Hirsch to author, Dec. 10, 1973; A. J. Friedlander, *This People Israel*, p. xxii.

13. A. Stanley Dreyfus, untitled personal reminiscences, courtesy of A. S. and M. Dreyfus; L. Baeck to A. S. and M. Dreyfus, Nov. 21, 1950, courtesy of A. S. and M. Dreyfus.

14. David H. Wice interview, March 12, 1975.

15. "Society for Jewish Study," *Synagogue Review*, Feb. 1951, pp. 173–4; I. Maybaum, *Face of God*, p. 127; Eugene B. Borowitz, *American Federation . . . 1973–74*, p. 24.

16. "The weeks in Palestine..." quote, L. Baeck letter to Rudolf Jaser, Oct. 12, 1947, in LBI/NY: LB Briefe, Rudolf Jaser folder; "If later history writers..." quote, "Aus dem Tagebuch von Dr. Willi Cohn, Breslau," p. 21, in LBI/J; L. Baeck letter to Ernst Ludwig Ehrlich, Oct. 22, 1947, courtesy of Ernst Ludwig Ehrlich; "The form which shall..." quote, Schalom Ben-Chorin, "Interview mit Dr. Leo Baeck," July 18, 1947, newspaper clipping; "engender nationalism and chauvinism..." quote, L. Baeck, "Religious Education of Children in Palestine," p. 42; "The state of Israel..." quote, L. Baeck address before the sixth conference of the World Union for Progressive Judaism, 1949, printed in *In Memoriam Leo Baeck*, pp. 41, 44; "We cannot stand by..." quote, in N. Bentwich, *My 77 Years*, p. 226.

17. "He walked briskly..." quote, H. G. Adler interview, May 27, 1974; "It was all that I..." quote, Herman Schaalman interview, Nov. 10, 1973; E. Spiro story, Ignaz Maybaum interview, May 29, 1974; "Many will remember..." account, "Erinnerungen an Rabb. Dr. Leo Baeck," by F.S.N., undated clipping, courtesy of Hazorea Kibbutz Archives.

18. Eugene B. Borowitz, *American Federation . . . 1973–1974*, p. 17.

19. "This ordeal has been so..." quote, L. Baeck, *The Task of Progressive Judaism*

in the Post-War World, pp. 1–2; "Only when resort..." quote, L. Baeck, "World Religion and National Religion," p. 6.

20. "It is one..." quote, W. Kaufmann, "A Biographical Introduction," in L. Baeck, Judaism and Christianity, p. 6; K. Stendahl quote, in his introduction to L. Baeck; Pharisees, p. xix; "Judaism means a question..." quote, in Common Ground, July-August 1953, p. 11.

21. "Judaism must not stand aside..." quote, L. Baeck before the fifth conference of the World Union for Progressive Judaism, 1946, printed in In Memoriam Leo Baeck, p. 39; "We should not be..." quote, L. Baeck before the eighth conference of the World Union for Progressive Judaism, 1953, printed in In Memoriam Leo Baeck, p. 52.

22. "was always that..." L. Baeck, "Our Religious Approach to World Problems," p. 10; "Every man is...", L. Baeck, "The Shema," p. 10; "I always advise..." from a transcript of an interview with L. Baeck, printed in Liberal Judaism, January 1948, p. 65.

23. L. Baeck, This People Israel, pp. 314, 315, 77, 399–400, 8, 370, 159, 37–8.

INDEX

INDEX